LIFE WITH
BIRDS

LIFE WITH
BIRDS
ROB HUME

D&C
David and Charles

To my father and the memory of my mother, who both so unselfishly dedicated their lives to their family. And for Marcella, without whom this book would never have been written.

Acknowledgements

Much of this book consists of acknowledgements of one kind or another: so many people are mentioned that it is clear how much I owe to them and I thank everyone involved, from family members to birdwatching acquaintances. Mic Cady, at David & Charles, Elizabeth Mallard-Shaw, who has edited the text, and Simon Barnes, who generously provided the foreword, have offered great encouragement. Mic has, consistently, urged me to continue, as has my wife, Marcella, whose support has been unfailing. I should also like to thank Chasewater Wildlife Group, the Kenyan and Zimbabwe tourist boards of some years ago, Mike Mockler, who in his past role with Abercrombie & Kent helped me to see some of Africa, Rhett Butler and Touch the Wild for inviting me to Zimbabwe, Swan Hellenic for taking me to Egypt, and Chris Durdin and Honeyguide Travel, and John and Vivien Boucher at The Painting School in Berdún, for help with the Pyrenees over many years. The RSPB has been a gateway to endless fascinating experiences and helped me to meet all kinds of fascinating people. People who are interested in or inspired by birds and other wild nature, and wild and beautiful places, tend to be interesting and pleasing people in themselves and I am especially indebted to those who work so hard to protect what so many of us enjoy.

A DAVID & CHARLES BOOK
David & Charles is a subsidiary of F+W (UK) Ltd., an F+W Publications Inc. company.

First published in the UK in 2005
Text and illustrations Copyright © Rob Hume 2005

Distributed in North America
by F+W Publications, Inc.
4700 East Galbraith Road
Cincinnati, OH 45236
1-800-0963

A catalogue record for this book is available from the British Library.

ISBN 0 7153 2181 1

Printed in Malta by Gutenberg Press
for David & Charles, Newton Abbot, Devon

Editor and Project Manager Elizabeth Mallard-Shaw

Commissioning Editor Mic Cady
Desk Editor Louise Crathorne
Production Controller Kelly Smith

Visit our website at www.davidandcharles.co.uk

David & Charles books are available from all good bookshops; alternatively you can contact our Orderline on 0870 9908222 or write to us at FREEPOST EX2 110, D&C Direct, Newton Abbot, TQ12 4ZZ (no stamp required UK mainland).

Contents

Foreword

Rob Hume is a rare man. Always has been. And not just because he has served his time on the British Birds Rarities Committee and made any number of make-or-break decisions on the sightings of rare birds. Rob's rarity is much more important than that.

In any field of human endeavour, you meet experts. People who are better than you. And most of these people can't wait to point this out: by tone, nuance, body language, clever remark, self-revealing anecdote. Good morning, I'm better than you. But in any field of human endeavour, you also find the experts who are so profoundly and meaningfully skilled at what they do that they can't be bothered with the game of one-upmanship. Their skills are not competitive, and are not needed for self-esteem. Their skills are pure. That makes them very rare, and therefore greatly to be cherished.

That's Rob for you. I have written a book called *How To Be A Bad Birdwatcher*. On that subject, at least, I am an expert. No false modesty. But I'd sooner talk to Rob than talk to anyone else about birds, not only because he knows more than most but because he shares more. No side, no nonsense, no snobbery. He has no need of such things. And in this book, which is filled with Rob's own gentle regrets and his gentle humour, you can learn what being a *good* birdwatcher is really all about.

As you read, and especially as you read the extracts from Rob's notebooks, you begin to understand that looking is in itself a skill. Rob looks better than you or I do. He is better-looking than any of us. He has refined looking into a way, not just of telling one bird from another, but of understanding the bird and the landscape it is in. He sees things that the rest of us don't notice; or if we do, we are not aware that we notice. He picks up small nuances of behaviour and tiny variations of plumage. He does this, not to find rare birds and create a big score, but because he sees the world in beautiful, clear, painterly detail.

Reading Rob's book, it seemed to me that I have been seeing birds in black and white all my life, or perhaps on fast-forward, or that I have never quite got my binoculars in focus. Rob slows the process down, makes everything clear. And it's not about rare birds; it's about all birds. It's about life. It's about a real love of the overwhelming biodiversity of it all, a real affinity for the mechanism of life.

I am reminded of something that students of extinction call the rivet-popper hypothesis. A jumbo jet can fly across the sky even if it has lost a rivet or two. Or three. Or four. But there comes a point when an aeroplane that has popped too many rivets will simply fall out of the sky. The planet is the jumbo jet, and the rivets are species. Rob has made himself one of the great experts at the understanding of rivets. That is to say, the things that hold our planet and our lives together. This is something that makes his work a very profound matter. Without making any such claim himself, Rob is telling us – in exquisite, perfect, Hume-esque detail – about the meaning of life.

In one of the many field guides Rob has written, I recall his line that the wings of a swift 'may shine paler in bright light'. Stoned, I thought. The dear man must have been boiled as an owl when he wrote that. Everyone knows that swift's wings don't shine. Then one evening, watching swifts over a cold beer in Cadiz in the unforgiving Mediterranean sun, I noticed something I had never seen before. Caught in the flashbulb light, I saw a swift's wings shimmer in a thrillingly hallucinogenic way. Noticed it again and again after that. And my understanding of the meaning of life was advanced by another micron or two.

Rob does that sort of thing. It's his – well, it's his *nature*.

Simon Barnes, 2005

Beginnings – Brooks and Byways

The white post-war prefabs stood in a long row like worn-down teeth along the top of a slope. Widely separated from their mirror image across the road, they looked down over a few narrow fields to a southern outlier of Cannock Chase called Gentleshaw Common. Few places I've known have a better name than that. My mother's name was Birch; I was born and lived in Oak Lane, in Burntwood, before moving to Lime Grove and then to Willow Avenue; I now live in Cedar Gardens. Perhaps I should have made a living from trees.

At the end of Oak Lane, turning left downhill past The Miner's Arms (since renamed The Concorde and then the Forester's Arms, thus divorcing it from any relationship with local community life), you come to a junction, with a diagonal bridge beneath it, at the bottom of the common. The Redmoor Brook runs through this culvert from the common, having sprung from the edge of the Chase, and continues south-east towards the edges of Burntwood and the Nag's Head, where we called it the Nag Brook. Later it joins the Maple Brook, grows a little into the Bourne Brook and eventually feeds the River Trent close to King's Bromley. The West Coast main railway line runs through here, via Tamworth and Lichfield Trent Valley station, although the Trent itself is some way north of Lichfield. The little brooks are often not much more than road- or field-side ditches, with overgrown banks where wrens nest and lines of alders where siskins feed in winter. Here and there they spread into wider, pebbly shallows where, once or twice a year, a green sandpiper might feed, or a grey wagtail might appear, wagging its body in concert with the ripples of the stream. This bit of southern Staffordshire was home to me, and I love it still.

Gentleshaw Common – 'the shaw common' we always called it – is a bulbous slope of heather and peaty bog, with a little 'peak' of sandstone that must once have been quarried: the old Ordnance Survey 1:25,000 map sheet SK01 marks it as a gravel pit. We called it 'Windy Peak'. Not only is it a bit of a local landmark, with its exposed pink-red rock and sand, but it was a good place to slide down on tin trays (although I'm not sure I did so very often, being very small and not very brave). The brook winds below it, alongside a rough, low hedge; beside it ran a rough track, which, I suppose, is still there.

'Brook' was a good word for this little stream, with its 'br' running into a vowel with a throaty full stop. I was always fascinated by words, how they look and how they sound. It was definitely 'brook', with a short 'oo', although for many years the big black bird of the fields and trees round about was a 'rook' rhyming with 'luke' (and a school teacher from up north, I remember, pronounced 'book' and perhaps even 'cook' the same way). There was, I think, a period of some confusion with 'roof' ('roofe' or 'ruff'), and it was a while before I rhymed rook with hook.

Although the surrounding countryside is nothing exceptional, this bit of Staffordshire is, to me, as good a bit of midland England as you can get, with tall church spires dominated by the fine three-spired Lichfield cathedral – tall and romantic as a sea cliff – lovely woods that become intensely rich in reds, browns, purples and gleaming sandy-orange in winter, green fields with dairy cattle and rabbit warrens, and tall hedges on raised banks beside winding little lanes that sometimes dive between outcrops of dark, damp sandstone. We had miles of it to the north and east of us and I walked miles from the age of four or five. Many of the fields I knew then – where we spent hours, whole days, out of doors – are now housing estates.

There may be a recurring theme in this book: the loss of rural countryside to development of one sort or another. Every bit of compromise to development is a loss to the open landscape; there is never a gain. Oppose a development of 500 new buildings, settle for 250, and you think you have won – in fact, you have lost, as more countryside goes under the concrete and tarmac. People criticize NIMBYS – 'not in my back yard' merchants – for trying to fend off development and put it elsewhere. I think NIMBYS are great – we need more of them. They fight for their beloved local countryside, which no one else does (certainly not the local councils, which seem to concentrate on nothing but more and more growth even where none is needed, more and more retail and industrial parks). Much has been written about the loss of birds to changing farming practices, but what gets most people, most of the time, is the loss of simple open countryside to buildings and roads.

Having said this, I'm not sure most people are very bothered about it if they ever think about it at all. I'm quoted in a recent book as saying that most people would prefer to have a new superstore, a car park, an access road and a roundabout. But some of us are deeply disturbed by this loss, which is accelerating. It began early in my area. At the bottom of the garden of the second house I lived in was a bramble and hawthorn hedge and a tall old oak. Beyond were large fields, grazed by fine Ayrshire cattle and surrounded by ditches, hedges and an abundance of tall oak and ash trees. Later, when the cattle were gone, the fields grew tall grass but the ditches, hedges and trees survived. Today, the garden oak and a few brambles are all that remain – the fields have long been covered in houses. I've nothing against houses, and I have no easy answers. But it is a sad loss, all the same.

I do not subscribe to the notion that there is any real division between 'country people' and 'townies'. Life is not so simple. But many people who make planning decisions live in towns – nothing wrong with that, I do myself – and really have no particular liking for the countryside. So they cannot see why the whole country should not be covered with buildings and roads and roundabouts and concrete. Why not? What's the problem with 750,000 new homes, largely on greenbelt land, in south-east England? Who says there will be no water to go round soon, no space on the roads? We'll build more roads – simple enough. So, the green turns to grey. They like grey. Someone, though, needs to put the opposing view, and do it soon.

We walked on the roads. There was, after all, no traffic. Little gangs of us – I don't know now, perhaps three or four or five – up to no good (but doing no harm) around the hedge banks and the brooks and the woodland edge. I don't think we ever penetrated the woods much: we kept mainly to the footpaths if we left the road at all. We were too timid to do much scrumping of apples and pears and damsons. There were one or two green lanes. Springlestyche Lane was metalled for the first few yards and had its name confirmed by a cast-iron sign on the house at its end; others we knew by names that might, for all I know, have been of our own invention. One was Cumpsey Lane, another Rough Dick's, where I clearly remember hearing my first green woodpecker laughing above the drifts of little, pale, wild daffodils. These lanes passed between high hedgerows and rolling fields, and two had small ponds (Bott's Pond in the case of Springlestyche), but I was never comfortable walking along them. Nor am I still, quite: they are a bit mysterious, making me feel a bit anxious, as if they might be haunted or as if someone unpleasant might be encountered walking the other way.

We didn't trespass into fields except those behind the house in Burntwood, where we roamed fairly freely up and down the hedgerows, played in the dry ditches where we made little roofed dens, and clambered about some huge English elms and ash trees. Elms have long gone from the countryside, a massive loss to the landscape. I occasionally look at a video of steam railway archive film and many scenes remind me of what it used to be like in the 1950s and even early 1960s: everywhere billowing trees, like dramatic cumulo-nimbus, thrusting powerfully up from the earth.

We used to cut a short stem from an ash tree and make what we called a throwing arrow with it. This would be thick and heavy at one end (which had been cut to a sharp point), and long and tapered at the tail end, which was split to take a simple cardboard flight. Just below this, we would cut a notch to take a long piece of string, with a knot near one end. The string was wrapped around the notch and passed over the knot; its other end was coiled around two or three fingers, so that when we threw the arrow, but held on tight to the string, it would act like the throwing stick of an Aborigine or Kalahari bushman. We could fling the arrow what seemed to be prodigious distances – it ought to be an Olympic sport.

Sometimes we had a home-made catapult, too – a forked stick with a length of quarter-inch square black elastic bought from a hardware shop and a piece of leather threaded onto it to hold a stone. I don't think any of us ever hit anything much with these fearsome 'catties', apart from our own thumbs. Blue-black, throbbing thumbnails were commonplace. The most proficient users of catapults that I've ever seen were kids in Cuba, who threw fish to attract royal terns, which were then hit, with a mighty thwack, with a stone. The terns usually continued flying, but with one droopy wing, or in visible discomfort, no doubt with several broken ribs and untold internal damage. There was little I could do but move on, just as in Turkey where I once watched middle-aged men 'fishing' for Mediterranean gulls on baited hooks. They reeled them in and broke off their beaks before releasing them.

Another trick we often tried with no success at all involved balancing one side of a garden sieve on a small stick and then scattering bread underneath it. Then we would tie a length of garden string to the stick and retire to the shed. The idea was that when a sparrow – a spuggie – came to get the bread, we would pull the string to dislodge the stick, releasing the sieve to trap the bird. What we would have done had we ever caught one I've no idea. I think the use of this kind of simple sparrow trap was probably widespread, especially in farming areas, although it may have been a West Midland thing, as the region has long been a centre of illegal bird-trapping, especially for 'green linnets' (greenfinches), 'brown linnets' (linnets) and 'seven-coloured linnets' (goldfinches).

We shot each other with plantains. For this we would pick a good, tall plaintain stem, wrap the bottom half of the stem tight under the flower head and then 'pop' it off a few yards; or we would pick wall barley spikes and throw them to stick on each other's Fair Isle woollen pullovers. Cow parsley stems, cut neat and sharp, with the soft pith removed, made excellent peashooters.

Where the Redmoor met the Maple Brook there was a deep, narrow channel of red brick, perhaps with fittings for a sluice gate at one end, leading one stream into the low, wide, shallow meandering of the other. We called it the Sheepwash, close to Cresswell Green by The Nelson pub. The Nelson now has a small restaurant; a sign proclaims the 'Eatery', which, at a small distance, looks unfortunately like 'Cattery'. The sluice was a good spot for competitive leaping across the rushing brook after rain, but the wide stream below was a bit too wide to jump. I remember being caught in a storm, on the wrong side of the brook, and crying because I couldn't, or wouldn't, get across, so my big brother had to pick me up and piggy-back me over. We were all wet through as we walked back home and stopped in the shelter of the side door of The Miner's Arms, where someone (the landlady I suppose) gave us all glasses of fizzy lemonade. Last time I saw it, the Sheepwash and its brick sluiceway were so overgrown that I could scarcely see the water. The old, splintered tree in the nearby field, where tree sparrows used to nest, has followed the tree sparrows into oblivion, but the countryside round about, the paddocks with beautiful horses, has changed little. The old cottages now have BMWs and Mercedes in the driveways, but they are better like that than falling down.

The Redmoor, with steep little banks between the hedge on one side and the track on the other, was made for damming. We collected stones and clods of earth and made long, effective banks across the stream, backing up quite sizeable pools of still water. Then we would break the dam in the middle and watch the whole lot get swept away before we went home for tea.

It was here, too, that for some inexplicable reason we took to catching grasshoppers. Catching them was not so shameful – they were everywhere, making their lovely little shuffling chirrups from the grass, that are now so infrequently heard (they make my wife shudder) and would hop up from under our feet as we walked through the grasses – but we also killed them. Why we did this I don't know, but I suppose someone started it and the rest of us followed. We used to throw them hard into the ground and watch them bounce and, if that didn't do the trick, we'd pick them up and do it again.

Strange fun for four- and five-year-olds, a bit like pulling the legs off spiders (which we never did).

The lower part of the hill was a mixture of grass and deep heather, with a flourishing growth of bilberry and cowberry. The red cowberries were a bit sharp, but the bilberries were traditionally picked in late summer by many people from the nearby villages and cooked in lovely pastry pies. My father, from Essex, had no bilberry tradition in him, and he's never liked them much, but the rest of us adored them. These were real bilberries, not the fat, cultivated 'blueberries' we get now. It took a lot of picking and a lot of berries and purple-blue fingers to fill a big Kilner jar with its rubber-sealed glass top; eating as many as we kept didn't help the speed of progress. It was years later that I found there were cranberries, too, sprawling across the sphagnum on the boggier spots, and sundews, colourful orchids and bog asphodel growing in the wettest peat. I don't know if they still do, but there's a good chance, as this is now, I think, an SSSI (Site of Special Scientific Interest). It needs management – tree-pulling or burning or grazing – to keep the heath open and free from scrub; I don't recall anything being done, or any animals grazing, when I used to play there.

The upper part of the hill, up towards The Windmill was flatter and drier. (This is getting to be a list of pubs; we never went in them, and I've been in very few of them since, but they always make good landmarks and The Windmill provides a good meal and a tasty pint of Staffordshire Bass.) On this section of the common many broadleaved trees had been planted, yards apart, each surrounded by a little ring fence of iron palings that bent over and outwards in a flourish at the top. As far as we could see nothing ever grazed the common, and these palings were far too large to protect the trees against rabbits; they were more like barriers to sheep or cattle, or perhaps deer. Something about them scared me. I rarely went that far up the common: these scrubby little trees in their Gothic black iron fences spooked me. I think they still might.

One warm sunny day we set fire to the common (well, only a little bit of it). Someone may have had a match or two but it is more likely that we burned a piece of paper by focusing the hot sun onto it through a magnifying glass. We used to do this onto our arms until we had burned a little brown spot on the skin. Once we had a few sparks, we pulled tufts of dry grass stems to set light to, and then went round setting crackling fire to the grass – rough, tough, dry stuff we called 'feg' – in a wide circle on the lower edge of the hill. We controlled it well: we never let it spread and used our feet to stamp out anything that might have threatened disaster, pounding the orange flames into aromatic, dusty black ash. Perhaps it is pushing it a bit to say that burning the common was somehow part of our relationship with nature.

It was here that we used to take birds' eggs. The whole area was full of birds, but I have little recollection of any specific ones or of being able to put names to any at that time, before I was six. Most of us 'took only one' from each nest; whether that was one from the nest between us, or one each, I can't recall. Even then I was reluctant and tried to argue the case for leaving some, but we were all eggers then. We judged the freshness of the egg by testing the way it floated in the brook; we would then puncture it at each end with a thorn and blow out the contents. The eggs we called 'addled' were, no doubt, well incubated with developing embryos. Over the next couple of years I collected eggs of blackbirds, song thrushes, yellowhammers ('scribblers'), pheasants and grey partridges. I well remember a chaffinch's nest found near Hammerwich, a beautiful construction of mosses and lichens and fine white hair, and that really started an argument as I wanted it left alone, or just to take one, but by the end we'd taken all the eggs and 'ragged' the nest – leaving me with a feeling of guilt and sadness.

We swapped eggs, so I can't remember which, if any really, I had found for myself, but between us we found nests that I've hardly ever seen since. We used to walk along the hedgerows, looking upwards through the twigs and foliage, against the light, until we found the tell-tale dark blob of a nest. If it was untouched, we might find eggs; if someone had been there before, it was usually 'ragged' (rhyming with lagged not jagged) and we were too late. One year, someone noticed a woodpecker's hole in a roadside oak. We went there armed with a chisel from someone's Dad's shed. My brother clung to a sucker growing from the bole of the tree and climbed up with his feet on the trunk; then he had to work his hands along the sucker to bring himself close to the hole. The sucker snapped and he fell off, banging and cutting his head against the tarmac. Whether anything was in the hole, we never found out, as we both went home crying, his hair matted with blood.

My egg collection was kept in a lovely little metal tin, golden-brass inside, black outside, with the bottom and the hinged lid both edged with a little cornice that was striped with red and gold. I lined it with cotton wool and kept the eggs safe inside, so there couldn't have been very many! If I remember right it was eventually knocked to the floor and the eggs were broken, but by then I wasn't much interested. There was a strangely musty, but slightly sweet, smell that came from the egg tin whenever I opened it. I can still smell it now. I still enjoy the sight of an impossibly perfect bird's egg, such as the sky blue with intense inky dots of a song thrush egg or the soft, blurry spots and lines on the

Song thrush nest and eggs.

egg of a chaffinch, but I rarely see them. Did egg collecting encourage an interest
in birds and nature, as many people insist it did? I have to say no, in our cases. So
far as I know, none of the other lads who collected birds' eggs then ever went on
to have the least bit of interest in the natural world around them. I was already
developing it, but would have done so, anyway, without the eggs.

Soon my parents bought us a bird book. It was for my brother, really, but we
shared it. It was an early Ladybird book of birds, with a pale pinky-buff patterned
cover inside the dust jacket and paintings by A. W. Seaby. Here were birds I
could only dream of seeing, such as the bullfinch; what a splendid bird that
looked, bright pink-red in front and blue-black on its thick, heavy bill and cap.
And the yellowhammer: fabulous, golden yellow and rusty brown with black
stripes. There must have been some mention of its eggs, which have irregular
black scratchings on them, and its country name that these gave rise to, the
scribbler. This book was the start of a combination of things that have stayed
with me ever since: a fascination with the bird itself, a lasting interest in the
paintings, and a deep impression made by the names. Yellowhammer. That, to
me, is a wonderful word. It sounds just right, it rolls off the tongue beautifully

and, of course, now it takes me back to my childhood and that Ladybird book. Little wonder, perhaps, that I am firmly opposed to changing English bird names. Leave them alone! Other names that I particularly liked (and still do) included redwing and brambling. I was illogical enough to think (without reading the words, I suppose) that brambling must have derived from bramble, the blackberry, and so I looked for bramblings around bramble brakes in my many walks across the fields on the various public paths.

Early efforts to identify birds were unsuccessful in the main. I tried too hard and I was sometimes reduced to real 'stringing' – exaggerating or glossing over a bird's features so that I could persuade myself that it fitted the description of a particular new species that I wanted to see. I recall seeing finches playing around in a hedge and flying up to a roadside oak one Sunday afternoon. I wanted to see a hawfinch, so I persuaded myself that they *were* hawfinches, thinking the beaks looked ever so big, their body colour was really tawny not pink. I'm sure now that they were chaffinches and I think, to be fair, that I had told myself that's what they were before we got home for tea, so these delusions didn't last long. But it is no surprise to me at all how easily people can delude themselves; how easy it is to get it all wrong, even with a barrage of modern books, CDs and video guides. Everyone has tales of mistakes that they've seen other people make. Once I overheard two people in a hide as they looked at a greenshank. Its bill curved ever so slightly upwards. They looked in their field guide and flicked through to the waders. 'Is it a redshank?' 'No, it's bill is curved, not straight.' 'Oh, yes. So it's a curlew, then.' Never mind up or down; the beak was curved – good enough.

My family had an interest in the countryside. My father had grown up on an Essex farm. Since the war he had taken on a career in industry, but his love of open spaces and farmland never diminished. My mother was my greatest support, wholeheartedly backing everything I did and said. Every Sunday we went for a walk – not just a short stroll, but a walk of several miles. Looking at flowers, butterflies, birds and so on, was something we just did. There were no experts among us, but the surrounding countryside was beautiful and we appreciated it. Being born on the edge of Cannock Chase was clearly crucial to my later outlook on life.

The local villages had grown up around the coal mining industry, and round about there were the remains of spoil heaps. One area, grassed over but still rough and wild, was the perfect place to ride our imaginary horses (a palamino and a paint) around the rimrocks, down over the bluffs and through the waist-deep purple sagebrush, on across the wash, through groups of Indians and into a box canyon, to find safety in the thickets of cottonwood and hickory. The landscape and language of the Wild West were as important to me as the action in the films and books.

Miners generally liked to have a hobby that got them out in the fresh air, away from the horrors of the deep black mines. In winter, many of them wouldn't see the sun for days on end. When I left school each afternoon in Chase Terrace, one of the shifts would be just finishing and I would see lines of miners, still black-faced with coal dust, white circles around the eyes, riding home on their bikes, their helmets and safety lamps on the handlebars. It doesn't surprise me that many miners have always been interested in pigeons, cage birds and fishing. Pigeons take them up into the sky, wild and free and beautiful as the sun burnishes them bright against the blue, such relief from being deep underground. My mother was from a mining family. My grandfather on this side was long dead, I think from the effects of long years down the pit, and an uncle had been killed in the mine long before I was born. Two others had died of influenza. But another uncle, Henry Birch, who spent his working life from the age of 14 in the mines, and lived to be almost 93, came to see us every week, without fail. He would take me and my brother for a walk, which is probably what eventually gave rise to our regular Sunday afternoon family walks. Later, we would drive somewhere first, then walk from there, thus extending our home patch into much of central and parts of northern Staffordshire. To the south was Birmingham, and we didn't often try to get through or around it: the Black Country conurbation was an effective barrier. We penetrated it only on alternate Saturdays when Walsall played at home and we stood, squashed in like sardines, on a bank of pit spoil at one end of Fellows' Park.

Uncle Henry went fishing, too. When I went to his house (it must sometimes have been around a Sunday lunchtime, probably after our walk, as we listened to *The Navy Lark* and *Take it from Here* on the radio), I often looked at *Mr Crabtree Goes Fishing*, a book that he had acquired for my cousin. I didn't know it was a publishing phenomenon, a massive bestseller published by the *Daily Mirror*. Again, there was a combination of lovely places, painted in Bernard Venables's delicate watercolours, large and unheard of fish, all that mysterious and colourful fishing tackle, and the magic of a combination of words and pictures that left indelible impressions in my mind. Many years later a series of coincidences led to my making contact with Bernard Venables, a year or two before he died, when he was 94. Our little bit of correspondence, and his various other books, made me realize how much his views about the development of fishing agreed with some of mine about the development of birdwatching: how similar the two pursuits can be. Although I didn't look at *Mr Crabtree* again for many years I did often think about it. Then I rediscovered it – the original copy, which I had somehow commandeered – some years before it was eventually reprinted.

Bernard Venables wrote about the joy of catching his first wriggling, sparkling little perch, a simple enough pleasure, but one that was a moment of magic for a small boy. Now anglers seem to start straight away with specimen fishing, going for the big ones; they have trailer-loads of expensive tackle, sometimes two or three rods at a time, with electronic bite-detectors. They sit down under a tent, switch on their gear and go to sleep, or read a book, until a buzz tells them they have a bite and the fish is practically hooked automatically. They happen to be present when the fish is landed, and not much more. In *The Illustrated Memoirs of a Fisherman*, Bernard Venables wrote that modern fishing:

> … is all so simple, so undemanding in terms of experience, skill, instinct, judgment. Small boys can do it, as can those unskilled of all ages. Consider those boys. They are cheated boys: so young they are ruined. Not for them the long magical sequence from first novitiate to experienced angler. That joy they can never know. They will never have that sublime experience when, the very first time, a small fish, probably a bristling little perch, is drawn pulsing from the riddle of the water.

There is a remarkably similar trend in birdwatching, thanks to the advent of birdlines, then pagers, then websites; 'twitching' takes over and dominates many a birdwatching career from the start. The initial magic of discovery has

Four woodlarks beside the runway at Farnborough Air Show.

been lost for many people (not, of course, for all) and, like the first wriggling perch, it is an experience that can never be recaptured. In one of his handful of typed letters to me, in 2000, Mr Venables wrote: 'It is painfully true that there is this parallel between bird watching and angling, and I think it's indicative of a blanketing thing which tends to spread over all spontaneous responses to such wonderful blessings that we have from Mother Earth. I sometimes think we are fighting against this tendency with inevitable defeat. But let's not accept that.'

I owe a considerable debt to Bernard Venables, for creating Mr Crabtree, and undoubtedly to my uncle Henry Birch, who introduced me both to the book and to the pursuit of fishing. With him, too, I increased my interest in aeroplanes, already sparked by my father who was in the RAF in the war. Always my uncle was aware of and pointed out to us aircraft flying overhead, usually DC3s, now and then an Anson. The drone of an old piston-engined aircraft still sends me outdoors to look. We went on Harper's coach trips from Heath Hayes to Farnborough Air Show for several years – a long trip then, going via Banbury where we stopped late at night on the way back – and at the back of the coach there was usually someone playing the Jew's harp (I've not heard one for donkey's years). In later years, Mum and Dad drove us there by car, and we went to Battle of Britain day displays at Gaydon, too. The best birds I saw on these trips were four woodlarks on the grass by the runway at Farnborough. Dad and Uncle Henry often joked about the way that everyone was looking to the right at some aeroplane while I looked left at a little show of my own.

Fishing meant going to Norton Pool, or, as we always called it, 'the pool', about which there will be much more later in the book. One day, from the houses over in Norton Canes at the northern end of the pool, I heard a local councillor broadcasting his election promises through a loudspeaker in the streets. 'And another thing,' he said, 'they want to take Norton Pool and call it Chasewater. We mustn't let them – it is Norton Pool and always has been Norton Pool and always will be Norton Pool.' I don't think anyone cheered, particularly, but I did so in my head and often think of what he said. The name was changed, of course, to Chasewater, for simple commercial reasons: it sounded better, ready for development as a water sports centre and whatever else anyone could think of to attract visitors, taking it away from any connection with the local villages. In fact, it was earlier known as Cannock Reservoir, or Cannock Chase Reservoir, and Norton Pool was perhaps just a local tag without much 'official' credence anyway. But who cares about official? It was Norton Pool to us, and that is where we went in search of big perch and roach and watched others fish for pike. I rarely tried for pike and never caught one. Sometimes we tried spinners and spoons, for the glistening lures themselves had an unmistakable appeal. But live baiting was not for me, Mr Crabtree notwithstanding, although we did sometimes turn over stones to catch bullheads (miller's thumbs) and stick one on a hook to tempt a big perch.

One time in my early exploration of Norton Pool, the water level was low, and on the southern shore there were, I recall, little brown birds running about on the exposed mud and grass. This, I think, must have been in 1957, when I was just seven. The dry summer had caused the water level to fall, making it a great year for dunlins, ringed plovers and other waders. I read about the birds years later, in old West Midland Bird Reports bought up to make a set. The southern shore had a deep inlet, perhaps (I'm hazy about this) with the remains of a boat. This boat had once taken people on trips around the reservoir, which is well over a mile long and quite a substantial sheet of water. The inlet and its adjacent 'headland' (being just a spit of land a few yards long) was later developed a little, with stone facings, a footpath, and a silly little stone 'castle' at the end. It has since been changed forever by the Birmingham North Orbital Road, which runs alongside, while the local authority has 'developed' the south shore by heaping loads of bulky waste onto it, covering it with earth and grassing it over in wide, round, unnaturally smooth domes. The rather rare (for the West Midlands) and quite ancient sward of shoreweed has been buried, while the topsoil has already been eroded, leaving bits of dangerous metal and unsightly brick poking out at all angles; an unnecessary footpath, which takes people right along the new shoreline, has done for the waders completely. Such is progress.

There was much more development on this shore after the castle was created. In the south-east corner, a creosote-scented pier was built, with a black and white painted wooden tower at the end, made to look like a lighthouse, with a spiral stair inside to a balcony at the top. Beside it was a floating wooden pontoon affair, the remains I think of another attempt to introduce a boat trip around the pool. Here we used to fish, just us kids, on summer days, when loudspeakers from the 'lighthouse' broadcast the hits of the day. There was Frank Ifield singing *I remember you* several times every Saturday afternoon and this, I think, was when I became hooked on the Everly Brothers' *Cathy's Clown*, which I still play. Either song will in an instant take me back to Chasewater and the joys of little slippery perch, their scales rough when rubbed 'against the grain', spiky gill covers and painfully spiny fins.

With Uncle Henry I used to explore other bits of the several miles of shoreline. We went by bike, our rods tied in neat cloth bags along the crossbar and a tackle bag slung over one shoulder. (Now people drive, or sometimes take piles of heavy gear, seats and umbrellas in little trailers behind their bikes.) First we'd have dug some lobworms from the garden. That was usually my job. Now and then I'd try the compost heap for something more exotic and find little red or stripy worms, which went into the tin with a bit of moss and soil. We might take some bread, too, for making 'paste', and very occasionally we might buy a few maggots, or a bag of split hempseed (little round, dark seeds with a split in one side that revealed a soft, white pith when they were boiled). Mostly, though, we were teaching worms to swim.

The craft and hobby shop in Lichfield, just across the road from the Friary school, had all we needed. I had an old rod from Uncle Henry and later bought a fibreglass tip from the shop. Eventually I had the old, yellow, varnished, whole cane and cork butt, a dark-brown split cane middle section, and a pale-green fibreglass tip. It was an inelegant hotchpotch that more or less served its purpose. I learned something when I bought the ferrules and was asked whether I wanted a male, a female, or both – this seemed to add credence to some unlikely rumours going around at school. We bought rings for the line and wrapped them onto the cane with red silk thread, from Mum's embroidery box, stuck a ferrule at each end and wrapped that around with silk, too, before covering the whole lot in clear varnish.

A substantial stick of some sort – a bit of narrow dowel – made the base of a float; several corks were pushed on to it and cut with a knife into a rough, central, elongated egg shape. These were painted with a tiny pot of bright enamel paint, the tip intense Day-Glo orange, red or yellow. At the bottom we added a little metal eye, also wrapped around with silk and varnished, to take the line. It needed several swan-shots to make it sit up nicely in the water and it made for very heavy tackle, but then we were casting out as far as we could from the flat shore and fishing at very long range. If the wind was right, the float would drift out to the limit of our line.

This was how people fished here; nothing very delicate about it. Now and then the float would bob and drift, tilt and sit up, then slowly sink sideways – wonderful! I've not fished for decades and don't think I will again, but I can still appreciate the magic of the moving float (fishing with a ledger on the bottom, and no float, was never so much fun). If the bait was a worm, the strike was a little delayed – it would be a perch and it needed time to fumble about with the bait and decide to swallow it. If the bait was paste or a maggot, or a boiled hempseed, it was likely to be a roach, and quicker reactions were needed. I'd read Mr Crabtree! That was about the limit of my expertise and over a few years I caught almost nothing: a few perch, once or twice big enough to persuade

Mum to cook them for tea. But, mosquitoes apart ('Dusk' insect-repellent never worked), those long evenings at the pool were marvellous. Nothing can quite bring back the atmosphere of those early fishing expeditions and the long ride home in the dark.

The deeply indented north shore of the pool was closely fringed in places by steeply sloping heaps of mining waste, the largest of which we called 'the Mount'. Beyond that, out on a headland, was a small mound, 'the Target', which was used as a target for shooting across the reservoir as early as the 1880s. To get to the Target was a real effort, with bikes and tackle, crossing streams and a sluice and climbing up and down the heaps of spoil. I'm not sure if it was really worth the trouble because I don't think the fishing was ever any better.

Below the reservoir is a canal. The reservoir is, in fact, a canal feeder, not a drinking water reservoir, supplying water to top up the canal system that goes north-east to Lichfield and branches into Walsall and the Black Country, which is laced with canals and their towpaths. We used occasionally to fish the canal, too, especially the 'canal basin' below the dam, where the canal widened to allow the long coal boats to turn. At the age I was then, I was just in time to catch the last of the horse-drawn narrow boats, although the old stables farther along the canal remained for some years.

In those days, both reservoir and canal had crystal-clear water. In the reservoir itself we could watch shoals of perch and flashing roach, and spot little jack pike hanging motionless in the shallows. In the canal, we watched the crayfish and mysterious groups of roach. But I could never catch much, so I resorted to fishing under a road bridge where I could easily pull out a few gudgeon and ruffe (little, spiky fish that I've never clapped eyes on since). If we spotted a crayfish, we would find a piece of string, attach a stone or button to one end, and drop it down in front of the strange crustacean, tempting it to make a grab for it. Every so often one would hold on long enough for us to pull it right up to the surface and swing it across to the bank. After any gale the shore of the reservoir itself was often littered with dead and dying crayfish, which dried out and changed from tough, dark olive green to skeletal, brittle, bluish white. On a calm summer's evening, the water was dimpled by scores, sometimes hundreds, of fish rising for insects on the surface. In later years, I never saw fish like this again, never saw so many roach and perch in increasingly fuggy water, and the crayfish all but disappeared.

Fishing alternated with trainspotting. While my interest in fish has remained, even with an absence of angling (I love fish-watching), my interest in steam disappeared for many years to be revived again (too late really) in the preservation era. Now I am a volunteer on mainline steam excursions and edit a periodic magazine for patrons of a steam preservation trust. We watched steam on the West Coast mainline at Lichfield and hardly realized how lucky we were. This was towards the end of steam, in the very late 1950s and early 1960s, with various experimental diesels – the massive prototype Deltic in sky blue with cream stripes was always exciting – and standard Class 4 diesels gradually taking over from the big 'namers' on the expresses. Names on a few of the diesels themselves, such as *Scafell Pike*, *Great Gable* and *Ingleborough*, were not the same. I took the numbers, of course – I always like to know 'what I've seen', especially with birds – but it was a purely aesthetic, physical thing for me. These were fabulous speeding monsters but, equally enchanting, were the 'duck sixes', the old Class 4 freights, that clanked along with endless lines of loose-coupled coal trucks, creating beautiful music all of their own.

The mainline was several miles from home – something like a four-mile bike ride each way – and the journey involved going through Lichfield city centre, which I did with my brother when I was just nine and ten years old. I'd been doing the countryside walks, with no parent in sight, two or three miles from home when I was just four and five. It seems inconceivable now: how many ten-year-olds go off on a bike, through the local town and out the other side, with a packet of sandwiches, a bottle of Vimto and a grubby Ian Allan abc of locomotive numbers?

At the back of the garden the fields changed from pastures for cows to tall ryegrass; I don't remember it being cut for hay. We used to play football and cricket when the grass was short, with rolled up pullovers for stumps or goalposts, a heavy, laced, leather ball – a 'casey' – weighed down by mud and wet, and big, long-studded boots with huge metal toecaps and long laces that wound under and over and round through a loop at the back several times. We religiously cleaned the boots and anointed them with sweet-smelling dubbin on a rag, and doused our bats in lovely, aromatic linseed oil. Later, when the grass grew tall and tough, we rolled in it, over and over for yards, and created our very own crop circles by flattening it down in complicated patterns that shone in the sun.

All of this fishing and watching locomotives and going on the bus to watch Walsall play on a Saturday afternoon changed when I turned my attention to birds, but it was a continuation of the same thing: a slow, fascinating, enthralling journey of discovery.

Secrets and Magic in Essex

Two things began to influence me very strongly as my interest in birds grew. First, there were books in the local library at Chase Terrace and, later, in the school library. Second, there was my relationship, at a distance, with my two older and more experienced birdwatching cousins in Essex. They were far more experienced birdwatchers than I was. They were not many years older, but a few years at that age means a lot. I was getting to know more about what they did (and they had a different set of steam engines down there, too, their numbers beginning with six instead of four, although they were never so handsome as 'ours'). We wrote letters and now and then we met on holidays with them in Colchester. This was a massive spark to my early interest; I could compete, in a small way, and I could copy. In other words, I was learning from them and they spurred me to do more.

My education took many forms. Cousin John was writing a regular bird diary (a log) and I copied its format (which I have hardly changed since). For many years I kept a regular diary of anything interesting. It was never a printed daily or weekly diary but rather a bound notebook so that entries could be made only when something was worth mentioning: there was no point having pages of 'blank' days with occasional pages that did not give me the space to write all I wanted to say. The chronological nature of this system has the great benefit now of allowing me to relive particular days, but there is the huge disadvantage that information on particular species or locations is scattered through the years. So, if I want to find notes on Chasewater, or find out how many firecrests I've seen, and when and where they were, I have to start at the beginning and plod through day after day for years. But, should I wish to know where I was in January 1967, there it is, in an instant, along with what was seen.

My cousins also had binoculars and I was soon wanting some of my own. We (that is, Dad) bought some Japanese Regent 10×50s after seeing an advertisement in a newspaper, although for a time we used a borrowed pair of wartime 7×50s, complete with cross-hair sights, which were fantastically bright. Then we had a lovely little pair of British Wray 8×30s, which I lost some years later when I left them on a bus in Swansea after a day out. I couldn't believe it and was mortified, ashamed to have to write to tell Dad.

When I saw my first ever waxwings (three of them) in the 1966 invasion, I wrote a letter boasting about it to David, the younger of my two birdwatching cousins. He wrote back, saying 'Three? A mere three?' There had been 24 in his school yard. We compared notes on colours and shapes, for these birds never seemed quite like their pictures in our books, their subtlety of colour and shape too difficult to capture on paper. I wrote back about the wildfowl on Blithfield Reservoir; he replied with news about birds at Abberton Reservoir and on the Essex coast. My birdwatching career was taking off in a way that now seemed unlikely to peter out after a few months' interest. It was my aunt in Colchester who suggested that she might enrol me in the RSPB as a Christmas present.

Holidays in Essex were wonderful. My father returned when he could to his own bit of Essex, a bit farther south than Colchester. I can just remember going to Whitehall Farm (now replaced by a spanking new farm building) near Fobbing, with its sticky grey-muddy farmyard and grey Ferguson tractor, and a bull that had learned the trick of hoicking the gate off its hinges with his horns. But it was Great Wakering and Foulness Island, east of Southend, that left an indelible mark and was where most of the family lived. This was magic to a child, especially as Foulness was accessible only by War Department permit and was full of atomic weapons research establishments. From Shoeburyness great guns fired across the Maplin Sands, making the windows rattle and shudder as if they would fall from their frames. From a battery behind my uncle's house on Foulness, anti-aircraft guns were tested, firing at a target hung between two tall pylons, with shattering reports. It fed endless fantasies for a small child, but strangely never any fears.

The house on Foulness was a wooden, clapboard-walled affair, with a chemical toilet out the back; there was an ancient tree stump, and a big woolly dog. Before that, there was a different house and, near by, a large chicken shed, where I would go in to collect the eggs and always find the china egg that induced the hens to lay. Even sleeping in a bedroom beside a proper road – as we did in Great Wakering – was strange (we lived in Burntwood at the end of a cul de sac, with no passing traffic). Seeing the headlights of cars light up one end of the ceiling, then fan out in rays through the gaps in the curtain tops and swing across to the other side of the room as the car went by, was new and exciting;

and, if it were going towards Foulness, perhaps, after dark, who might be in it? It must be a spy at least ...

Uncle Ron was in the Royal Observer Corps (ROC) and filled our heads with aircraft. He would go off some evenings in his smart blue uniform and cocked cap to the ROC meetings. His magazines were packed with exciting pictures, including pages and pages of tiny, blurry, black-and-white photographs of distant aeroplanes that had to be identified, including exotic Russian ones such as Fishpots and Fishbeds, Bears and Blinders. Sometimes I wonder how much this influenced my approach to bird identification and the use of bird books. This aeroplane recognition business used much the same techniques: first you looked at shapes and formats to narrow a plane down to a few possibilities, then you used the detail and a process of elimination to pinpoint the only possible conclusion.

The marshes and fields round about, the sea walls and muddy creeks, the borrow pits inside the sea walls where waders fed – all were brilliant for birds. I was shown a night heron on a pool on Foulness, close to the church, when I was eight. I've looked up the books, which confirm that it was there. But I can't remember it. It is the only species I have seen in Britain that I can't remember seeing, as I've never yet seen another one here. I've not ticked it. Sometimes we swam in the sea at Shell Corner and watched passing porpoises; often we sat on the Quay Loading, a small, concrete jetty on the banks of the River Roach, opposite Wallasea Island, and watched swarms of large yachts go by from Burnham-on-Crouch, their big, gaily coloured spinnakers round and shining in the sun, collapsing and clapping as they turned and emptied of wind.

Driving on to Foulness meant, as it still does, stopping at the 'police hut' to show our War Department pass, without which there was no access. Then we would go along a narrow, straight road partly made of concrete, which made a distinctive rumble and rhythmic thump-thump-thump as we rode over the joints; then there was a long, low, narrow bridge and another long stretch of road, which at night was populated with hares and rabbits. On either side old farmhouses stood in the open fields, each with a little copse or shelterbelt; it seemed that someone in our family had been born in, or lived in, most of them at some time or another. The black Jerry barn, now demolished, stood beside a little wood to add some relief to the flat landscape. Flat land can be dull and boring, to be sure, but this flat coastal area, long ago claimed from the sea and still defended by its sea walls, has a magic all of its own and it still tugs at me.

There were days when we rode around on combine harvesters; others when we played around the outbuildings of the Quay farm (properly, Monkton

Barn). Inside was a new-fangled caterpillar tractor as well as a couple of Massey Harrises, Fordsons or Fergusons. The smell of any old, oily tractor still takes me back there in an instant: smells are wonderfully evocative. The last time I visited this farm I was distressed to see it in a dilapidated condition, with broken windows and missing roof tiles, abandoned in the consolidation of smaller holdings and outposts into giant farms served from some central headquarters. But the old school, which my father had not visited for 80 years, is now the Foulness Heritage Centre, the walls inside plastered with old photographs. I had never seen any of them before this recent visit, but here there were four of my aunts in one school photograph. Others showed my uncles (both now dead) driving their combines and Marshall tractors, or unloading sacks of wheat, in their blue overalls and black caps, exactly as they always were. Heroes.

Foulness has a network of ditches in which there were usually eels to be found. The locals would catch sizeable eels; whether they used eel forks, long sticks with a fork on the end, or traps of some sort, I'm not sure. Sometimes someone would come round with a bucket of live eels and we would later be served lengths of fried eel for supper – an exceedingly rich, tasty meal. Long lines might be set out at low tide on the mudflats, to catch Dover sole, plaice, flounder and dabs on the incoming tide. It was not without its dangers: a photograph in the heritage centre shows a local man who was drowned while attending his lines.

Another cousin lived in a farm opposite Rushley Island, to which cattle were taken out by swimming them across at low tide, like something from *Rawhide* or one of the countless cowboy films we watched at Chase Terrace in the Saturday matinées. One day, some years after my first visits (it was 29 October 1965), I walked to the farm and on my way back, towards Landwick, discovered a great grey shrike hunting along a line of small trees. It was new for me, and a beautiful bird: a stunner. I wrote in my notes that I was surprised that a black, white and grey bird should look so beautiful. Black, white and grey birds often do. I've loved shrikes, in particular, ever since. Of course I wrote to David about it. He quoted from the Essex bird report, which detailed 22 records the previous year and said that the species was no longer even a lesser rarity in the county. It has since become one again, if not a major one.

That same day I saw a flock of small brown birds, perhaps two or three hundred of them, along the sea wall. I didn't get great views, and I put them down, initially, as redpolls; later I inked in two question marks, added 'plus Twites?' and then crossed that out and pencilled in 'TWITE for sure'. The next day I also wrote down redpolls, but was puzzled that I saw neither the red caps nor the black chins. I put this down to the long-range view, although I did add that the habitat seemed better for twites; later, I corrected the record to twites. It seems odd to me now that I was not more convinced at the time. And while I was struggling with twites and redpolls, I could easily identify a much rarer bird, the superb shrike (although that is, of course, pretty well unmistakable). It shows that a 'good bird' can turn up in front of anyone, however incompetent.

Things in Colchester were just *different* from home. Just as the family in Great Wakering talked of such unknown things as 'the arterial road', so in Colchester it was 'the bypass' that cropped up in conversation, equally a new concept for me as a youngster. We had fresh herrings and plaice for tea: no better than at home, but different. The trains from Colchester station out to the coastal towns were electrics, which hummed and crackled. And there was this birdwatching business. We often popped down to 'the reservoir', which was Abberton Reservoir, for many years rated among the very best inland waters in Britain for wildfowl (although, to be fair, it is pretty close to the coast).

Colchester in spring (Easter holidays) and summer (long summer holidays) was very important in my formative birdwatching years. I had no contact with anyone really expert in birds at home, so these visits were like short, intensive courses in how to find and identify birds properly, and how to keep records of them. We usually went on day trips to the beach at Clacton and Walton on the Naze, where we built the world's best and most realistic sandcastles, with moats that were filled by the tide and towers that collapsed as the incoming sea washed around them, but somehow birdwatching walks developed as well. Walks to Birch Lake and nearby areas were always fascinating. We walked through deeply entrenched green lanes from Shrub End and Stanway Green to the Roman River valley, which sounded enticingly mysterious, passing Olivers Farm and going on through Chest Wood. It is not much different even now.

Birdwatching was a bit hit and miss at first. We walked past some derelict buildings, Baymill Cottages, and, from the evidence of the already broken windows, we were by no means the first to throw a stone or two through the remaining panes of glass. Kids doing what kids do came first, birds second, but as we grew up a bit it gradually turned the other way round. Mostly the birds were common ones, but I was becoming really aware of them for the first time. Early on I was trying too hard, as usual. I saw a brownish bird in a treetop, flitting about in the foliage, and decided it could be – ought to be – a spotted flycatcher. It was pretty undistinguished, basically dull, plain brown, so it was easy to twist into a spotted flycatcher – early 'string' – but I had taken no real note here of behaviour or posture. I don't mean displays and intricacies of direct or indirect scratching or whatever, just that spotted flycatchers sit upright, stay still for long periods, then fly out, catch an insect and return to a perch. They are alert and bright-eyed. They don't 'flit about' in the foliage, let alone slip quietly between the leaves in a horizontal pose, as this bird was doing. Obviously, it was not a spotted flycatcher; but when I got back (for some reason I was on my own this time) and described a sober, brownish, small, slim bird, John kindly agreed that it might have been one, as spotted flycatchers were usually around there at that time of year. It was a simple mistake, compounded by excess enthusiasm and a desire to see something new. I think, at the time (I must have been 12 or so) I probably knew what I was doing, even while I was watching it: pushing things a bit towards what I wanted to see, as I was to do with the 'hawfinches' in the Staffordshire hedgerow. I'd vaguely heard of a spotted flycatcher, I had not, to my knowledge, seen one, and here was my chance.

Now and then there was something different. We found a small brown and white bird with white wing bars on the edge of a wood one August. It was, David said, a bit like a female chaffinch in colour, but with only one wing bar, and it was slender and thin-billed. It was with some satisfaction, later, that David read from the trusty *Collins Pocket Guide* that the female and young pied flycatcher look rather like a hen chaffinch without the white shoulder patch. I don't think that recent field guides have made such a comparison, but this one was spot on with our own impressions at the time. The most recent Collins guide, the super-impressive *Collins Bird Guide* by Mullarney, Svensson, Zetterstrom and Grant, jumps in at a much higher level, assumes you know it is a flycatcher already and then discusses the separation of different age and sex categories and elimination of various other 'pied' flycatchers from across Europe. We were nowhere near that stage, operating in a different league. 'Like a hen chaffinch without the white shoulder patch' was good enough for us then; Richard Fitter had hit the right mark with his pocket guide text – something that is immensely difficult to do.

There were some quite good birds early on. We once drove to Ring Mere and East Wretham heath in the Brecks. We parked beneath a group of Scots pines. I wasn't really aware of what might be there, but I heard some clicking and quiet splintering noises from the tree above and John said, 'That's what we're on the lookout for.' There were crossbills feeding on the cones. This was April 1963, when I was still 12. I had seen my first red-legged partridge, nuthatch, siskin and brambling the day before, when I also recorded a chiffchaff for the first time. My first blackcap and tree pipit came on the same day as the crossbills, and my first noted meadow pipit a few days later. This was a good spell. This in part reflects the fact that I was just beginning to keep notes as much as see birds, although some of these were undoubtedly firsts, or at least the first time I had seen them and realized what they were for sure.

It wasn't until September 1965 that I first saw a collared dove, at Birch Lake near Colchester, at a time when collared doves were still rare and localized, and still practically absent from Staffordshire. (In my copy of *The Birds of Staffordshire*, 1962, I wrote in collared dove by hand: it was unknown in the county at the time the book was published.) It is easy to forget that, not so long ago, this was a bird that people travelled to see, not one that they would write to the RSPB to complain about and suggest a nationwide cull to relieve them of the monotony of their calls. (They do.)

By 1965 – I was 15 – we were visiting some more productive and interesting places in Essex. It seems strange now: many 15-year-olds are already on their way to having seen 400 birds in Britain and have travelled the world. It was not like that in the mid-1960s, or at least not for me. (I must remember that there were precocious teenagers who were remarkably expert, but this was not by any means the norm.) In August we went to Goldhanger on the Blackwater coast just east of Maldon. Foulness had already implanted in me a love of the Essex marshes, and this kind of walk around a sea wall, with mud and salt marsh on the seaward side, borrow pits and grassy meadows and long fields of golden corn stubble inland, reinforced my lasting delight in such coasts, Essex in particular. I recently went to Old Hall Marshes, an RSPB nature reserve that has, because of access problems, escaped what some may see as excessive development as a visitor attraction; it has not become a 'Minsmere' but has remained almost untouched (in the way that many RSPB reserves are if they are not 'A list' and heavily promoted). The reserve is a superb piece of old Essex, although its salt marshes outside the sea walls remain under threat from sea-level rise and erosion: around it, much of the character of the coast remains, but much has also been lost. Near by there are experimental areas of 'managed retreat': fields that have been opened up to the sea for the first time in centuries and that will help to replenish the shrinking marshes. This is a great idea and excellent for birds, but for the moment, inevitably, a little bit unnatural in appearance.

At Goldhanger I was noting most of what we saw: two magpies, a sedge warbler and a whitethroat are on the list alongside 120 oystercatchers, 10 wheatears, many dunlins, 20 to 30 turnstones (my first), 25 shelducks, 250 curlews, including a flock of 46 and another of almost 200, a common sandpiper, a female yellowhammer, and so on, in random order. Two grey plovers (I well remember their *tseeoo-ee* calls), two green sandpipers (also calling loudly as they flew up from the channels inside the sea wall) and two golden plovers were noted as new birds that day – 'lifers' to use a word that I never normally use.

Later, at Abberton, we noted two ruffs, two little terns, gadwalls and a long-tailed duck, which I had first seen, as a new bird for me, a week before. It was at close range, in moult, and 'allowed detailed observations to be made'. Odd how I had already adopted a somewhat pompous birdwatching turn of phrase when writing my notes; it is so obvious how, at a young age, we copy such things from books. (What books I'm not sure, but the language bears comparison with the unnatural, formal speech used by police or fire officers on the news when giving details of an incident; birdwatchers have their own kind of jargon from the start.) I'm not sure whom I was writing for, but the semi-official tone persisted for years. Was it for me? For my own enjoyment later on? Not exactly. It was as though I was writing for some unknown reader (although no one ever got their hands on these books of mine! – the last thing I wanted was that anyone else should read these bird diaries and they remain all but secret).

These notes are in an exercise book, covered with brown paper, written in blue ink with a proper fountain pen. I later added little asterisks alongside some bird names in black ink – this could have been done months afterwards.

Long-tailed duck. My first at Abberton was a juvenile.

Asterisks were something I began to use quite early on in my notebooks; this was my own addition to John's logbook format. They were used to highlight 'good birds' and 'good views'. For example, on a trip to Kings Forest in Breckland on 29 August, we saw and heard a few run-of-the-mill birds, so no stars were awarded; at Blythburgh the next day (on the Suffolk coast) the list was more interesting but only red-legged partridge got a star (a good view, perhaps, or just that I didn't see them at home), while later in the day, at Benacre Broad, a star highlights 'Bearded tits 2 (several more heard) (New Bird)'. The asterisks and the (New Bird) [underlined] have survived in my notes until now. New Bird is self-explanatory. At that time, there were many but I needed to pick them out somehow and a red underline did nicely.

I also changed John's 'triangle' symbol (meaning present, but no estimate of numbers made) to SN and LN, meaning 'small numbers' and 'large numbers'. These guesstimates have no great meaning (I still use them) but give a vague idea of abundance – 'SN' for something such as dunlins on the coast might mean 20 or 30 or 50, while 'LN' for something such as whitethroat, say, or blackcap, might mean ten – they are shorthand for 'quite a few about' or 'just a handful' and assume a knowledge of the likely abundance of the species concerned. Or, I should say, they are written in the context of my own knowledge of such abundance; since they are not there for anyone else to read, I need make no such assumptions for others.

The idea of the shorthand and particularly the asterisks was to give me more to go on should I refer to these notes at a later date; a straightforward list was never very satisfactory. A list gave an impression of what we saw but no real idea of how well we saw anything: was this the best view of a ruff in my life or just a fleeting glimpse of something flying overhead? It seemed to require a bit more than just a name. For a year or two I even went through the notes seeking out the days with the most asterisks so that I could list them as 'best days of the year', but enthusiasm for this soon waned. I added notes (such as those on the long-tailed duck at Abberton), which sometimes highlighted something special. For example, at Goldhanger: 'We saw a weasel on the sea wall, which we could easily have caught' (some chance!). I also took notes on plumages and unusual patterns of behaviour now and then. One remarkable bird on these early walks was heard but sadly not seen. It was near Stanway, after a long walk towards Copford (all built over now), where we heard the unmistakable calls of a corncrake. It was autumn, and this was a migrant (why it was calling I can't imagine), and it was not until 1970 that I actually saw one, in Scotland, for the first time (although I heard many in 1969 in Ireland).

It was late October (half-term) in 1965 that we were again in Great Wakering and went to Wakering Stairs, on the coast, where the public road ended just before the gateway to Foulness Island. 'The Stairs' run down to the shore where a trail used to lead out over the mudflats, turn parallel with the coast and go several miles north-east before turning back into dry land on Foulness. This trail, marked with big bundles of sticks, like giant besoms, stuck upright in the mud, and called 'the Broomway', was used by my father when, as a child, his family moved off Foulness by horse and cart. I wrote that there were at least 10,000 (doubly underlined) birds along the shore. Owing to War Department restrictions and soft mud (Oh yes, the Thames has some lovely soft, black, stinking mud) I couldn't get close enough to identify many, but I thought I had never seen so many birds at one time. I was not up to much, even by then, as I noted down an assortment of waders including green sandpipers (still using the triangle symbol to mean any indeterminate number from 'a few' to 'many'), which I later crossed out in pencil. On Great Wakering Common the next day there were perhaps 300 goldfinches and a similar number of greenfinches in a mixed flock. (This kind of thing was usual then; finch flocks are harder to come by now.) Later on in the week I watched 50 to 100 goldfinches, 300 to 400 greenfinches and 400 to 500 linnets on the common; close by I saw a redwing, surprisingly my first. This was the week I struggled with the twites (thinking they must be redpolls) but found the great grey shrike (which really *was* a good find, the first scarce bird I had discovered, and a fine bird at that).

Wakering Stairs, without a telescope, proved frustrating. I wrote in my notes a few days later that I could hardly hold my binoculars in the right direction, let alone steady, because of the strong cold wind, and – in this vast, exposed place with no cover at all – I could never get close to many birds. Birdwatching was not easy and it still isn't, very often, despite the lure of instant success if you join this or that society or club, or buy this book or that guide. It is something that I am acutely aware of in writing articles or leaflets or posters for the RSPB, or books: they offer such delights to people who take up birdwatching but give little idea that it needs a bit of dedication and, above all, *time*.

I was doing quite well, still struggling at times, on my own, with inadequate equipment, inadequate clothing, and inadequate books. But I was having a whale of a time. In 1966 I was back at Abberton and wrote down 'White-headed stiff-tail, 1 male (New Bird)'; 'American ruddy duck?' was appended at the time or more likely a little later and confirmed, in blue ballpoint pen, some time afterwards. It was, of course, a ruddy duck. I'd forgotten about that until I looked back through these old notebooks. I well remember seeing ruddy ducks at Chasewater later on, and had thought that these latter ones were my first. Abberton was good later in the year, in August, with black terns several times, shovelers, a goldeneye, a kingfisher and then, on the last visit, three little gulls (New Bird underlined in red). They were superb. This was an example of a bird that would have been entirely unknown to most of my family – my parents, my uncle – even those who were interested. I was now seeing things that they hadn't even heard of.

Our local walks from Shrub End produced wheatears, blackcaps, spotted flycatchers, that first pied flycatcher (in Chest Wood), which we saw again the next day, another one the following day at Birch Lake, treecreepers, marsh tits and tree sparrows. At Baymill Cottages (the derelict red-brick buildings), there was a buzzard soaring overhead. This was a real find, as the 1964 Essex bird report (the latest we had to hand) reported only two in Essex all year. That made it, for Essex, better than the great grey shrike at Great Wakering, but, for me – and nationally, of course – the shrike was much the rarer of the two.

Another new opportunity was the chance to watch whitethroats, lesser whitethroats, garden warblers and blackcaps visiting the garden to feed on the honeysuckle berries. These were great birds – real warblers, and not just willow! – and gave excellent close-up views. I'd seen nothing like this at home (and, come to think of it, I've rarely seen such a regular line-up of warblers feeding on honeysuckle since). Young lesser whitethroats were established as favourites then – so smart, so simple – and remain so.

Our trips to the coast that August were excellent. Little Oakley was one superb place, close to Dovercourt. The tide was very high when we arrived (whether this was by chance or by dint of our good planning I can't remember), and birds were roosting in ploughed fields inside the sea wall. A flock of 250 or more grey plovers was outstanding: most were still in breeding plumage, 'handsome blue-grey, black and white' as I described it, crisply ink black below, white around the face and spangled black and silver-grey above. The grey plover, in breeding plumage, is another one of those 'black, grey and white' birds that looks exceptionally well designed.

I noticed that many of the dunlins, golden plovers and turnstones were also in breeding colours, while 25 sanderlings were all silvery grey. There were 19 eiders, unexpected so far as I was concerned by an Essex marsh, but not so unusual there. More impressive then was a male marsh harrier, a new bird for me and 'very unusual in Essex'. I put an asterisk and a double vertical line in the margin beside it, 'New Bird' in the customary brackets and underlined in red, but just a couple of lines about its flight. It certainly was unusual in Essex then:

At the time I sketched this Caspian gull on an Essex tip, it was not yet on the British list.

in 1966 marsh harriers were at a very low ebb in Britain and a few pairs bred up the coast in Suffolk. Indeed, the next day we were in Suffolk, exploring the exciting marshes at Walberswick, and saw two marsh harriers as well as a couple of bearded tits. Now, of course, there are scores of pairs in East Anglia.

We went back to Little Oakley a week later. I was impressed by large numbers of waders although they could be counted only in hundreds, not thousands. I wasn't yet counting things very accurately and recorded 'many' and 'very many' for some of the commoner species; later, I would at least estimate, if only roughly. But there was a good selection of waders, including green sandpipers and greenshanks, bar-tailed godwits, whimbrels and a little stint, none of which I saw very frequently back then. There was another migrant pied flycatcher, encountered just a few days after I had seen my first ever.

Essex certainly widened my experience of birds. At the end of the notebook I have for much of 1966, I entered a few 'life list' totals. I had seen 152 birds by 30 August 1965, 162 by 9 April 1966, 174 by 8 August, and then 188 by 18 November 1967. These were poor totals really, but at the time they were not so bad. After all, my travel was limited, although another element had boosted my experience: holidays in Scotland. Somewhere along the line Chasewater changed from the place where we went fishing to the place I went to see birds (probably at first, at least, also with my uncle). This was where I really began to learn, to make mistakes and correct them, to get things sorted out to my own satisfaction.

Another uncle on my mother's side had a car (before the rest of us did) and a camera that took colour slides; and he went on foreign holidays. Uncle Sam gave us a slide show of a holiday he had taken in Europe – Switzerland I think – with pictures of the Rhine. I had read about the Rhine and was already an 'angry young man' (young boy) on environmental matters. 'Just think that half of that is sewage,' I said. It stopped the conversation for a moment. It was a stupid and ill-judged comment, but I was trying to do the right thing: as I say, the beginnings of an environmental consciousness (and conscience) were showing through, in its blundering, inept, adolescent sort of way.

Uncle Sam was very keen on Wales and hillwalking. Although he lived just a couple of miles from me, he had a closer relationship with the Colchester side of the family 150 miles away than he did with us. But now and then he took me with him to Wales – not hillwalking, but just good days out in his powder-blue Austin Cambridge. Once Dad had a car, we went off to Wales as a family many times. Sometimes we went in convoy – two or three cars full of Humes, Birches and Thompsons, occasionally joined by the Thorogoods from Colchester. During one of these trips I misidentified jackdaws as hooded crows (this was in the 'early period', when I – almost knowingly surely – allowed what I wanted to see rule what was actually in front of my eyes). At Capel Curig we found and photographed (with a Kodak Instamatic taking square-format colour pictures of surprising richness and quality) a common sandpiper's nest. There were, I think, dippers and grey wagtails, too, and buzzards.

John also experimented (to great effect) with colour photography, taking excellent transparencies. We gathered one Christmas and his parents unveiled the big present – a slide-projector and screen. They said they had taken all the best advice, and, as they always did, had looked into the subject as much as they could to make sure everything was right. So the disappointment was profound when the glass-beaded screen proved to show nothing but a blur of colour in the middle no matter how much John fiddled with the projector's focusing. Then, what relief! It was, after all, a misted-up lens: the projector, in its box and wrapped in Christmas paper, had been in the back of a car for a day or two over a cold, damp night. All was well, and pictures of holidays in Scotland became regular and much-enjoyed events, despite all the effort of rigging up the slide show paraphernalia in cramped rooms full of people after a vast Christmas dinner and equally vast tea, just before the beef and ham sandwiches, pickles and Christmas cake for supper.

Ladybirds and Libraries

There were bird books in the local library and, later, a surprising number in the school library. The first bird book in the house was my brother's Ladybird book, written by Brian Vesey-Fitzgerald and illustrated by Allen W. Seaby. There were two such volumes, dealing with 24 common birds; then there came a third, illustrated by Roland Green. It is probable that we borrowed all three, but perhaps we owned the set. The Ladybird books had lovely full-page pictures of such exotic-looking birds as male bullfinch and yellowhammer: what could be better?

I don't recall borrowing any identification guide from a library, but library books were always in the house for as long as I can remember. I owe my love of good books to my mother, who devoured novels and travel books (especially about wild animals and savage tribes in Africa) for years. From the library at Chase Terrace, after I'd selected Mum's regular half dozen books, I looked for Romany. Romany, G. Bramwell Evens, was a radio personality long before I was born, but his books, written in the 1930s and 1940s, and illustrated with a few black and white photographs and drawings, were still current. Romany wrote about the countryside in a simple, direct way, describing what he saw and adding a sometimes rather obvious message. His simple technique was a little bit like Mr Crabtree's in his supreme fishing book. In talking about wildlife to children, he used conversation and entertaining dialogue:

'That's the cock [chaffinch],' I said, 'with the fine pink breast and the white shoulder-knots on his wings. There's his mate doing the weaving of the nest. See how he keeps bringing her the material. He is the labourer, and she is the architect and builder.'

'She is a poor-lookin' thing,' said Tim. 'Not much smarter-lookin' than a sparrer. No pink or blue about 'er.'

'There's a reason for that, Tim. You can see how conspicuous he looks with his gay colours. If she were as highly coloured, an enemy mighty see her as she hopped onto her nest, or even when she was sitting on it. Nature keeps her drab-looking so that she may not be seen so easily. All soldiers, you know, used to be dressed in scarlet and blue, and now they wear khaki, to make them less easy to see.'

Mr Crabtree took his son fishing; Romany rolled up in his vardo, the gypsy caravan, pulled by Comma, with his spaniel, Raq, and took little boys and girls off to the woods and moors. It wouldn't do to try to write books like that now, but I read several, including *Out with Romany by Moor and Dale* (which introduced such unusual birds as curlews to my imagination), *Out with Romany* and *Out with Romany Again*. Romany's *Out with Romany* series was particularly popular, followed by another short series written by his son after Romany's death, including *Romany Muriel and Doris*.

This 'talking to children' technique was the ideal way to teach young readers without their noticing that they were being taught. He talked about birds' nests and hares' forms and all kinds of things that he saw while out and about in the countryside and, cleverly, it was often the children who made the discoveries that Romany could then explain. He wrote about rabbits and hares; one in particular, with a smudge on its face, he called Smut. My brother and I had a pet rabbit each (how badly we neglected those poor rabbits); mine was Blackie, while Alan's was mostly white, with a dark patch on its nose. We wanted to call it Smut (Alan must have been reading Romany books then, too) but Mum wasn't keen. We couldn't understand why. Romany's rabbit (well, a hare, actually) was Smut, wasn't it? What could be wrong with that? Eventually we got our way and painted the names on a board over the wooden hutch, 'Smut and Blackie'.

Romany was a Methodist minister in the north of England. His caravan, or vardo, is still kept in Wilmslow, Cheshire, where his dog Raq is buried (although he had a series of at least four dogs called Raq as well as a bitch called Ruin!). He still has quite a following. Many dogs are still called Raq and there is a thriving Romany Society. I mentioned it in the RSPB's magazine a few years ago and the society received more than 300 enquiries as a result.

The Ladybird book was soon replaced by *The Observer's Book of Birds*, which we had when I was about 12. It sold some three million copies. Young birdwatchers now have the best in field guides, CD-ROMs, videos and websites to learn from; when I was 12, any little book was a treat! We already had *Birds' Eggs*; it's on my shelf now (although it has my brother's signature in it). W H Smith in Lichfield was then a neat little bookshop, and in one corner it had an even neater little shelf bearing a long line of fascinating little books in white paper covers, all the same size and shape and design: the Observer's set. Only a week ago, as I write, I saw a lady on a tube train in London reading *The Observer's Book of Music*, still in its white cover with a coloured band at the bottom. *Freshwater Fishes* was an early acquisition, followed by *Birds' Eggs*, *Birds*, *Cacti*, *Ships*, *Railway Locomotives*, *Astronomy*, and *Aircraft*. Only *Astronomy* (by Patrick Moore, another long-time hero) has managed to keep its paper jacket, but this was a far later acquisition (February 1967), when it cost six shillings.

In the back of the bird book I find some interesting notes in an assortment of smudged blue ink and black biro. My first written record of a bird I had seen was in an exercise book (lined pages alternating with blank ones for drawing pictures), noting a jay that flew over one of the pools on Sutton Park, where we were out on a hired rowing boat on 10 June 1962, a few days before my 12th birthday. For a while I noted nothing else but I underlined the names of birds I had seen in blue ink in the Observer's book. The book was written by S. Vere Benson, 'Hon. Sec. of the Bird-Lovers' League'. A complete rewrite of the Observer's book in 1987 was later one of the first books I ever wrote – for a one-off fee of £200 – after a visit to see the editors at Warne's office in London. The original was first published in 1937. The 1962 reprint of the 1960 revision that I have has a series of famous illustrations, many in colour but some in black and white, that came from Lord Lilford's *Coloured Figures of the Birds of the British Islands*. Many are by Archibald Thorburn, some by J. G. Keulemans, and these same pictures were used by Warne in their *Birds of Wayside and Woodland* and *The Birds of the British Isles and their Eggs* by T. A. Coward.

The preface to the original Observer's book is interesting. Miss Benson wrote that she had often been asked to recommend a really inexpensive pocket textbook of British birds and had found it impossible to do so. T. A. Coward was acknowledged as the inspiration (as D. I. M. Wallace has noted, Coward was ahead of his time and well ahead of the more famous guides in producing accurate, concise descriptions that were useful in identification). Miss Benson goes on to acknowledge Mr Richard Kearton, an early bird photographer, as a hero among naturalists. She says of him:

> ... the 'Old Naturalist' who observed without being observed, but was always on the spot to come to the rescue when his feathered friends needed his intervention. ... Personally, I consider the bird-lover who cannot tell a Sparrow from a Kingfisher more worthy of admiration and emulation

than the unscrupulous collector, however much technical knowledge he may possess.

She goes on, however, to give useful hints about identification and says, 'All this joy might be lost if we had no eye for family traits', and 'As we notice more of these things our interest and pleasure are greatly increased.' She clearly saw that a little knowledge opened up possibilities of greater enjoyment and satisfaction: knowledge does not reduce our fascination with birds; it increases it.

The original foreword to the book was written by Lady Warwick:

There was a time – and it is not very long ago, either – when a love of birds and interest in their habits and peculiarities were practically confined to a very small section of the community – a group of persons whose circumstances and environment enabled them to indulge their inclination to watch and study birds in flight, feeding and nesting.

How different it is to-day! Almost everyone entertains a kindly feeling towards birds and likes to know something about their modes of life.

The reason for this, Lady Warwick surmised, lay in modern transport, coupled with a backlash against 'high-pitch city life', and was reflected in the increased number of books about birds being published. 'I have read many of these books, for I love birds (I have over four hundred in my aviary here, which I have "rescued" from unsuitable conditions in captivity).'

It is certainly true that interest in birds was growing, but since this foreword was written it has increased dramatically. The RSPB now has a million members. Soon after I joined (at the junior rate of ten shillings) membership was 22,000 and the society celebrated its 75th anniversary. Since then, bird feeding has become big business (a few years behind America but catching up fast). Birds are big business, too, and birdwatching paraphernalia in all its forms – from books to bird boxes to binoculars and telescopes – generates a huge turnover. How much stronger is the conservation movement? In Britain, it is undoubtedly stronger; worldwide it is strong, albeit to a lesser degree. But in the bigger things – such as saving the rainforest – we have gone backwards fast: 2004 was the worst year on record for destruction of Amazon forest, for example. Two weeks ago I read of the president of the Democratic Republic of Congo travelling around Europe on a business trip, trying to sell logging rights to 60 per cent of the Congo rainforest in an effort to stimulate his country's economy. In 2003, I visited, for the first time in decades, the Ideal Home show in London and was dismayed to see acres of furniture made of solid mahogany and acres more of garden furniture, proudly labelled as being made of 'prime teak'. It was all so depressing.

But back to books. There were other books in the Chase Terrace library. Part of the fun of borrowing a book was in watching the young lady librarian with very long, varnished nails manipulating a shallow, circular, revolving tray – a large wooden carousel affair – in which there were innumerable little card pockets, one for every book, with a slip of paper inside. She would swing the carousel, then flick through the cards, like a bank teller counting notes, nails flashing and clicking against stiff paper, until the one relating to the book I had chosen was found. It had a kind of hypnotic effect on me – young woman, swirling tray, clicking cards, flashing nails – and I stood quiet and motionless hoping that it would last a few minutes more.

I developed a liking for Joseph E. Chipperfield books, illustrated with pencil drawings by C. Gifford Ambler. A few years ago, I bought a second-hand one to renew my acquaintance with these books, although it took me a while to find it. They were mostly about the dramatic, wild Torridon region of north-west Scotland, or Skye – titles such as *Greeka, Eagle of the Hebrides* and *Rooloo, Stag of the Dark Water*. The drawings seemed hugely realistic and were the only reproductions of pencil work that I was aware of. Pencil is still poorly represented – and poorly reproduced – in most books. When I was editing the RSPB/AA *Complete Book of British Birds* I asked Ian Wallace to do some pencil illustrations (pencil being suggested by my co-editor from the AA, now commissioning editor for David & Charles, Mic Cady, after his boss, in turn, had used it in a previous book), and he was delighted, telling me that this was his favourite medium, but one that he could rarely find an outlet for. Having tried to find second-hand Chipperfields, I now have *Grasson, Golden Eagle of the North*, one that I can't recall from my schooldays and that, sadly, doesn't quite recapture the old magic. But these books enhanced my interest in birds and especially a growing interest in Scotland and all things Scottish, which was to continue.

I have recently found and re-read space adventures by Capt. W. E. Johns. Captain Johns wrote a hundred or more Biggles books, many of which I read, but the space adventures captured my imagination the most. (My taste for aerial battles was met more often by little war comic books with remarkably lifelike and accurate cartoon strips, full of excellent aeroplanes.) The space stories are fascinating little books, full of environmental asides, particularly stressing the dangers of meddling in strange or untouched environments and habitats that might be damaged or destroyed by things introduced by humans, whether artificial pesticides or alien creatures. There is a lot about evolution and the 'survival of the fittest', much of it simplistic in these short, quite matter-of-fact stories, but with quite a bit of sound common sense. And there is a lot about the danger of mad scientists risking the destruction of the Earth with their seemingly unstoppable desire either to blow it up with nuclear bombs or wreck it by over-exploitation, including deforestation, oil pollution of the seas and excessive pollution of rivers. I can hardly claim that space adventures did much to encourage my interest in birds, but there was much food for thought here that probably stimulated some early concern for the planet. Anyway, along with books by Patrick Moore, and *The Observer's Book of Astronomy*, they certainly helped stimulate a lifelong interest in the stars and planets around us.

In my early teens, I discovered books on birds in the grammar school library in Cannock, in particular a pristine set of *The Handbook of British Birds* by Witherby and his collaborators ('The Handbook' to everyone then, long before 'BWP'). I frequently referred to *The Handbook* but probably didn't realize how lucky I was. It was way beyond my means to think of buying a set and, sadly, I never did, much to my regret. Later the school even began to collect volumes of *The Birds of the British Isles* by David Bannerman, illustrated by George Lodge. So far as I know, no one but me ever looked at any of these. Bannerman was always fascinating to read, and the Lodge paintings – while sometimes a bit quirky in terms of pose and shape – show lively, colourful birds in habitats that were beautifully evoked with an energetic painting technique. Each painting was on a full page glossy plate, protected by a sheet of tissue paper, and each book had a sweet, new smell about it that I can still remember.

Also in the school library was a slim volume entitled *Wing-tips*, by Roland Green. It was about the identification of birds in flight, and it was profusely illustrated with the author's line-drawings (although these did not greatly impress me at the time). I also read the odd book by 'BB', or Denys Watkins-Pitchford, who was also a great illustrator in strong scraperboard, but I can't remember any specific titles and don't think I ever tried hard to read everything I could by him. He was, in any case, a wildfowler and wrote for shooting magazines, and that undoubtedly sullied him in my eyes. But books with drawings, paintings and scraperboards such as these were developing my interest in bird art, too.

I devoured Henry Williamson's *Tarka the Otter* and *Salar the Salmon*. Such was the impression that these books made upon me that at school I wrote an essay called 'Vanellus the Lapwing' (using the bird's generic name in the title). It was clearly based on the Williamson style but doubtless awful. Henry Williamson wrote many other books, several with later editions illustrated by Charles

Tunnicliffe, but of these I have no recollection. *Tarka* (1927) and *Salar* (1935) were the famous ones. I did, though, much later, read *The Story of a Norfolk Farm*.

My aunt, uncle and cousins in Colchester had a shelf with interesting books on it. *Mereside Chronicle* by Charles Tunnicliffe was one (it's now worth a bit). I didn't look at it much, partly, I think, because I didn't dare: we all had a reverence for books and were careful about how we handled things, and this was clearly expensive, not mine, and best left on the shelf. Charles Tunnicliffe wrote several books, but I had none of them. I now have several, including a later edition of the classic *Shorelands Summer Diary*, with its magnificent illustrations, and a host of Tunnicliffe books that came out many years later, including his field sketches, his measured drawings and various exhibition works. Noel Cusa wrote the text to some of these. Noel was an artist whom I got to know when he lived in a brick-and-flint cottage in Letheringsett, Norfolk, where several original Tunnicliffe paintings adorned the walls, including a superb upright eagle owl, a flock of curlews in the rain (Noel showed me how he did the rain, with lines of masking fluid) and a flock of lapwings, golden plovers and dunlins.

Noel was a friend of Tunnicliffe's and joked about the view sometimes expressed that he was himself a sort of poor-man's Tunnicliffe, or a copier of Tunnicliffe's ideas and compositions. Of course, he was influenced by Tunnicliffe, but Noel was a wonderful watercolourist and produced a fine body of work over many years. I have several, a couple of which I commissioned (he was not expensive). It is a great shame that most birdwatchers remember Cusa, if at all, only for the paintings he did for *The Birds of the Western Palearctic*, which were severely criticized and did not do justice to his abilities. He was trying to create impressions, while the handbook required precision.

Tunnicliffe illustrated a great many books (including books on farming, such as Sidney Rogerson's *Both Sides of the Road*, with superb animal drawings and paintings) and the well-known PG Tips tea card series; he also painted every cover for the RSPB's magazine *Bird Notes*. So I could hardly fail to notice him, and *Bird Notes* was still going for a couple of years after I joined the RSPB. I have them here. The covers start with a wing-waving dunnock in January 1964, and go on through summer-plumaged black-tailed godwits, a lovely nightjar, guillemots and a razorbill on a sea cliff, a fabulous waxwing (still easily as good as any that anyone has painted), a gaggle of turnstones and so on. They end with a couple of male smews with their typically yellow reflections in cold, steely-grey water.

So Tunnicliffe was everywhere. But was I strongly influenced by him? I'm not so sure, now. It seems to have been the stories, rather than the paintings, that caught the imagination in the early days, although I was rarely without a pencil and piece of paper to draw on. I was given a couple of large books, published in Italy, with full-page paintings of birds. The drawings were amazingly detailed and realistic. We all thought they were wonderful, and I copied them in great detail in pencil and ink. However, I soon realized that, realistic though they were, they showed precise renditions of dead, stuffed birds, nothing like the living thing. But they encouraged me to draw and to look at feather patterns in great detail.

My cousins in Colchester had two field guides. It was about time I had one, to replace the rather inadequate Observer's book. I looked at what they had: Collins Pocket Guide to British Birds by R. S. R. Fitter and R. A. Richardson and A Field Guide to the Birds of Britain and Europe by Peterson, Mountfort and Hollom. I thought the pictures in the field guide were a bit unnatural. I remember thinking the moorhen looked like a cardboard cut-out and was surely the wrong shape. I opted instead for the pocket guide, which seemed to me to have more realistic paintings in it – less regimented poses. I didn't realize that the regimented poses were there for a purpose, for ease of comparison, and that the field guide was a classic, a huge step forward in European bird books. It was many years later that I met Richard Fitter and told him that, although I had met Richard Richardson a couple of times on the famous East Bank at Cley (and lent him my telescope once – my claim to fame!) I had never been able to buy a line-drawing of his and wished I had had the opportunity. A couple of weeks later, a small package came in the post with an original drawing of a lapwing, by Richard Richardson, that Richard Fitter had kindly sent to me.

In fact, Richard Richardson once made a sketch in my notebook, but stupidly I lost it. It was at Cley when, with my friend Pete Garvey, I was looking at a strange wader. The bird appeared to be remarkably uniform, pale brown above, but shaped like a grey plover. It raised a wing and showed a black armpit, proving it was indeed a grey plover, but it still looked so odd that we wanted to make sure. Did some other wader have black axillaries too? R.A.R. appeared and came over to look at the bird. It was, he explained, a particularly badly worn and bleached individual, perhaps one that had missed its moult and retained a set of feathers for longer than usual. He took my book and biro and sketched a whimbrel, to show me how the pale 'notches' along the edges of each feather wore away more than the stronger, darker feather centres. Look at a photograph of a whimbrel or curlew on the nest, he said, and you will see this sort of saw-tooth wear on the feather edges. This removed the pattern, more or less; then envisage months of sun and salt spray on the remainder of the feather and you can imagine how the dark brown colour would fade away to a paler beige. This was what had happened to our odd plover: the pale feather-edge spots had worn

Gannets 'passing by the hour ... a procession many a league long'.

off, and the dark centres had bleached paler, giving it this uniformly grey-buff appearance. Don't worry, it's a good find, he told me. If only I could find that notebook. Richard Richardson was one of those rare birdwatchers universally admired by all the others; no one had a bad word to say about him.

The Collins pocket guide had its birds arranged in groups by habitat, within which were sub-groups according to size, and there were keys that tried to separate birds by colour, pattern, beak shape and so on. I didn't use the keys much, and habitat is always a difficult thing to use (for example, it is common to see woodpigeons, pheasants and blue tits knocking about in and around reed-beds), but the book was a godsend and gave years of good service. It was full of Fitter's experience and in many ways, I later thought, much better written than the subsequent *The Birds of Britain and Europe* by Heinzel, Fitter and Parslow, which was too compressed and had some ambiguities that I could never resolve (such as the Egyptian goose that, compared with the ruddy shelduck, 'has white shoulders instead of wing-patches'). This later guide appeared in 1972 and, with the arrogance of youth, I was pretty disparaging about it at first. In fact it, too, was a breakthrough in its own way and brilliant at the time.

John Parslow was to interview me at The Lodge and was still RSPB director of conservation for a time when I went to work there. Herman Heinzel I have met only once, at an art exhibition, after the publication of a new, much-improved edition of his guide, with many new subspecies added. Some of his published work (tiny thumbnail illustrations in large, not very good books) seemed to me to be poor, but he is really a fine artist and his field guides are excellent; so, to me, he was a star and to meet him, if only briefly, was a great pleasure. When I saw Richard Fitter in 2005, he was working on his computer on three books and reading bird and ecology journals avidly – at 92! He is an inspiration.

Roger Tory Peterson effectively invented the field guide for wildlife groups (not just birds) in the USA, and his European bird guide, with Mountfort and Hollom, was a huge milestone. I bought it pretty quickly after the Fitter and Richardson book, and I used both, much to my benefit, for years. It was soon clear that I had misjudged it: the paintings were actually remarkably good and accurate, and the flat, patternistic style, rather than the realism and variety of Richardson's work, was of great value when comparing similar birds on the page.

A later edition, revised by Ian Wallace, with some improved paintings, remains a great book (although let down by some poor printing), and it was the celebration of this that led to the great trio, Peterson, Mountfort and Hollom, getting together at an RSPB members' weekend (their appearance arranged by their publisher at Collins, Crispin Fisher, and the weekend arranged by my wife, Marcella). They sat at a table and signed books and prints for a great queue of people. Only recently I found out that Peterson was not at all happy with the revisions of the book by Ian Wallace. Ian had moved the book on a little from the basic identification guide to a more intensely analytical one, and this was not what Peterson intended. The Peterson guide was made for its own time. Later books took more account of the greater interest in the minutiae of plumage and the more general use of high-quality telescopes, so that we can all now look up the length of the tertials or the colour of the fringes of the outer scapulars – features that we can often see with ease on the real bird. Peterson's guides were made for people with low-powered binoculars, looking at the bigger picture, often at a bird in the distance. More recently, identification guides have relaxed a little and have gone back to a more general appreciation of the bird, which is perhaps a good thing.

Later, after an RSPB conference, I had the great honour of driving Roger Tory Peterson and his wife, Virginia, on a week-long lecture tour in England. It was a big disappointment to me that, despite our best efforts at advertising the events to local clubs, the talks (although the halls were quite full) were not attended by many really active 'birders' – the kind of people I knew from bird clubs, twitching and so on, who I thought would really appreciate seeing the great man. The first half of his lecture told of the history of the field guide and how he had developed the concept. Most of the audiences were not especially taken with this, although I was fascinated. The second half, mainly about penguins and other Antarctic subjects, illustrated by scores of Roger's own slides, went down much better. It's a pity that the people who benefited most from his work didn't appear to pay tribute to him.

Back in the Cannock Grammar School library, there had been another Peterson book, *Wild America*, written together with James Fisher, father of Crispin, who had helped get the field guide trio together at Warwick. It was a good story: the two giants of ornithology travelled around North America, seeing and listing birds as they went. It was an unusual book, a readable book about watching birds, something already falling out of favour with publishers. Another Peterson and Fisher collaboration was a huge, colourful book on the birds of the world; this was also in the school library (which was, I begin to realize, well blessed with good books). James Fisher wrote many other books, including *Sea Birds*, one of the early Collins New Naturalists, with Ronald Lockley, and *The Fulmar*, a massive monograph that details the history of the fulmar, so far as he could reconstruct it, at every colony in Britain and Ireland. It took him years to compile and, he later admitted, could have been cut by half. This was a book about a seabird, a brilliant bird, that lived on islands and sea cliffs on the remote coasts of Britain, especially in Scotland, so it had all the attributes to make it a favourite of mine and the book was a dream. It had been published in 1952; fortunately Collins reprinted it as a paperback edition in the 1980s so people like me could buy it.

There was to be another book by James Fisher, *The Shell Bird Book*, published in 1966, which became a favourite. Only once did I ever see James Fisher: he was speaking in Birmingham and selling signed copies of *The Shell Bird Book* and his *Nature Lover's Atlas*. I fancied the Shell book but Dad didn't want to buy it — it was quite expensive, I realized, so I was not too upset, but it would have been nice to get the signature. I didn't really want the atlas. Only later did I find that my parents had already bought a copy of *The Shell Bird Book* for me, before hearing about this event, hence the unwillingness to buy another. It is a fascinating book, a one-off. The first chapter is 'A Bird's Eye View of Britain', a review of prehistoric birds and the relationship between man and birds in our islands. 'Birds, the most observable of the animals, are a litmus paper of a country's state of native culture.' It is a slightly different take on the usual 'birds are indicators of the state of the health of the countryside' that is now so familiar. Then follows 'The Naming of the Birds', the history of ornithology in Britain and the gradual expansion of the recorded list of birds recognized in the islands, and 'The Peculiarity of British Birds', which reviews unique subspecies to be found here. Other chapters include: 'Bird Protection'; 'Bird Gardening'; 'Bird Song'; 'Birds in Literature, Music and Art'; 'A List of Bird-Watchers' (in which

Fisher acknowledges heroes and demolishes others); 'The Ornithologists'; and 'The Shell List of British and Irish Birds', which Fisher claimed to be the first decent list since the official 1952 list produced by the British Ornithologists' Union (BOU). I used it as my life-list for a time, with my first dates alongside the species I had seen. My 1962 jay remained the earliest record. My life-list reached 177 (plus ruddy duck, Greenland wheatear and Scottish crossbill) on 20 January 1967, 214 by 9 October 1969 (including the ruddy duck, by then) and 245 by 23 March 1973. That is pedestrian by today's standards, and even by my early twenties I had seen remarkably few birds.

The Shell Bird Book was brilliant. It taught me about Charles Waterton, Alfred Newton, Henry Seebohm, Ernst Hartert, Edmund Selous, Eagle Clarke, John Walpole-Bond, A. W. Boyd, and a host of other luminaries whom I might otherwise not have heard about for years and whom most young birdwatchers know nothing of. (Many I know have never heard of Eric Hosking or Peter Scott). Here was a history of birds and birdwatching in Britain in a form that was as entertaining as it was informative. Who else but James Fisher would have done it, or even thought of it? And it had dozens of colour illustrations (albeit tiny ones) by Eric Ennion, and full-page pictures by Charles Tunnicliffe and Peter Scott. One, by Scott, was repeated on the cover: it is a freezing cold, snowy picture of Slimbridge with geese flying over the fields, with lovely white-fronts, and a surprisingly hard to spot (exactly as they are) red-breasted goose near the front of the V. This was great stuff: random, erratic, not an encyclopaedia or a handbook or a school textbook that began at the beginning and worked through to some sort of end, but a book that covered Fisher's chosen subjects, things that he included because he liked them and thought them worth exploring.

One more school library book, one that I bought as soon as I could afford it, was Collins New Naturalist volume, Number 6 – the sixth in what was to become a colossal and eminent series, *The Highlands and Islands*, by F. Fraser Darling and J. Morton Boyd. I bought mine in July 1967. It was part of my love affair with Scotland. I had already been to Scotland a few times by then and was besotted with the Highlands, so this book fed my existing obsession and added still more fuel to the fire. I never became a collector of New Naturalists and have read rather few of them. Nevertheless, this is still (if not often read, to be truthful) a favourite book and one that came along at precisely the right time (it was published in 1964), when I was getting into birds and getting into Scotland in a serious way. The cover, designed by Clifford and Rosemary Ellis (as all New Naturalists' jackets would be for many years), features a black-throated diver – surely the most immaculate bird in Britain.

Other books I recall being keen on include *Birds in Britain*. Written by Scottish author Kenneth Richmond, this was quite a large book with no pretence at being a field guide or a handbook; it is simply a good read about birds. It was set out in more or less systematic order, a paragraph or two about each species, with a series of black and white pictures by the author. These photographs were not all of top quality but they captured the character of the birds well, as did the text: for example, I liked 'eagles in Wagnerian settings' in the western Highlands. A similar book, by Frances Pitt, didn't take my fancy at all.

Once I joined the RSPB I was open to its sales catalogue and advertising in *Bird Notes*. I didn't go for much, although I acquired a glossy leaflet on birds in the Midlands and a booklet on the return of the avocet (with more Tunnicliffe paintings). But I did buy another book, one that I still pick up and browse through with much pleasure. It is curiously bound in hard white boards, adorned with Robert Gillmor drawings, with a spine of dark-green cloth. *Birds and Green Places: A Selection from the Writings of W. H. Hudson*. Edited by P. E. Brown and P. H. T. Hartley, and illustrated by Robert Gillmor line-drawings, this 1964 publication draws together some of the best passages from Hudson's work and introduced me to a natural history writer of great skill and renown, albeit one that came into the 'demolished' category in Fisher's Shell book. Fisher thought he was intolerably ignorant. I find the writings here are still capable of taking me to lovely places in England and bringing to mind the minor details of the life of birds, mammals, snakes and insects in the countryside with great impact and veracity. The first item, the longest in the book, is about the birds of the Itchen valley in Hampshire, written from the cottage loaned to Hudson by Edward Grey, Lord Grey of Fallodon, author of *The Charm of Birds* (a book that I did not discover in my youth). It is an unbeatable evocation of summer in the Hampshire woods and meadows at a time when cirl buntings sang lazily from the trees near by (the buntings long since gone). But I love, especially, the descriptions of gannets over the sea off Cornwall, the gatherings of geese in north Norfolk, the encounter with a glaucous gull, and minute descriptions of gorse and other heathland flowers.

> … I have watched the gannets passing by the hour, travelling to some
> distant feeding area or to their breeding haunts in the far north; a procession
> many a league long, but a very thin procession of twos and twos, each
> bird with his mate, following the trend of the coast, each bird in turn now
> above the sea, now down in the shelter of a big, incoming wave, and every
> curve and every rise and fall of one so exactly repeated by the other as to

give the idea of a bird and its shadow or reflection, with bird and reflection continually changing places.

Why is it that that passage still raises the hair on the back of my neck? I loved that book from the very start, even though it is not a book that anyone would expect to be read and appreciated by a young teenager: it is of a style that is out of fashion, now, as it was already then, but it caught my imagination and held it for years. It was said by Joseph Conrad that Hudson wrote 'as the grass grows'; he seemed to have an easy style, a simple turn of phrase, but, as the extract above shows, he was not afraid of long and complex sentences (which are, now, rather frowned upon). In fact, he apparently wrote and redrafted and rewrote again and again until he was satisfied with what, it later appeared, flowed freely from his pen, just right first time. (I have had a little correspondence with Bryan Nelson, seabird expert and author of mammoth volumes on the Sulidae and truly excellent books on the gannet. Euan Dunn, now a colleague at the RSPB, tells me that Bryan Nelson does sit and write his books, which are intriguing, exciting and informative reads, longhand, in pen on foolscap paper, with barely a revision – they 'come out right' first time.)

Another bird book came my way some years later. I was always ready to copy what my cousins were doing – a few years ahead of me in the birdwatching game (they must have groaned) – so on seeing a fabulous-looking book that David had somehow bought I decided I would like it myself. The chance came along when I passed my A levels and was awarded the school prize: thanks very much, how about a copy of Nelson's *Atlas of European Birds* by Dr K. H. Voous? I'm not sure why I wanted it, except that it was so big, and full of photographs and maps, and of course David had it (it wasn't envy, just imitation, which I hope was more flattering). The maps were a bit basic by today's standards, but they were the best that could be achieved then. The photographs made a fine collection, although most were small and all black-and-white. The text was quite scientific, as this is an academic work, not a popular bird book. It made me feel that I had gone up a step or two. And, to be truthful, it was, despite its scientific style, a good read and full of stimulating ideas. One, I remember, was that the Mediterranean gull was a species in the process of extinction; it certainly seemed so at the time. Mediterranean gulls played a large part in my birdwatching in later years, and thankfully still do, home and abroad, so I am pleased that the range of this handsome species has expanded and seeing one is less of a rare event than it once was. I have even seen a full summer-plumage adult hawking for ants over my Bedfordshire garden. My copy of the book has a neat, pale-grey and green sticker on the front page, with 'Live Worthily, Cannock Grammar School' curled around the oak leaf and acorn crest, above 'A Level Prize, Presented to Robert Hume, 1966–67'.

There was another book on the school library shelves that was to have a much more direct influence on me, despite its being a minute volume of merely 40 pages, bound in green cloth. On the shelf it is far slimmer than the average county bird report and apt to disappear; in gold blocking (easily worn off) on the spine the title is *The Birds of Staffordshire (1962)*. On the title page it reads 'by J. Lord and A. R. M. Blake 1962 published by The West Midland Bird Club'. I'm not sure when I first saw this, but I bought a copy in 1967, some years later. It was a huge breakthrough in my local birdwatching 'career'. It is simply a county checklist, little more: most species have from three to six lines of text, some a few more, in a very abbreviated summary of the status of each bird in the county. For the first time, however, I could relate birds to my own home area. No longer did I have to put up with 'common in southern England'; I could find out their status in Staffordshire. It came as something of an eye-opener: I hadn't realized that such local information was available. Not only that, but here were places mentioned in the text that I knew about; above all, there were constant references to Cannock Reservoir and Blithfield Reservoir.

Where, though, was Cannock Reservoir? There was a map. The key said 'C.C.R. – Cannock Chase Reservoir', and there on the map was Norton Pool, 'the pool' to me, Chasewater. So, this Cannock Reservoir place, Chasewater, where I went fishing just a couple of miles from home, seemed pretty good. The very first bird in the book, black-throated diver, had occurred in seven of the years since 1947 at Belvide (another south Staffordshire reservoir) and in five of the years at Cannock Reservoir; the next, great northern diver, had been seen there in eight of the years since 1947. There were records at Chasewater of Slavonian grebes, a Leach's petrel, red-crested pochards, scaup, long-tailed ducks, eiders – the first for the county – a kite for goodness sake, a dotterel … no end of good things. And I could see that wheatears and white wagtails appeared on migration, even such oddities as Lapland and snow buntings had turned up from time to time, and there was a regular flock of twites, at Chasewater *and nowhere else*. This was amazing. I lived next to the best place in the county.

This book changed things completely. Now that I knew about the West Midland Bird Club, I wrote to the RSPB and asked for its address, and I joined. And I knew that two people in the club had written a book: J. Lord and A.R.M. Blake (he must be something special, to have three Christian names). Soon, I was to meet A.R.M. Blake himself – an author!

A Television World
of Adventure

I'm not sure when we got a television at home, a wooden box with a small, bulbous, greenish screen. From the start, I went for programmes that featured animals, in the same way that, while I had a few tin soldiers, I preferred to play with model farm animals. When we moved house and dug out a plot for the new lawn, Dad and I cleared off every stone and, for a few days, I had the whole patch of dusty loam to myself, with roads and tracks and raised hedges and fields full of tin livestock. While other kids may have liked the Andy Pandy day on *Watch with Mother*, it was *Rag, Tag and Bobtail* on a Thursday for me. I don't think these earliest children's programmes, when I was four or five, can really be cited as influences on the development of a 'naturalist', but who knows?

Muffin the Mule was on television from 1946, and he was already 12 years old then. (Muffin had been created in November 1934 and stored – as yet unnamed – until he was rediscovered by Annette Mills, sister of actor John Mills, in a 1946 edition of *For the Children*.) Muffin was a big hit. I don't remember much about his puppet friends, which included, among others, Mr Peregrine Esquire (a bossy penguin), Louise the Lamb, Willie the Worm, Poppy the Parrot, Katy the Kangaroo, Monty the Monkey, and Zebbie the Zebra. But Prudence Kitten, who later had a show of her own, made a bit more of an impression, if only as something I didn't much like – too girly for me. *The Flowerpot Men* were on *Watch with Mother* on Wednesdays and have become minor cult figures in the decades since their first appearance in 1952. They lived in giant flowerpots at the bottom of the garden, behind the shed, either side of a large flower called Weed. They had a tortoise friend called Slowcoach, whom I cannot recall. It was better than Andy Pandy and Looby Loo anyway.

Rag, Tag and Bobtail – some 'new friends for the very young' – were brought to the screen in 1953. These stories, written by Louise Cochrane and told by Charles E. Stidwell, featured a hedgehog, a mouse and a rabbit. Real animals! I remember making rather embarrassing excuses about why I wanted to watch it ('I wanted to see if they used real flowers' was one that still haunts me), when I felt I was really too old (about five or six). I had already started school, so I was, presumably, watching during the school holidays. Well, it was wildlife wasn't it?

Real wildlife on television was an important early influence, but very different from what is available to the aspiring naturalist now. Along with the television, there were usually books about the programmes; Mum used to borrow these from the library and I read them eagerly. They generated an early interest in Africa, I remember, and there seemed to be many programmes and books that featured African tribes and their way of life, as well as wildlife. I was knocked out by the music: those rhythms, the drums and simple percussion created something magical, just as the steam engines and their long trains of coaches or freight wagons had done over the clickety-clack rails at Lichfield Trent Valley. I went so far as to write to the BBC to ask how I might buy records of African tribal music. I had a helpful reply, but the chances of getting recordings from the places they suggested seemed so unlikely that I failed to follow it up, although I did much later borrow some from the library. I would have been years ahead of my time in appreciating 'world music'.

Wildlife television was simple and direct, but it often achieved great impact despite there being little technology beyond a camera and tripod. Film-makers could use simple techniques to show what they saw, but they could not create virtual reality – they couldn't put cameras on birds and animals or inside elephant droppings or do many of the other things that are routinely done now (often with little benefit – I tend to avoid them). When the natural history unit of the BBC celebrated its anniversary with a review of old programmes, the first few wobbly notes of an old theme tune were enough to bring instant recall of *On Safari*, which featured Armand and Michaela Denis. They were Belgian wildlife photographers, and I remember the characteristic strong accent of Armand and the glamorous Michaela with her long, blonde hair. Their programme, which was launched by the BBC in 1957 and ran until the mid-1960s, took them to Africa and South America, although it is only the African subjects that I remember – in particular, a famous black rhino with an immensely long, forward-pointing horn, called Gertie.

The Denises had a flat in London, a house in Kenya and a penthouse in New York, but to me they were always out of doors in the African bush, pushing their luck with dangerous animals that stood, unsuspecting, just beyond the next acacia, likely to turn and charge should Armand cough at the wrong moment, or tread on a dry stick. Armand had used the royalties from his invention of a volume control for radio to set up his adventurous lifestyle. He had worked as a cameraman in Hollywood before spending six years filming in Bolivia, where he met Michaela, who had come to study native textiles and ceramics. Within 12 hours of their meeting they were married: quick work!

They visited Britain in October 1953. They were featured on *In Town Tonight*, telling of their travels and adventures. This led to their wildlife series, with assistant cameramen who went on to become wildlife stars in their own right, notably Des and Jen Bartlett, Alan Root and Hugo van Lawick. They travelled around Africa with a car, two trucks and five cameramen-technicians. Apparently Michaela was never without her make-up, even in the deepest jungle. She was mauled by a gorilla and half-strangled by a python, but the pair continued to bring wildlife to the screens of the BBC in a remarkably direct and exciting way. They were not hunters – as so many of the older wildlife experts in Africa had been – and had strict views on killing animals, even for meat: they didn't do it. If they were faced with a dangerous situation, they relied on their knowledge of animals and the ability to climb the nearest tree; Michaela, it is said, often damaged her silver nail varnish when such desperate measures were called for.

Armand Denis died in 1971. Michaela, then Lady Michaela Denis Lindsay, died at the age of 88 at her home in Nairobi in 2003. I believe I once saw her in a restaurant in Africa: a lady came in and sat at a table, and looked for all the world like Michaela Denis, elderly then, but with a great presence. Could it really have been her? I like to think so.

While Armand and Michaela Denis brought millions like me face to face with elephants and rhinos, Hans and Lotte Hass did the same with wildlife under water: they were the predecessors of Jacques Cousteau. They were German naturalists and divers who made exciting underwater films. Their first series was broadcast in 1956, with film from the Caribbean, the Aegean and the Red Sea. *Undersea World of Adventure* followed in 1958 and *Adventure* in 1959 and 1960, a trio of documentaries from the Indian Ocean.

Years ago, if anyone said they worked in any way with birds, a likely question was 'Have you met Peter Scott?' Peter Markham Scott, artist and ornithologist, was the famous wildlife personality on television for many years; he was, as David Attenborough later became, the voice of wildlife on TV and radio, and that was but a small part of his amazing contribution in so many fields. He was both a scientist, with a special interest in wildfowl, and a conservationist, able to speak to politicians and international conferences at the highest level. He was gifted in many ways but, above all, he had the perfect voice for television. (Younger people now don't have any recollection of how famous and influential Peter Scott was on television, if they have heard of him at all.) His series, *Look*, was the first wildlife series on British television, beginning in 1955. Until it was axed in 1969, it gave cameramen, scriptwriters and producers the chance to push wildlife filming to new heights, without being unnatural and contrived. *Look* and *Faraway Look* also created as spin-offs the fat books that we could get from the library, but Peter Scott went on to much greater things in the world of conservation.

And yes, I did meet Peter Scott, a few times, in small ways. He used to appear from time to time in the hides at Slimbridge, the centre of his Wildfowl Trust (later the Wildfowl & Wetlands Trust). Once I thought I had found a lesser white-fronted goose among the white-fronts, but it was sitting down, asleep, and the extent of white on the head and its eye-ring were difficult to assess. At that moment Peter Scott appeared, so I pointed it out to him and asked his opinion. At first he said 'I'll buy that', but later he wondered if it could even be a hybrid, as the features that suggested a lesser were not really sufficiently clear cut. I jumped the gun, as I so often did (and do) and wrote a short note to *British Birds* about a possible hybrid Lesser white-fronted × white-fronted goose at Slimbridge, citing the opinion of Peter Scott (without even asking him!). Rightly, of course, the editors asked him what he thought and, also quite rightly, he said that, although it was a suggestion that he had made at the time, the evidence was very far short of conclusive. So my notes and sketches were (I'm glad to say) never published.

Years later he agreed to speak at the RSPB's members' weekend, organized by my wife, and I was able to carry a small pile of Peter Scott books into his room for Sir Peter and Lady Scott to sign for me, which they did with great patience and kindness. He had been a speaker before, at the RSPB's AGM, using a joke that I have since used myself a couple of times, with rather less success than he did: he said he knew little about the RSPB and its members and would like to have the audience broken down by age and sex; he was assured that most of them were. He also showed the audience his red socks. He always, he said, wore red socks for luck when giving such talks, a long-standing superstition that he maintained as much as he could.

One of the graphic designers who worked on the RSPB's magazine *Birds* before I did used to be scathing about Peter Scott's paintings. I don't think she understood their significance, although she had every right to her opinion about their technical qualities. It was years later that I heard Keith Shackleton, a close friend of Sir Peter's, talk about his work to Peter's daughter (and Keith's god-daughter) Dafila. He emphasized the way that Sir Peter broadened the perspectives of so many wildlife artists, who had been used to the traditions of Thorburn and Lodge and now saw, almost for the first time, wild birds set in the landscape, as part of the landscape rather than as portraits of individuals. Peter Scott painted wildfowl against magnificent skies and these, hardly through any fault of his, became copied and turned into a clichéd form of wildlife painting by people who had only a tiny part of his talent. (One of these – well known and saleable through Boots and Woolworths – Keith once described as 'absolute bedrock'.) Sir Peter also painted many more subjects and, in my opinion, produced some extremely fine work, with marvellous colours and textures that have always fascinated me; and his simple illustrations of wildfowl exhibit a brilliant eye and exceptional drawing skill. Keith described how Peter would set himself a real problem, when drawing, for example, a portrait of a human face. Most artists, Keith explained, would make an outline of the face and lightly sketch in the eyes, nose and mouth, taking great care with their relative sizes and positioning, before building on these features to create the face. Peter Scott, he said, would draw an eye, and then work on the eye until it was almost complete in full, intricate detail, before starting on the other eye, completing that, and then taking the next feature and so on. Every item drawn and completed in this way had to relate exactly to the rest in proportion and position, with no room for error and no outline sketch to guide him.

On one occasion Peter Scott asked me if I had ever been diving or snorkelling. I said that I had not (being neither much of a swimmer nor someone that had ever been to exotic places where I might do such things, I might have added). He recommended that I should: go to a tropical island and you might see 20 or 30 species of birds, which would be wonderful; but dive into the sea and there would be 100 or 150 species of incomparably beautiful fish. His underwater paintings of the fish of coral reefs, and later also of whales amongst which he dived, were ahead of their time.

Peter Scott was, in my youth, the most famous of the television animal programme presenters, but there were others. George Cansdale, who wrote the Ladybird book on British wild animals, brought live animals from London Zoo into the studio and I remember them, dimly. James Fisher presented *Zoo Time*, a series from zoos around the world. He was, I remember, a fine television performer, with a suitably refined BBC voice, but he was also a serious ornithologist and prolific author of bird books, sometimes in collaboration with the great American birdwatcher, writer and artist, Roger Tory Peterson. However, it was Johnny Morris who took children's animal programmes to the peak of their popularity. In his programme, *Animal Magic*, he brought animals to the studio, but he would also go to the zoo. In his role as a keeper at Bristol Zoo, he would interact with the animals in a new way that brought them to life – or made them sentient – for millions of viewers: he would imagine what the animals were thinking and then speak for them, using a voice that you could imagine the animal using if it could talk. It was a technique that eventually became pretty much outlawed on television because it was considered pure anthropomorphism, something that was declared unacceptable; but he turned tens of thousands of children into nature lovers. He said that he always learned as much from the animals as he learned about them.

Johnny Morris had a unique way with words, and his conversations with animals, based on a deep and genuine respect for them, were inimitable. His 'regulars' on television included Dottie the ring-tailed lemur, an elegant and graceful creature that was usually draped about his neck or over one arm and likely to do something unexpected at the wrong moment. He put humour into animals without degrading them; the humour, as a rule, was aimed at himself. This is extraordinarily difficult to do. I find it hard to emphasize the humour that can be seen in the natural world because I am scared of this risk of degrading the subject. While I may see humour, I tend to avoid it for fear of

Dotty the ring-tailed lemur was a regular studio companion of Johnny Morris.

destroying the natural dignity in wild animals. So I am, I suppose, too po-faced about it. Johnny Morris was not: he managed to hit the right spot, making us laugh, without ever making fun of the animals themselves, or making us laugh *at* them.

Animal Magic ran for 21 years and more than 400 editions before it was chopped, with no warning to Johnny and little or nothing in the way of a thank you for all he had done for the BBC and its ratings. Keith Shackleton was the resident 'guest artist' on the show for years and still finds the BBC's treatment of Johnny Morris distasteful. When the programme was dropped in 1984 – when the anthropomorphic approach fell out of favour – it was reported that Morris 'was not really sad about it', but that he did not like the way the 'whizzkids' were now running things and that everyone was expected to have 'official qualifications'. He said he had none, and claimed to have a mental age of seven, which was why, he believed, he could relate to children so well. It was also reported, though, that he was in fact deeply upset by the way that he had been dropped with no explanation or thanks.

Johnny was also a fine radio and television journalist: his wit and sharp observation gave a unique style to descriptions of such mundane events as the village jumble sale, for example, while he also had other radio and television series such as *Johnny's Jaunts, Oh, To be in England* and *Around the World in 25 Years*. The word 'unique' is quite justified. Johnny Morris's development as a broadcaster and wildlife man is interesting. His first job was in a solicitor's office, followed by spells on a building site and as a salesman – nothing much there to train him for his future career, but an interest in animals must have been bubbling underneath because he became the manager of a farm in Wiltshire. His first broadcast was in 1946, and soon he had a regular radio show, *Pass the Salt*, broadcast from the BBC's West Region. His television shows were filmed without sound, and Johnny added a sharp commentary, including the 'voices' of the people that were featured. His companion was 'Tubby Foster', in reality producer Brian Patten. They travelled to the Pacific, South America and through France. As the *Hot Chestnut Man* in the 1950s he brought to television the narrative skills developed to such effect on radio. He was in demand for narration, including, most memorably, *Tales of the Riverbank*, which was based loosely on characters from *Wind in the Willows* and featured live animals – Hammy the hamster and Ratty the white rat – in place of cartoons or puppets.

When I was still working in the development department at the RSPB, which among many other things ran the annual members' weekends and AGMs, I was pleased to persuade colleagues that Johnny Morris would go down well as the members' weekend guest speaker. While I was entertaining him – mainly at the bar – before the evening, he told me about the emergence of towns and villages near his home (at Hungerford near Newbury in Berkshire), as commuter towns for people who worked in London and raced home each evening on the motorway. He was unhappy about the urbanization and despoliation of his beloved countryside and, although by then he was in his eighties, he later demonstrated against the building of the Newbury bypass across beautiful water meadows and unspoiled countryside near his home.

He did, incidentally, go down a storm as our guest speaker, performing exactly as we hoped he would and enchanting his audience of close to a thousand people with his stories of a life in broadcasting and working with animals. My wife was the conference organizer, and I'm pleased to have a copy of Johnny's book, *Just Like You and Me*, neatly inscribed 'To Marcella, with best wishes, Johnny Morris'. It was a bit of a gamble for the RSPB. After all, we did not much favour the anthropomorphic approach then, either (and wouldn't entertain it, now), but it was a chance worth taking and it worked.

A final story about Johnny Morris illustrates his character well. Married in 1944, he was by all accounts blissfully happy for 45 years. When his wife, Eileen, died in 1989, she was buried at the bottom of the four-acre garden they both loved, and for the rest of his life he visited her grave every evening to tell her about the happenings of the day.

Keith Shackleton was a handsome, fair-haired, barrel-chested young man, made for television. Like Peter Scott he was blessed with the perfect voice, but he featured less than he should have done (except for those appearances on *Animal Magic*). Keith submitted pictures to RSPB art exhibitions and, when I took over organizing these when Carl Nicholson left the development department, I was able to contact such well-known figures to ask them to send paintings for exhibition and sale at RSPB members' weekends and other membership events. I also persuaded my boss, Trevor Gunton, that Keith would make an excellent speaker, which he did, at the RSPB's AGM in London.

One day a lady arrived with several large paintings, none of which I liked. She came into our small office and arranged the highly priced canvases against the walls before proceeding to tell me about their exceptional qualities as wildlife paintings (they were of domestic doves) and the deep meaning that could be discerned within them given prolonged and intelligent contemplation. The lecture lasted quite a long time, but I discerned neither deep meaning nor the least hint of technical competence in these unattractive pictures. Doubtless it was my fault. Shortly after she left, Keith Shackleton happened to arrive. He had a couple of large oil paintings under his arm. He dropped them down face-to-the-wall, apologised for not having anything more worthwhile to show, then walked across to the desk opposite mine and looked at a picture on the wall. It was an original Mike Warren, a golden plover used on a *Birds* magazine cover. Keith was entranced by the Warren: if only, he wished, he could paint like that.

When he spoke at the AGM, we also had another artist on the programme, Peter Hayman. Keith talked about wildlife in the southern oceans and illustrated the talk with stunning paintings of albatrosses and penguins and extraordinary southern land-, sea- and ice-scapes, pictures with phenomenal power and impact. I stood at the back with Peter Hayman, who had recently returned from a trip to New Zealand to research a proposed book on the identification of the world's seabirds (a book that never appeared, sadly, as it was beaten to it by Peter Harrison's ground-breaking *Seabirds*). Peter was talking about his *Birds* magazine series, 'What's that bird?', with Mike Everett. The series used Peter's highly detailed and exquisite paintings of birds in various plumages and poses to build up what Ian Wallace calls the 'multiple image' of each species. Peter looked at Keith's slides of his oil paintings and said 'I wish I could paint like that. When I was sailing round New Zealand looking at albatrosses, it was so rough I couldn't make the pencil hit the paper let alone draw what I was seeing – how does he do it?'

Later, I stood at the back with Keith while Peter was at the front giving his talk. Predictably, Keith looked at Peter's watercolour pictures and said 'I wish I could paint like that. Look at the delicacy, the detail – how does he do it? I couldn't begin to paint such fine work.' I remembered the lady and her awful pigeons, and the way she spent all her time talking about her own splendid work, before Keith appeared and enthused about the pictures by other artists hanging on our walls while ignoring his own. In the vast majority of cases, I have found bird and wildlife artists to be lovely people, ever ready to talk about other people's work rather than their own, and quick to praise other artists (although, when confronted with something poor, the odd groan or whispered judgement is not unknown). Keith, I would suggest, is one of the best, in every way.

Keith Shackleton served in the RAF in Europe and in the Far East and painted war scenes with the Army and Naval Coastal Forces. After the war he worked in the family aviation business as a salesman and pilot: he delivered planes to the field at Old Warden, a few miles from where I am writing this, now the base of the Shuttleworth Collection. During this period he was a 'spare-time' artist and developed considerable skills as a writer. In the 1950s he published two books of paintings, drawings and essays, *Tidelines* and *Wake*, largely concerned with small boat sailing and neither of which I came across. Like Peter Scott, Keith was a skilful yachtsman and represented Great Britain on several occasions in international dinghy racing.

He became a full-time painter at about the time that he joined Johnny Morris on *Animal Magic*. He illustrated *Birds of the Atlantic Ocean*, by Ted Stokes, a large, expensive book that found its way into the college shop at Swansea and first brought his work to my attention, but this was not a book of dramatic paintings so much as an identification guide, with mostly gouache, field-guide-style illustrations of seabirds. A few pictures of birds over the seas, however, showed what Keith could do with his use of light and colour, including striking reflections of green and blue on mostly white birds; it opened my eyes to the endless effects of varying light on living birds.

Keith travelled extensively as a naturalist with several cruise vessels, notably the *Lindblad Explorer*, mainly in the Antarctic but also in the Arctic, on the Amazon and in the Atlantic, Pacific and Indian Oceans. He has been president of both the Royal Society of Marine Artists (RSMA) and the Society of Wildlife Artists (SWLA) – of which he was a founder member – and chairman of the Artists' League of Great Britain. At the 2003 SWLA exhibition, he described to me the difference between the SWLA and the RSMA: the wildlife artists, he felt, were always taking risks and moving forward (we were beside a painting by Kim Atkinson, which he described as 'a fizzing good picture'), while the marine artists had become too static and were mostly painting scenes of ancient battles and events that none of them had ever witnessed, rather like old sailors putting model ships into bottles.

To contradict any such judgement of his own marine paintings, anyone who was there has only to remember his 75th birthday retrospective exhibition at The Mall Galleries in 1998, which I found astounding. I had been used to the SWLA annual exhibitions at The Mall Galleries, just around the corner from Trafalgar Square, in which three or four large Shackletons could dominate a wall, or the whole gallery. Now the gallery was full of nothing *but* Shackletons, all stunning and powerful, pictures such as the view of large yachts with highly coloured, sponsored spinnakers in *The Fleet of the British Steel Challenge, 1992*, or a magnificent broad-bill swordfish skittering across the surface of a blue sea in *Exuberance in the Banda Sea*, majestic albatrosses and shearwaters against dazzling waves, polar bears on pack ice, old aeroplanes such as the Miles Messenger in a field in *The Farmer's Wings*, North Sea oil platforms, commandos on exercises, elephants in Africa.

Many of the pictures can be found in his book *Keith Shackleton: An Autobiography in Paintings*. For a short time, in *Birds* magazine, I ran a series of short articles, headed 'By invitation', and for one of these I asked Keith to write something, as he is a writer of great talent as well as a supreme artist and accomplished speaker. His essay, 'Water Worship', is included in his book. Another of Keith's books is *Wildlife and Wilderness: An Artist's World*. This has many examples of his muscly dolphins, frolicking penguins and dramatic albatrosses against strong light, the kind of pictures that, even on a printed page, have the ability to dazzle, almost to make me shade my eyes against the reflected sun. I have a postcard from him above my desk at work, a tiny reproduction of an albatross painting, and it has exactly the same quality.

James Fisher's son, Crispin Fisher, was natural history editor at Collins. The reason for introducing him here is that he was the editor of the books written for Collins by David Attenborough, and this would prove significant for the RSPB. In wildlife television, Attenborough is the giant of all time, but he is also vice-president of the RSPB and an RSPB medallist for his services to conservation. However, he always claimed to know little about birds, so year after year he turned down all RSPB requests for him to speak at the members' weekend. Crispin, bless him, said he would sort it; just leave it to him. He did. But it took about 11 years. Eventually, David Attenborough did indeed agree to talk at the members' weekend, which, as it happened, would be held at the University of Warwick, near Coventry, rather than at the generally favoured venue of the University of York. This was fortunate, in a way, because Marcella was able to arrange a performance by the Coventry Cathedral choir before the Attenborough lecture. We had a number of guest celebrities, too. I disgraced myself by trying to move a lady from near the front, where she was not supposed to be – well, she was *not* supposed to be there, to be fair – but when I asked who she was, I was reminded (as I well knew) that she was Dorothy Hosking, widow of bird photographer extraordinaire Eric Hosking. (I had rarely met either Eric or Dorothy, but should have known better: Eric, incidentally, when he did occasionally visit the RSPB to show me some of his recent pictures, was the most charming man.) When all were settled, the Coventry Cathedral choir produced a brilliant performance before Sir David appeared on stage, draped himself across the lectern very naturally (before this became the contrived posture adopted by choreographed politicians), and talked about the earth, our one and only planet, a tiny dot in space, and how we should try harder to protect it, before it was too late. He received a standing ovation that lasted for several minutes.

David Attenborough's *Zoo Quest* on BBC television began in 1954: for almost my whole life he has been a massive presence in books and in television documentaries. The *Zoo Quest* series had their spin-off books, which we duly read, borrowing them repeatedly from the library in Chase Terrace. The television programmes had me spellbound to such an extent that, though I hesitate to bring it up, I occasionally fantasized about being a television or radio wildlife star myself; I began to play at being David Attenborough. When I was still under ten years old and at Chase Terrace school, I waited for the bus home to Burntwood beside a patch of waste, grass-grown ground, next to Sankey's Corner, where there was the old cinema that showed Saturday matinées of cowboy films (I'm still addicted to them, too). In that patch of grass, I once found a large, round, pale buff-coloured stone. I mentally described it, its lifestyle, and how I had come to find it. I was Attenborough, describing a strange, exotic, hitherto unknown creature, which in reality was – a stone.

I think this happened for a few days, perhaps spread over a period of weeks. The stone sometimes seemed to have moved, probably rolled over or kicked by someone passing by, and I had to 'rediscover' it. I would locate it and, in my head (never out loud), go through the behaviour patterns that had taken it to its new spot. I gave a good commentary about this wonderful creature that no one had succeeded in filming before. I was bringing this – er, this stone – to the notice of the British public for the first time. I remember, too, being an indri (a Madagascan lemur) – a large, long-legged, rather humanoid one. It had strange calls and was elusive and wild. I sat on the bend half-way up our stairs, one arm hanging over the banister, and watched until someone appeared in the hallway below. It might have been Attenborough seeking me out. I bounded up the stairs in a couple of leaps, to evade the camera: now I was not David Attenborough but the wild animal he was trying to film.

A few years ago, when David Attenborough was preparing his series *The Life of Birds* – the first series he had ever done solely on birds – I decided to write a feature on it for *Birds*. I was given a phone number for his appointments secretary and told to find out if he would spare half an hour to talk about the article, to promote the television programmes. Rather nervously, I phoned the number, only to hear Sir David, himself, answering the phone. I explained that I thought I was ringing his secretary. Yes, he said, I was, but she was actually his daughter and she happened to be out. He was at home and, yes, he would like to do something for *Birds*: why didn't I come to see him next week?

So I did. Sir David asked me in, sat me down, made me a pot of tea and gave me a plate of home-made biscuits. Not wanting to eat and speak at the same time, I ungratefully left them half-eaten on the plate. He made the interview incredibly easy, but it was not a good one. The article in *Birds* was better, after a bit of work. One question I could not get out. I didn't know how to phrase it, and still don't. I think I asked him if he liked wildlife. Good question! He kindly answered it very well, recalling that, in one location, he had heard there were some whale sharks just a short journey away. He wanted to see them – there was nothing he would have liked better than to go to see them – but he hadn't the time, so he couldn't do it. What I had meant to ask was whether, like me, he did his homework before a foreign trip – trying to learn the birds and the animals – or did he know them all already? In particular, did he know everything he had seen before and get excited, specially, about seeing new things? If he saw a lesser kudu, say, and it was a 'tick' for him, was he always aware of it in this way (having, I presumed, seen practically everything there was to see on earth anyway). Did he think 'Ah, look at that, I've never seen one of those before!' I admit that, even having seen so very many species fewer than he has, I sometimes have to look up my records – usually a book with 'ticks' against animals' or birds' names – to be sure. But I didn't want to come across as a lister, or a 'ticker' – I'm not, really – but this recognition of something new, something never before seen, is nevertheless important to most of us. Was it equally important to him? I never asked the question properly. (Neither did I mention to him that I had played at being David Attenborough, although I did put it in the article. He was kind enough not to refer to it when he commented on the draft.)

We talked about conservation and the loss of habitats worldwide. He admitted that it was easy for him: if he wanted to film a bit of rainforest, he went to the rainforest; he didn't go to a place where the rainforest had been felled. So he saw the world through rosy spectacles and freely admitted that was the case. If, perhaps, he went to the worst bit of development in Bali, where he had seen pristine habitat before, he would be heartbroken. But he didn't; he didn't go back. Other people go back, are profoundly shocked and saddened, but have no way of expressing their anger, their fear. I hear stories now of people who go to South-east Asia, see a bit of forest and think 'I'll look at that on the way back' and, returning two weeks later, find that it has been felled. No further comment is really necessary; but the way the world is going, I wish people who had real influence could be shocked into action, somehow. There needs to be a United Nations task force around every bit of surviving forest to fend off the illegal loggers. The governments are never going to do it, and half of them seem to be in cahoots with the criminals. But, in the end, there is no other source of timber to meet the demand: controlling demand is the only way.

Sir David Attenborough is an astonishing man, influential at the very highest level in the BBC and responsible for many ground-breaking programmes, from *Pot Black* and *Match of the Day* to *Civilization* and *Life on Earth*. He was very much involved in introducing colour television to Britain. But his wildlife programmes have been so many, so diverse, so ambitious, so fantastic, that there can be no one in the UK who has not seen them and enjoyed them and been influenced by them. His contribution to the awareness and enjoyment of wildlife has been incalculably immense. He has the uncanny ability, in his presentation and in his writing, to explain the most complicated things in a way that is at once simple, understandable, inspiring and enjoyable; he makes science entertaining, and scores of us lesser beings have tried hard to do the same without a tiny fraction of his success. In the RSPB editorial section, we often talk of 'the Attenborough effect', wishing we could convey a story or a particular concept in the way that Attenborough would do it, but knowing full well that we can't. But we try, and that is one of the great contributions that David Attenborough has made: he has raised the game for everyone else; he has moved the goalposts, broadened our horizons, extended our ambitions.

Another hero of mine began his record-breaking television series in 1957. *The Sky at Night*, introduced by Patrick Moore, is not a wildlife programme, but has, in a sense, the whole of nature as its subject. It began six months before Sputnik was launched and I have watched it, and enjoyed Patrick Moore, ever since. As editor of the Young Ornithologists' Club (YOC) magazine, *Bird Life*, I used my position as an excuse to write to him and ask for a feature on binoculars. He replied, using his ancient typewriter on which he has written scores of books, that he didn't know a robin from a mute swan, but would gladly do the article. A postcard later arrived, simply 'Did my article reach you all gight [sic]? I don't trust the post! Regards Patrick Moore.' I'm pleased to have the card with his signature inside a copy of one of his books on my shelves.

A West Midland writer of magazine and newspaper articles and many books, as well as an occasional television presenter (most famously of *One Man and His Dog*) is Phil Drabble. I admit I learned more about him from my parents, who read his columns in the local papers and often read his books, than from reading his work myself. At one time, though, he became increasingly worried at the prospect of the land adjacent to his own private nature reserve in Staffordshire being taken over by Center Parc (why can't they spell it properly?) and developed as a tourist destination. The thought of the disturbance to his heronry and badgers made him distraught: it was the worst period of 'worry guts' in his life. So he turned to the RSPB, offering to sell or give the land to the society to manage as a reserve.

Oddly, to my mind (as it had a huge heronry in its lovely woods), we turned him down, which was not to his liking. I was sent to interview him, to give him space in *Birds*, partly to placate him and partly to fend off any criticism he might publish. So, one early spring day, off I went to mid-Staffordshire, to see the area that I still thought of as home and talk to Phil – perhaps a bit of a daunting prospect. I pushed my way through his gate and was immediately met by two enormous dogs. One, a big, glossy black German Shepherd, bounded up and planted its forefeet against my chest in a friendly greeting. Phil was just the same: potentially difficult and dangerous, but, as it turned out, the perfect host. He showed me where he fed the badgers and had a camera on the spot, which, once a badger arrived, lit up a light over his television set so that he could turn off the programme and watch pictures of the badgers on screen instead. We had a big lunch and then walked around the woods and meadows around his home. I could see exactly why he needed some assurance that this would not be ruined after he was gone. I understood all his worries.

I wrote a feature on Phil and his herons, and his work with local schools (he soon saw that this would do him a bit of good and help fend off the developers). He rewrote what I had done and sent back an article that was pretty much like many others that he had published elsewhere, which was a pity. But the idea was still good and he wrote a lot of good sense. However, it was the prelude to some difficult times as he then tried to use me in his personal battles with local authorities and especially the South Staffordshire Water Company, which wanted to develop part of Blithfield Reservoir at the time. Phil wanted me to endorse his own opposition to this, in the name of the RSPB. I entirely supported what he was doing, but it was not an RSPB priority and I was not able to bring the RSPB into it. I was torn between Phil and my own ideas and the RSPB, and the RSPB had to win. It was all a bit unsatisfactory, and I felt I had let Phil Drabble down. He sent me reams of paperwork to support his case; files of it built up on my desk. Eventually it stopped and I suspect he gave up on me, realizing it was pointless trying to make any more of such a bad job as I had turned out to be. I still feel bad about it, but pleased that I met him. He is, especially in the Midlands, a great influence on the way that people look at and enjoy the countryside around them.

Board Rulers and Beanstalks

The best days of your life? Not for me. School was not my favourite place. I recently went to see a school play, and the sound of the bell and the sight of the playground, the dark-brown brick building and smooth-tiled corridor walls brought it all back. It was as much as they could do to get me in. Certainly, school, apart from the inexplicably good collection of bird books in the library at Cannock Grammar School, did little for my interest in birds.

My first day at school was a disaster for everyone. I was being taken away from home, taken from my mum, and I fought against it (it was only to be for a few hours, but how was I to know that?). I wrestled with the headmistress, brown-suited Miss Sparkes, her grey hair tied back in a bun, and kicked her hard on her thin, brown-stockinged shins for all I was worth. And I was sick in the corridor for good measure. Take that! I started as I meant to go on. Several times I ran away from school and went home; once I hid under the teacher's desk. OK, so a nice lady with a hooped blue and yellow sweater read us bits from *The Hobbit*, and I drew pictures and made cardboard castles from cornflake packets painted in thick, grey powder paint, but that couldn't make up for it, nor could the nice days at harvest festival and Christmas: school was a place to be hated. I'm still not sure why. But I did get a copy of *Tom Sawyer* as a prize for good attendance.

A very tall, very thin lady, clothed head to foot in very dark brown, with a 1930s' tight, round hat, was Miss Latham, or 'Latherbottom', who had taught my mother and brother but was about to retire. Mr Dennis the headmaster was pleasant enough and he had a shiny black Ford Prefect, ECH 322 or similar. He once gave me a gift for selling programmes at the inter-school sports day, a softback school atlas. Before he let me take it, he opened each page, drew a line through it with a flourish and wrote 'Out of date' in big blue letters over maps that still revived fading memories of the red British Empire. But he gave many pupils six of the best with his cane, across the palm of the hand. One boy was often in trouble at home or with the police and, should Mr Dennis find out, he was hauled up onto the stage in front of the morning assembly and caned for good measure, sobbing and dribbling in front of us all. Another Mr Dennis was a dead shot with a piece of chalk and had the cheery habit of grabbing boys by the hair above their ears, twisting it and leading them out to the front of the class where they could properly be made examples of if they did not copy their letters properly from his blackboard. Should Mr Derry, the sports master, wish to punish anyone, he would use a short, thick, wooden bat, a 'stool ball bat' and hit as hard as he could, so the unfortunate lad would be in tears for the rest of the day and hardly able to sit down. It was, for a moment, barbaric.

Fortunately I did not suffer such punishments, although I once or twice had the blackboard ruler across the backside from Mr Foster. He broke his big, yard-long, yellow boxwood ruler on me before he got his new, thicker, dark-brown, three-foot rule that stood up to the punishment much better. I think I recited 'Dr Foster went to Gloucester, in a shower of rain', unfortunately within his hearing (and starting '*Mr* Foster …'), and he didn't appreciate the humour, so it was the board ruler in the right hand, my neck in his left hand, bending me down to be hit. But I wasn't such an easy victim. Bent double, I ran round in circles, ahead of the ruler, making him even more furious and frustrated as he spun round with me, trying to get in a good shot. Not much chat about birds in the garden there, then.

The playground had a pile of coke by the boiler room which we would climb and slide down in a grubby heap. Someone regularly picked out bits of grit from my grazed knees. There were long, shallow, concrete gutters running to metal drains – ideal for racing Matchbox cars. I had the older Maserati, Alan had the new style Ferrari – the sublime magic of bright-red Italian racing cars still remains. We used to bend over, feet wide apart, and, after several swings to get the line and trajectory right, send them back between our legs as hard as we could – a good throw would speed the little car along the gutters and it would even take a bend; but now and then, exuberance or lack of skill would send the car spinning off to one side, sometimes, horribly, inexplicably, to fly up and off to one side and hit a plate-glass window. Even the staff-room window. Time stood still; but no great damage was done.

We had free milk, first in little bottles, and later in strange three-pointed cardboard cartons, and for a few years I went to a place near by to collect free orange juice, the best orange juice I can remember. I went home on the bus, unless we decided to spend the one-penny bus fare in Dewsbury's, the baker's, across the road, on a penny cob, and walk home instead.

What about my peers? I can't recall talking about birds with anyone at infant or primary school, where our 'biology' lessons were pretty dreadful from what I remember. Miss Wright, an awful, big, smelly woman, coughed and spat and spluttered all over everyone in the front of the classroom and occasionally waved around an eyeball, plucked from a poor beast at the local slaughterhouse, in front of our faces. That was it I think, apart from a few tadpoles and growing a bean in a glass jar with wet blotting paper, so we could watch the progress of the roots, and collecting and drawing some sticky buds from horse chestnut trees. That was good: I still remember the little horseshoe shapes and the dots left where the sap ran through channels into the leaf-stalk.

Later, at Cannock Grammar School, biology was one of three subjects from which I could choose only two to take as far as O level; history and geography were the others and both had more appeal as neither involved killing frogs or sitting in the biology lab, in a dreadful stench, cutting up rats. So, biology was dropped as soon as possible and I didn't ever study it or anything like it again. There was really nothing, except that surprising library, to encourage anyone to take an interest in wildlife of any kind. There was a small round pond, but that served only as a means of potential punishment by the sixth-formers, who threatened to throw first-years in if they didn't do as they were told. Nor was there any likelihood of finding anyone else interested. I don't think anyone else in the whole school was a birdwatcher. I didn't talk about it, really, as it was better to do without the insults and unfunny comments. I think it was here, though, that I first began to get the 'birds – ah, the two-legged kind I suppose' kind of comment that has continued ever since (I never have discovered any kind with more or fewer legs than two). It never ever raised a laugh. Jokes about birds and birdwatching have never been very good and, after several scores of times, such pointless comments are tiresome in the extreme – but naturally everyone who makes them thinks he is the first.

No, school did nothing for my interest in birds, although by the time I got to A level, geography was much better and I was happy with art. Actually, I'd done quite well with the O levels, even in difficult subjects such as physics, and A levels went along swimmingly. After my O levels, I remember the maths teacher (I'd passed maths, somehow), Mr Pearman, meeting me on the road outside and smiling genuinely as we passed each other, his black gown flowing behind him. It was one of those odd moments: I no longer did maths, he no longer had any responsibility for me; instead he just smiled at me as any ordinary person would. Teachers, perhaps, were human after all, and I had grown up a bit.

I remember a geography field trip to Snowdonia, which came about purely at the suggestion of a good teacher, Mr Douglas. We camped at Beddgelert and climbed Snowdon, which was stunning, and probably had some sensible conversation about the birds we saw, but there was never very much of that as far as I can remember, although I was watching the birds there quite closely. I don't think anyone else ever so much as looked at the bird books in the school library. These were 'reference only', so they could be read just now and then in free periods. There was no mention at any of my schools of the Young Ornithologists' Club or RSPB (even though I was an RSPB member myself from the age of 14); and there was certainly no involvement with RSPB education, either in the school or out on nature reserves, not even in the ubiquitous pond dipping (I sometimes wonder what it is like to be a tadpole or a water beetle, swept up into the sky several times a day into a net and bundled about by clumsy little fingers – Oh no, here we go again).

I do remember, though, helping to illustrate a school magazine (*Chenet*), which had a poem in it about oil pollution and dead birds on the beach; a diver was mentioned. Where did that come from? Come to think of it, I believe I wrote it myself. The art teacher asked me to 'do a bird shape, looking dead', as a line-drawing, so perhaps there was a little more awareness of my interest in birds than I tend to remember. We also discussed the tendency to draw birds in a realistic, accurate-as-possible way. David Merrills, the art teacher, asked me what I thought was wrong with Kokoschka's purple seagulls, which he considered worked very well in his paintings. I probably scoffed at the time, but there is, of course, nothing wrong with them at all.

What did seem impossible at school was going in on a Monday morning and telling someone – anyone – what I had been seeing over the weekend. I often needed this; everyone does. Even at home I would sometimes go in bursting with excitement about some new bird I had seen, or something at Chasewater that was unexpected, and wanting to share my discovery, but no one really knew much about what I was talking about and more often than not I had to give up and sit down to my dinner. It's the same as being the only Rolling Stones or Bob Dylan fan in the family, or the only one interested in post-impressionist paintings, or any other special subject. It was all too easy, too, to resist encouragement. It must have been frustrating for people who told me I was good at drawing, for example, to hear me come right back and say no, I wasn't. It was very unfair of me and I am still the same, still hard on others: I accept compliments grudgingly, feeling they are unwarranted, based on a lack of judgement. It upsets people who are close to me; it is a strange, ungrateful and unattractive kind of arrogance – you say it's good, I know it isn't, don't bother, I know better than you. But it was also difficult as a schoolboy to show off drawings of birds to my parents' friends and relatives, having been egged on to do so, when I thought – no, I knew – they were not so very good, and all too often copies of something else, never coming close to what I hoped might be my potential. It must sometimes have caused embarrassment all round, despite the best of intentions.

Yet somehow I persisted through all this lack of encouragement at school, and even through some resistance to my interest in birds, which came in the shape of the occasional bit of ridicule – birdwatching was, if anything at all, seen as silly, a bit wet, by my friends – and I was always their second-best friend. It could be the same even now, I suspect, in many schools, although there is much more interest in the world around us than there was in the 1960s. I'm not sure the kind of teacher who might say 'It's a beautiful spring day; let's go out to the local lake and see if the swallows have arrived' ever existed outside a few fortunate schools where nature study and even bird clubs thrived in the 1940s and 1950s (and a few persist even now). And today it is almost impossible to do anything like that for fear of health and safety regulations – there is always the chance that a child might slip on a muddy bank and fall in the water, which might prompt a parent to sue.

There is now, though, a risk – I'm not sure how great a risk to be fair – that what used to be called nature study (now deadeningly called 'biodiversity' or 'the environment' or whatever it might be) might be viewed as just another subject, another exam to get through and forget. It has become something to slide into the school curriculum in as many places as possible, but it doesn't seem to be enthralling, absorbing, inspiring. It fills a gap or two in the weekly timetable and meets a few objectives. I don't know how lasting the effects might be, unless a child happens to come into contact with a really dedicated and inspiring teacher, someone who can identify a particular interest, a special talent, and has the time to work on it. There will always be a few loners, like me, who just get on with it on their own. And I get some letters from parents about their children who are just as excited by real wildlife out of doors as I ever was.

The old Junior Bird Recorders Club (JBRC), which was founded in 1943 and developed into the Young Ornithologists' Club (YOC) in 1965, and now the RSPB Wildlife Explorers, have influenced vast numbers of children. More than a million people have been members at some time. The YOC regularly had well over 100,000 members, and recently the RSPB celebrated 60 years of youth work of one kind or another, a record to be immensely proud of. Advertising standards prevent its being said, now, just in case it can't be proved, but the YOC was certainly the largest wildlife club for children in the world.

The Junior Birdwatcher, which began in 1955, was the first JBRC magazine, and it has developed and diversified from one all-encompassing production to separate, specially tailored ones for under-eights, 8- to 13-year-olds, and older teenagers. For some years I edited *Bird Life*, which catered for all the youth members. It was good fun. Amongst other things, I was able to commission illustrations from young artists who have since become well known in the field-guide and wildlife-art field, people such as Ian Lewington, who, I believe, had his first work reproduced in colour in *Bird Life*, which I commissioned on the advice of the leader of the Vale of White Horse RSPB members' group, Harry Lemon. Ian has become one of the most respected bird illustrators in Europe, while his brother is the number one insect painter, renowned for his butterflies and moths.

Through its organizer, Peter Holden, the YOC had excellent contacts with the BBC and especially with *Blue Peter*. In 1978 the YOC/*Blue Peter* Birdwatch attracted 32,000 children, and 1,600 became members. A couple of years ago, 16 per cent of RSPB staff had been YOC members and many claim that they would not have taken a conservation career had it not been for the YOC. Peter, who has been heading youth work for the RSPB for 30 years, can be justly proud.

RSPB field teaching began at Vane Farm, a reserve on the edge of Loch Leven, near Perth. It now operates at many reserves the length and breadth of the UK, with recent and planned expansion especially at nature reserves within easy reach of urban centres. There are also many local groups that cater for children under the RSPB umbrella. These have always influenced some children deeply: many people with conservation jobs can cite a YOC group, or a YOC leader, as an early, defining influence on the direction they have taken in life. We are not entirely sure how many who leave birds and wildlife take it up again as a serious interest later in life, or may lobby against a damaging development close to home, or campaign for the protection of a wood or meadow.

The JBRC took groups of birdwatchers on field trips and courses at bird observatories. Although its membership was small it was in its way remarkably influential. It managed to hit the right note straight away, involving its members in a way that gave them rapid feedback and a chance to see their own work recognized, even in print, and their own bird records published in JBRC bulletins. My Colchester cousins were JBRC members and their bird records, with their names or initials in brackets, were published in its magazines. It seems

Spring – the swallows are back.

to me that the JBRC engendered a great sense of purpose and of belonging, but perhaps this could only work with a relatively small membership.

Today, RSPB Phoenix (the older teenager branch) members can be involved in running the club itself (through the Phoenix Forum) and some have represented the club as far afield as the Earth Summit in Johannesburg. Some have even gone on to become junior MEPs. Will they become movers and shakers who remember wildlife in their business careers? Or even sympathetic politicians, who can give birds a bit of a boost?

Why, I don't know, but without any help from school I survived well enough on great encouragement from my parents, periodic encouragement from aunts and uncles (including the suggestion that I join the RSPB), and correspondence, with its element of friendly competition, with my cousins. Organized activities for young birdwatchers passed me by, and this probably contributed to a spirit of independence that is still alive and well. If a nature trail leads birdwatchers to one side of a lake, I'll most likely walk round to the other. It's always been more fun, and usually more productive, that way.

North to the Highlands

One summer day in 1964, we left home at 5 o'clock in the morning and reached Kinlochleven on the Argyll coast at 7.15 in the evening. It was the start of a love affair with Scotland that has, in a way, survived, despite a lack of visits in recent years. As we drove into Kinlochleven for the first time we saw simple little houses dotted around the loch, painted pink, yellow and white under grey slate roofs, and we all began to sing *Little Boxes* ('made of ticky tacky, and they all looked just the same'), which seemed childishly appropriate (it was a minor hit at the time, if you can believe it). The Highland Games were taking place on a field by the loch and bagpipes were being played. The peaks around Glen Coe were topped with cloud and mist and there were a few spots of rain, but such gloomy weather enhanced its mystery and drama. What better landscapes can you find than these? The place left an indelible impression on me, and I have devoured books about its history (John Prebble I particularly like), admired a multitude of photographs, studied maps and generally felt an affinity with Glen Coe ever since.

In that first year, we stayed in a caravan near Kinlochleven between Glen Coe and Fort William. In Kinlochleven we found the McAngus sisters, who took us to our caravan 20 yards from the loch side on a low promontory beside a stream. I noted the Gaelic names of all the visible peaks, together with their heights in feet (so much more impressive than metres) and was in my element from the start: this was Joseph E. Chipperfield country come to life.

David kept holiday diaries, illustrated by postcards, so I kept a diary too. The first year's was a scrappy affair, but later ones were larger, and we collected local postcards (Valentine's and J. Arthur Dixon, the local publishers, did well out of us) and took our own black and white photographs with a Kodak Brownie 127. Daily mileages in our Ford Consul were religiously noted, along with details of the weather and precise routes.

Our first Sunday morning was basically a rest after the journey (duly logged as 416.8 miles). We scrambled through a wood of birch and willow up onto the open hill, about 800 feet up behind the site, from which height all the hills around looked even more impressive. There was a golden eagle high over Am Bodach. I made little of this, except to say that it looked marvellous, soaring and gliding, but soon going out of sight. Postcards sent to Essex with news of several golden eagles were politely received but, I'm sure, quite rightly, not entirely believed. A golden eagle glimpsed from the campsite on the first day? Some of my first 'golden eagles' that year were undoubtedly buzzards, a mistake that is perhaps understandable in an excited just-14-year-old. But this very first one, soaring high over Am Bodach, an unlikely spot for a buzzard, I can still remember and it was a golden eagle, sure enough. Because the bird notes were copied into my later format some years on, extracted from the narrative diary, I admitted that some of the eagles (of about five claimed in a fortnight) were buzzards, but added 'I remember vividly the bird over Am Bodach and am sure it was my first real eagle'.

This was typical of my early birdwatching, doing it on my own, learning by trial and error. It was ill-disciplined and it would have been better if I had had someone to keep me on the rails now and then, as with one or two of these 'eagles', but it was far better than being led by the hand and shown birds that were identified for me by someone else. The bulk of the notes for my first fortnight in Scotland are made up of typical common birds such as wheatears,

Rock dove – handsome resident of northern and western coasts.

whinchats, buzzards, eiders and mergansers, hooded crows, common and Arctic terns, common and black-headed gulls, redshanks and curlews, rock pipits and the like. Many were new or almost so.

One day we drove up to Loch Garten, and new birds there were ospreys and crested tits. Ospreys had not been nesting for many years at Loch Garten but were already popular. Since then a couple of million visitors have been to the osprey centre; the nesting tree has been sawn through and burned, the old centre itself burned down, eggs stolen. On this first visit we parked as best we could beside the narrow road and walked along a boardwalk, made of railway sleepers, to a sturdy but rudimentary hut. Giant binoculars on heavy tripods gave good views of the nest. Volunteers ran the observation hide and nest-protection rotas, with tents and caravans for accommodation.

Most memorable, in many ways, were the evenings beside the loch. None of us had experienced anything quite like this before. It hardly got dark; even late in the evening it was still broad daylight, and whatever the weather had been during the day it usually settled down by the evening, when it became wonderfully calm and quiet. The loch, so often whipped into choppy grey, with those curious lines of white surf parallel with the shores that characterize western Scotland, became mirror smooth, the hills reflected in perfect replicas of their shapely form and richly textured colours. Oystercatchers piped on the shores and their calls echoed from the hillside behind. It was sheer bliss. Despite many subsequent holidays, nothing ever beat this; in its own, small way, it was the epitome of the western Highlands.

On the way home we met my uncles, aunts and cousins heading north for their holiday in Scotland, and I quickly swapped cars and joined them for another two weeks. How lucky could I be? This pattern was to continue for a few years: I usually had four weeks, once even five, in Scotland each summer and, over the years, covered much of the area north and west of a line from Loch Lomond to Aberdeen. We were simply finding our own way to see what we could, although David would put in some homework beforehand. For example, he clearly worked out from books roughly where the Slavonian grebes must be and then we went along and found them. It was this kind of thing that was not exactly hit and miss, but it was, looking back, surprisingly unprepared. We knew there were crested tits and capercaillies around Speyside, and we went, used our maps, found some suitable looking woods, and saw them. We didn't have guides to birdwatching in the Highlands, or lists of RSPB nature reserves, or birdwatchers' maps. Nor did we have any information from anyone else: no websites listing likely sites for all the rarities, no trip lists, no grid references. We did our own thing, so we missed out on quite a bit, but we were much happier making our own discoveries.

The business of finding divers was managed by the simple expedient of driving beside lochs and staring out across them at every opportunity. We found a lot of divers. I kept a map of all the accumulated diver sightings: black-throated, red-throated and occasional sea-going great northerns, too. Finding eagles was a matter of stopping at likely vantage points, or walking along suitable quiet, remote glens, and staring for hours at the sky, especially along the distant skyline. We had many great views of eagles. I would watch them with my telescope from two or three miles away; sometimes it proved to be as many as five miles when we measured the distance to a peak on the map after seeing a minute dot sail dramatically but majestically behind it, 3,000 feet up (never a buzzard). Once when I walked from the high road to Applecross, over 2,000 feet and into ptarmigan habitat above the pass of Bealach na Ba, to the nearest great cliffs of Sgurr a'Chaorachain, an eagle passed by at really close range: a stunning bird, so big, so dramatic, its wings marbled with pale gold where its old feathers had bleached in the sun.

Having said all this, we had days when we saw few birds, but since these were family holidays, not major birding trips, it mattered little. Many of the better days for birds, though, were on the coast. I was recently back in Caithness, on the clifftops at Dunnet Head, Strathy Point and Duncansby Head, and this brought back exciting memories of past visits. On such days I could bring together and make use of all my reading of James Fisher's book on the fulmar, Fraser Darling and Morton Boyd's 'New Naturalist' on the Highlands and islands, the hours spent poring over maps, and my interest in geography (physical geography rather than any other kind); and of course I could indulge my especial delight in seabirds and seascapes. In short, everything I liked best seemed to come together on these cliff-bound coasts, where kittiwakes wailed and fulmars cackled, guillemots crowded the ledges, and rock doves spiralled out of sight into hidden sea caves, all above the surge and sweep of the blue and white sea and the tang of salt and fishy guano.

What a place Handa Island was. On 4 July 1966 we arrived too late to land and walk over the island, but Mr Munro, the boatman, took us out in a small boat to the base of the main cliffs and the black water at the foot of the famous stack of Torridonian sandstone. We were just six feet from guillemots and razorbills beside the boat. Puffins stood on grassy screes at the top of the cliffs, fulmars sat on broad, stony ledges and peered out to sea, where they really belonged, and shags lined the flat rocks at the edge of the deep, black sea. Thousands of kittiwakes wheeled above us and hundreds more stood in close ranks on seaweedy rocks at the edge of the surf. Mr Munro told us of the waves that crashed against the foot of the cliffs in winter, sending roaring spray towering right up and over the tops; it did seem to be a place where nature was in control. Stupidly we had left the camera in the car. On the way back later we saw two black-throated divers, a short-eared owl and several buzzards.

On later visits we landed on the little sandy beaches, said goodbye to the boat, which puttered back to the mainland, and walked to the Stack, dodging great and Arctic skuas that were just beginning to colonize the island (they nest in large numbers there now). The views north and south along the Sutherland coast were superb, the sea incomparably blue, the beaches unoccupied, wild and untouched. In many places we could look across gullies in the cliffs to see guillemots, razorbills and fulmars on ledges opposite, fabulous birds at really close range. Now and then we would surprise a shag on a nest and it would wave its head and snaky neck, hissing and cackling at us until we left it in peace. Cormorants and shags are rarely anyone's favourite birds, but I have always found them remarkably handsome, especially in spring when their facial colours and wispy plumes are at their best.

In 1966 we were staying by the shore of the Cromarty Firth. I learned that England had won the World Cup by overhearing a fisherman's radio in Invergordon. Each evening we had roding woodcocks overhead, and redpolls sang around us each morning (this was where I learned the redpoll's calls and reeling song-flight). We drove out to Glen Affric and saw golden eagles, and to Loch Torridon where there were red deer stags as well as eiders and black guillemots. I took notes on displaying red-throated divers and on 13 July saw two new birds in quick succession as a young peregrine flew beside the car above the cliffs at Berriedale and a rock dove flew up near Ulbster. We went to Duncansby Head that day, and saw hundreds of fulmars, kittiwakes, puffins, guillemots, razorbills and herring gulls, and then to Dunnet Head, its higher cliffs the most northerly point in mainland Britain, where there seemed to be even larger numbers of most of these super seabirds. Here, too, stocky, black-faced rams backed off each other before a slow, deliberate charge and a solid crack of skulls and horns, fighting like wild ibexes. The cliffs and clifftops were remarkably rich in wild flowers, which we duly identified from our Collins pocket guide and noted somewhere in long-lost pocket notebooks.

I was back in Scotland at the end of July, staying at Bunchrew, where there was a single summering whooper swan; the following week there were four. We watched crossbills – which species? – dippers, black-throated divers everywhere.

By Stac Polly there was a golden eagle; next day, near Loch Maree, there were two more, and the day after, at Torridon, another. At Findhorn Bay there were crested tits and, far out over the sea, an Arctic skua (at that time a new bird for me). I'm not sure what I thought about the crossbills then; Scottish crossbills came later, in the big pines of Rothiemurchus and Abernethy (and in Easter Ross) with fat, muscular cheeks and big bills. But were they really Scottish? In recent years it has become clear that common, Scottish and parrot crossbills all breed in these magical woods, where the ground is deep in bilberry and cowberry, and juniper grows between the majestic Scots pines. They are hard to tell apart, even by the specialists; now, I suppose, if I saw crossbills there I would be left floundering. It is perhaps as well I 'ticked' Scottish crossbill when I did …

Some of these 'new birds' became the norm in later years. We saw many peregrines, a lot of skuas, and a great many rock doves. Hen harriers, short-eared owls and merlins were frequent, and we had magnificent views of all the divers on many occasions. Ospreys were seen in new places, not just at Loch Garten. One very wet day we had travelled a long way north, seeing little in driving rain, and I was disappointed and depressed – and imposing my mood on others (as I am too apt to do) – when suddenly, alongside the River Laxford, an osprey appeared, chased by lesser black-backed gulls. Ospreys then were still rare and close-kept secrets. A little later, near Durness, there was a great northern diver and, in improving weather, we watched fulmars in Smoo Cave (later checked in Fisher's book), red- and black-throated divers, greenshanks and golden plovers.

I had never seen a Manx shearwater (perhaps not surprising – where would I have seen it?) until one evening, near Melvaig on the west coast, a small, dark shape skimmed the sea and, before it could be identified, disappeared into a patch of dazzling reflection. Then several more were seen, straight- and stiff-winged, black above and white below, like little black and white crosses tilting from wing-tip to wing-tip low over the waves, very much in Fitter and Richardson's pocket-guide fashion. I remember the smile of satisfaction when we finally clinched the identification and the birds matched the book to perfection. Shearwaters somehow seemed to be difficult and challenging, and to get them was a triumph. In subsequent years we saw hundreds of shearwaters, especially opposite their great colonies on Rhum, and from a few points off the far north-west coast occasionally found a few sooty shearwaters with them (and even, once or twice, some storm petrels).

On 13 July 1967, Dad and I were walking around a low-lying loch in northern Caithness when I discovered my first genuine rarity: not only the first

*Mountains with eagles, a pinewood with capercaillies and crossbills,
and black-throated divers on the loch.*

'rarity list' bird I had seen, but the first I found for myself. To be sure, it was easy
to identify: not much can be confused with a summer-plumaged adult white-
winged black tern! What was it doing so far north, in mid-July? It was pretty
stunning, and it came as close as ten yards. My notes and drawings were proudly
submitted to the Rarities Committee and my first rare bird was accepted.

How, then, did I get to submit a gull-billed tern and have it rejected? I made a
complete botch of this, whatever it was. It was long after I should have known
better although, to be fair, my rarity experience was slim. It was in August
1968, when I was 18 (an age when birders now know everything about Pechora
pipits and the subtleties of soft-plumaged petrels). At Chanonry Point, in the
Moray Firth, Arctic skuas, kittiwakes, Sandwich terns and gannets had held
my attention before what I took to be a gull-billed tern flew by with a group of
Sandwich terns. The bill was 'shortish' and all black, the head white with a bold
black eye-patch (noted as tapering a little up towards the nape, not a good sign).
The general shape and wing pattern seemed good. Looking back now on the
notes in my book, I can see that they are very brief and scrappy and convincing
only in the sense that rejection was a foregone conclusion! I somehow got
mixed up with two birds, one presumably a young Sandwich tern (if this one
was not) and messed the whole thing up. Whatever, whether there was a gull-
billed or not (and I'm still not sure there wasn't) it is obvious that a summer
white-winged black, however much I added subtleties of shape and flight action

to the blindingly obvious plumage features, was a doddle compared with the challenge of a more difficult tern a year later.

There were other mysteries over the years. I'm sure we once saw a gyr falcon, but John and David – who were naturally less pushy than I was on the subject of identification, more experienced, and better – were not convinced. It was, though, a whopping big falcon, 'as big as a buzzard', lead-grey (not bluish) and with little more of a moustache than the average kestrel; but how much I can really remember all that and how much I am remembering what I think I remember, who can say? Once it's gone, it's gone.

Other things were easier. David suffered a bad attack of mumps one year and John and I left him in bed at the Crask of Aigas and went to the nearest bit of coast, in quite thick fog. It was August 1969, close to Inverness. Up to 50 bottle-nosed dolphins were leaping from the surf and chasing enormous salmon, rising in long, low arcs and occasionally making vertical leaps high out of the water. These dolphins, which we had entirely to ourselves, have become a regular tourist attraction now; they even have a website. A skua passed by; there were a few kittiwakes, terns, fulmars, a red-throated diver – not a great deal about in the calm, misty conditions. But a small gull drifted along on the tide, swivelling and picking from the surface as it went, in the manner of a giant phalarope. It sailed past us, then flew back upstream, to repeat the performance. I have the scribbled sketches I made in my small, ruled notebook at the time, with a black biro, featuring a detail of the closed wing-tip, a full side-on view, a larger, close-up view of the bill, head, neck and breast area, a sketch of the back of the head, an upperside flight view and an underside one, and details of the tail.

It was, in any case, unmistakable: a Sabine's gull. It is still quite a remarkable record, for there had been just three records in Scotland in the previous 57 years. It was accepted as the 14th for Scotland. Like some other summer or early-autumn Sabine's gulls, it was in an interesting, transitional sort of plumage, and was presumably a year-old bird – we did not know much about the moult sequences of these gulls at the time. The back and wings were clearly fully adult, without a trace of brown or scaly feather edges, but the tail had some dark-tipped feathers and the head was clouded with mottled lead grey; a dusky, brownish mark on the hindneck continued as a dark grey smudge down the side of the breast. It was the wing pattern that was so astounding, as is always the case with any decent Sabine's. I wrote: 'The wing pattern was very obvious, striking because of the contrasting black, grey and white and the very clear-cut borders between these shades. It was immaculate and a really beautiful flight pattern, even better than an immature kittiwake.' (I still had not grown out of writing in the slightly formal, detached style that had characterized my notes when I was much younger.)

We climbed some hills and found our ptarmigan; we walked through pine forests and found our capercaillies. We used to see these giant birds in a small wood beside Loch Tulla, south of Glen Coe (a place where we sometimes watched as many as six golden eagles at a time, well past the 'is it a buzzard?' stage). But the capercaillies disappeared once the wood was enclosed by a high deer fence. It seems highly likely that this is what did for them: it was a small, isolated population, but they survived all right until the fencing came. Such fences are lethal to capercaillies and, within a year or two, a small number could easily be wiped out simply by fatal collisions with the wire. I told my old friend Tony Blake about this wood as a place to find a capercaillie. Pleased as I was that he saw them, I couldn't help being a little jealous when he told me that a 'rogue' male had come out of the trees and chased him off.

As I skim through the holiday diaries and my bird logbooks, so much comes back, thanks to my daily-diary style of making and keeping notes; a card index or some other more sophisticated system would be far less evocative. (No doubt a computer system would now be able to do everything in one go, daily notes, species by species, highest counts, lowest counts, sightings on Tuesdays when there is an r in the month or whatever, but I'm not going to start transferring everything onto computer now, thank you very much.) More books added their own slice of enjoyment to the mix, as I began to find out more about the ecology of the Highlands. However, it is a pity that it was not until much later that I began to read Seton Gordon. The expert ecologist and ornithologist, Adam Watson, at eight years old, found Seton Gordon's *The Cairngorm Hills of Scotland* in the local library and is quoted in a biography of Seton Gordon:

> Books are one of the pinnacles of human culture and achievement. Few things have a more revolutionary effect on the attitudes and beliefs of young minds in a receptive mod. That was so for me, with Seton Gordon's books. Only perhaps twice in a lifetime may a brief event, such as a glance at a book, or a sudden union of two like minds, become a clear turning point which transforms the rest of one's life ... From then on I saw Scotland, its wild life, weather, skies, people and culture, with this different eye.

In August 1967, in my second fortnight that year, we set off one day from Bonar Bridge, where we had rented a cottage in the village. I noted a couple of buzzards and a kestrel on the way north, then some swifts at Thurso, before we

Field sketches of red-necked grebes, showing black and yellow bill patterns, and velvet scoter. Alberlady Bay, Firth of Forth, 17 August 1974.

reached Dunnet Bay. Here a huge sweep of clean sands, backed by dunes, offers magnificent views out over the sea to Orkney – where the Old Man of Hoy is a prominent feature – and of the cliffs approaching Dunnet Head. My asterisk system draws attention to what were the good birds at the time: 25 sanderlings (ridiculously tame, as waders often are), 37-plus eiders, a pair of scaup, two great northern divers, three red-throated divers flying over, one or two pale-phase Arctic skuas, and many Sandwich terns. The red-throated divers breed on inland pools but feed on the sea, and seeing them flying (and hearing their staccato, quacking calls from high overhead) is not unusual. The scaup were first seen flying over the bay and naturally, I suppose, taken for tufted ducks until they settled with the eiders quite close in, when the female showed the characteristic white face and pale ear-patch as well as a rather reddish-brown overall colour. The skua chased a few kittiwakes and terns. Arctic skuas were rapidly established as great favourites and still, to me, represent perfection in terms of shape and elegance in the air.

Dunnet Head itself was, as always, a delight, although getting good views of the cliff face beside the stubby white lighthouse is not easy there. Again, the asterisked birds – 50-plus twites, a dozen golden plovers, 4–5,000 puffins, 4,000 kittiwakes, 1,500-plus fulmars, ten great skuas, six Arctic skuas, an immature peregrine – give an idea of the fare. The supporting cast included black guillemot, a curiously low figure of ten guillemots, plus gannets, shags, rock doves and rock pipits. We made quite determined efforts to get the numbers roughly right – not detailed counts, but at least an idea of what we had seen. It always seemed important to me to do this (once I was past the earliest months of serious birdwatching when I tended to put 'many' or 'few' – or John's triangle symbol – rather too often). This has been something of an obsession since. When I have been lucky enough to see miles of African savannah covered with wildebeest, I've always wanted to know, roughly, whether I was looking at 100,000, 200,000 or half a million. It was just the same with the train-spotting: I never wanted to see 'all the Scots' or 'the full set of Jubes', particularly, and I wasn't especially interested in how many engines I had seen, but if I saw a locomotive, I wanted to know what it was and to underline its number in a book to record the fact. Had I seen it before, or was it 'new' – a cop? It seemed to me to be odd, somehow, *not* to want to know, and, in just the same way, I needed to know whether I was looking at 500 puffins or 5,000 – or 3,500. It was a matter of putting the record straight, getting it right.

There was another element in my notes: I wanted to do justice to the birds. I needed to say not just that here were 5,000 puffins, but that 'they looked very handsome'. Everyone knows what a puffin looks like, I knew what a puffin looked like, but, whoever these notes were for, I needed to show that I enjoyed these puffins, appreciated them – they weren't just numbers in a book, a name in a list. Was this being pompous, trying to make more of it than was really the case? I don't think so. I was not aware of 'listers' (certainly not 'tickers') then, so it wasn't an effort to show that 'I'm not one of those'. It was to express more about my reaction to these fabulous birds – thousands of puffins, and didn't they look fantastic! It is still just the same. They deserve something more; I have to pay homage to them one way or another and, if I can't draw them, paint them or photograph them, then they must at least be described. For here were the seabirds that James Fisher wrote about, the birds whose photographs I'd examined in all the books I could find and that I'd studied in field guides and read about in Bannerman's *Birds of the British Isles*. Here in Scotland – a country whose rocks and coastlines I had studied, together with the unpronounceable place names, in hours of looking at gorgeous 1-inch Ordnance Survey maps – I was at last seeing them all at first hand. I couldn't quite believe it, and I had to say something more than '4–5,000 puffins'.

The peregrine that I had noted was described as flying quickly out to sea, before returning to the cliff where it attacked a group of 'feral pigeons'. I had also listed three rock doves. What, then, were these pigeons? Surely they were really wild rock doves. Were there some mottly pigeons as well, up here, as far north as we could possibly get? Surely not – I hope not. I have always liked real rock doves, which seem to me to be smart and attractive birds, sadly being pushed out of existence in most places by the march of the escaped domestic variants such as might be seen in any town square or railway station.

Many of the best birds are in the eastern Highlands and we did have holidays based in places such as Banchory and near the Spey. These were good for crested tits, crossbills, black grouse, capercaillies, ptarmigan and ospreys. But I always hankered after the north and the west, particularly the west, where the hills are so much more spectacular to look at, at least from the bottom. (The Cairngorms, obviously, are stunningly large and awesome from the top, with dizzying drops and spectacular corries.) The west, though, generally has fewer birds and the days' lists are, in many cases, pretty thin. In some areas I fear to go back now: the growth of windfarms is not to my taste and I wonder about the wisdom of putting these in so many areas of astonishing beauty. Wind farms raise the hackles of many people, for and against. A few turbines in certain areas can be spectacular, even beautiful, but I've also seen the wind farms in California that spread for mile after mile over otherwise open hilltops and utterly destroy any landscape quality that might have been there before. The idea that wall-to-wall wind turbines should clothe Ardnamurchan or Inverpolly – some say de-registered as a National Nature Reserve in preparation for such a fate – is anathema to me.

The weather, like the midges, could be appalling, but often it was sublime. We climbed Ben Nevis, straight up and steep from the east, eschewing the popular tourist path, and stood on top in shirtsleeves, with not a breath of air, bright sun and views marred a little by the haze of a hot day. We sunbathed by the roadside in Glen Etive and by Loch Tulla – 'Go on, sun, burn me!' Dad said. We were so often drawn to the west coast and its unbeatable views across to the islands on magnificent days. One of the early trips serves to illustrate the point. It was the day I saw my first gannet, and looking at one of my various bird lists I find it was 1 August 1965. The first line is: 'The day started sunny and clear, and if anything it improved as it drew towards afternoon.' We headed west, to the most westerly point on the mainland of Scotland (as far west, I wrote, as the Lizard in Cornwall) – Ardnamurchan Point.

The trip entailed a drive around Loch Eil, west of Fort William, to begin with. Common sandpipers and what was presumed to be a hen harrier started off the bird list, followed by red-breasted mergansers and shags, eiders and oystercatchers, curlews and buzzards along Loch Linnhe. This was classic Argyll coastal scenery: lowish hills, backed by higher ones inland, scruffy bits of birch and oak woodland, much overgrazed grassland with black-faced sheep, rocky shores covered with orange seaweed, and little sandy bays edged with close-cropped swards of vivid green, dotted by pairs of common gulls.

The road out to the Ardnamurchan peninsula became a favourite with us, fabled in later years for its narrowness, its twistiness, its blind summits and hidden bends. How dare anyone want to improve such roads as this! In a book written in the 1930s Seton Gordon refers to a road farther north that has, he says, 'mercifully not yet been turned into a wide, soulless highway'. When I went to Forsinard in 2003, to write a feature for *Birds*, I stole this line when describing the road up to Thurso from Helmsdale (although it was not nearly so narrow and nowhere so twisty as the Ardnamurchan one). When my colleagues in the North Scotland office read the draft, they quite properly asked that I remove the reference: the road, and its improvement (or lack of it) was a prickly subject up there, to say the least. How dare a tourist from the south say that it was best left as it is!

But Ardnamurchan in the 1960s was an adventure. We had trouble getting petrol, I added in my diary. We often did, and we often wondered if what we had from the hand-operated pumps had been watered down because the cars 'pinked' so much and stumbled on the hills. Far to the north the Cuillins of Skye became visible, an early indication that visibility would be good on this late summer day. Mull, Tiree and Coll could be seen from our lunch spot as we approached the headland; then we walked out to the far point with its tall, elegant lighthouse, a slender column of pinkish-brown stone, widening slightly at the top before a broad, white balcony and dark glass dome. My first gannet sailed past then. It was already flying away when I first saw it, but it remained in sight for many minutes. This great, white bird, visible for miles, was a stunner.

Most lighthouses are now hard to reach and unmanned. But on this day the lighthouse keeper was only too happy to invite us in. We climbed the 140 steps of a narrow spiral staircase and then two steep ladders to get to a small room at the top and out on to a little balcony, 120 feet up. This was more than enough for me: to go any higher would have meant climbing the ladder that went up outside the light itself (to facilitate cleaning of the glass), and we didn't fancy that idea. Here on the balcony the view was astounding. The keeper ran through the names of all the islands in a magnificent sweep: here we could see Skye, Eigg, Muck, Rhum, Canna ('the wee flat one'), South Uist, Barra, Coll, Bac Mor – the Dutchman's Cap, which I drew in the book – the Treshnish Isles, Mull. I wrote stuffily in my diary, 'Though we could tell most of these the lighthouse keeper told us each name.' As if. It remains a memorable experience.

The glorious day was topped by a fine sunset, which turned the tops of Bidean nam Bian, above Glen Coe, and Ben Nevis rose pink as we headed for home. Such days had a simple, pure quality that is hard to recapture. It is easy being a 15-year-old, driven by someone else, who does all your cooking and washing, buys the food and the petrol and pays for the holiday. All I had to do was read about lighthouses and islands and watch gannets, write my diary, stick in a postcard of Ardnamurchan lighthouse and note carefully that we had done 163.3 miles in the day. Although in later years I did go to Scotland on the odd winter trip, the curious thing is that our holidays and the approach to them did not really change much. The birdwatching was never much more advanced and we carried on enjoying bumping into the occasional peregrine or hen harrier or golden eagle in just the same way, while wandering around looking at the scenery. That's not quite true of every day, I suppose; here's another sample from a much later holiday, in 1973.

We were based at Polbain, a little village close to Achiltibuie on the far north-west coast. My first notes include long lists of the local wild flowers. On the first Sunday we went to Reiff, out on the coast not far away, no doubt at my instigation. (I was, certainly, pushing the agenda towards including the places with the most potential for good birds. And it usually worked.) I found a comfortable spot against a rock from which I could do a bit of seawatching (not the random scanning out to sea in the hope of another gannet as at Ardnamurchan nine years before). Not a lot passed by, but I recorded black guillemots (always good to see), a few red-throated divers, 100 fulmars, some gannets and, although there was only a single presumed Manx shearwater, a sooty shearwater flew south (at 4.31 p.m.). The sea was flat calm and the conditions rather misty, so this was a bit unexpected, but I had seen sooties here before and no doubt hoped for more. Anyway, I had a good view and took some useful notes, as this was still a bird I had very little experience of.

On another seawatch at Reiff, from 6.25 to 7.45 p.m, the weather was mixed and included heavy rain and strong winds, but there was also bright sun, which made things difficult against a dazzling sea, although it made the western seascapes as dramatic as ever (the Atlantic coast of Scotland beats anything the Mediterranean can offer). It was great: 500 fulmars going south, 77 Manx shearwaters also heading south, two sooty shearwaters (which was what I was hoping for), three or four storm petrels (almost unheard of for me to see these offshore, then, rather than from a ship), 50 gannets. The sooties were again described in detail, as I learned more about this pretty exciting species. The next day I was back: fulmars going south (290 per hour), just the one Manx and a single sooty, 60 or so gannets, a couple of red-throated divers heading south, too, quite a mixture of waders including a whimbrel, and an Arctic skua. I wouldn't mind an hour and a half like that again now if I could get it.

While I was clearly much more aware of possibilities and probabilities, and much more disciplined in my recording of what I saw, other days were much as they had been when I was younger: merlins, buzzards, ravens, divers and black guillemots, always the pleasure of fulmars on ledges or out to sea and oystercatchers piping along rocky shorelines, stonechats on wires or clumps of gorse. I was keen to record 'good' rock doves – none of your feral pigeon rubbish here. Stoer lighthouse was great (although one of those you 'couldn't get at', unlike Ardnamurchan in 'the old days'), with plenty of shags, hundreds of fulmars and a passing bonxie. I watched two golden eagles in the Inverpolly area, first picked out above Cul Mor, using 7×40 binoculars, at a range of five miles! These were Carl Zeiss Jena Septarem wide-angle binoculars, new and optically brilliant. They remain optically superb but they had an early form of retractable/extendable eyepiece for spectacle wearers. These eyepieces were too big: retracted, they were fine, but extended, as I used them, they overbalanced the whole binocular, not least causing the objective lenses to rub against clothing and wear off the coating. I used these for many years and found 7× magnification was not a drawback except in a few circumstances where birds were always 'long range'.

With a telescope the distant eagles were still worth watching – I always think golden eagles are worth watching – and I watched for a quarter of an hour or more as they sailed about and passed behind Stac Polly, about three miles off, then disappeared. I reckoned they had covered three miles of ground, between about 2,000 and 2,800 feet up. There were more eagles near Polglass; another near An Teallach, and another on the same day near Dundonell, which twice gave wonderful views; there was a brief view at Kylesku, then the pair again at Polglass, which merited a full page of closely handwritten notes (in my best Rotring black ink) and half a page of detailed sketches – some of the best views I've ever had of eagles, above quite low coastal slopes. I was especially taken by the way the huge wings seemed to 'ripple' from the base outwards, rather than simply 'flap', giving a wonderful impression of size and power.

In later years, while the rest of the family carried on going to Scotland, one way or another I dropped out and did different things, began to take separate holidays, and my Scottish adventures stopped. Foreign holidays took over, which are marvellous, but Scotland still has a spell that is unlikely to be broken and that will, I feel sure, lure me back in my later years.

Chasewater – Wildfowl, Waders and Spoil Heaps

Chasewater is a canal-feeder reservoir in south Staffordshire between Brownhills and the A5 to the south and Chasetown to the north; Cannock is a few miles west and Lichfield a few miles east. It helped shape my interest in birds and my opinions about wildlife and wild places. If I had been living a few miles farther away, in any direction, I doubt whether I would have developed as a birdwatcher in the way that I did. As it happened, Chasewater was within a good walk or an easy bike ride.

Chasewater, by Norton Pool and out of Cannock Chase Reservoir, has changed over the years, not always to my liking. I have not been back for some time. The thought of facing the North Orbital Road and the M6 toll, which cuts across the south shore, is too much. Associated developments (industrial and retail parks, services, roundabouts, new access roads and junctions) have so altered the area, seemingly for miles around, that I find it deeply depressing. My route on bike or foot to Chasewater has changed out of all recognition: the one green space separating Burntwood and Chasetown from the Birmingham conurbation is filled in. Even before the M6 toll was approved, there were 80 planning applications for industrial and distribution sites around Wharf Lane, the last bit of open land by the 1990s. The same feeling of anger, helplessness and disenchantment must have struck thousands of people all over Britain at various times.

In the 1500s large areas of heath flanked 'Canke Wood'. Felling of woodland formed larger heaths from Stafford south to Sutton Park. Around the 1790s, much of the heath was cultivated, creating a broad 'ridge and furrow' effect. This I have only recently learned. It explains the ridges and dips and little bays and promontories along parts of the north shore of Chasewater, which add to the complication of the shoreline as the water level rises and falls. Towards the end of the 18th century, mines were sunk to supply the iron and steel industry. Coal proved plentiful, but transporting it was difficult. In 1794, a canal was built from Wyrley, near Cannock, to Wolverhampton. The canal had eight locks to lower or raise coal barges by 50 feet. Every barge that passed through meant a loss of 25,000 gallons of water downhill. Such locks can only work if they can be replenished. South Staffordshire coal could in theory be transported cheaply to Hull and Bristol or to the industries of Wolverhampton, Walsall, Coventry and Oxford, but, shortly after the canal opened in 1797, the company had no option but to close it again: the whole system was running dry. It was a potential disaster. A reservoir was desperately needed. So, at a rent of 3s. 6d. per acre per year for an area of 'unenclosed open fields and barren bog', 156 acres were acquired for the construction of a canal-feeder reservoir.

Construction began in 1796. A second long embankment was built, to the west of the main dam, to create a reservoir up to 35 feet deep. In 1797 the dams were completed and the Crane Brook filled the reservoir. This was fine until June 1799 when the dam burst, washing away roads and bridges and drowning livestock. A new, thicker dam, lined with limestone, was built and in March 1800 the reservoir was refilled. In the 1890s subsidence caused by the mines flooded surrounding areas and a further embankment was built to protect Norton to the north-west, strengthened by the addition of Black Country slag – waste material from the iron foundries – shipped across the reservoir. This western embankment allowed the weir at the southern end of the dam to be raised during the early 1900s to enlarge the reservoir. This, plus more subsidence, created a smaller northern pool, Jeffrey's Swag, which is now easily viewed from the road into Norton Canes and linked to the main reservoir by a tiny channel. Thus Cannock Reservoir took shape.

In the mid-19th century more coal mines opened around the area and canals were used to transport the coal. The landscape was modified by mounds of mining spoil, especially to the north, and by the creation of embanked 'lagoons' or slurry pits into which coal washings were dumped. Eventually, railway lines practically encircled the reservoir. (When I first began to visit, many disused lines were still intact.) The line around the west and north sides, along yet another large, long embankment, was built in 1871; it has been restored as the Chasewater Light Railway. In 1898 a steamboat was launched to provide cruises on the lake, but it was soon left to rot on the shore. By the 1920s several mines had closed; another local one, the Fly Pit (hence Fly Bay on the northern shore) closed in 1940, but in 1947, when the coal industry was nationalized, numbers 3, 7, 8 and 9 pits ('threes', 'sevens', 'eights' and 'nines') were still working.

In 1844, Robert Garner (author of *The Natural History of the County of Stafford*) described the reservoir as 'the fine pool, near Norton, on Cannock Chase, one mile long by three quarters broad'. However, *Where to Watch Birds* by John Gooders referred to Cannock Reservoir as 'Set in an industrial landscape of slag heaps and desolate waste ground. Even its regular species, which are mainly numbers of diving duck, do not hold much excitement.' Those of us who knew it didn't much approve of his assessment, although it was not far off the mark (after all, it was the irregular species that were exciting). Maps of 1883 named the reservoir 'Cannock Chase Reservoir', a name that persisted in bird reports until the 1950s, becoming shortened to Cannock Reservoir for a time. Maps also marked a rifle range used by the South Staffs and North Staffs regiments, including the mound of earth that gave the local name to the 'Target' headland on the north shore.

A local history website quotes from Charles G. Harper's book, *The Holyhead Road: the Mail-Coach Road to Dublin* (1902):

We have reached that abomination of desolation called Brownhills. Words are ineffectually employed to describe the hateful, blighted scene, but imagine a wide and dreary stretch of common land surrounded by the scattered, dirty and decrepit cottages of the semi-savage population of nail makers and pitmen, with here and there a school, a woe-begone chapel, a tin tabernacle, and a plentiful sprinkling of public houses. Further imagine the grass of this wide spreading common to be as brown, and innutritious as it is possible for grass to be, and with an extra-ordinary wealth of scrap iron, tin clippings, broken glass, and brick-bats deposited over every square yard, and all around it the ghastly refuse heaps of long abandoned mines. Finally clap a railway embankment and station midway across the common, and there you have a dim adumbration of what Brownhills is like.

Mr Harper obviously liked the place. It had character and always has! My own adumbration of Chasewater, if not Brownhills, was that it was a great place to be.

In 1834 the area had plenty of 'grouse'. These were presumably black grouse, then common on Cannock Chase (a British record bag, killed there in about 1860, accounted for 252 of them), although red grouse persisted on Cannock Chase longer than black (I believe I saw a small group at about the end of their presence on the Chase in the 1950s). Other good birds were recorded, including a great skua, shot in 1896, and a ruff shot in July 1897. Most early records refer to birds that were shot by F. Coburn and G. H. Clarke. There was a turnstone in 1904, a white-fronted goose near by in 1906 (which Coburn thought was a lesser white-front – it wouldn't surprise me, Chasewater being what it is!). In July 1907 comes a really intriguing report, dug out from somewhere by Graham Evans, who will appear later in this story. G. H. Clarke shot one of two jack snipe at the Plant Swag and two days later found a downy youngster from the same place that differed from the skins of common snipe. (The Plant was a local coal mine; a 'swag' is a pool, created by subsidence, more or less like the ings of Yorkshire). Graham Evans, who has amassed much of the history of Chasewater and its birds and flora, says that this is 'not quite conclusive evidence of the only breeding record of jack snipe in Britain'. Clarke later shot several grey plovers, while six whimbrels and a probable brent goose were seen in 1908. Four little terns, three Sandwich terns, a wryneck and a grey phalarope were shot in 1909 (and a pomarine skua, shot 'prior to 1909', was mounted on a lady's hat); then in 1910 came five brent geese, snow buntings and a crossbill in the area. It is amazing how such reports have a 'Chasewater' feel to them even now: odd and unexpected records of the kind that the place is known for.

In 1948 there was an article about the birds of Cannock Reservoir in the West Midland Bird Club annual report. The place had been 'discovered' by a small group of 'modern' birdwatchers, including the late, great H. G. Alexander, who wrote a little about it in his book *Seventy Years of Birdwatching*. The article includes the following:

The water, which has an area of about 210 acres, lies at the foot of Cannock Chase in the midst of the South Staffordshire mining district. There is an attractive area each of sandy beach, gravel, marsh and mud around the flat and easily flooded shores, which provide suitable feeding-grounds for several different species of bird. Along the north shore grow a few stunted bushes, and in the immediate vicinity is an extensive area of heathland.

Old records, dating from 1907–10, give an attractive list of rarities, many of which, the late F. Coburn stated, occurred there regularly. It was with ever-increasing pleasure, therefore, that we found as the year advanced that most of these species were still visiting the pool.

The chief attraction of this reservoir lies in the facility with which migration may be observed actually in progress. Many of the waders

recorded were seen arriving or departing; many did not stay, while on May
21st, Messrs. Norris, Lambourne, and the writer [G. W. Rayner] watched
a flock of seventeen Common Sandpipers flying over and around the
reservoir. This species is rarely recorded in flocks of quite this size.

No less than eighteen species of wader were recorded during the
year and eleven kinds were seen on one visit in May. Common, Arctic,
and Black Terns were observed on both passages. As winter came on a
few Twite appeared and a flock of nine was resident from December. A
single Snow-Bunting stayed throughout December. In November, two
Eider Ducks were present, and in December, a duck (female) Red-crested
Pochard. Other notable records are: Great Northern Diver, Slavonian
Grebe, Shag and Merlin, the latter being recorded on one or two occasions.
Perhaps the most interesting bird was the Lapland Bunting which appeared
for four days in early December.

Cannock Reservoir, known also as Norton Pool, lies within easy reach
of Birmingham and Wolverhampton and should prove a popular resort
for week-end bird-watchers at all times of the year.

More good birds turned up, notably a red kite in 1953, when red kites really
meant something, being exceptionally rare in the UK. In 1956 a sailing club was
formed and Brownhills council bought Norton Pool from the British Transport
Commission for £5,600, including 272 acres of land and water and a couple of
cottages. A further 170 acres of land to the east was leased from the National
Coal Board, followed by another 128 acres in 1957. The reservoir's name was
changed to Chasewater, and at an opening ceremony it was announced:

It may indeed seem bleak and dreary at present but I want you in your
imagination to travel forward with me to a time when the bleakness and
barrenness will have disappeared under a scheme of ordered development
and beautification.

It sounds awful to me. There was a petition of 3,400 names against it, but
a funfair was approved for the south shore and then plans unveiled for a
'pleasure precinct', a golf course and pitch-and-putt course, and a landscaped
area with chalets on the west side. It was the first of many such plans, and the
development of the southern shore began with a hotchpotch of buildings,
concreted shores, a mock castle, pier and lighthouse. In 1959 a powerboat
club was established in the south-west corner, and in 1960 a go-kart track was

added. For some years powerboats included hydroplanes and then big, fast, undoubtedly impressive, racing boats; there were sometimes 24-hour races but the noise and disturbance caused to local residents did for these and the club reverted to water-skiing in the main.

The railway over the causeway between the main lake and the northern pool, Jeffrey's Swag, was last used in 1961, and the causeway soon became dilapidated; the last load of coal was transferred by canal boat in 1962. My glimpses of horse-drawn narrow boats must have been from about that time. Between 1968 and 1972 fields between the western embankment and the looping embankment of the railway to the west were scraped bare and filled with power-station ash and stinking sewage. Later, at the northern end, refuse was tipped, so that the whole stretch of rushy and marshy fields where I often saw good birds was buried for good.

In 1970 there was another grand plan: a report proposed a range of sporting and recreational facilities at a cost of £336,669 (I admire the precision). A surprisingly large stadium was built near the A5 entrance to house a trotting track. With no real following, it didn't catch on and the stadium became empty and semi-derelict, adding to the unkempt and dilapidated feel of the whole southern shore area, before it was eventually demolished. For a while in 1971 the northern pool, the swag, was used by water-skiers, with a ski-jump ramp parked in the centre. I well remember my anger when I saw it. It seemed an unnecessary extension to cover the whole of the water surface with speeding boats. Could there be no freedom from noise and disturbance anywhere? Fortunately, this was quite short-lived. It was the sort of thing that sparked off pointless but feverish letters of complaint from me to the council.

In the early 1970s the area east of the main dam was being filled in with domestic refuse, with plans for more 'recreational facilities' including a golf course, but this was stopped when the wildlife value of the marsh was realized by the Nature Conservancy Council. The boggy patches included sphagnum bogs with interesting plants, such as sundews and cranberry; the marsh had water shrews in it, and the thickets of willow had willow tits and occasionally roosting long-eared owls. The tip, for a time, was obviously generating heat and became alive with noisy house crickets; one day I watched a great grey shrike hopping about on the ground, eagerly feeding on them.

Meanwhile, large areas of grey and orange mining spoil were being restored to the north. Much material from these steep-sided heaps was pushed sideways to lower the spoil, rather than remove it, so that intervening stretches of ancient heath were buried. It showed such ignorance of what was there, what was important. What used to be a mixed landscape with an abundance of boggy spots, little pools and heaths became uniform, smoothly contoured, sterile grass, suitable for walking the dog for a few minutes before going home. The wilderness and opportunities for adventure were under attack. My local doctor wrote a letter to the *Lichfield Mercury* praising the admirable work being done to restore and revitalize the Chasewater hinterland (but then he did have a Jack Russell to take for a walk) and I wrote a fierce response (not published) against this 'destruction' of much more exciting and valuable habitats. Any kid then would far rather play cowboys and indians, ride a bike, dam the streams, hide in the bushes and scramble up and down the mounds than walk about on plain, dull grass. And for me, the abundance of wild flowers, butterflies and birds made it a place to treasure, not to trash.

In 1984 another master plan was published. At last the wildlife value of the place was recognized (Graham Evans had a lot to do with that), and the northern end of the lake was scheduled to be a nature reserve. But a seven-year programme costing £26.2 million was proposed for the rest. The consultants said:

One's first impression of Chasewater is of a vast, relatively unused stretch of open water set in a desolate landscape of spoil heaps, electricity pylons, low-income housing, and a rag bag of assorted recreation facilities that bear little relationship to each other.

It is interesting to note the implication that things have to be 'used' and cannot *ever* just be left alone. Councillors everywhere see 'growth' as the only option.

In 1987, with Graham Evans pushing as hard as he could for proper recognition of the wildlife value (putting me to shame), some of the heath was scheduled as a Site of Special Scientific Interest (SSSI). The development proposal was deferred while the Birmingham North Orbital Road was planned, cutting across the southern shore of the reservoir. In 1991 the county structure plan proposed a country park at Chasewater while, remarkably, opencast mining on a huge scale began a mile or two to the north, long after the deep mines had all been closed. The country park was opened in 1999 and work began on the obligatory cycle path around it (oh dear).

In 1995 the Chasewater Wildlife Group was formed to combat some of the threats to the remaining areas of interest, of which, surprisingly, there were still many. Such roughly wild places have a pleasing habit of developing all over again and regenerating themselves. Graham Evans continued to work hard to get Chasewater's natural history importance recognized and properly valued, decades after a representative of the West Midland Bird Club had told me that they had more or less given up on the place and the RSPB had shown no interest at all.

For me, Chasewater was where I went fishing. Later, it became the core of my birdwatching experiences, and remained so for years. One early diary entry gives an impression of one day in November. It was dull, cold, with grey mist thick over the water. The reservoir was flat calm and lead grey as I approached from the eastern corner, at the north end of the dam, and looked over the gravelly embankment. Out on the water, an exceptional number of ducks caught my eye. I counted and recounted and settled on 179 pochards. Normally there might be one or two: this was one of those occasional late autumn arrivals, birds on the move that might stay a day or two and then be gone. I was amazed. Chasewater at that time was not a great place for ducks. Then a group of swans appeared: their squeaky, bubbling, conversational call notes meant Bewick's, 11 of them, two grey juveniles and two adults with bills so richly coloured that the basal patches looked orange rather than yellow. Bewick's swans here were really wild and exciting birds and gave a satisfying feeling of achievement, not like the flocks that come to be fed at the Ouse Washes or Slimbridge, lovely as they are. After walking all round the pool, I counted 450 lesser black-backed gulls. This was ten times the usual count only a few years before – perhaps a new high for Chasewater. With them were three or four great black-backed gulls. Arthur Jacobs, long-time Chasewater regular, had not seen the great black-backs. Secretly, I felt pleased that he had overlooked them and I had noticed they were there. Great black-backs were unusual birds there then: unexpected.

Also in my notes for this day I see there were two or three goldeneyes, a tufted duck (just the one), four unidentified ducks that were perhaps mallards (which remained rare for years) and seven dunlins. The water level must have been fairly low that year, as dunlins would not have been hanging about in November unless there had been an unusual amount of sticky, black mud. I can still smell the matted waterweed and algae that makes Chasewater mud quite choice in the little bays between swards of spiky, fleshy leaved shoreweed and headlands of clean yellow gravel where the crayfish drifted ashore and bullheads hid under the stones.

A few days later I saw an eider, the first I had come across at Chasewater and a genuinely good find so far inland. Dunlins had gone up to 11, pochards down to 12; the Bewick's, surprisingly, were still there. Bewick's swans are great birds.

No wonder they were Peter Scott's favourites. I enjoy seeing them at Slimbridge or around Welney on the Ouse Washes in their hundreds, but in these places they are simply there: you just roll up and see them. There's nothing wrong with that, but I like to find them in unexpected places, such as Chasewater. In Staffordshire, they were not common, and nowhere had a regular wintering flock. Chasewater would not see Bewick's swans every year, by any means. To discover them was a great treat. They were exciting, evocative birds, straight out of the Arctic, wild and wary as could be.

This was how Chasewater was for years. I was hooked from the start. My fishing expeditions gave me a rough idea of what most of it was like, but much remained unexplored until I started birdwatching in earnest. Then came the *Birds of Staffordshire 1962* book in the school library, by Lord and Blake, which told me that Chasewater, aka Cannock Reservoir, known to me as Norton Pool, 'the pool', was a seriously good place for unusual birds. On 21 November, with the 11 Bewick's and the eider still there, I met a birdwatcher on the shore. It was Tony Blake – A. R. M. Blake, member (although I didn't know it then) of the British Birds Rarities Committee and co-author of that slim book. I wrote in my notes: 'I met Mr A R Blake of the West Midland Bird Club. He helped write the "Birds of Staffordshire 1962".'

So began several years of good friendship with Tony Blake, whose obituary I would eventually write, with great sadness and three times the requested length, for *British Birds* when he died relatively young. For a long time, though, I met him only by chance (although it was not quite by accident, as I did my best to engineer meetings). I could recognize his car and would scan the reservoir, looking at likely spots in the hope of finding it parked there. On seeing it I would guess which way he might have walked round, and set off in the opposite direction, so that I could 'bump into him' and we could walk back together. After all, I had no birdwatching friends, no one to share my excitements and discoveries with, no one to learn from except at a distance.

The same happened with other people I began to meet. Finding out who these people were (Tony Blake apart – he introduced himself that first day) was a matter of trial and error. Regular monthly bulletins from the WMBC dropped through the letterbox from autumn to spring. They always had a few pages of bird news and, at the end, a list of contributors. Certain names cropped up regularly and were there when I had seen someone at Chasewater while an interesting bird – good enough to appear in the notes – was also there. This couldn't have been very helpful, but one way or another I worked out who was whom. The annual West Midland Bird Report was more useful but much slower: it came out months after the end of each year. It did, though, have people's initials after most entries and a key to observers at the back, helping to confirm my suspicions, but it was a slow process.

Although telling anyone who I was never occurred to me – and asking them who they were seemed quite out of the question – I spoke to birdwatchers I met and began to know several regulars quite well. Chasewater, much to my surprise, was not just a place where Uncle Henry went fishing; it was clearly somewhere that birdwatchers visited quite often. Alan Dean and Paul Hyde came by bus to 'do' Chasewater in the morning, then perhaps go off to Belvide in the afternoon (some miles west along the A5, along which they would walk some miles from the last bus stop). The next day they would sometimes go to Blithfield Reservoir, north of Rugeley. They would go by bus from Solihull to Rugeley, then walk – a trek of several miles before they even reached the reservoir, and several more round half of it, before walking back for the bus home. This was dedication, and since Chasewater was on the regular circuit for them it must have been better than anything nearer Solihull could offer. It was obviously worth watching, and I was visiting every weekend, usually twice a weekend, sometimes twice a day. In school holidays I would be there several times each week.

Tony Blake used to say that, although its regular birds were quite few, Chasewater was the best place in the West Midlands to turn up something unusual. When I wrote to the WMBC to add my notes to its bulletin, I would be reminded of this by the secretary, Alan Richards, with whom I corresponded for years before we ever met. Alan recently found an old letter of mine and sent it to me, for my amusement. I had written to him when I was 15:

Dear Sir
I have some records of birds at Blithfield and Chasewater (Cannock Res.) On March 6th a Red-throated Diver [underlined] was at Chasewater. It came quite near to me and I could see the tilted bill, and I could also compare it to the Black-throated Diver which I saw some months ago [this had been seen by many people before me]. I also identified it from my book, comparing it with illustrations and descriptions. On March 7th the diver flew off, circling the water before going off to the north. A Bewick's swan was also present there, among a group of mutes.

On March 7th at Blithfield a drake merganser was present, among goosanders [both species underlined]. Also there was a dabchick and a white wagtail ...

There was quite a lot more, including an account of two men shooting at ducks (their pellets peppered the water in front of me). I remember the brent geese very well – there was no question about them, nor about the divers, but obviously I was having trouble with distant goldeneyes. On a grey day, against silvery water, a goldeneye can look very dark overall, with just a small lozenge of white on the closed wing, close to the tail. This I thought might be a velvet scoter. I wasn't trying too hard for the rarer species, it was just that here was a dark duck with a white wing patch, and the goldeneyes in my book were illustrated as pale grey, with brown heads, white collars and large patches of white along the sides. It was a good lesson that birds very often do not look like their idealized pictures in the books.

Later that same November, after my Bewick's swans and 179 pochards, I drew a map of Chasewater. It included the names for the bays and pools, which I had picked up over the years spent fishing: Fly Bay (derived from the nearby coal mine, the Fly Pit), Jeffrey's Swag (I never knew how to spell Jeffrey's, nor why it had that name), the Target – and others that I made up for my own reference – the Brownhills side, the Chase side, Chase Bay, the Chase dam, the Norton dam, the speedboat club, the sailing club. 'The cinder'ole' was one I didn't add to the map – it must have been 'the cinder hole' but that scarcely seemed classy enough for my map, so I left it off. It was a deep pool, formed by several adjacent spoil tips (of cinder, or shale and ash) pushing water up against the edge of the heath. A narrow stream flowed from it into Fly Bay, with a disused brick sluice, which had to be crossed each time I walked around. It gradually became overgrown with willows and more difficult to scramble over, especially with a bike, but the spoil heap overlooking the willow thicket was a nice spot to sit and watch for autumn migrants. Spotted flycatchers, whitethroats and lesser whitethroats, the odd blackcap or garden warbler, once or twice even a redstart, gave it the air of a genuine migration spot, as redstarts would not normally have been found within several miles of there. Beside the map were noted which groups of birds were likely in which area and the additional comment, 'usually interesting birds are few and far between'. Indeed they were, but this place had great charisma and was clearly addictive.

The spoil heaps were mostly soft and shaly and eroded by rain. I compared the deeply chiselled water channels with the models of rivers we had in geography at school. In places there were humps and deep, steep-sided hollows, with footpaths worn into them, which I usually attempted by bike (although I sometimes had to stop, or I simply fell off). It was a hundred times better than a manufactured cycle path and still would be. Make that a thousand times.

Chasewater's main dam is on the eastern side, falling away to a swampy area that became increasingly overgrown with willows, and a low spread of hummocky mining waste thick with nettles, brambles and rosebay in which sedge warblers and whitethroats nested and, sometimes, early arriving grasshopper warblers crept like mice. This area was bordered by the canal on one side and another embankment, carrying a railway, on the other, which overlooked a small area of grassy fields, one of which was used as a motorbike scramble track. It was a few years later that I found a mossy, boggy patch, quite small and round, below the dam near its northern end, with sundews, marsh orchids and cranberries.

A narrow, rough road crosses the dam, on a kind of ledge a little below its top level, between the old water tower, which controls the sluice into the canal, and a large house, perhaps the home of the sluice operator and watchman but earlier the first large coal mine in the area. A steep, bushy bank above the road ends in a narrow footpath along the top, beside a wide, round-topped concrete wall (great for a telescope without a tripod) and the face of the dam, which was protected by random bits of eroded concrete, limestone and lumps of blue and white slag from iron-ore furnaces. The concrete wall gave essential shelter on days when the wind whipped the water into huge waves. On the path along the top I would frequently chat to retired miners, small, grey-haired old men with trademark flat cloth caps, who would spend their hours wandering around the pool, talking about nothing in particular.

Chasewater is not deep in a valley with a dam at one end, but high and open. The long western side is embanked, too, above what was originally a low-lying area of pastureland. Its altitude and exposure has long made Chasewater beloved by sailors. It can be a bitterly cold place, dramatic in extreme weather conditions, be they snow and ice or rain and gales. I just loved to be there on a day of westerly gales or storms of hail and stinging rain, birds or no birds. The southern shore was low and grassy, with little tall vegetation. It was developed into the park with concrete slabs facing some of the shore, paddling pools, the ridiculous 'castle' and a pier. Near by the go-kart track was built and fenced in so that it was invisible from outside; a road along the south shore passed through an entrance gate which, at times, was locked at dusk, something that became important to remember in later years when gull-watching became popular and the evening roosts were scrutinized by little knots of birdwatchers at weekends.

This whole place quickly became unkempt and run down. There was a miniature railway, abandoned almost as soon as it was built, and a cafe that closed before anyone got used to using it. It was not an area that I was keen to hang around in but, when the water level was lowered, the shore regained its natural bays of oozy mud and clean sand and was as good as anywhere around the pool for waders. The large car park on the south shore later became a place to meet, a place from which to watch the gull roost on a cold Saturday evening. The south shore, despite this development and disturbance, has always attracted some of Chasewater's best birds; one of the later ones that I saw (but did not discover for myself) was a shore lark. Much of the area, with its unusual sward of shoreweed, has been buried under waste in an ill-conceived attempt to 'improve' the shore, with an idiotically positioned footpath built right along the edge, as if specifically to disturb the waders.

To the west, the reservoir is constrained by its long, high embankment, crossed at its northern end by the railway, in a narrow X of steep-faced embankments, so separating the smaller, northern pool from the main lake except for a small bridged channel: this is Jeffrey's Swag, made famous by the first Western Palearctic lesser scaup. To the north, the hinterland was a magical mixture of heath and marsh – an isolated extension, via Gentleshaw Common, of Cannock Chase – with patches of heather, swampy bogs full of orange and scarlet sphagnum, and thickets of willows, mixed with small fields and long, ancient-looking hawthorn hedges and clumps of trees, one of the clumps around the remains of a demolished building with a few garden flowers (and dingy skipper butterflies). The north shore was low and grassy when the level was moderate, but high water took the margin up into the thickening growth of willows, making it quite a job to walk round anywhere close to the pool. The high fences of the sailing club, right against the water's edge, made it even more difficult in places, with the chop-chop of waves against the willows' feet trying to drown out the metallic clink-clink of cables smacking against masts.

Through all this ran the remains of the railways that served the coal mines and nearby sidings beside the mainline at Brownhills. These broad tracks curved around the reservoir in wide arcs and led to a number of smaller pools with not much bird interest as a rule, but you never knew … Some ran through low cuttings, so there were steep banks of various kinds all over the place, ideal for sun-loving plants and butterflies in summer. And dotted all over this whole area were the enormous heaps of mining spoil, chiefly shaly material, obviously quite limy and excellent for assorted lime-loving plants and butterflies that would not otherwise have been found there. There were also large, flat pans, filled with fine, black material from the coal-washing plants, the older ones consolidated and overgrown, the newer ones still oozy, black and bare. The banks, each with a footpath along the top, were a riot of rosebay, tansy, wormwood and mugwort, hawk's-beard, and scores of other wild flowers typical of such untidy 'waste'. One of the pans suddenly developed a reed-bed, which spread over it in a couple of years, but was lost to 'landscaping' soon after.

The shore itself was, in places, thick with shoreweed, a curious little, spiky-leaved, miniature-rush-like plant that carpeted the flatter shores. Bands of shingle made little headlands and shallow bays of gravel and clean sand. The shoreline could be littered with dead, dried-out, white crayfish after a gale, and we watched them creeping about the bottom in the sparklingly clean waters of the nearby canal. But for years the crayfish population seems to have become small or non-existent, the water in both the reservoir and the canal far less clear. Likewise, I often watched shoals of perch and roach, and little jack pike in the shallows, in the crystal-clear water of the reservoir. When we went fishing on a late summer's evening, the water could be dimpled by scores of fish rising to take flies, but that long ago ceased.

All this variety was wonderful for me to explore, and explore I did. Over the years I got to know every bush, every stalk likely to be used by a scolding whinchat, every grassy thicket where a grasshopper warbler might sing. I scanned the wires in winter for great grey shrikes and knew their favourite bushes. I watched the skies above the marshes for drumming snipe and knew where I was likely to see one standing on top of a telegraph pole, metronomically calling its *chip-per chip-per* note in spring. Here were elder bushes where blackcaps and garden warblers appeared late each summer to feast on tart purple berries. There were rough, grassy suntraps where I could find the dingy skippers and common blues, flurries of small heaths and small coppers. Here was the spot where a stonechat pair unexpectedly settled and nested, where I found my first stonechat egg at the end of a soft, narrow entrance tunnel. In this little boggy patch there might be a jack snipe; over there, go slowly and carefully over the bank because just beyond is a sandy spot where there might be a wader or two – a turnstone, perhaps, in the autumn, or a sanderling in summer plumage on a sunny, blustery day in May.

Here was the place to learn my butterflies and to sit down with the wild-flower guide and work out which plant was which. I watched water shrews, weasels, stoats. The patch of willows beside the dam was the best place for a March chiffchaff; the garden of the Old Vicarage near by was the likeliest place for a bullfinch or two, the taller trees and bushes alongside always good for a buzzy willow tit. Some things were oddly rare – I hardly ever saw a jackdaw, for example – but I mapped the willow warblers in spring, and the whinchats (several pairs, long since gone) that nested in May and June. One bird that was found regularly nowhere else in the WMBC area of old Staffordshire, Warwickshire and Worcestershire was the twite. Tony Blake's book says, 'Regular winter visitor occurring in the vicinity of Cannock Reservoir in numbers up to 50.' I found them favouring the flat pans of coal washings, the surrounding banks and sometimes the spoil heaps well to the west where an abundance of seeding wild flowers grew. Sometimes, as many as 70 or 90 might be found. Then someone landscaped the place. The spoil heaps were spread out to lower their angular, irregular profiles, to turn gullies and bluffs and canyons and pinnacles into rounded mounds that were seeded with grass and mown to keep the flowers down. The embankments were bulldozed. I saw a lorry tip a pile of spoil on top of 1,500 wild orchids. The twites were never seen again. The landscaping received plaudits and won awards for its value for wildlife and nature.

A few miles north of where I now live is Grafham Water. Here there are vast areas of mown grass and prettified car parks, and the all-round cycle track, which is, I know, enjoyed by many people. But near one of the car parks there used to be (perhaps still is) a minute patch of longer grass set in the sterile sea of mown sward. Beside it was a notice: it apologised – yes apologised – for the long, untidy grass, but explained that this couple of square yards of ground was left uncut because wild flowers grew there. Gee, thanks. I detest such places, and the way they are touted as being good for the environment. Signs proclaim 'working together for people and the environment' (be it a water company, a wildlife trust, an oil company or a manufacturer of baked beans). Wild places – even with their mining spoil if need be – are much more exciting and infinitely better for the insects, flowers and birdlife that can exploit them as well as for people who can explore them and, most importantly, find things for themselves.

There is currently a small debate going on about what Marion Shoard, author of *The Theft of the Countryside* and *Right to Roam*, calls the 'edgelands'. She would prefer to see them retained for the good of people and wildlife, to remain places where kids can play and where older children can learn and explore, as I did around Chasewater. The planners, though, would love to get their hands on them and realize their vision for the out-of-town, edge-of-city spaces: all green with cut grass, here and there a fountain, here and there a pitch-and-putt course, now and then a patch of lollipop trees, and, of course, the essential cycle track – not a bramble, or a thistle, or a nettle, or a bird or a butterfly in sight. Marion Shoard has written:

> Vast interfacial areas bordering towns from Bristol, Swindon and London Colney to Bolton, Warrington and Hartlepool, together with much of the edgelands of Romford, Rainham, Nottingham, Manchester, Liverpool and Sunderland, are to be transformed by courtesy of substantial grants into so-called 'community forests'. In England alone (and there are also similar forests in Wales and Scotland) the community forest programme covers an area of more than 1,700 square miles (4,400 square kilometres), or over twelve times that of the Isle of Wight. Not all of the land involved is interfacial, but the vast majority is. 'We're transforming the living and working environment of the North East,' proclaims a document which sets out how 101,000 acres (40,900 hectares) will be planted with 20 million trees to make the area more attractive for business and housing and to 'improve the landscape and the image of the North East'. The same document presents pictures of an old industrial landscape which has been bulldozed clear of any upstanding features or natural vegetation alongside the replacement landscape aspired to: a line of trim, brick houses surrounded by a liberal sprinkling of trees and new, screwdriver assembly factories.
>
> This, it is imagined, is the kind of scene that will lure industrialists and prospective homeowners alike, to fill the grim world of the edgelands with happy workers and laughing families. All over Britain, disused quarries, old industrial land and other varieties of unkempt wasteland are to be turned into something more respectable and legitimate – woodland. The intention for the community forests is not continuous forest: about 30 per cent of the land is to be tree covered, with the remainder 'a rich mosaic of wooded landscapes and land uses including farmland, villages and leisure enterprises, nature areas and public open space'. But the essential idea is that an undesirable landscape is to be turned into something else – green, but ordered rather than wild.

This is perhaps a bit unfair on the community forests and the well-intentioned drive to plant more woodland, but I see exactly what Marion Shoard means: miles of young trees planted in grid-iron patterns on farm edges and alongside new roads seem to be the best that can be managed, and I was dismayed to find that the new forests are all planted in the same utterly unimaginative way. Time will improve them, no doubt, if they are given the chance to develop in a more adventurous, rough and ready fashion, but I fear many will be kept trim and neat and boring.

Simon Barnes, several times voted Sports Writer of the Year for his inimitable column in *The Times*, called me from his mobile recently and said he was on a train, near Ipswich, passing a Nice Place. Like all such Nice Places, it was several acres of short grass planted with a few lollipop trees and surrounded by – you've guessed it – the cycle track. (It is only fair to say that recently I have been riding along a new cycle track between Sandy and Bedford, along the River Great Ouse, and enjoying it immensely. These things can be done well, and still leave a bit of life and liberty.) Some years ago now Simon approached me and asked if he could write a column in *Birds*. I readily agreed and he has been doing so ever since, upsetting some people and delighting others with his provocative words and good sense. I suggested he write about these 'edgelands', their untidiness, their richness in wild things – the thistles, perhaps, that Marion Shoard said are unwelcome in the town, even more unwelcome in the country and find refuge in the rough and ready places between the two.

As I said to Simon later, he wrote exactly what I wanted to say but couldn't, so I can do no better than quote from his page in *Birds* here:

Nature is not nice. The beauty of the blue tit eludes the caterpillar, the beauty of the sparrowhawk eludes the blue tit, the beauty of the tapeworm eludes the human. Your idea of nice may not be another creature's idea of nice …

Birds don't always like nice places. Why don't you find birds on that nice little park set up by the local council? It's got a nice green sward with a few lollipop-like trees stuck in it. There is a nice asphalt path running through them, and a nice new cycle track. It is what is technically known as a Nice Place. For most birds – for most living things – it is a howling wilderness. Might as well be the Sahara. Might as well be Oxford Street or Fifth Avenue. It is first class for the defaecation of dogs and the panting of the fearful middle-aged, but it is nothing to do with nature.

On, then, to the Edgelands. This is a term coined by a writer and conservationist called Marion Shoard. She draws attention to the strange places that are neither town nor country: 'vaguely menacing frontier land hinting that here the normal rules governing human behaviour cannot altogether be relied upon'.

The most striking thing about the Edgelands is their total rejection of anything in which a human could find comfort.

And that is rather the point. Some aspects of these Edgelands are stunningly good for non-human forms of life. They are ignored. They are unmanaged. And that alone is perfect for an astonishingly wide range of creatures. Shoard again: 'While town parks are grassed over for ball games and our national parks overgrazed by sheep, these truer wildernesses are allowed to find their own accommodation with nature, evolving silently and unhindered.'

There is an increasing tendency to create green spaces that are tame, nice, unnatural, unmysterious, castrated and lifeless. They are places that don't look good anywhere apart from on a planner's model. They are neat and tidy and well-organized. Just what nature abhors.

Well, they're for the kids, aren't they? Huh? When I was a boy, I loved the thickets and tangles, trees and brambles, for hunting games and exploring games and imagination games. In wild places, your mind can spin free: all you can do among the lollipops is kick a football and go home.

We do not come to terms with nature by trying to make it nice – neither with our mistaken minds, nor with the help of lollipop-fancying cycle-track-obsessed planners.

Putting in the Hours

There were two main routes from home to Chasewater, each with minor variations. Usually I went one way and back the other, long uphill grinds on the bike each way then long, fast descents: flat-out, pushing on to the top, taking a short breather, then racing on down at ridiculous speeds. The last half mile was an extremely rough, gravelly road with deep potholes, usually full of water if not iced over, so I was half-scrambling, half-riding and made something of a sport of avoiding the deepest holes in fast, sideways swings. Fantasies went through my mind, as I became champion at this one-man event, repeated day after day. If it was icy, or snowy, the test was even greater. These cycle rides did me the world of good physically. I was fit as a fiddle for years. The bike was a bit of a bind around the reservoir, so it was often left against a fence, rear wheel chained to the frame, but otherwise unprotected. It was never stolen, amazingly as I look back on it now, although I sometimes came back to find the saddlebag searched or the empty binocular case left lying on the ground, and once I returned to a cut tyre.

On my walks I would sometimes mentally commentate on what was seen. Just as I might now sometimes run through such paragraphs as this one in my head – while lying in bed, or eating my breakfast, or travelling to work – so I would describe the birds and what they were doing, or why they were there, silently, in my head, fantasizing some sort of radio broadcast bird walk. There was sometimes something a little similar on the radio, in *The Living World*, but it would be years before a broadcast bird walk would be attempted on television, in a short series featuring John Gooders (*A Day in the Country*), and a sit-and-watch in Tony Soper's *Birdwatch*, and a long time again before Bill Oddie would perfect the idea and become immensely more popular.

In my diary of 1969, I find to my surprise my youthful prediction that, in years to come, a particular Beatles song might take me back, in spirit, to these rides and walks around Chasewater. I was right: they do. 'Eight Days a Week' instantly takes me back riding along the western embankment through deep snow, over rutted, frozen mud, 'Mr Moonlight', Ringo's thump on a deep African drum, to the cold northern shore. Memories seem more often to be of cold days than warm ones – nostalgia isn't always about long, hot summers.

I had a thin, green, nylon jacket with a little quilted lining, which I supposed would keep out the rain but which was soaked by the least bit of drizzle. Without walking boots or anything else other than wellingtons, which were not suited to riding a bike, I went out in slip-ons with elasticated sides, pointed toes and shiny, smooth soles. I remember following Tony Blake down the side of the embankment and being quite unable to climb back up again, slithering about and sliding back down on the grass whenever I got close to the top. I had plenty of woolly pullovers (Mum was truly expert) and gloves, but I was still often bitterly cold and would return home with frozen fingers, face and ears that throbbed with intense pain as they thawed out by the fire (the dreaded 'hot aches'). Chilblains were the norm. Rubber boots rubbed the backs of my calves red and sore. I didn't wear a hat, and the hood of my jacket was not much use on a fast bike ride in pouring rain.

Nevertheless, I would plod on, religiously, noting everything I saw. It was my patch, and I loved it. That doesn't mean it was mine, exclusively, for it had been thoroughly watched for years. Once I began to collect back issues of the West Midland Bird Report I discovered the long tradition of watching Cannock Reservoir and the many people who had made a great contribution to our knowledge of its birds. No, it was not that I was going somewhere that others didn't, just that I was watching this one place more than I was watching anywhere else; it was my chosen place and I was sorting out for myself just what could be found there. For a long time there were days that produced remarkably little, despite all this effort. After the Bewick's swans, eider and pochards had gone, I was recording, for example, two goldeneyes, two tufted ducks, 152 coots, two to three great tits and three to four greenfinches (a specially bad day!), but often staying on later and adding a few notes about the gulls that gathered each evening. But it had not, then, occurred to me to stay until dark and study the gull roost properly.

On 9 January 1966 I caught up with a twite for the first time but made a bit of a meal of the identification (as I had done on the sea walls of Essex). Later, the Chasewater twites were to become quite special. On 16 January I met Tony Blake again, and Eric Clare. Tony had again seen a great grey shrike that I had missed, but, as we walked along the south shore he picked up a bird flying overhead and identified it by its call: 'Snow bunting! *Tirililip—teu!* Lovely!' This was impressive: it would have gone unidentified, if not perhaps quite unnoticed, had I been alone. This was a new bird for me. Later that day I saw another first – waxwings – near Blithfield, when we happened to see half a dozen people watching something in a tree in a farmyard by the road and stopped to find out what was going on. The next week I saw the snow bunting again and took notes. It was not what I expected because, as winter snow buntings do, it showed much less white when it was settled, and much more rusty red and orange tan, than I had imagined from field guide illustrations. This was not a brown and white or grey and white bird: it was richly coloured with bright browns, orange-buff, grey and black, with a dark-tipped, bright-yellow bill.

On 30 January 1966 Tony saw a bird overhead and said, 'I bet that's the first you've seen this winter.' It was. In fact, although I didn't like to say it, it was the first I'd seen, ever – a sparrowhawk. It seems hard to believe how rare they were then, barely recovering from the devastating effects of pesticides. I noted that many skylarks were singing – more than 150. It is a number I find hard to credit now, but I did ride through large areas of arable farmland. I wish, though, that I had kept better notes, or made better counts. Such a number of singing skylarks would now seem almost impossible as they have crashed to just a quarter or so of their past numbers and, in many areas, seem to have all but gone.

New birds were coming along at intervals, some identified with other people's help. My first jack snipe was flushed from a rushy pool north of the reservoir, which had been pointed out to me as a likely spot, so I was primed and hoping for it. A black-necked grebe: 'I could not really identify this, but two men came up and identified it with a telescope. I later saw it fairly well.' The next day I saw it again and wrote that it was in the middle of the pool and would probably fly off, as there were water-skiers and speedboats about. A couple of weeks later a female scaup was another new one for me. I'm not entirely sure I realized it at the time, as it is written in my list in the usual blue ink while the asterisk alongside and the essential '(New Bird)' annotation is in a different colour, added later.

I came to hate the water-skiers. They often disturbed birds deliberately. In later years, when whole groups of us would watch the gathering gull roost in the hope of seeing a glaucous or Iceland, a boat would appear with a sneering driver and a single skier, to drive through the flock and scatter the gulls to the four winds. When I was on the British Birds Rarities Committee (BBRC) a record was queried and the observer's ability questioned. Keith Vinicombe, who made the often tedious process so entertaining and bearable, said that the observer had twice been to court and fined, once for hitting a policeman and once for throwing stones at a water-skier, so he couldn't be all bad. That sums up most birdwatchers' views of water-skiers. A skier doing his 'tricks', towing himself along by his toe, skipping sideways or turning momentarily to face backwards, seems to me to be the type specimen of a total idiot.

As I began to find out more about the wildlife of Chasewater so, intolerantly, I began to be more annoyed by the constant disturbance. Plans to develop the shoreline with hotels, even casinos, golf courses, a railway around the lake and improved road access regularly appeared in local papers, and I would fire off letters saying that the wildlife should be considered first. It got me nowhere. I see in my notes a plan put forward by Sir Billy Butlin, which I had quite forgotten about ('it was almost accepted but he was not allowed to buy the actual pool, only the land'); but a plan for an army camp, which would 'take over the area between Norton and Fly Bay to practise landings in amphibious vehicles' was more successful, as an army camp did appear for a time, even though the landings may not have taken place. The camp could be overlooked from the top of the biggest spoil heap, a great spot to watch kestrels playing in the wind.

I see in my early notes the same error twice repeated, once at Chasewater, once on Cannock Chase. I heard a long, metallic, trilling sound. It was clearly metallic and mechanical in quality, so a 'metallic rattle' didn't seem too far off an accurate description. As a result I wrote down 'corn bunting'. The corn bunting's song was described as a metallic rattle, like a bunch of keys being shaken. Hmm, it wasn't quite how I would describe it, but that must be what it was. What I actually heard in both cases was the song of a grasshopper warbler. It was, indeed, metallic and rattling and could, vaguely, be described as a bunch of keys being shaken, but the difference is that it continued for 20 or 30 seconds, even a minute or two, without a break or change in pitch or pace. It is a 'reeling' sound, described in the books as being like the sound of a fishing reel. My fishing reel, a nice, new, pearly grey fixed-spool job, never made a sound other than the well-oiled roll of ball bearings (a vibrant, liquid sound that I can still hear). Nor did my bike tick when it was freewheeling, although that comparison was more useful. Still, I find it hard to think that I was so far out with my identification at first. It is a useful thing to remember when writing about identifying birds by voice: it is easy for the author to know what he means, but a different thing altogether for the reader to cotton on to it.

On 15 May, Tony Blake told me about a bird atlas scheme and asked me to write down all the birds I could prove to be breeding around Chasewater. This was the West Midland Bird Club atlas of breeding birds in the West Midlands,

Waxwings at Blithfield. They have appeared several times in Sandy,
even seen from my office window.

Great grey shrike.

which was a pilot scheme for the national atlas that was to be run a few years later by the British Trust for Ornithology (BTO). Not for the first time, the WMBC was ahead of the rest. Later, I wrote to Dr Swindells, who happened to by my father's boss at work, as he was the organizer of the atlas work in the area and wanted me to be involved. I went to see him at his home and was given a small supply of record cards, which I duly filled in for the national grid square referenced as SK00. In the full-scale national atlas, I was to fill in smaller, more refined cards with details of birds possibly, probably or proved to be breeding, mostly in remote spots that might not otherwise be fully covered, such as parts of Scotland, and send them in to the organizer. Another survey of mine at Chasewater was the national wildfowl count, once a month from autumn to spring – the 'duck count'. This was a Wildfowl Trust (now Wildfowl & Wetlands Trust) initiative so that all areas of water should have regular counts of its wildfowl in a coordinated fashion. A population estimate of ducks, geese and swans across Britain could be built up, but it also allowed sites such as

Chasewater to be classified as 'Category 3' – meaning, more or less, that the area was useless – so it was not necessarily a good thing.

Autumn was great because then the waders would drop in. A day later, they would often be gone, but there could be common sandpipers, ringed plovers, dunlins, greenshanks – who knew what might appear? The point was, it was important to keep going, over and over, because no two visits were the same and the birds were not any more likely to be there on a Saturday or Sunday morning than, say, a Wednesday evening. Visit after visit after visit was the way to find something. Common, Arctic and sometimes black terns appeared, too. Common and Arctic terns were often around for long spells and I was able to work them out quite well, as a rule. I never did like putting down 'commic' tern (an aversion to such abbreviations that has stuck with me, as well as a desire to know what I was seeing and not give up, even with this difficult pair).

In October 1966 came a typical Chasewater record: I came across seven eiders in a tight group, diving for shellfish and crayfish. Two stayed for a few days and were watched by many people – Chasewater had no ducks to speak of, so if any did turn up it was as well to look at them. After a week, 'I arrived to see a man carrying off one of the eiders, obviously [crossed out and replaced with possibly] shot and bleeding from the breast. He had a dog but no gun. The other eider was wary and looked perplexed, and was continually approached by yachts, causing it to dive frequently and fly about at times. I counted at least six men shooting.'

On 22 October in 1966 I was really excited. The previous winter I had missed it several times, but now I found a great grey shrike. It was fabulous – according to my notes, 'an outstanding bird'. It was a year almost to the day since my first one in Essex. I saw it first in the morning and this made it a 'two visit day', with more views in the afternoon. It was several visits later before I glimpsed it again. This was the way of it with shrikes, which returned to Chasewater for several years, one, sometimes two, easy to see on some days but impossible on others. Trying to show a shrike to someone else was hardly ever worth the effort. They just appeared, out of nowhere, or they didn't. When I did see a shrike, it was often a stunning view.

A great day was 5 November: there was the eider, and two Bewick's swans, which flew in from the north and landed briefly on Jeffrey's Swag, before going on down to the main dam and settling in alongside three mute swans, which seemed to calm their nerves. Another pochard influx totalled 105, and I saw a short-eared owl, the first one I'd come across at Chasewater, and my best view yet of the shrike. Another new one for the area for me was a great spotted woodpecker. Tony Blake told me he'd only seen one there, many years before. I was to remember this woodpecker a year later, on 18 November 1967. I was walking with Tony near the northern end of the reservoir when I saw a medium-sized bird with broad, black and white wings fly low over the ground. Instead of saying 'Look at that' or something equally vague, I said 'A woodpecker!' even though I knew it didn't look like one. Tony instantly recognized it as a hoopoe. It was a great find – one of the more amazing birds in my Chasewater career – and several people saw it later. When Tony told Alan Dean, Alan thought he said 'whooper', a swan that would have been quite good at Chasewater, too, but not *that* good – not as good as a hoopoe in November.

At the end of February 1967 I find two interesting notes in my bird diary. One was about a mixed flock of birds alongside the rough entrance road to the east in a grassy field, long grass growing up through some sort of corn stubble. Arthur Jacobs told me that he had picked out some corn buntings by first hearing their song (corn buntings were then rare in the West Midlands). My notes reveal that the flock in this field comprised 30-plus reed buntings, 300-plus greenfinches, five to ten redpolls, 100 house sparrows, five to ten yellowhammers, 700 starlings, and the four corn buntings. Later in the day I also saw a collared dove – my first in the area. It was the great grey shrike, however, which was again 'bird of the day' by far.

This sparrow, finch and bunting flock was a good one but not so unusual. Now it would be hard to find one quite so varied and numerous in most English farmland areas. My walks to Chasewater in later years regularly produced several hundred sparrows in wheat fields in late summer. There were no

scandinavian rock pipit and unusual 'meadow pipt'. Chasewater, Staffordshire, 4 April 1975.

tree sparrows there, but they were not far away in fields around Burntwood, and in one year there was a large flock at Chasewater. Now they have all gone. Later that summer I found corn buntings singing near Burntwood and Hammerwich, beside one of my routes to or from the pool. This area was to have quite a concentration of them for several more years, during a period of rapid expansion in Staffordshire, before an equally sudden contraction and virtual disappearance that mirrored their losses elsewhere in Britain, from the south of England to the Western Isles.

My second note of February concerns a conjunction between Venus and Saturn. For some time I had been interested in the stars and planets, and I was always reading space adventure books as well as factual books about astronomy. I saw the four visible moons of Jupiter on the same evening as the conjunction, as well as the Andromeda nebula, that great tilted cartwheel galaxy that looks like a faint smudge in the night sky, despite a near full moon. But I wrote, 'The conjunction was what I had hoped to see through my telescope, but as yet it has not arrived, being some days late.'

There were then on the market two new German telescopes that made the brass and leather ones look old fashioned; both were black-painted metal and plastic, looking very smart and beautifully made. One was the Hertel & Reuss 20–60×60, with simple draw tubes and a focusing ring at the eyepiece; the other was the Nickel Supra 15–60×60, with two draw tubes and a focusing knob on a little roof-like projection beside the eyepiece. I chose the Nickel. At that time it cost £38. 9s., which Dad forked out, generous as ever. On 27 February it arrived, but the weather was so bad that I was unable to go farther round Chasewater than some wooden shelters on the southern shore. It hung around my shoulders on a narrow leather strap in a neat, upright, tan-coloured leather cylinder. It gave me options between 8× and 60×, I wrote, combined with the 8×30 and 10×50 binoculars that I used. I'm not sure what I had then, but presumably I had by that time acquired the Wray 8×30s to supplement the old, heavy 10×50s (although I never took both out at once). When I first went out with it I met Eric Clare who saw it immediately and said, 'Ah, you've got yourself a telescope – now you can see what you're looking at.' The next night the skies were clear and I used the telescope on the stars: the Pleiades looked mighty impressive, as did the Hyades, the Orion nebula; the Andromeda nebula remained disappointingly faint, but Jupiter was now an obvious disk with its four moons, just about revealing darker bands across it.

The Nickel was quite short and I didn't use a tripod; that came much later. No one used tripods then. The usual thing was to lie back on the ground, with one or both knees raised, and balance the end of the telescope held against a knee by one hand, while focusing with the other. The longer brass Broadhurst Clarkson jobs were easier for they could be used in the time-honoured manner of the stalker with his spy glass. The new Nickel was too short, even compared with the Hertel & Reuss, but I managed. Over time, the Nickel became stiff. The smaller draw tube pulled out from the larger one, with a fibre seal of some sort to keep out the dust and moisture, but this seal always became hard and dry and slowly broke up. Eventually, it was all but impossible to pull the draw tube out at all: you had to grip the far end of the telescope between your feet, grab the focusing knob housing with both hands, and heave as hard as you could. Pushing it closed was just as bad. And the Nickel was not a good telescope optically, either. I later bought a second Nickel because, despite everything, it was convenient, light and easy to carry, but it was a silly thing to do.

Still, I had my telescope and was naturally very proud of it. I hope I was as grateful for it as I should have been. There followed many more notes on the night sky, comparisons from night to night to reveal the movements of Jupiter's moons and a brief dash round some of the more obvious star clusters and nebulae. By working out its movement night to night, I was pretty certain, too, that I could identify Uranus. Cold, clear nights with sparkling stars were accompanied by 'Penny Lane' and 'Strawberry Fields For Ever'. Beatles' songs infallibly welded themselves to my activities and recapture the enjoyment years afterwards. A clear sky, a beautiful view of Orion, or Capella high overhead, will nine times out of ten bring 'Penny Lane' unbidden into my head.

And, so far as birds were concerned, I watched everything with it. My first chiffchaff of the year was on 21 March, first day of spring – 'seen through telescope beautifully'. Despite its limitations, the Nickel Supra opened up a new world. Decent optics are always a joy to use and I was revelling in this telescope, zooming up to a soft 60× magnification whenever I could. Having been restricted for years to 30× with my current Optolyth, I still miss the 60: blurry or not, it gave that extra size to a dot on the horizon that could make all the difference. Did my eyesight pay for this? Opticians say no, but my right eye soon became weaker than my left, never quite sharpening into focus. After prolonged staring through a telescope, it was usually a minute or two before it got back to normal at all, remaining a little blurry. Years of staring at gulls on gloomy winter evenings may have done some damage. Eventually I worked out that leaving the left eye open while I looked through the telescope with my right reduced the strain and, peculiarly, seemed to brighten the image seen through my right eye. I used the left eye at times, to even things up, but found it was less convenient;

also, remarkably, it showed that my eyes see slightly different colours, the right slightly 'warmer', the left cooler, more bluish or greenish in comparison.

There were not many good birds in these early months, even with my telescope, but I did see a great deal of the great grey shrike. How lucky we were! For several years one, sometimes two, wintered at Chasewater and one, sometimes two, on Cannock Chase. Several times I saw them at both places on the same day. Despite my seeing them with such regularity they never lost their appeal. If I walked all round Chasewater all day long and saw nothing else, the shrike made it a good day, even if I had seen it only the day before, and the weekend before that. Shrikes are super birds: aesthetically they are unbeatable. Later, they became very scarce in Britain once again and deserved their high rating even more.

Once the evenings became light enough, I was at Chasewater day after day. The spring was full of birds – sand martins and willow warblers arriving in a rush, pied, white and yellow wagtails on the shore with meadow pipits, rock and Scandinavian rock pipits, grasshopper warblers and whinchats, and migrant waders, which seemed to be the real prize. The water level fell and the shore became suitable, in places, for a feeding dunlin or two, or a common sandpiper – once even a knot. Little ringed plovers appeared, then, in May, several turnstones, ringed plovers, sanderlings in a short, concentrated passage that is typical of a Midland spring. The wader passage was a good one and lasted almost into June, better than in many subsequent years. Black, Arctic and common terns once again showed that almost anything might turn up here, while sedge warblers, meadow pipits, spotted flycatchers and linnets, coots, moorhens and great crested grebes were nesting.

By 21 June 1967 the waders were on their way back: a dunlin and a common sandpiper, not counting the flocks of lapwings that had already passed over for a week or two. Black terns were back on 24 June (this was early). There were still birds that left me puzzled, still some that I now think were wrong. A wood warbler at Chasewater seems distinctly unlikely. I think I was pushing it a bit, trying to get it on my local list. Then a strange duck, which I described and sketched in my notes, in late July. I still have a letter from Alan Richards in response to my report to the bird club, expressing the view that it was a moulting and abraded common scoter, quoting from the Witherby Handbook in support. I'm sure it was, but a bright-pink bill still seems odd. In August seven juvenile shelducks arrived. They were a puzzle for a bit, but easily resolved. Then, to my dismay, someone came along and shot one – 'No police near, little could be done.'

It was on 4 November that my old friend the great grey shrike returned. Alan Dean found it; he was excited too – he, like me, loved shrikes and soon became an international authority on them. We stalked it and got quite close, and I greedily turned my telescope onto it and took detailed notes and sketches. The sketches, like most of my field sketches of the time, I no longer have. The next day was classic Chasewater after a night of rain and gales: cold, grey, remorselessly wet and blowing force 8 from the north-west. An Arctic skua! It was a stunner, a dark-phase adult, no doubt about it – a real seabird, blown inland by the terrific storm. Then, to confirm the remarkable qualities of this exciting day, a kittiwake appeared. Marvellous! Better yet, a flock of birds flew over the dam and across the water, to settle in the distance with much fluttering and flapping of wings – 25 to 30 more kittiwakes! This was really something, so how could I not have made an accurate count of such an important flock of birds? I still can't work that out – but the wind, the rain, the excitement and the distance conspired against me, and 25 to 30 it had to be.

Later that day I went to Blithfield. (During the summer I had discovered the delights of Blithfield and its large areas of mud, which attracted many waders and did not suffer from the constant disturbances that plagued the Chasewater shore.) There, too, the gales brought rewards. There were two, probably four, kittiwakes, and there was a huge skua with large wing patches – a great skua, surely, a great big bonxie. But everyone else there said it was an Arctic. I couldn't believe it. I knew both from Scotland, and only a few weeks before I had been watching them in Caithness. But these people were all more experienced than I was so I must be wrong. It is down in my notes as Arctic skua – crossed out, reinstated as great, with a big black asterisk. A couple of days later, at the bird club meeting in Birmingham, someone told me that the Blithfield party had changed their minds: it had, after all, been a great skua, and I had been right.

The field where the finch flock had been the previous winter, with the four corn buntings, was still really good: 60 skylarks, 40 reed buntings, 40 chaffinches, a brambling, 400 greenfinches, 400 house sparrows, several tree sparrows, 10 yellowhammers, 200 starlings, a couple of collared doves. Such a gathering, such a mixture, would be astonishing now. The loss of farmland birds has been a major talking point for several years at the RSPB, but younger members of staff have no idea what we are really talking about: they never experienced flocks such as this.

Back at Chasewater the next weekend were gulls and some Bewick's swans. I counted the gulls as precisely as I could: not huge numbers, by any means, but I was doing my best to get it right. Gull roosts would become something of an obsession in later winters, a kind of sub-obsession to my whole Chasewater one. On Boxing Day the Bewick's had increased to nine, and the shrike was close and confiding for a change. Next day I found no fewer than 70 twites, first located by pinpointing their wonderful twangy flight calls. This took the famous Cannock Reservoir twite flock into new dimensions, and yet two days later they hit 80 or more, feeding on weed-seeds on the black coal dust in the flat pans to the north. Their rich tawny throats and bright-yellow bills made them attractive little birds, just my kind of thing: streaky, strongly textured, rich in varied tints of brown, buff, tawny and orange. As they flew up over a shaly pit heap I noticed that 'they seemed to double their number owing to the sharp shadows of each bird, then they all pitched on the shale, each bird on its shadow – a peculiar sight. Then slowly the flock drifted back to the slurry bed and began to feed again, the birds moving across the ground in waves, those at the rear closing up, then the front birds spreading out again, and so on.' I'd been reading my W. H. Hudson book.

In the new year, twites reached 85 to 90; and a jay was exceptional for the area. Tree sparrows were commoner than I now remember them, 20 or more being noted but not picked out as anything remarkable. In mid-March there was a kittiwake. Several subsequent springs produced kittiwakes, and I wrote a note about the overland passage in early spring for British Birds. I had noticed that Horace (H. G.) Alexander mentioned such a movement in his book Seventy Years of Birdwatching, and I referred to this in my note. A little while later I was astonished to receive an airmail letter from America, a handwritten note from H.G.A., who was by then almost blind, thanking me for noticing his kittiwake theories and hoping that I could find out more about the direction taken by these seabirds that seemed so determinedly to pass over the middle of England every spring – where from? Where were they going to? Sometimes, in a late-winter gull roost, the unmistakable call of a kittiwake would ring out, but more usually a few birds would appear during the day, crossing the reservoir but not stopping on their way north-east. In subsequent years this kittiwake passage has been noticed many times, and one year in the West Midlands, long after I had left, there was a huge influx, with scores at many places.

After some weeks' apparent absence (but who knows) the shrike reappeared and I saw it again several times. A goldcrest gave me 'the best views I have ever had of the species: all details could be seen in good sunlight at very close range … once the bird scratched its neck and, as it did so, the crest was erected and fluffed out, showing a brilliant orange centre'. More notable, it produced a prolonged, varied, but subdued subsong, quite unlike the usual song of a goldcrest with its rhythmic pattern. I learned willow-tit song, too (the wood-warbler-like repetition of a simple, sad note). Spring brought other goodies, such as a summer-plumage black tern, singing grasshopper warblers, sanderlings, a whimbrel and a bar-tailed godwit that stayed for several days, common scoters, and a mid-May scaup complete with the summer ear-patch in addition to the white face.

That summer my notes became vastly more extensive. I was describing a dead kittiwake, the displays of cuckoos, the habitat of flocks of linnets (more than 20 of them, in mid-July), and writing detailed plumage notes on more common scoters and reams of stuff on kestrels exploiting a strong wind around the spoil heaps. And yet more common scoters. Like the kittiwakes, these seabirds seem to have an intentional overland movement, often in July. Goldeneyes had summered the previous year, apparently injured, and now one was back as early as August. In the autumn there was a black-necked grebe, only the second I had ever seen, shortly after both Slavonian and red-necked in Scotland. Through September my appetite for Chasewater was at its strongest, after a summer lull; I was there day after day after day. There were redstarts and lesser whitethroats in the bushes, black terns over the pool, and then a new bird, a super bird, only the second ever recorded at Cannock Reservoir – a Temminck's stint. Ah, what joy to find for myself a rare wader, and a really good one at that. I saw it first in the morning, and I was back in the afternoon for much better views. I got the lot – a full plumage description, the flight pattern, the distinctive calls. It was even with a common sandpiper, which it rather resembled superficially, for comparison. It was there again the next day, and the next, and for ten more days after that, and each day I was there to see it. It was at 15-yards range, at 50–60× magnification with my Nickel Supra. This bird took me to another level of observation and understanding, and it was a beautiful little bird, too. I was over the moon. This was a good autumn. There were small birds in good numbers, such as 50 to 60 redpolls (where are they now?) still in superb, bright plumage, loads of linnets, goldfinches, an assortment of warblers in the willow thickets – who needed the coast?

March in 1969 would not have been complete without its kittiwake, its great grey shrike, its twites. But from the beginning of April I was away until late July, and again until mid-August. No matter, it would be a good autumn, perhaps. Two little gulls! – my first in Staffordshire – together with nine black terns (Chasewater was never more than moderate for black terns). Scoters, shovelers, a ringed plover or two, a few shelducks – actually, this was not so very special. I noted a whitethroat on 15 September, the only one of the autumn. It was the year in which whitethroat numbers crashed: the Peggy whitethroat, common in every hedgerow, had become a rare bird, courtesy of a drought in the Sahel. But I got two new ones for the pool on one September day, a Sandwich tern and a purple sandpiper. There was a funny warbler, too. I can't remember it, but the notes are intriguing: 'Like a chiffchaff, except perhaps for a longer eyestripe [superciliary, no doubt, presumably a juvenile] and a yellower rump. However the call was very different, loud and ringing and repeated every few seconds, a loud, clear *tsweeoo* or *tsi-ooo*'. I was experimenting with call annotations, using something that I had seen in a Peterson guide to American birds: a line above each syllable, in this case going steeply upwards over the '*tswee*' and down over the '*oo*' to indicate the change of pitch. It is hard to reproduce in a field guide, but still a good way to show on paper the inflection of a call, so I still use it from time to time. That December brought several scaup, a kittiwake, twites, a merlin and two water pipits on several days: good experience. The twites reached 80, but I found no sign of the great grey shrike. In January I counted 228 tufted ducks. Remember that, not long before, there would often have been just two or three!

My first visit to Chasewater after the annual Scottish holiday in 1971 was on Monday 9 August. (These long summer breaks from university were such a treat!) There was not much about. I walked around the north shore, going anticlockwise, then all down the western embankment to the powerboat club

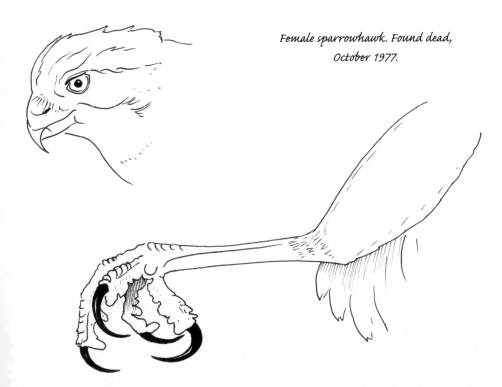

Female sparrowhawk. Found dead, October 1977.

in the south-western corner. The water level was low and I hoped for some waders, but only a couple of birds were on the shore. One was a common sandpiper; the other was, well, odd: immediately, it was just not right. It was tiny: a stint. Right, but no rufous, so not like a little stint. It had grey on the tail, not white; but, when it settled, it showed pale legs, like a Temminck's! But a pale V on its back: how could that be? Not a little, not a Temminck's. So what was it? I was trembling. 'I realized I had a peep on my hands, which was a real shock!' The sandpiper (as sandpipers usually did), flew away, but the mystery wader curved back and settled again quite close:

> I watched it for an hour and took a description [thank goodness I always had a notebook]. It was clearly neither a Baird's sandpiper, nor a white-rumped, so it had to be either a least, western or semi-palmated. I thought semi-palmated had a stouter bill and remembered that western sometimes had rufous on the scapulars and a longer bill – but I couldn't really say at the time which it was. With a glance at the field guide [when I got home] it became quite clear that it could only be a least sandpiper because of a) the pale legs, b) the pale v, and c) the small, fine bill.

In a way, it was easy. Fortunately it was not one of the other two. I had nothing to judge it by except for a short paragraph in the back of the Peterson, Mountfort and Hollom field guide – no picture – but luckily I had one or two issues of the John Gooders part-work, *Birds of the World*. I didn't take it regularly, but I did have some of the waders, including the small American waders ('peeps') with an illustration by Robert Gillmor. That helped clinch it.

I phoned Tony Blake – I had never done this before, but this was the time. I had to walk up the road to do it, of course, from a phone box, as we didn't have a phone. 'I know it sounds silly, but I think I've found a least sandpiper,' I told him. I went back to Chasewater to meet him and his wife, Dorothy, with Saab their Afghan, on the shore by the car park. There were children about and speedboats coming out from the club compound; but, wonderfully, the bird was still there where I had left it. We watched it for an hour. Tony, properly cautious, agreed with my identification but wanted more people to see it. The next day, I arrived to find several people watching the exciting wader – an adult least sandpiper. Next day, it was seen by dozens of people. This was the 17th British record. Later reviews and rejections promoted it to number 14. It was beyond my wildest dreams. And a few days later, I was back again in Scotland. It had fitted neatly into the slot between my two holidays.

September was nothing special, but Blithfield was good. I went there many times, borrowing Dad's car when I could. There had been many good birds, but on one particular day I hit the jackpot. I saw the sensational sight of a crane flying over. It was just amazing. It was, I think, the first Staffordshire record. Two people were picking blackberries near by. One I recognized as Dennis Munns, whom I had seen at bird club meetings. Just in time I ran over and pointed out the departing crane. 'I think,' Mrs Munns said, 'you mean a heron don't you?' But they saw it well enough to confirm my identification and enjoy a good bird. There was one more day before I would be heading back to Wales (I was now at university at Swansea). At Chasewater it was hot, flat calm; a mild, mild day. No matter, with the least sandpiper I'd seen the best bird I'd ever found and now, with the crane, I had topped it off with another 'first' for the county. I'd have just one last walk. Little did I know that I would find the most astonishing bird I would ever find at the pool, least sandpiper not excepted.

The water level was low and there were several little points and bays, which I tended to follow quite close to the shore, rather than taking obvious shortcuts, in case there was a hidden wader somewhere. At the 'Target', I wandered along the shingle beach and, four yards in from the water's edge, found something large and brown. I think, momentarily, I guessed it might be a skua (once I realized it wasn't an empty sack), but almost instantly it was obvious that this was something stranger even that that. It had a big, pale bill. It was a Cory's shearwater! So far as I can tell, this was the first Cory's shearwater ever recorded inland in Britain (and it is probably still the only one). I was at a loss to know what to do, apart from sit and look at it and scribble some descriptive notes. A kind of euphoria ran through me; it was a real high. It was a Saturday, and, within a few minutes Graham Evans, some years younger than I was but by then a regular Chasewater watcher, appeared on the far side of the bay with his bike. I waved him over.

Graham had no camera; I had a simple Instamatic at home. After a panicky discussion we decided that I should ride home on Graham's bike and fetch the camera, while he stayed with the bird and hoped it didn't fly away. It did fly, a little, while I was gone, fluttering across a little bay to another bit of shore. But it was sick, exhausted, or simply disoriented, so when I returned we were able to get within a few feet of it. It showed no sign of fear, but when we looked at it from the front it would rear up and half open its wings. Sometimes it would get up on its toes and move forward in a peculiar, shambling waddle, its wing-tips crossed over its tail but its inner wings lifted clear of the body: a typical shearwater stance (being made for the air and the sea these birds are unable to do much more than this on land). Having fetched the camera I took a few photographs of the bird on its little shingle beach. Looking at the pictures now brings it all back: excitement, amazement, but also sadness for the poor bird. I tried to phone Tony Blake but he was out; as I had seen Dennis Munns at Blithfield the day before, I called him, and he came to see the bird at the reservoir. Then, I borrowed Graham's saddlebag and put the bird inside (it struggled and pecked) and Dennis drove me home, with Graham following on his bike.

Later that evening John Lord came to see the shearwater. I had not met John until then, although he was one of the most regular birdwatchers at the pool and contributed a huge number of records to the West Midland Bird Club report, which he also edited; he was also, of course, co-author of *The Birds of Staffordshire 1962* with Tony Blake, the little book that had meant so much to me. The next day Tony came to see it in the morning (I still wrote 'Mr Blake' in my notes). I was particularly determined that he should see it. I'd taken quite good notes but measured the bird with a ruler, in inches, hardly a proper 'in the hand' procedure. The wingspan was exactly four feet, with the wings a little flexed and not strained, while bill to tail it was a little over 18 inches. If I remember rightly the bill was two inches long: a large, heavy, hooked beak that would be quite serious on a fit bird, but this poor creature was weak and managed little more than a nibble. We tried to feed it on tinned fish.

On the Sunday, my return to Swansea was a bit awkward. After three years in a hall of residence I was about to begin three years of post-graduate research and I would now be in digs out in the town for the first time. This was all sorted, but Miss Owen, my new, rather elderly, landlady, would perhaps not take kindly to my turning up on the first day with a big bird in a box. Still, it was obvious that, as I was heading to the coast, the bird should come too: I had visions of its sailing off out to sea, with a last look over its shoulder to thank us for our efforts.

When we reached Swansea it was raining. The shearwater had survived. We drove out to Mumbles Head and found the sea crashing against the rocks in a huge, rolling surf. I put the bird on a rock by a little bay. It did nothing, so I picked it up and put it in a rock pool to get it used to sea water again. It crawled away. It still seemed lively and strong when I held it up and opened its wings, but it made no attempt to fly. I had seen fulmars, grounded in tall grass above a beach, successfully 'launched' (in the same way that stranded swifts can be) by being tossed into the air, so in one last attempt to get it to go I picked up the shearwater, faced into the wind and threw it up in the air. Instead of opening its wings and gliding off, it came back down like a lump of earth, smack, onto the sea, where it rolled onto its back and was swept away by a wave. It sank, before being washed back onto the rocks, half-dead if not entirely so. A miserable end for a beautiful bird.

Then, Cory's shearwater was an 'official' rarity, a bird that required a submission to the national British Birds Rarities Committee. It is not now, but it is still, in practical terms, a very rare bird. It was then something that many people would not have seen in Britain; the big listers now have seen it, although it isn't quite so easy to pin down as a land bird. Now, a captured Cory's would be photographed and videoed; digital pictures would be on the internet within hours and several magazines – *Birding World*, *British Birds*, *Birdwatch* and *Bird Watching* at least – would feature it, with pictures. It might make a regional newspaper if not the dailies. Goodness knows how many people would have turned up at my parents' back door. It would be thoroughly well documented, although it is likely that very few people would know anything about who found it. In 1971, I made two phone calls: one to Dennis Munns, the other to Tony Blake, my obvious choice. That was it. So far as I can recall, five birdwatchers saw it: these two, myself, Graham Evans, and John Lord.

The report was first made public in *British Birds*, in the few pages devoted to *Recent Reports*, more or less a monthly essay written by Pat Bonham, something that I later took on myself. The reference reads:

> Great and Cory's Shearwaters were recorded off Co. Cork – 250 Cory's on 5th–6th [of October] in flocks of up to 70, and 520 Great on 15th – but a Cory's off St Ives (Cornwall) on 19th, a Great Shearwater off Hilbre (Cheshire) on 31st – the first county record – and 20 Greats between the Wolf Rock and Isles of Scilly on 21st were notable records for British waters. Still more remarkable was a Cory's Shearwater picked up alive at Cannock Reservoir (Staffordshire) on 2nd and later released on the sea at Swansea: this was the first record inland in Britain and Ireland and we understand that it was of the North Atlantic race.

Yes! – fantastic.

This was special, really special. I hadn't had the heart to report (or the guts to admit) that the poor bird had died: 'released on the sea' was economical with the truth, let's say. Later in the same report, there was just one crane for the month: 'at Blithfield on 1st'. Terrific.

Gulls and Great
Grey Shrikes

My love affair with Norton Pool, Chasewater or Cannock Reservoir had gone through several phases. Fishing first, then increasingly regular birdwatching visits, sometimes twice a day, with a concentration on winter weekends, and then late summer and autumn when I could get out every day. School holidays meant I could be out all day long, and even my year at the art college in Stafford made little difference, as I was home every weekend. (I gave up after the foundation course when it became clear that the college would not tolerate my interest in birds – I must be committed to art and nothing else!) The big change came when I went to Swansea as a 'proper' student: then I was home only for a couple of weeks between terms and then for a longer period in late summer and early autumn, which coincided nicely with the autumn wader and tern passage. Much of this period was still taken up, though, by holidays in Scotland. So, while Chasewater was still a priority, my visits were erratic, at best.

Nevertheless, this was a period when I could concentrate on the birds there and my notes improved considerably, despite following the pattern established right at the beginning of my serious interest in birds. There were several reasons why I could do this. One was that I didn't do much else. I didn't go out drinking or clubbing (well, Burntwood didn't have much to offer!), and girls were frightening creatures and I was hopelessly lacking in confidence. This seems a trivial point with little relevance to birds, but it is a fact that I spent much of my time watching birds and had no other distractions, much as I might have wished for them. Like any obsessive interest that requires plenty of practice, birdwatching demanded a lot of time and a lack of competition. Had it been different, I would not have been a birdwatcher in quite the same way that I was.

This was true for years. Even six years at a university didn't change me in that respect and I left Swansea as inadequate socially as I was when I went there. But I could do waders.

A second fact, equally important, was that I sponged shamelessly off my parents for years. While others got part-time jobs during the vacations, I did nothing. It didn't really occur to me that I should. This gave me the time to spend outside, watching birds. Nor did I do what some students did and sign on the dole for ten weeks in the summer. However, with a research grant I somehow managed to pay for my lodgings and books and even buy myself a car – a Reliant! (a three-wheeler meant just £10 a year road tax). I was mobile.

Graham Evans had found a marshy spot to the north of Chasewater, by a pig farm, from which all kinds of slurry flowed into Jeffrey's Swag. Jack snipe were suddenly regular here, in good numbers, but you had to climb a barbed-wire fence and wander around in the muddy pig fields to flush them and hope you weren't chased by a pig. There were water rails here, too, regular for the first time at Chasewater. This may have been the beginning of a significant change at Chasewater: this was when the water became thicker, not nearly so crystal clear, and also, perhaps, when the fish numbers declined. Yet wildfowl numbers began a remarkable rise, something that is still happening. Whereas I used to see two or three tufted ducks, there have since been hundreds in winter for years – in December 1971 there were just two! Goldeneyes had increased a bit, well into the twenties, hitting a new highest-ever total of 38 on 31 December, but soon reached a hundred or more for long periods in the winter.

For some birds, this was a great time around Chasewater. The famous twites are much in evidence in my notes, usually around 65 to 70 of them, but they could be hard to find and often missed altogether at weekends. Where did they come from? Were they from the Peak District, which might, in part, explain their subsequent disappearance as the Peak also lost most of its breeding twites? Wintering stonechats, grey wagtails and water pipits always added interest. At the end of 1971 my notes concentrated much more on Chasewater's gulls. Numbers were not large: half a dozen great black-backed, two common gulls (not common here), three or four thousand black-headeds and 1,500 each of herring and lesser black-backs. There were increasingly regular records of glaucous and Iceland gulls from other Staffordshire reservoirs, notably Blithfield, but I was not seeing them. Then, in January 1972, I found a glaucous or Iceland, at Belvide, a place I visited only irregularly. I suspected then that it was an Iceland and feel now that it must have been, going by my brief notes and sketch, but it was too far off to be certain.

There were still new things to see. I found lapwings with chicks that summer, the first at Chasewater for years. A black-tailed godwit was only the second I had ever seen there, and little gulls in August were likewise my second record at Chasewater, where the species is strangely rare. That August I counted an astonishing 650 sand martins; I don't think such numbers could be expected now. Then, shown to me by Graham Evans who first found it, there was a dead long-eared owl. This was entirely unexpected here, but it presaged a series of winter records of small groups of owls roosting in the willow thickets. That Chasewater was a peculiar place, whose birds are somewhat unpredictable, was proved again when I saw a green sandpiper – common enough at Blithfield and Belvide – which was my first ever there. It remains a rare bird at 'the pool'.

On 22 December I saw my next Staffordshire glaucous or Iceland gull, this time at Chasewater. It was an adult, hunched, with high tertials and drooped white primaries. But for some reason I had no telescope, and seeing it at 7× it was again not certain enough to claim as Iceland. The differences between glaucous and Iceland are subtle, depending upon shapes, bill size and facial expressions, not on plumage patterns or colours. Next morning I was back and saw 70 twites, but it was a return visit in the afternoon that excited me, as I hoped to see the mystery gull again. And so I did. This time I was with Dave Smallshire, who watched Belvide as often as I did Chasewater but rarely came here. The white-winged gull dropped into a small gathering of gulls very early, at 2.50 p.m. I saw it from the far side of the reservoir and hurried round – a couple of miles' fast walk – to get a better view. It was hard to see a pale bill, on a

Wing of dead black-headed gull, showing state of moult. Chasewater, 16 August 1975.

pale bird, against pale water, a long way off in fading light. The demands of gull-watching on inland reservoir roosts were beginning to make themselves plain. It was an adult Iceland, though, and my first.

This was a good spell: the highest number of goldeneyes (61), a long-staying snow bunting, a scaup, and a superb if distant first-winter glaucous gull; a pintail ended the year well. The new year began with the snow bunting and a bearded tit in the pig-farm marsh. Others had seen two in November and it was another excellent bird to add to my Chasewater list. Keep on watching and they keep on coming. The large, young glaucous gull reappeared, the Iceland on a couple of days shortly afterwards, then I saw both of these northern gulls (and two snow buntings) on 7 January.

It was in summer that year, 1973, that I took much more notice of the wild flowers and butterflies and started to keep more detailed notes than I had done before. Although my walks were not always along the same routes, I kept detailed counts of the butterflies I saw, which are interesting, but not as comprehensive as they later became. I didn't know of anyone who counted butterflies at the time and had no real idea what numbers to expect – other than what I guessed there might be – so a bit of precision was sometimes eye-opening. There were 220 small whites along the western embankment on just one day; usually there were a few small tortoiseshells and walls, small heaths and small coppers, now and then common blues and meadow browns, red admirals and peacocks. But some species that I saw regularly, but hadn't actually totted up before, proved to be remarkably few. The following year was better, and I was noting every butterfly I saw. Late-August walks produced scores of wall browns (54, 67), in places where now there might be one or two. Even in mid-September there were 25, 32, a dozen or so. In 1975 I was around all summer and finding orange-tips, dingy skippers, large skippers, more common blues, meadow browns by the score, then by the hundred, then the main emergence of wall browns (66, 71).

Around this time I was seeing less of Tony Blake at Chasewater, but I bumped into Eric Phillips and later John Fortey. Eric was a different animal from the others: he was a twitcher, in the proper, original sense of the word before the media picked up on it and misused it as a definitive term for a birdwatcher. Eric travelled the country in pursuit of rarities, but maintained his regular visits to local spots in the West Midlands and began, increasingly, to come to Chasewater. John I knew from his initials – J.E.F. – in my collection of old West Midland Bird Reports. He had been a Chasewater regular in the past and was now returning after a few years' break. It soon became clear that both men were thoroughly expert, and J.E.F., E.G.P., became a frequent pairing in the bird reports. We still didn't have a phone at home, so I began to get into the habit of walking half a mile up the road to the nearest phone box to call Eric every Friday evening. If there had been anything about during the week, he could not have called me and I would not have known. So my Friday calls – a weekly ritual in advance of the weekend – became my link to the national grapevine that centred around Norfolk's Dave Holman, top twitcher of the time and a genuine identification expert. But we usually met, anyway, at the Chasewater gull roost in the mid- and late 1970s.

Pencilled into my notes on 11 August 1973 I see '738', which means my 738th recorded visit to Chasewater (that is, the number of days on which I had made some sort of bird notes). By 15 July 1975 it had become 1,000; a few years later, I passed the 2,000 mark. A couple of weeks after visit 738, I saw seven Arctic skuas; this was completely unprecedented in the West Midlands. Chasewater was interspersed with frequent trips to Blithfield, which was proving great for waders. It was late September when I saw a wood sandpiper there, remarkably my first ever: seeing it at last got rid of a bogey bird that had haunted me for years. This was a period of intense birdwatching. There were daily notes, with Chasewater at their centre.

After a long period of suspecting a difference, I was now concentrating hard on proving a difference in upperwing pattern between adult common and Arctic terns. The field guides of the time concentrated on the underwing, reasonably enough, with the different primary-tip patterns and translucency being invaluable clues (first described by Richard Richardson). I had been noticing that common terns – or some terns, anyway – had a dark mark on about the fourth or fifth feather from the wing-tip, a narrow 'wedge' of darker grey against the pale upperwing, which was not present on others (Arctics). For example, on 15 August I wrote 'tern identification [common] confirmed by bill colour etc, but upperwing pattern quite clear even at long range: definite dark wedge on 5th/6th primary area. Inner primaries being moulted.' I had not, at this point, noticed that the moulting of the primaries at this date was also a definitive characteristic for common and not consistent with Arctic, which moults much later.

This led me into correspondence with Peter Grant, with whom I had already had some contact regarding gulls. I had been impressed by a paper in *British Birds* by Peter Grant and Bob Scott, on the identification of juvenile common, Arctic and roseate terns in the autumn, which had transformed my own observations. Peter added to my observations on the upperwings with some studies of his own (chiefly on the effects of abrasion on tern feathers) and together we wrote a short paper on the subject for *British Birds*. Only then did we find that a European bird journal had previously carried a feature on this wing-pattern difference, so we had been beaten to it by a few years; no one, however, had, picked this up and referred to it in the field guides.

December 1973 was an especially good month for gulls, both at Blackpill, Swansea, and at the pool when I returned home again. The gull roost was turning up trumps: an immature Iceland a couple of times, then two nights with an adult (followed by first-winter glaucous and Iceland together at Blithfield). January began with the immature Iceland at Chasewater the first two nights, an adult the next. But then I was in Swansea again until April, when another totally unexpected bird came in the shape of a hooded crow – a bird far from annual in Staffordshire, and the first ever at Chasewater.

At the beginning of August 1974 I left Swansea and joined the ranks of the unemployed. Chasewater was back on the daily agenda. I wrote off for jobs, even had interviews, and worked desultorily on my research work, with little confidence or ambition; after seven years as a student, I had no strong direction. Had my postgraduate work been a great success, or had I found a good job straight away, things would clearly have been different, but as it was I stumbled on, watching wildlife. My father often says (although I can't recall it myself) that he once told me that I would never make anything of myself looking at birds. Whether or not he said it, he must have thought it often enough. Eventually, people at the DHSS felt sorry enough (or exasperated enough) to give me a job there, and for a while I worked in Lichfield, earning the princely sum of £23 a week. At last I was paying my keep and I could afford to run my old Reliant.

On 2 November 1974, we had one of those great Chasewater days that make so many ordinary visits worthwhile. I bumped into Tony Blake, but we saw many of the birds separately. There was an adult yellow-legged gull – a good bird. I missed a snow bunting and, something I had quite forgotten about, a hoopoe (another November Chasewater hoopoe some years after what remains my only one in Britain). But then there was a great grey shrike: brilliant. I had not seen one at Chasewater for a couple of winters (although I had watched one on Cannock Chase), and it was a joy to see it. While looking in vain for the hoopoe (it says in my diary) I saw a much larger bird, being chased by four or five crows. It was pale beneath, with obvious black carpal patches, and it had a slow, relaxed flight, gliding with wings in a V, sometimes suggesting a short-eared owl. But it was just flying away and I couldn't get a clear view – it was,

Common spotted orchids. Chasewater, Staffordshire, June 1975.

though, no owl and obviously a buzzard. As it tilted over, it surely showed white above the tail? Such poor views left me a bit frustrated – it was obvious what it must have been – but luckily, Tony Blake was right under the spot where it had been flying and had excellent views for several minutes. It was, he said, a perfect rough-legged buzzard – only the second I had ever seen, a first for Chasewater, and about the fourth ever for Staffordshire. A few days later I saw the fifth, on Cannock Chase, as well as one if not two great grey shrikes.

I also saw a new bird, but couldn't count it as, sadly, it was very dead: a little auk, found at Rugeley. At Chasewater I saw a bird that I had not previously seen away from the coast, a shag, which stayed several days. It was the fourth for Chasewater and the first since 1954, which gives an idea of how scarce the bird is in Staffordshire. In December, I found a Mediterranean gull in the black-headed gull roost: at last, a different 'small' gull. I had watched the black-headeds many times, hoping to find something different. I think I would have seen a Mediterranean now and then had they been regular in the roost, as it was sometimes possible to see thousands of black-headeds streaming in and to 'tick them off' as they passed by, mentally acknowledging that there was nothing different there, night after night. Now, at last, I had found a Mediterranean, although it was not my first in the county (I had found one at Blithfield in September 1972, itself a 'first' for Staffordshire).

Gull-watching took on a heightened level of intensity. Glaucous and Iceland were the stars, and many people came to see them. I joined forces most evenings with Eric and John and frequently Tony. The gulls went on through the winter into late March. In April I was watching summer water pipits and Scandinavian rock pipits. In May I added a new bird to my Chasewater list when I heard a racket from some small birds and a mistle thrush, went to investigate and flushed a tawny owl. My notes describe many calls and songs. A lesser whitethroat interested me because, apart from the book by T. A.

Coward, the usual texts said that the lesser whitethroat has no song-flight and has a soft, quiet warble audible only at very close range, before the usual hard, monotonous rattle. This one sang very vigorously with whitethroat-like phrases before each rattle and once even gave a full song-flight, including both warble and rattle. Four singing lesser whitethroats made the best ever total for the area, perhaps increasing as old hawthorn hedges became taller and more dense; a singing tree pipit was a first. Lesser whitethroats appealed to me but, as I wrote, 'unless I always see aberrant birds, I still fail to see the blackish "mask" – at best the ear coverts seem only slightly darker than the rest and any dark impression seems generally to be caused by the eye itself.' As late as 2 June three sanderlings appeared, just one in breeding plumage, on the north shore by the sailing club. Arctic, common and black terns all appeared in June, too.

My notebook is full of sketches of orchids. Common spotteds proved highly variable in flower colour and pattern (with one beautiful flower almost solid purple with sharp white edges) while marsh orchids seemed to include a few early marsh types among the majority of southern marsh flowers. Part of the main orchid colony on the black slurry beds was burned, but I could still count 850 to 900 orchids in flower at the end of June. One September day at Blithfield, with the water level low and the shore heavy with the scent of a profusion of water mint, I counted 770 small tortoiseshells, a quite phenomenal total, in a short walk (with just eight red admirals and three painted ladies). Now I tend to see far more red admirals than 'small torts', which, in the areas I visit, seem to have suffered a bit.

In August an unusual 'escape' appeared (there were not many obvious escaped birds at Chasewater) when a sacred ibis flew west. A particularly good day at Belvide, with John Fortey, produced a superb red-necked phalarope and a spotted crake, while Blithfield was good for waders, with a good scattering of curlew sandpipers and little stints, black- and bar-tailed godwits, greenshanks and spotted redshanks, turnstone and sanderling, and an unusual 13 grey plovers. It was a fine autumn. At Blithfield, there were garganeys and early pintails, my first inland little tern, Sandwich, black and Arctic terns, a regular peregrine and an osprey. At Chasewater, another escape was a Chilean flamingo, which appeared in September and stayed for months when it became injured; I half suspect it was shot. I watched it closely for a long while, escape or no, as it was a fascinating and beautiful bird, yet with a touch of the grotesque.

After earlier red-throated and black-throated divers, a great northern appeared at Chasewater in November, my first there and the first reported since 1960. It merited a lot of notes and some drawings, especially of the head and bill.

It stayed into December, then, after just a one-day gap, was replaced by a black-throated. 'That will separate the men from the boys,' said Tony Blake when I told him. It got far more notes than the great northern. At that time, too, there were fine birds such as red-crested pochard, velvet scoter (excellent inland), scaup, two Iceland gulls and yellow-legged gulls, and great grey shrikes. It was a classic Chasewater year.

These notes could go on for ever. In subsequent years, gulls were always good, with regular glaucous and Icelands. The usual thing was to sit in the car and listen to the football on the radio while watching the roost gather. It was then a race against time, in the fading light, to try to find anything interesting amongst many thousands of black-headed gulls and perhaps two or three thousand herrings and lesser black-backs. At its peak, the roost contained 4,500 lessers and two or three thousand herrings; gradually great black-backeds built up to the several hundreds before a long, slow decline in all the big gulls. They were enjoyable purely aesthetically, these black, white and grey gulls against the water and sky, sometimes paler, sometimes darker, with endless exciting lighting effects, often against the backdrop of a fine sunset. I never tired of watching them, and the reward was usually there in the shape of a glaucous or two, an Iceland or two, or some new, strange variation in herring or yellow-legged gulls. These variations, the way the birds behaved, the way the roosting birds arranged themselves, often with older birds in the centre and younger birds at the edges – even the way that something unusual might seem 'out of tune' with the rest, so that a glaucous, or perhaps a Mediterranean, might be left at one end of the flock as the rest moved about, or left on the water after everything else had flown up – all this gave me enough material for several notes and papers in *British Birds* and my later lectures on gulls around the bird clubs, as well as for reams of notes in my books. For example, one extract from a 1975 diary reads:

> I settled in for a gull-roost watch but had little hope of seeing much because a powerboat was on the water. The early roost didn't develop but in a group of gulls which appeared as early as 3 o'clock was an Iceland – why can't it come in so early on a quiet weekday? It drifted away to the north. At 3.45 another flew in – by that time there was no boat and several hundred gulls were on the pool near the northern end [I was at the southern end]. I drove round to the west side for a closer view but the Iceland was definitely not on the water. The roost remained quite small and well to the north of the middle of the pool [where it might normally form], though the boat had

Iceland gull at dusk.

long gone. It seems very strange that if the first arrivals are not allowed to settle in the centre the roost never really develops properly, as if the birds can't recover from the initial disruption. The late arrivals cannot know about the earlier disturbance but either join the birds in the northern part or just drift off elsewhere – why do they not settle in the centre as usual?

Another extract:

I saw a first-year Mediterranean gull. Though I say it myself (but wouldn't say it to anyone else of course) I think it was pretty good – I saw it fly in over the western side, from the road close to the south shore car park [a mile away] and felt pretty certain of it from long-range flight views before it settled well towards the northern end. I then drove round and confirmed it. One of my best 'spots'. The fifth for Staffordshire, my third!

Thirty years on I can allow myself to boast a bit, for this was a small, not particularly easy, gull, amongst several thousand others, in dull light, at very long range. At this period, after countless hours watching gulls at Chasewater and much experience of Mediterraneans at Blackpill, I was 'at my best'. People will often say 'Oh, you must have good eyesight' or 'Your binoculars are much better than mine'. I'm sure I need not say what I think about such comments. I know very well what my abilities are and where my limitations lie. I know, too, when I have found something more creditable; that is really satisfying, and such was the case with this 1975 Mediterranean gull.

The mid-1970s proved to be a brilliant period for me at Chasewater. I found other birds from time to time, to keep the Chasewater list going, such as red-footed falcon and white-winged black tern, while some regulars, such as the twites and shrikes, petered out. I still went to Chasewater very often, even after I'd moved to live in Bedfordshire in 1978. The old place produced a first for Britain — a first for Europe! — in the shape of John Fortey's lesser scaup, which I went to see in spring 1987.

It still produces the goods: as I write there are five velvet scoters and a glaucous gull, and last year a red-necked phalarope hung about for a long time. Graham Evans and his group maintain impeccable records. Yet, for me, something has been lost: the wildness, the roughness of it, the sense of discovery. And once you have a job, a mortgage, a wife and responsibilities, things inevitably change. The intensity of my birdwatching in school and student days could never continue, but to have been so close to Chasewater was a piece of good fortune that can never be overestimated.

Swansea and the Gower

Swansea Bay is a marvellous sweep of mud and sand backed by rolling hills each side of the Tawe valley. Swansea fills the low space where the Tawe rather hesitantly gives itself up to the sea. Dylan Thomas's old seaside town spills up and over the hills to the west; compared with how it was when I lived there, it has spread much farther north and the centre has been developed out of all recognition. Much of it was already relatively new, having been blitzed into oblivion during the war and since rebuilt. To the west, a great block of limestone – a vanilla slice topped with several ridges of red sandstone that stand up above the green pastureland as rough, heathy hills – hangs off the middle of the South Wales coast: the Gower peninsula. To the west of that is Carmarthen Bay; to the north is the long, triangular estuary of the River Loughour, the Burry Inlet, half cut off by a great spit of dunes and marsh from the south, Whiteford Burrows. It is a wonderful place for a geographer and naturalist.

My first visit to Swansea had been from school, on a geography field trip, when we were based at the university in September 1966. So when I decided to apply for university, Swansea was my first choice. Despite the horrors of what was then UCCA forms (Universities Central Council on Admissions) – even the paper they used seemed strange and disturbing – I applied for a course in geography. I was interviewed at Hull and then offered a place without interview at Swansea. The university is on the western edge of Swansea, where the shore runs west-south-west and begins to curl southwards to the little notch that is the exit of Black Pill (better known as Blackpill), a small stream from the Clyne valley. The outer limit of the university grounds had a pond (the 'physics pond', as I would come to call it, where I might later sometimes see a water rail and once found a storm-blown and exceptionally tame common scoter). From here you could pop out of the gate, across the road and under a little culvert onto the beach. Or you could walk along the road towards Blackpill between the beach and the university playing fields, where gulls and waders often gathered if the tide was especially high.

On the first day, I had a few moments to walk from the college campus to the beach. A short walk down to the main road and across a narrow strip of dunes took me to the edge of Swansea Bay. The bay curves round beautifully with the humps of Mumbles Head at the outer end. Far beyond that, on a good day, could be seen the low, grey shape of Exmoor; on a really good day, with my telescope, I could watch farmers ploughing their fields in Devon. The bay, like everywhere else, is now scheduled for development into a windfarm. All I noted on this first expedition were oystercatchers and five species of gull, although I later queried lesser black-backed – I'd probably put it down out of habit. The next day I investigated a little more. As the tide rose, birds gathered on sandbanks opposite Black Pill to the south-west. Whenever I go anywhere – whether it be to see birds, or to go to a grand prix, a concert, or an air show, whatever it might be – I suffer from nervous tension, as if the thing I am going to see might be gone before we get there. I have to rush. People with me are always saying slow down, wait for us, but I need to get there before whatever it is disappears. As I saw Blackpill and its birds, I felt the same thing: I wondered if, in my next three years at Swansea, I might be able to get there and see the birds some time. Would they still be around at the weekend? It looked a mile or so away. Might I manage to get that far from the college? Dare I walk on the beach?

Sandwich terns, 660 oystercatchers, chiffchaffs and a grey wagtail promised better things. And two days later I went back to the beach and walked towards Blackpill to see what I could see. I knew nothing about the area, having done no homework on the birds of Swansea Bay – I'd not seen a local bird report, or spoken to anyone who had been there. It was a case of starting from scratch, finding the right places for myself and seeing what birds turned up. I'm not really sure how, back home in Staffordshire, I could have done much in the way of preparation – no websites, back then. It was not difficult. Anyone could see that this was a bay full of gulls and waders and that Blackpill was the high-tide roost. But I can't imagine doing it the same way now, without knowing quite well where to go and what to expect in advance.

Fortunately I was walking to Blackpill as the tide came in, so I was treated to a show by hundreds of waders – more than are there now. So my regular walks to Blackpill began and after a couple of weeks I walked out as far as Mumbles Head, a good eight-mile return walk unless, as I sometimes did, I took the bus one way and walked back. (Later I did it by bike until the beloved Falcon Black Diamond, with real Italian Campagnolo gears, was stolen and the £19 insurance

When a flock of black-headed gulls takes off, and the clean white under-wing of a Mediterranean gull catches the eye, it is always an exciting moment.

payout was insufficient to replace it.) At Blackpill the little stream wound out between concrete banks and spilled onto the beach in a broad, shallow gleam of water, which varied over the years as the combined effects of the stream and the tides constantly changed the detailed topography of the sand. Here the sand-flats between high and low tide can be a full mile wide, but a few hundred yards from solid land were long, low banks of purer sand, parallel to the beach, which are the last bits of beach to be covered at high tide; often they were not covered at all. The edge of the beach itself here is just a little higher than elsewhere, so Blackpill is naturally the spot to which all the bay's waders and gulls resort twice a day when they are forced off the sand-flats by the incoming sea.

At Blackpill the beach, stony now, takes a further turn almost due south, as far as Oystermouth, where the long, tapered spike of Mumbles Head swings south-east, to complete the enclosure of the western half of Swansea Bay west of Swansea Docks and the Tawe. Mumbles is a ridge of limestone, which falls almost sheer to the bay, with a narrow ledge along its foot occupied by a road and the old railway track, making good walking all the way from Blackpill to Mumbles Pier. The road sweeps up above the pier and pops out over the top to give a magnificent view from the coastguard area above Bracelet Bay, fresh and windswept and wonderful. Beyond the pier are two islands, the Middle Head and Mumbles Head proper, with its squat white lighthouse.

My first less than usual bird was an eider, under the pier at Mumbles, but more impressive by far that day was the sea in a strong westerly gale: it was sensational and something I have never tired of watching over the years. Being able to watch the sea is something I've missed ever since, living, once again, a couple of hours' hard drive from any coast. The day of the eider, I met Jerry Tallowin and Pete Garvey, my first encounter with birdwatchers in Swansea. It gave me someone to talk to about birds and we soon found that there were half a dozen people around who were pretty keen. None of us, though, had any contact as yet with local birdwatchers, although Pete was just about on nodding acquaintance with one or two, and Jerry had been out with scientists studying the Burry Inlet oystercatchers as part of the controversy over the effects of oystercatchers on the cockling industry there.

A year or so later the three of us went out on the Burry with the oystercatcher ringing team, led by Peter Davidson of the Ministry of Agriculture, Fisheries and Food. I was sceptical, as I thought Davidson represented the 'pro cull' side of the oystercatcher–cockle argument and I felt uncomfortable about giving them a hand. We met in the warden's hut at Whiteford and drove out to Weobley on Llanrhidian Marsh, then out across the marsh to an old tower at the edge of the open mudflats. This was a good spot to look for a roosting peregrine. The old brick tower stood up on piers and was reached by a rickety old ladder. Several hundred yards from the tower we set out eight cannon nets intended to catch roosting oystercatchers. We rolled out the nets, sorted out leader lines and weights and dug them in; then Jerry and I tested the circuits on each of 24 cannons, which would launch the nets over the birds. These were also dug in and connected in a single circuit, ready for firing. Each cannon was about 30 or 36 inches long and we camouflaged them as best we could with bits of spartina. After wiring the whole lot up to our base in the tower, we retreated to The Greyhound at Old Walls (something that had completely gone out of my head, rediscovered in a diary) to recover from four hours' work in rain, mud and cold wind. Everything, ourselves included, was covered in wet, grating sand.

Later Pete, Jerry and I were left in the tower while the others went to meet representatives from the Wildfowlers' Association of Great Britain and Ireland (WAGBI) and the Nature Conservancy, who attended as observers (quite why the wildfowlers were there I'm not sure). We all communicated by radio as dusk began to fall and the oystercatchers started to arrive in their thousands, many settling near the farther nets but all avoiding the nearer ones, some of which looked conspicuously white. Then the whole lot moved off; Peter Davidson, in his Land Rover, drove them back, although none came into the firing area. It was all to no avail. The tide was coming in strong and fast, aided by the westerly wind. Whether there had been a miscalculation I don't know, but the nets and cannons were all flooded and the exercise was rendered useless. To cap it all, I was standing on the ladder beneath the tower and had the main battery and firing gear passed down to me, which slipped from my cold, numbed hand and fell into a pool of salt water. So ended my one and only effort to cannon-net waders. In a way, I think we were all glad not to have several thousand oystercatchers to put in canvas bags ready for 'processing' in the dark.

I was lucky in that the room I had been allocated at the university was in Neuadd Sibly, a hall of residence at the back of the campus, looking across Singleton Park. Homesickness had been instant from the time I arrived, and it was slow to subside, but I was enjoying Swansea Bay, exploring the beach along from the college via Blackpill to Mumbles whenever I could, and getting in walks around Singleton Park as often as possible, too. The park is a large one, with huge expanses of grass separated by bands of mature trees and ornamental gardens. In the autumn it was glorious. For a time I made regular circuits, counting every bird I saw on a fixed route; it would be fascinating to go back and repeat the exercise. On the bay I was counting the waders regularly, but the birds' own movements around the bay and the frequent disturbance from walkers on the beach could be frustrating. How often in the next few years would I get three-quarters of the way through a wader flock several thousand strong, only to see the whole lot fly up and readjust their position as the tide rose a little too high, or see a new flock fly in and settle amongst those I had already counted, or watch a dog chase through them and send them off beyond Swansea Docks? Nothing for it but to start again ...

Steadily I found out more about the local birds. I was told that two snow buntings had been at Blackpill, but I'd missed them. I was still birdwatching on my own and seeing the others back at college, or purely by chance, rather than going out with them. Fortunately the snow buntings were back the next day; I watched them for a long while and took detailed notes, over several days. Another student birdwatcher was Adrian Lewis, a geologist, whose friend Pete Curry was a student at Cardiff. Pete came over to see the snow buntings – they were quite a draw – and I remember his strong West Country accent and big Stetson-style hat as we watched them in dreary rain and wind. Later he was to work for several years in Australia and contribute a good deal to the knowledge of birds there.

I believe Pete carried an umbrella. It was years before I ever used an umbrella while birdwatching – it had never seemed practical – but then I discovered that it was perfectly possible to watch birds while sheltered from a downpour beneath one. When I wrote a book on how to watch birds, I put in a paragraph about this, but it was deemed to be so odd that it was edited out. This is a feature of writing books that I got to know well: you put something in that isn't in any other books because it is a bit different and it gets cut out because it isn't in any other books … Meanwhile, people will pay hundreds of pounds for waterproof jackets when they might buy an umbrella for a fiver and watch birds quite happily without getting wet.

By mid-November my notes refer to Blackpill four or five times a week: I had settled into a routine between lectures, despite persistent rough and rainy weather. It still surprises me how little I had seen up to then despite some years of continuous effort back home. I just wasn't used to some of the birds I was now seeing. One day my book says, 'a real quality list!' It was an interesting day, but nothing so special. I saw the snow buntings, then walked up the valley behind Blackpill and found a blackcap (a bird I had not seen before in November, so 'wintering blackcap' was good), four or five siskins (which I really rated – great little birds), a dipper (unusual) and a buzzard. Fine views of a great spotted woodpecker and a male bullfinch in bright sunshine cheered me up, too. I was probably still struggling with being away from home and seizing on good views of common birds to enthuse about even more than I might normally have done.

On 17 November I went out to Whiteford Point. This must have been with Pete Garvey and probably a few others who were in their second year at Swansea and knew the place already. It might well have been our first day out with Mike Goddard, now wing commander (retired), who, wonder of wonders, had wheels! He owned a battered Ford Anglia van and, with one passenger in front and three or four squeezed in the back, we had some productive trips out together. For me, Whiteford Point and Llanrhidian Marshes were all new and marvellous, although the huge open spaces, and the fact that the tide was rising and things were becoming interesting just as we had to leave, made it difficult to get to grips with. The best birds were red-breasted mergansers, a couple of brent geese and two excellent Slavonian grebes. This was a breakthrough in my exploration of the Gower proper and an introduction to the woods, dunes, marshes, creeks and sandy beaches of the northern shore, the whole complex of the Burry Inlet, which we were to explore so often.

The following weekend we journeyed even farther: Cors Tregaron! It was a lousy wet day, horribly dismal, but ravens, buzzards, a great grey shrike (quite a find) and a red kite made it special. The kite was my first ever. At that time there were not many kites in Wales; to see one was quite an event. Now people can drive up to a farm, where kites are fed, and watch 200 at a time. I can't help feeling that although the success of the kites is phenomenal, it is almost too easy. I am reminded of Bernard Venables's words about the child's first wriggling perch. On later days at Tregaron we would see five or six kites, usually one or two at really close range, which were magnificent, but mostly at long range over the surrounding hills. I never took my binoculars off them as long as they remained in view. These were, after all, some of the rarest birds in Britain, with a long and difficult history of persecution and protection, as well as being amongst the most attractive and spectacular.

This first trip to Cors Tregaron was a poor day, really. There were, we were later told, six kites and four or five hen harriers around in the valley, and peregrine, merlin, red and black grouse and whooper swans should have been likely as well. This information came from Pete Curry and the Cardiff birdwatchers, via Adrian Lewis. But I was happy with my kite, my 200th bird. Within a few years, I'd be expecting my 200th species of the year before May! On 4 October 1969 I saw a red-crested pochard, perhaps an escape, but new for me anyway – and my 200th bird of the year: things were changing fast. That year finished with statistics that I now find amazing. It was the first year in which I saw 200 birds (about 203), but they were from a total life-list (over several years) of just 217; only 14 of my life-list were missing from that year's list and yet I had added only 14 new ones.

My next new bird followed soon afterwards. I'd heard that there might be purple sandpipers on the rocky island that supported Mumbles lighthouse. With Pete Garvey, who was fast becoming my regular birdwatching companion, I went out there at low tide and searched the rocks with no success. Fortunately we walked on into Bracelet Bay and found a purple sandpiper with a large group of turnstones finding food amongst the seaweedy rocks and bursting spray at the edge of the tide. I was impressed. It was not quite as I had expected from the field-guide illustrations (less plump, rather browner and paler below, legs and bill base more yellow-orange than yellow) – for a 'dull little bird' the sandpiper was a gem. Purple sandpipers have a real individual character and their subtle plumage patterns are lovely.

As we stood on Blackpill beach, Adrian Lewis turned to Pete Curry and said, 'Eh, Pete, would you believe it, he's seen 200 species and still hasn't seen a white-fronted goose!' Adrian meant that 200 species was quite impressive: it was the lack of the goose that shocked him. Well, Pete and Adrian were from near Bristol and used to going to Slimbridge, so white-fronted geese were standard fare. But where would I have seen a white-front? I hadn't been to Slimbridge and white-fronts were rare in the West Midlands, so I was hardly likely to have seen one; but there was a place, not far from Swansea ...

On 7 December, only a couple of months after my arrival, we went to Llandeilo in the Towy (Tywi) valley, and on foot to Golden Grove. We walked from the bridge in Llandeilo along a disused railway track, looking out across the flat fields of the river floodplain hemmed in between low and attractive hills each side. This was a remarkably rich place for birds; it is not nearly so good, now, even though the landscapes of South Wales remain beautiful. There were 11 white-fronted geese, and they received my standard asterisk and (New Bird) accolade as the first I had ever seen. However, better by far were 2,000 golden plovers and 1,000 lapwings, and the list was amplified by 175 curlews, a green sandpiper, four buzzards, three dippers, a kingfisher, a brambling, willow tits, and an assortment of finches, wagtails and pipits. The geese were seen briefly as they flew over the valley – viewed well enough to identify them but a disappointment considering that 800 were there in January 1967. (I must by now have been looking at Welsh bird reports or something similar to get this information.) It was the flocks of plovers streaming up and down the valley that remain vivid in the memory. On later visits we did much better with the geese – seeing up to 1,200 or so – with a few barnacle, pink-footed and bean geese with the white-fronts. Sadly, this outposted flock has gone, now, as white-fronts have largely withdrawn from Britain into the Low Countries in winter.

We explored our surroundings as best we could every weekend. Birds were not exactly an escape, but certainly a welcome break from days and nights of work, and I could certainly escape from other pressures – from the awkwardness of this new life – into things I was good at. The students' bar had awful beer at a shilling and eightpence a pint (more expensive Youngers Tartan was an option only if one of the tutors bought us a drink, which was rare), and I couldn't afford much or to go very often. Student life generally was not something I took to. While the music was great, I was glad next morning to escape from the terrors of the disco and terminal shyness and get out in the wind and rain to see some birds – to be where I felt I belonged.

In mid-January, I returned to the Burry Inlet at Penclawdd and the magnificent Llanrhidian Marsh. My notes begin:

A day which involved long walking and much difficult going through Llanrhidian Marsh, in driving rain and a freezing cold wind for much of the time. We walked right across the marsh, having many difficult creeks to cross and innumerable ditches and pools.

I was never that keen on a hard day in the field like this, although I loved the marshes. For me, the best part was often towards the end of the day, when we walked up the steep slope from the base of Whiteford Point to Cwm Ivy to get the bus, and paused to look back. Far out over the grey marsh, Whiteford Point's iron lighthouse stood out in the grey sea; white surf rolled in against the beach and could just be heard as a low, uniform roar. The marsh was vast and dark, split by innumerable creeks, flat and always quiet and still whatever the weather, solid as rock. Below us, horses turned their backs to the wind in the green, muddy meadows, while a buzzard or a raven might fly over in the last of the winter's afternoon light. It remains a memorable image: a scene of great tranquillity, perfect peace after a hard day out, miles of walking in mud that sucked your boots off – better still if there were a few good birds safely in the notebook. Then we would ride back on the bus and dash – usually Pete and I – to the snack bar just before it closed, to feast on a pasty and the last of the half-solid baked beans or, if we were unlucky, a potato croquette and chips. That would be the main meal of the day, blowing the budget.

It was with Pete that I saw my next new bird, along the cliffs west of Mumbles as we walked towards Langland Bay one day in late January. A gull came by. Look at that, cream wing-tips, big pink bill with a black tip – a glaucous gull. I later referred to the 1967 Welsh Bird Report (a very flimsy offprint of a few pages) and found that there were no Iceland gulls and only one glaucous in Wales that year: this must be good! Although I wrote it up as an 'immature' my notes and painting show that it was a second-winter, with a clear grey back, the rest being mostly 'Morning Coffee biscuit coloured'. The second glaucous I ever saw, also in Wales, was to be the following April, in Saundersfoot Harbour, while I was on a geology field trip. It flew by, then circled and landed on the beach, as we were being told about the geological interest along the shore.

Whiteford, if the tide was right, proved a great place for seeing small numbers of birds such as red-breasted mergansers, common scoters, eiders, the occasional long-tailed duck or scaup, goldeneyes, Slavonian and black-necked (rarely red-necked) grebes, and great northern divers. These would drift in with the tide and back out again an hour or two later, often close in, in front of a ramshackle hide built into a hooked dune on so-called Berges Island. On the walk to and from the point there was a good chance of a hen harrier, sometimes a merlin or a peregrine, and usually stacks of wigeon, knots, bar-tailed godwits and the like. A small flock of brent geese was established in the area and would grow in numbers over the years. We had some brilliant days. In summer, too, Whiteford was superb, with a great variety of butterflies and rare flowers in the dune slacks to search for; there were fen orchids, as well as marvellous shows of colour from spotted and marsh orchids, marsh helleborines, centauries, rest-harrow, bloody cranesbill and stacks more.

February 1969 was quite a month for weather. It opened with increasing cloud in light north-westerly winds that quickly turned to near gale force in the late morning, with heavy showers of rain and sleet. My diary says that, out at Whiteford Point, it was cold with winds force 8 or even 9, heavy showers and hailstorms; we arrived just as the longest, heaviest shower passed over. The next day dawned a lovely Sunday with sunshine (although overnight frost had left ice on the puddles), but by mid-afternoon it had turned much colder and had begun to snow heavily. Little settled in the park or around the university buildings but the roofs up on Town Hill were all white. The next day was calm and clear, Exmoor very clear and covered in snow, then a crisp night sky with a full moon and brilliant Jupiter.

The week continued with calm, sunny spells between squalls and storms of rain, but on Saturday 8 February it snowed. There was a foot or so in Swansea and heavy snowfall all over Britain. I awoke to see the unexpected brightness of snow through the closed curtains and a magical world across Singleton Park, followed by a brilliant morning with blue skies and bright sunshine. The trees in the park were astonishing, all covered in snow, bright orange-white on the sunlit side, cold blue in shadow. Not for the first time I gave up any real attempt to describe the effect in my diary and wrote 'indescribable – superbly beautiful' in the hope that it would evoke something of it and emphasize the exceptional conditions. It was, luckily, a Saturday, and I watched the movements of thousands of birds overhead, heading west to escape the severe weather. In a couple of hours I had seen up to 10,000 redwings, 5,000 to 10,000 skylarks, 100 fieldfares, 200 starlings and 3,500 lapwings go over, as well as small numbers of assorted finches and meadow pipits. I went down to the beach and watched an exhausted skylark heading in across the waves. Every few seconds it settled on the water for up to eight seconds at a time. Eventually it was heading parallel to the beach, seemingly unable to make any headway towards safety and, after one more dip in the sea, it drowned.

By half past eight the next morning, it was snowing heavily beneath a lead-grey, hazy sky that seemed to be full of snow. Pete Garvey, Robin Woods and I caught the bus west towards Whiteford but it could get no farther than

Oldwalls, beyond Llanrhidian. We were reassured by the driver that things would not get worse, that he would tell the inspector that we were 'out there', and that the bus would get through at least as far as Oldwalls for 7.15 that evening to bring us back. So we walked on to Cwm Ivy and down to Whiteford Point in deep snow, then back to Oldwalls by 7.15, but no bus came. We phoned the bus station and heard that all services were running; certainly the roads were by now quite passable. Eventually we walked a few miles farther back and by good fortune found a bus at Llanrhidian. The day was all in all pretty good for a February day. According to my notes, there were 69 species seen and two or three heard. The list included woodcock and jack snipe, merlin and hen harrier, Slavonian (two) and black-necked grebes (nine), and a bullfinch that distinguished itself by singing. I've still heard very few bullfinches singing. It made 'a double pipe, low and vibrant like a policeman's whistle, followed by faint warbling and creaking noises'. It was in the wood beneath the tor near Cwm Ivy and I remember it well.

In the Clyne valley, behind Blackpill, a small stream or ditch ran beneath a clump of alders. In the tops there might be siskins, sometimes quite a good flock; underneath I discovered water rails. These were great birds. I watched them very closely and took a lot of notes. It was all part of getting to know a new set of species well and building on the progress I had made at Chasewater, which had been fine but had left a lot of gaps. Moving to a new area, with new habitats, was crucially important. Whiteford was the place where I could really sort out my grebes and divers. Here I was sketching them, finding them in intermediate plumages between winter and summer, learning for myself – not just from the books – how to separate them. The small grebes (Slavonian and black-necked) were often sailing by at speed but quite close as they came in on the tide, the sunlight sparkling in their cherry-red eyes, sometimes even highlighting the curious white inner ring of the iris. What views we had. We were getting to Whiteford almost every weekend now. But my notes were equally about the pre-roost flights of hundreds of jackdaws over Cwm Ivy woods, the way that redwings hopped about and fed like song thrushes scattered evenly across a meadow, the songs of marsh tits and dippers, the display flights of collared doves and the timidity of these doves when chased by a house sparrow.

So far my birdwatching had been confined largely to Blackpill, Mumbles and the Gower, and only limited bits of the Gower at that. It was not until the following May that we first ventured east to Kenfig Pool and Eglwys Nunnydd Reservoir, which were then still quiet and undisturbed (before the M4 motorway was built along one side). These were very much in the province of the Cardiff birdwatchers. Gower- or Swansea-based people rarely seemed to go, if at all, and this was indicative of an uncomfortable relationship, then, between the Gower Ornithological Society (which published its own report) and the Cardiff Nats (who incorporated Gower records in their comprehensive Glamorgan bird report). Sometimes, we students became embroiled a little in these local politics as we were bold enough to try to deal with both sides. We also looked at the new Port Talbot breakwater, designed to allow much bigger ore-carrying ships into the steelworks. Built of gigantic boulders, it apparently attracted some interesting birds, including little gulls. One time we drove in with Mike Goddard past the security policeman on the gate, who agreed to 'turn a blind eye'. On the way out, although we could have driven away, Mike thought he would acknowledge this kindness, so he made a point of catching the policeman's attention and waving to him; unfortunately, it was a different policeman, and we were stopped and hauled in for questioning.

At Blackpill the waders were in splendid summer plumage, and kittiwakes began to come in and sit about on the beach. By the end of May there were 480 of them – remarkable, for this flat, sandy beach, far from any nesting colony. A young little gull hung around with the young kittiwakes, a bit of a needle in a haystack. In June, kittiwakes increased to more than 500, with two young little gulls.

There were several regular birdwatchers at Swansea now and we organized ourselves into a society within the Students' Union, not least because we could then hire the union minibus to get us to places such as Whiteford and Tregaron more easily. We had a meeting and, by virtue of drawing a short straw, I was elected chairman. Soon we were officially recognized by the union, I drew up some posters, and we had an inaugural meeting. It went very well, attracting a surprising 28 people on a Friday lunchtime. We later had some posters properly designed and printed by the union print room. I wrote to 'Hargreaves' who was famous for his cartoon birds in *Punch* and asked if he might send a sketch for the poster. He sent some excellent drawings of one of his 'birds', one proudly showing off a sparkling new ring on its leg, another eyeing a worm, about to disappear into its burrow, also with a shiny ring; I have them on the wall beside me, as I write this, 35 years later.

Our field trips were mostly excellent, although there were one or two odd people coming along. One strange girl used to borrow our telescopes but was unable to see the details we were pointing out. Eventually she gave up and said 'It's all right for you, this telescope is only in black and white.' For a while we organized visiting speakers and entertained David Saunders from Marloes, near

Haverfordwest (a pity the handle came off the door of Mike's van in David's hand), David Hunt from the Isles of Scilly and Peter Davis, the great kite expert and past warden of Fair Isle, who attracted 110 people. But our funds, enthusiasm and list of potential speakers ran out pretty soon. Eric Hosking, the great bird photographer, replied that he had given up public speaking long ago, as he would be so overwhelmed by requests, but sent me an order form for his new book. Spike Milligan (via his agent, Norma Farnes – how did I get the address?) said he would love to come but was just about to go off to Australia. We generally resorted to slide shows from our own members (Mike Goddard's bird-ringing on Fair Isle, Robin Woods's studies on the Falklands); few people came to see them and it all petered out.

Despite this, there was a genuine feeling that we ought to raise awareness of conservation issues. I remember buying a cheap paperback about what would now be called 'green' ideas – everything from saving petrol, water and electricity to buying rubber dustbin lids to reduce neighbourhood noise – and putting a poster in the union building encouraging everyone to buy a copy. There was, at that time, generally very little awareness that anything like this mattered, or ever would. As part of our geography course we had a visiting lecturer who argued quite sincerely that the answer to all the world's pollution problems was to burn everything and send the smoke up in giant chimneys to disgorge into the air, to let the atmosphere take care of it: he believed that the atmosphere (like the seas) was so vast that we could just throw anything and everything into it and it would all be absorbed and neutralized. But I had recently read of puffins in the middle of the Atlantic being poisoned by PCBs – which got there precisely by being released into the atmosphere through smoke – and felt that the 'what goes up must come down' argument was more telling. In a tutorial (one tutor and three or four of us students) I mentioned that penguins in the Antarctic were being found with all kinds of pollutants in their bodies, but this was pooh-poohed by the others – who cares about penguins? – but fortunately not by the tutor, Mr Rouse, who could see the implications.

Contact with the 'locals' was difficult at first. For some reason Pete and I called in to see Bob Howells, the Gower Ornithological Society (GOS) chairman, but he was out, at a GOS meeting in Swansea. We thumbed a lift into town and belatedly got to the meeting in the museum, then had a lift back with Harold Grenfell, who (according to my diary) 'never spoke and did not acknowledge any of our records or my recent letter', which was probably about roseate terns on the beach at Blackpill (I had submitted them for inclusion in the local records but the committee rejected them as uncertain). These diary entries seem funny now: Harold and I later became good friends, only occasionally meeting but frequently corresponding.

Bob Howells was a real phenomenon. Single-handedly he has counted the waders, wildfowl and gulls at Blackpill and on the whole of the Burry Inlet for decades. He was at Blackpill almost daily. Once I offered to help him with the bird counts on the Burry Inlet. He looked a little unsure about this and then told me he wanted help only from people who could tell a common gull from a black-headed gull, which even then I thought was a bit harsh. But I'd been put in my place. It was a year or two before we also became pretty firm friends. Certainly I have huge admiration for Bob's work – and he did treat it almost as work. He said, for example, that he didn't ever go to Kenfig or Eglwys Nunnydd 'because other people cover them'. He was interested in recording birds in important areas and dedicated his birdwatching to doing just that, as accurately and as often as possible, in the course of which he has produced a most remarkable series of counts. He was less interested, it seemed, in just birdwatching for the pleasure of it, in the way that I was, although he enjoyed what he was doing every bit as much.

The pattern was set for the next few years: intense watching at Blackpill, frequent visits to Mumbles and, as often as possible, to the Gower (with greater concentration on Oxwich as well as the Burry and, now and then, a trip to Rhossili and Worm's Head), with days farther afield usually focused on Llandeilo or Tregaron. January 1970 boosted my geese a bit, with 1,500 white-fronts at Llandeilo and 16 pink-feet (new) and three barnacles (also new) there, followed by three to four thousand white-fronts, a bean goose (new), two barnacles, and a brent at Slimbridge. Waders increased at Blackpill, as did the purple sandpipers at Mumbles, and we seemed to see much more at Whiteford as a rule, although there were still some duff days. My old friend, a great grey shrike, turned up at Oxwich, only the third Gower record.

In April 1970 I was delighted to see more little gulls at Blackpill, up to 15 of them, perhaps linked with those at Margam breakwater. Detailed notes and sketches compared all the various faded and mottled plumage patterns of young little gulls with similar stages in the Blackpill beach kittiwake flock. But 10 May that year was a bit of a turning point: Pete Garvey and I found an odd gull on the beach. It had us puzzled, although Pete had a pretty good idea what it was. My notes are quite extensive, and sketches show the bird at rest and in flight. It was a first-summer Mediterranean gull – a new species for us both – and we spent ages watching it. At the time, this was quite something. This very first bird had all the character that Mediterranean gulls later displayed in full at Blackpill:

the thick, droopy bill, a 'pirate patch' through the eye, a high-stepping walk and run, aggression to other gulls (rushing at kittiwakes, common gulls and black-headeds with stabbing pecks), and a mixture of features between first-year common and black-headed gulls. We looked for it again but couldn't find it for some days (although I did find a female Kentish plover, a scarce bird then, a real rarity now). It was back again on the 23rd. Its head had developed much more dark coloration (it is possible it was a different one, but more likely that summer plumage was still developing fast). Already, close scrutiny over long periods had given us a real feel for the species: from a puzzling bird at first, it had become 'unlike any other bird on the beach' and full of Mediterranean character and charisma. It was seen on four more days, then disappeared, but then along came a second Kentish plover, this time a male – this was a good spring.

All of this was punctuated by a trip out from Mumbles Pier on the boat that used to give pleasure cruises in summer around the Bristol Channel. We did the Swansea–Ilfracombe–Lundy–Ilfracombe–Swansea section and (as in subsequent summers) saw a handful of storm petrels mid-Channel, then ten between Lundy and Ilfracombe on the return trip. These were the principal targets for the venture and Pete and I were delighted with them – they remain favourite birds. One year, too, Pete and I took the ferry to Cork and back, in October, and saw some good birds including fabulous great shearwaters.

We went too infrequently to Oxwich (purple heron was a good find, a rarity then, and later bearded tits), and to Rhossili and Worm's Head (marvellous for scoter flocks, a few breeding seabirds and many purple sandpipers), to the Gower downs (where long, whaleback ridges gave phenomenal vistas across the Burry into South Wales and out over the channel to Lundy and mainland Devon), and to the south Gower cliffs. One wonderful evening I spent an hour or two on Cefn Bryn, listening for nightjars, as the sun went down beyond Worm's Head and Lundy and all the pinpoint flashes of lighthouses and light ships along the Bristol Channel came on, one after the other. Worm's Head on a rough day was exhilarating, even if sometimes we didn't appreciate it.

After missing both breakfast and lunch, Pete and I went to Rhossili. Dull, not very brilliant, but some spectacular waves in Rhossili Bay and just south of the Crabart. Also, a spectacular show by the Worm's Head blowhole, spray rising to a full 200 feet and spreading in the wind.

Unfortunately it was cold and uncomfortable, too windy in most places and, by Kitchen Corner, though to some extent sheltered, difficult to sit and look out – the ground all at steep angles and often rather jagged, the birds seen very poorly at great distances. I had a nail sticking in my foot, had no food to speak of and had paid out over 6 shillings for this – not the greatest of successes. Joined the Scottish Ornithologists Club (10/-).

Six shillings on a bus fare and a ten-shilling subscription made that a pricey day. That January (1970) my grant was £98. 18s. 1d., of which £61. 13s. 4d. went immediately on the hall fees. By the following autumn the fees had gone up by £5 but the grant had gone down to £89. 13s. 4d. Amy Heathcote, the county recorder in Cardiff, sent me a copy of the annual bird report and I posted her 5s. 6d. for it, including postage; she returned it, saying it was a complimentary copy for the university society as a thank you for all our records.

There were not enough weekends for everything and, for most of the time, no transport apart from the bus services. No, it was Whiteford and Blackpill that caught my imagination most, with a small sprinkling of birds, flowers and butterflies from the local woods and, especially, the beaches, cliffs and limestone ridge of Mumbles. From my room in the third year in Neuadd Sibly I could see out across the bay and even identify common scoters offshore. I watched the ships beyond Mumbles and those that came in to Swansea Docks, and I bought the *Evening Post* once a week on the day that it published the expected arrivals and their various tonnages. With my telescope I could read their names and watch the comings and goings of the dock pilot in his yellow cutter. Everything about the sea and the shore seemed to be fascinating. Mumbles was a rough bit of land, really, but great for such things as common and small blues, brown arguses and dark green fritillaries, and a variety of lovely limestone plants. One day I found some bee orchids there. Back at the university, I went to tell Martin Davies, but he was out, so I left a note and sketch map. He went off to see them and saw, instead, seven *bee-eaters*. That hardly seemed fair.

Another new intake of birdwatchers saw the best by far of the Swansea students of that era, Keith Vinicombe, arrive from Bristol. Keith was clearly in a different league, but he lived in a hall near Blackpill, not in the main campus, so we saw relatively little of each other except on the odd trip or at Blackpill itself. Martin Davies, who still works at the RSPB in the next building to me, was there, too, and Dave Waugh, known for his international conservation work, was a long-time friend and colleague. Dave and I once found a huge angler fish dead on the beach; there would sometimes be small ones, and lumpsuckers, washed up, but this was a monster, with a vast mouth and a great array of needle-sharp teeth. Dave, in a flash of genius, put it in a bag and we carried it up to the halls of residence, somehow got ourselves into the women's hall, and put the fish tail-first into a lavatory, its gaping maw neatly filling the whole pan. We put the lid down, made our escape and sat back, waiting to hear the fuss. Disappointingly, we never heard a word about it.

Keith and I, especially, studied the Blackpill gulls endlessly, seeing glaucous and Iceland at times and Mediterranean gulls day after day after day, sometimes several together, with quite a number of immaculate summer adults knocking spots off all the other birds on the beach. In February 1970 I watched a yellow-legged gull near Blackpill. It was a 'herring gull' with a darker grey back (darker than a common gull), a more brilliant bill and dull-yellow legs. The only thing I could find that fitted was *Larus argentatus omissus*, a race that has since been questioned or discredited but that was detailed in the old Witherby Handbook as a rare vagrant with six old British records. I fired off a letter to *British Birds*. James Ferguson-Lees replied, saying that:

> … although individuals belonging to other races – notably *taimyrensis*, *michahellis* and perhaps *heuglini* – may occasionally have wandered to Britain and Ireland, there is no definite record of any subspecies other than nominate *argentatus* in this country. In this connection I should perhaps explain that 'omissus' which is given as a rare vagrant in the handbook is no longer treated as a separate race. There is a cline running north-east from *argentatus* to *heuglini* with the populations becoming darker on the mantle as one goes further east. The western part of 'omissus' is now sunk in nominate

Ring-billed gull (left) is not the easiest bird to find and identify amongst a flock of thousands of other gulls, including common gull (right). The pale eye is a critical feature.

argentatus and the western part (with yellow legs) in *heuglini*. The description of your bird seems closest to *heuglini*, but more than that I cannot say.

I was left puzzled. In my diary, I wrote:

As Mr Ferguson-Lees says, the determination of races is really a matter for the museum. However, surely a very dark (very uniform and immaculate) mantle and yellow legs (no doubt at all about that) precludes *argentatus* and must indicate one or other of the foreign races? As such, surely it is worth publication somewhere?

This is interesting given that we were talking about Swansea, an area where yellow-legged gulls were really rare. I saw several more at Chasewater and, when Peter Grant became involved with *British Birds*, began to publish notes on them. Now, the yellow-legged gull *Larus michahellis* is almost universally treated as a separate species.

And it was at Blackpill, in March 1973, that I found a ring-billed gull, the first for Britain (and, I thought at the time, for Europe, but there was an earlier German record). This was when there was no mention of the species in any European bird guide and, although a paper on it came out in *British Birds*, dated the same month, it was not actually in print until some time later. Peter Grant, who had written it, came to Blackpill to see the bird a few days after I found it and brought a proof copy with him; and it was a phone call to him, from Pete Lansdown, that revealed that an all-important feature was the pale eye. My sketches showed a pale eye, but I had made no mention of it in my notes!

This needed confirming, but the next day I could see no trace of the bird. The following day I was able to show it to one or two other people; the next weekend a large gathering arrived. It did not appear for hours; but then, when all hope seemed to have gone, I saw it on the water amongst the common gull flock, on a very high tide, fortunately close to a protruding post. 'Get the post; then a common gull to the right, then a black-headed, then a common, then – the next one.' What satisfaction and relief I felt when I heard Tony Smith say, 'Yes, tick off pale eye!'

That summer, after I had gone back to the Midlands, Keith found another one – a young one – and after that ring-billed gulls were regular each winter. On subsequent day trips back – after I had left the area – I saw them as 'old friends' on the Blackpill beach. Blackpill was exceptionally good to me and the Gower was an absolute joy. I miss the area still.

Join the Club

B irdwatching alone is fine, but there is something special about 'belonging'. From the RSPB I found a contact for the West Midland Bird Club (WMBC) and joined. In terms of membership, it was (and probably still is) the largest of the many regional bird clubs that cover Britain and Ireland, and it also covered a large area (the old counties of Warwickshire, Worcestershire and Staffordshire). The West Midlands, as a county, came later.

The club produced a cyclostyled bulletin, which came in a neat brown envelope that I could identify before it was opened. I remember the smell of the ink, barely dry, the feel of it. It was important to 'belong' to a club like this, to be part of something, and eventually to make a contribution to the bulletins and reports (there was a free annual report, and my initials began to appear against records in the main list). After a while we got to some of the meetings. It was a mad dash after Dad got home from a long day's work, and sometimes we would park the car and have to run to the art gallery in Birmingham city centre, where the meetings were held, to get there in time. There was the smell of Dad's suit, aftershave and the leather seats of the Ford Consul – a heady mix – as we drove into the city, frustrated by traffic delays and anxious about where we might park.

Years later I was on the bird club research committee, which met in a room above a Birmingham pub. On one occasion someone half-jokingly suggested that perhaps we might change the name of the committee, so that we need not have to do any research ... The WMBC did do some good research, and had a history of cooperative surveys such as the Breeding Bird Atlas, which helped organizers of the later, nationwide British Trust for Ornithology (BTO) atlas to sort out their techniques. Occasionally I attended committee meetings of the Staffordshire branch, which, in many ways, was ahead of the rest of the club in its conservation activities. Bird clubs generally were naturally more interested in seeing and recording birds than in conserving habitats.

This lightweight committee work led to a more onerous task, however: involvement in editing the annual report. The report had started out as a thin booklet, but it was now maturing into a substantial publication with a thick spine. As the job grew and grew, the editor needed an assistant. Far more people were submitting records and some sent in stacks of excellent material. Piles of paper record-slips would come in a shoe box and needed to be put into some sort of sensible annual review, a paragraph or two of dense narrative and lists of dated records for each species, with tables where numbers permitted. Analysing the reports was an increasingly demanding job, but here was such a wealth of material that it was crying out to be used, not simply listed. Because county bird reports included so many one-off reports and 'unscientific' observations, decades worth of perfectly good information from thousands of wholly reliable people seems to be largely ignored in current studies, which is a sad situation.

Working on these reports for a few years gave me an insight into the workings of a large bird club at a time when it was taking on a more important role in the organization of birdwatching locally (with permit schemes for several sites, club hides and so on), in translating the needs of national surveys (principally BTO-organized) into local support, and in regional conservation issues. Alan Richards was often secretary, bulletin editor, indoor meetings organizer, spokesman, publicity person and several other things rolled into one. Many clubs must have been the same: without a handful of willing people, they would have collapsed. Now the WMBC, like many other clubs, has its own website, and its reports, if sometimes a little tardy, remain among the best in the country. While I was not a county bird recorder as such, editing the West Midland Bird Report involved judging other people's records. This was fascinating, illuminating and difficult. All clubs, or report editors, have some such system: reports of locally scarce or rare birds go through a semi-official review before they are deemed acceptable for publication. Once published, they become part of 'the record' – written history – so it is worth a bit of effort to get it right.

After a few years in Swansea I was invited – much to my surprise as I was a real 'outsider' – to join the records committee of the Gower Ornithological Society. So for a year or two I was on another records committee, continuing to review other people's records. It is, by its very nature, a conceited position to be in: who was I to judge others? Who, on the other hand, were any of these people to judge me? There is always room for unease in these situations. There are people who just refuse to submit their reports to be scrutinized in this way by any committee, self-appointed or elected. But most birdwatchers accept the sense of it and play the game, although they naturally become a little uppity at times if one of their reports is queried or thrown out. It is, to some extent, just a game. Does it matter terribly much how many firecrests have been seen in Staffordshire, or how many roseate terns have turned up in West Glamorgan? Does anyone analyse the records to draw conclusions more valuable than a simple histogram showing monthly occurrences or yearly trends? But if we want to play the game, we should at least play by the rules.

I have certainly had records published that should not have been. Brief descriptions of great shearwaters in Scotland were accepted, and they made the annual reports there, but I have grave doubts whether they were correctly identified. On the other hand, I have had records rejected that were 100 per cent, cast-iron certainties. My first ever roseate terns were on the beach at Blackpill in Swansea Bay – an adult, with a red-based black bill, almost full black cap and even a pink flush in October, along with a juvenile complete with dark forehead, dark bill, barred upperparts and blackish legs – but the local committee rejected them as uncertain. In the end, it is better to be cautious – if in doubt, throw it out. These things tend to balance out in favour of accuracy. Many such reports are voted upon in records committees across the country: good ones go out through lack of support; bad ones go in with a majority of one overturning common sense. But, I suspect, most get it right most of the time and not many babies are turned out with the bathwater.

Undoubtedly many decisions are influenced by a committee's perception of the knowledge of the observer (for all that recorders and committee secretaries may say otherwise). 'We judge solely on the evidence' they may say – but part of that evidence is the person who sends the record in. My old Staffordshire friend Tony Blake was the kind of observer found in many areas, out in the field week after week, solid and thoroughly reliable, but he was even better than that: he was perceptive and able to pick up many birds that 'solid and reliable' types might miss. Even Tony, though, may have got it wrong occasionally. We all do. One story is interesting in that it highlights some of my concerns about the whole business of recording rare birds. Tony saw a strange kestrel on the western railway embankment at Chasewater one November. He told me about it a couple of weeks later and I was able to tell him that, oddly enough, Peter Lansdown (later rarities committee chairman) had seen something similar from his car in South Wales three days after the Chasewater one. Tony had watched his bird with binoculars and later went to the trouble of acquiring a stuffed kestrel, putting it in the same spot and looking at it from the same place in similar lighting conditions; Pete had seen his bird with the naked eye. Both thought they were lesser kestrels, and each account gave the other greater plausibility. And there was a third, in Sussex, on the very same day as Tony's. Each seemed to add further credence to the others. Lesser kestrels have always been exceptionally rare in Britain, and November reports were unknown – at this time of year they should be in East Africa. Here was something of an influx into Britain perhaps. They were accepted, but on a later review of lesser kestrel records all three were rejected and removed from the historical record. Whether any or all were genuinely lesser kestrels I can't really say – perhaps they were. Tony undoubtedly felt certain of his, convinced, for example, that on the bird he saw there was no trace of dark spotting above, which he could see easily on the stuffed male kestrel but which is absent from a lesser.

For there to be lesser kestrels in Britain in November, something odd must have happened. This was a significant event, surely? It was published as such and accepted for several years before the records were rejected. Well, was there a significant late-autumn influx or not? For three kestrels to be wrongly identified and submitted as lessers, within three days, all in the most unexpected of months, was itself a little unlikely. If there was an influx, it didn't seem to change anyone's lives; when it was decided that there was not, again it had no shattering consequences (99.9 per cent of us didn't notice). In other words, did anyone care? What difference did it make? What's the point of it all? I'm sure that most people involved in judging records will have asked such questions of themselves more than once, especially when another large, fat brown envelope thuds onto the doormat, demanding attention at a busy time – sometimes, if you were interested and conscientious, hours of time.

Richard Porter told me that my name had cropped up at a meeting of the British Birds Rarities Committee (BBRC) as a potential future recruit. The journal British Birds had started this committee in 1958 and it has since been copied in most countries across the world. I didn't know what to think, but I was put forward and, to my surprise, I was elected and served on the committee previously known as 'the ten rare men' (a description that encapsulated the perceived mystery of it all, although it has fallen out of use). I was on the committee for nine years, from 1988, as an ordinary member, and then as chairman until 1996. Being chairman also meant joining the meetings of the British Ornithologists' Union (BOU) Records Committee, the senior scientific body, which took responsibility for 'the British List'. I find it hard to believe I was on the committee at all, let alone chairman. It was a fascinating experience. Chairing the meetings was interesting, and sometimes a bit challenging. There were some dominant personalities and, in a small way, clashing egos; more importantly, there were differing views on how the committee should proceed. There were even resignations mid-meeting that were, after some persuasion from me, withdrawn before the end.

The rarities committee was and remains remarkably democratic. Each year someone retires, each year anyone can be nominated for election and, should nominations exceed vacancies, a ballot takes place. In theory top identification experts end up on the committee, perhaps with a leavening of organizers who can keep the show on the road and ensure prompt publication of its annual reports. A geographical spread across the UK is another desirable quality; there is a need for members to know individual observers or, if not, to know someone who does.

The BBRC faced a number of issues in a period when things changed fast, but the committee and its ways remained fixed. I several times brought up the fact that the BBRC was entirely male-dominated and had been throughout its history: could we find a woman as a candidate for a future election? We never did and the committee still can't. I sometimes suspected, too, that women had less chance of getting a record accepted than men. There were records that I chose to dig my heels in over, probably ill-chosen ones that stood no real chance, but where rejection seemed to be on the basis that this was an observer no one knew (and, moreover, it happened to be a woman). My unease might force a recirculation, which would result in a capitulation (usually by me, but sometimes by others, which would then reveal that there had been more support for my view than had earlier been apparent).

The BBRC was slow to advance technologically and it was beginning to show. It was a hard job to make much progress, but still, it worked, and the published reports were unblemished. There were regular suggestions that, to reduce the workload (or to bring it back to an even keel, as it had mushroomed alarmingly), we should take many more species off the official rarity list so that we could leave them to be dealt with by the counties. There was much support for this within the committee from time to time, but I was generally against it, perhaps unreasonably. The main argument against the change was that, after having amassed many years of reports on species such as Pallas's warbler, at the very time when their status was changing, and therefore was most in need of a national overview, we proposed to lose the opportunity to monitor the situation in a single, national, uniformly judged report. (The regular publication of excellent and detailed analysis of 'scarce migrants' has now filled that role admirably.) On the other hand, I had to agree that some species had increased dramatically and were no longer real rarities (it was not so many years since little egret was a rarity and it is now present in thousands and scores of pairs breed), while others that were not on the list had become so scarce that they were genuinely rare (for example, when we checked we were surprised by how few ferruginous ducks were being seen).

We demanded evidence for the identification of rare birds in the form of descriptions and supporting notes and, ideally, sketches and photographs. But there was a major problem developing that caused real disagreement in the birding world (and, notably, in *Birding World*, the magazine): many people were no longer very interested in taking reams of notes, and why bother anyway when there's a photograph in this month's magazine? Records were sometimes not submitted at all, even though the rare bird had been seen by scores if not hundreds of people and its photographs were in print for all to see. Some 'firsts' for Britain were well publicized long before submission and acceptance by the BBRC and the BOU Records Committee (which specifically dealt with 'firsts') but, as everyone could see the evidence for themselves (and many had seen the bird and bought the photo), what did it matter? In recent years it has been possible to go to see a rare bird and find half a dozen photographers selling pictures of it for a pound, in a mini car-boot sale, before you've even seen it. And more recently still, everyone seems to be taking their own photographs through the new technology of digiscoping. Ian Wallace sent me a card with a note at the bottom saying 'Digiscoping is killing field notes' – I think it had already killed them. Another complication arising from this is the spectre of a hoax. When I was on the committee we thought we had been conned once or twice, but now digital manipulation of photographs makes the possibility all the more real.

In short, while some people had always questioned the value and validity of the rarities committee, now more and more were asking what the point of it at all was. The response of the committee was that it was still better to have a committee of ten experts, democratically elected, than to leave the judgement of records to a group of self-appointed editors of one or other magazine (a situation that recalled the time when *British Birds* editors themselves were judge and jury, when there was no committee and no other magazines either).

Before I left we had changed things a bit. We introduced news items in *BB* and, more importantly, in other magazines, too, about the way the committee operated and the way recent rarity decisions had been made. A new occasional feature in *BB* was 'From the Rarities Committee Files', which put pages of original notes and drawings, comments by the committee, and research on identification matters, into the public domain. This dealt with one of the more important criticisms of the BBRC – that it was excessively secretive – but it also meant facing the problems associated with publishing comments about observers and suggestions that perhaps some of them had made a mistake, or were mistaken in their opinions, or were just not up to it in the field. The whole thing is now much more up to date, with email submissions (around 20 per cent by 2004) and circulations a matter of routine, and there is also a useful committee website. But I can't help feeling that the profile of the committee has lessened still further over the years. The mysterious image of the 'ten rare men' has long since gone – there are, after all, many tens of others who may know as much as they do.

BBRC work was demanding in terms of time and concentration but often interesting and nearly always instructive. Fortunately there was also a good deal of humour in it, and there were moments of light relief that were sometimes essential to keep us sane. Frequently the comments were really funny, but often unrepeatable – one reason why we were loath to make all our files open to the public. There would be cases when an observer would want to withhold his name, not because it might reveal the whereabouts of a rare breeding bird or some other legitimate secret but because he was worried that his wife might find out he was out on the beach with his girlfriend when he was supposed to be away at a business meeting. Often comments were far from politically correct: one report was queried by a member because 'if he still goes out with the same girlfriend he used to have, either his eyesight or his judgement must be at fault'. One field sketch of a drake surf scoter, showing a rear view of the head with its big white nape patch, was said to look more like a drawing of the rear-view mirror of someone's motorbike. There followed queries about the make and design of the motorbike, while another member bemoaned the fact that his wing mirror had been clipped by a passing van and did we know how much it cost to replace it; and on it went, the surf scoter all but forgotten. Such things were occasionally essential to lighten the load.

Summer on the Berwyns

It was a breakthrough year in 1976. With a lot of help from Derek Thomas, a keen birdwatcher and lecturer in pure (and obscure) maths in Swansea, I was picked up from nowhere by Roger Lovegrove, the RSPB's Wales Officer, and offered a contract job in Wales for the summer. My brief was to survey the best birds in much of the Berwyn Mountains range. There was no real money in it but my job at the DHSS was leading nowhere, so I jumped at it. It was the first step on the rickety ladder towards working for the RSPB full time, and, in any case, watching birds in Wales for the summer would surely be pure enjoyment.

Early in April a meeting in Newtown sorted out the general outline of the project. Then, on 23 April, I drove to Wales and met Graham Williams, along with Martin Davies, another old Swansea mate who was to go south to do a similar survey around the Elan valley. (He would later became well known for his invention and constant promotion of the British Birdwatching Fair.) Next day I was off on my own, in my trusty blue Reliant, via the office and a meeting with Roger, to set up home for a few weeks in a caravan at Llangynog, in a deep valley beside the Afon Mellte. That first night I camped in my small tent beneath the grey crags of Craig Rhiwarth, and I explored a bit around Blaen y Cwm. It was a splendid bit of mid-Wales, with wild and beautiful scenery. I had a great start with the birds, too, seeing two peregrines and two hen harriers, along with ring ouzels, ravens, buzzards, redstarts, tree pipits and wood warblers. I wrote up my notes in the car, including the admission that, already, I was missing a bit of company. A few days later: 'Getting into the routine now, but I could do with somebody to talk to. Even my radio has bust. I don't think the lonely life would altogether suit me – I like to go home at night.'

But here I was, in northern Powys, looking especially for peregrines, merlins, hen harriers, kites (there were none), ring ouzels, red and black grouse, curlews, lapwings, golden plovers, snipe, ravens, wheatears, stonechats and whinchats –

and any other 'good' upland birds that I might come across. In the event, I
noted practically everything, including tree pipits, wood warblers, redstarts,
pied flycatchers, dippers and common sandpipers, as well as butterflies, and
religiously recorded them on maps and in a detailed notebook, to be given
to Roger. This meant I had to write everything twice, as I still kept my own
notebook going (from which this account is culled), and I kept a normal diary,
too. I also recorded the state of the heather in each one kilometre square –
good, medium, poor or absent – and noted areas of hillside scrub, a rich habitat
that was under severe pressure as many hillsides were being ploughed up and
seeded with grass for yet more sheep. This was a period when much of mid-
Wales was undergoing rapid change. Great squares of vivid green were replacing
the heather, rough grass and bracken mix of the steep, hillside *ffridd* (roughly
pronounced freethe) zone, taking away vast areas of habitat suited to whinchats
and tree pipits, ravens and buzzards, black grouse and merlins, as well as
destroying an integral part of the visual appeal of Wales.

The Berwyns form a high, diagonal spine to northern Wales and are best
known to most visitors as the remote hills either side of Lake Vyrnwy (the long,
north-west–south-east reservoir that cuts through the south-west–north-
east range of hills near its southern end). The Berwyns are not mountains in
any real sense. They are mostly rolling moors, brown with heather, greener
in the valleys, although they have some deep and steep-sided valleys, and the
middle rises impressively to just over 2,550 feet (800 metres) at Moel Sych and
Cadair Berwyn, two central points. There are deeply scarred peatbogs, bracken-
covered slopes, extensive screes and some quite spectacular, sheer cliffs. Some
of the best valleys are long, deep and beautifully symmetrical, with a wide,
green bottom, typically with a rushing tree-lined river, pastures, trees and
hedges; some have wooded lower slopes – or more often quite open slopes
with bracken and scattered hawthorns and patches of bluebells – then a steep,
heathery upper slope, steepening even further to grey screes and broken or
terraced cliffs. These roll over to the wide open moorland plateau above,
with its deep, undulating heather, mossy hollows and shallow, rushy or
grassy valleys.

All in all, this was a large, varied and daunting tract of land to cover in
a few short weeks, much of it wild and far from anywhere, or anyone. The
RSPB office in Newtown could send mail for me to the post office, poste
restante, and I could phone in from a call box, if I could find one that worked
(always the old-fashioned 'button A and button B' type), but we had no day-
to-day contact. Before I went out on the hills I had been handed a compass and

a whistle, although it is questionable how useful these would have been in a remote place in a real emergency. This was made all too apparent when, on one occasion, I suddenly dropped vertically into a crevice that had opened up in the peat, hidden by long heather. Fortunately the bottom of the crevice brought me to a halt when I was about chest deep, so apart from wet feet and boots full of stinking, soggy sheep's wool I was undamaged. A couple more feet and I might have been in trouble. The whistle would have been of little use – I was far from any road or track.

April was a fabulous time to start. The banks and roadsides were awash with primroses – more abundant than I had ever seen them – celandine and stitchwort, while great patches of open hillside and woodland floor were turning mauve-blue with bluebells. By late May the bluebells were 'better than any I've seen away from Skomer' (the beautiful south-west Wales island that has the best, brightest, tallest bluebells ever, which leave you strongly scented for days after a walk through them). Stone walls were coloured by bright-green clumps of parsley fern and the tall stems and round, shiny leaves of wall pennywort. Wood sorrel grew profusely on some open slopes and golden saxifrage was everywhere along the streams. I was not entirely comfortable being so alone, but the area was just wonderful and I loved it.

The first full day, though, began dull, and a cold and windy night had not helped me sleep much. As I drove over the high moors, 'the prospect of surveying the Berwyns became more and more fearsome!' I tried the local pub that evening, an exceptional thing for me to do on my own, and without exception everyone was speaking Welsh, which was good to hear, but not much use to me. The first week or two were also remarkably cold and often drearily dull. At the end of April it was still frosty at night; on the better days 'the combination of warm sun and cold wind is awkward, as I'm hot and sweaty and cold and shivery all at the same time or in quick succession when climbing these hills'. The best thing about the cold was that it kept the atmosphere wonderfully clear and the views were constantly inspiring.

I scraped the frost off my face and got breakfast going – that reminds me, I've forgotten bacon and eggs *again* – and got out earlier than before. I walked through an old ruined farm and along a north-east slope with tree pipits singing all around – how did a certain field-guide writer come to call the song undistinguished? I cut up a steep slope and staggered across the moor (a thousand-foot climb) and walked over rough, knee-deep, tussocky heather, tussocky grass and boggy hollows – hard going – covering the upper slopes of Craig Blaen-rhiwarth (where I heard a twite and saw a yellow wagtail!). A major feature up on the hills, out of sight of all roads or buildings, when the wind dies down, is the absolute silence.

By early May there was still no sign of the great summer to come.

After a foul night and early morning the rain stopped and the effects of cloud shrouding the hillsides were very attractive. With the new leaves coming on the trees, red bracken on the hills, bright emerald fields lit by shafts of sun through the clouds, the whole area is outstandingly beautiful. ...

As it brightened up after a dismal start I decided on a walk up the Nant y Llyn valley. By the time I reached the upper valley I thought I might as well go on to the next rise – and then it seemed a good idea to continue to the top after all. So I climbed up the ridge south of Llyn Lluncaws to the top of Moel Sych and walked along the ridge to Cadair Berwyn. On Moel Sych the mist occasionally swirled around; on Cadair Berwyn it came down until visibility was less than 50 yards. A strong, roaring wind swept up the steep crags from the south-east, pushing up the white cloud at a rapid pace – quite a sight to look down from the ridge at the mist speeding up and coming over in clammy waves. It swept high over the ridge, then eddied back again from the west.

Even at the beginning of June it was wet. A local man passed me and said, 'Lovely morning – except for the rain of course.' It was. In fact, looking back at my diaries now, I realize that the 'long hot summer of 1976' really did not start before late June, and by the third week of July I had left the moors. Many of my days were spoiled by rain and low cloud, but in late June I was on the Horseshoe Pass hills enjoying views of Snowdon and the Glyders, Tryfan and other Snowdonia hills, and out over the sea across Colwyn Bay and Rhyl, farther east perhaps Liverpool or Ellesmere Port. From a caravan above Froncysyllte, I could see out over the whole Cheshire/North Shropshire plain in a magnificent sweep and decided I could see Cannock Chase and the north Staffordshire moors. A short walk added Wenlock Edge and the Wrekin to the view. To the west the views were less extensive, but perfect, along the valley towards Llangollen and high hills beyond: a pointed hill with earthworks on top, a winding valley, glimpses of the river, steep slopes, green fields, cattle, hedges, trees and woods – a lovely composition.

By late June I was complaining of 'nearly unbearable heat' and sunburn. On 28 June I wrote 'I saw a small cloud, briefly, this afternoon!' I described one walk as 'a real toil, battling through long heather and bracken and tormented by hundreds of flies. This heat is not my idea of enjoyment. I don't know if the stream is fit to drink, but it saved my life (even if it kills me). In the caravan, all evening, it has been almost unbearable.' Next day: 'Mercifully there is a cool breeze this evening, yet there is not a sign of a cloud. Of all things, I have a streaming cold.'

After a while in the luxury of the first caravan at Llangynog, despite the lack of heating, I moved across the village to an empty, disused school (which was kept in running order for periodic field trips from other schools and colleges). I had the choice of half a dozen tiny lavatories, made for infant schoolchildren, and could sleep in any classroom I liked. It was a touch spooky, but there was a cooker, running water and lights, but no electric kettle and no heating. There was a café at at Llangynog and I often dropped in there. I once broke the world record for the number of cups of tea (11) to be had from one tea bag in a steel pot, sitting there looking at Craig Rhiwarth, tired from some hours on the hill, not really wanting to shut myself away in the old school. After that, I moved north, via a night in the tent, to a caravan in a garden above Froncysyllte, near Llangollen, not far from the splendid Chirk viaduct. It had no water (I filled large bottles from a neighbour) and no toilet, but it was at least dry. This let me explore the northern end of the Berwyns, as well as occasional forays north to World's End and the Horseshoe Pass, where choughs nested in a deep quarry. Peregrines nesting above World's End were robbed by egg-collectors; the local birdwatcher, who ran a pottery business in the nearby village, saw the thieves and went up to intercept them. He told me that one of them was not so bad, as 'he asked the other one to put me down, and not throw me over the edge of the cliff'. That year was dreadful for peregrine robberies. A radio report in June claimed 35 to 40 pairs had been robbed of eggs or chicks.

It had been intended that I live in a 'derelict bungalow' for a time. I was taken up to it near Bryn Newydd, above Vivod, a couple of miles from Llangollen. It was along a steep, rough, winding track into the hills — a black speck on the OS map, named Plas-Rabbit — and had not been used for 70 years! It was dark, dirty and empty except for hay and bird droppings. There was a water trough at the top of a nearby hill. The track would have killed my old Reliant in days and I would have been much more comfortable in my little tent, so I gave up on the idea of living in the bungalow and tried to make telephone enquiries about a caravan I had been told about. The owner was out. I didn't know the address so tried to phone Roger Lovegrove to get it: no reply. Later, I rang his home number – he was out. I pitched my tent.

I visited Mr Best, the ageing owner of the Vivod estate near Llangollen – a man who held a prominent position in the local wildlife trust – to talk about the birds of prey and black grouse on his land. It was a bit tricky: if, as an RSPB employee, I asked for permission to walk about on the moors, it would be refused (I would have been seen as a spy). If, having been refused permission, or not having asked, I was found by a gamekeeper up on the moors, the reception could have been hostile. On a nearby estate, a gamekeeper had been in court recently for having fired a shotgun over the heads of a visiting Sunday school outing! On one occasion, on a public footpath, I came across a farmer standing beside the very first, closed, gate. My notes record that 'he immediately started off in a raised voice, swearing and going on about "your sort" and "you ramblers" and asking me where I thought I was going – and I was on the public right of way. He said there were three men on his side of the gate to deal with me if I tried to go through.'

Mr Best showed me some ancient game books and said he couldn't understand where the grouse had gone, as they used to shoot dozens of blackcocks every year and now there were hardly any – 'we only shoot about four a year now'. There was a big problem then concerning poisoned bait put out for foxes and birds of prey – I found dead ravens alongside such baits – and persecution of hen harriers in particular. He was entirely serious when he said that poisoned eggs laid out on the heather were beneficial, as the 'strain of hen harriers that ate eggs' would find them, be killed, and thus gradually remove the egg-eating habit from hen harriers, leaving a harmless 'strain' that could be accepted on the moors in future.

One day in the caravan at Froncysyllte, Tim Cleeves (of Britain's first slender-billed curlew fame) turned up. He was on his way north after doing an early summer stint in Pembrokeshire as a peregrine warden. Peregrines were then still scarce and likely to be robbed, so many nests were watched or wardened. On one occasion an eyrie near Rhayader was robbed despite having been under the surveillance of a well-known birdwatcher. Roger Lovegrove and the local police were brought into instant action: a rapid reaction force, out on the hills, looking for the culprits, helped by a team from the local motorbike scrambling club. A young peregrine was found hidden in a duffle bag in heather above the eyrie. The robbers were chased through the lanes of mid-Wales, Roger in the RSPB Maxi in hot pursuit, a police car trying hard to keep up in his wake. A local magistrate had a heart attack and died. The young peregrines were recovered and put back in the nest but disappeared a few days later – taken by a fox, officially, but I always wondered if they were not just stolen again.

Roger said afterwards, when he saw my notes, 'you really saw a lot of peregrines didn't you?' It was indeed a great summer for peregrines, which, then, were only just beginning to make a comeback in Wales after a period of great scarcity. There was still a great deal of secrecy surrounding their whereabouts. I got to know them very well, much more than ever before or since.

It was good for merlins, too. If they were nesting in an old crow's nest in a tree, they would sometimes be so noisy when I approached that they were easy to find, impossible to miss even. Yet, if they were nesting in thick heather on the ground, they could be silent and elusive: at times I could be writing descriptions of still-flightless juveniles scattered in heather a few yards from the nest and would neither see nor hear the adults at all. I found their plucking posts and sat and watched until something happened; and I found a nest or two, but they were easy to miss. One day Derek Barber met me in a teashop in Llangollen and we went up on the hills to meet Roger and Tim. We sat for half an hour on a slope above a little rounded valley, where I had suspected merlins, but saw nothing. When we stood up to leave, I found a brood of merlin chicks in the heather just a few yards away – the adults had not made a noise or put in an appearance. Yet merlins in trees would dash at my head with noisy, angry calls.

There was a broad heather bank at the head of a valley where I knew hen harriers must have been nesting, too, but I had not found them. Tim Cleeves suddenly bent down and raised a harrier chick high in the air, a triumphant gesture, and we all gathered round the nest as the furious male dived at us. It was always the male that attacked me there, never the female, the opposite of the norm. He never hit me, but came within inches of doing so with his fast, diving swoops that reminded me of a lightweight great skua, with equal venom. On other days at this nest I quickly photographed the chicks and noted down their main plumage and eye colours before leaving them in peace.

Male hen harrier flew up from the nest as soon as I came into view at 4–500 yards. Began to call; female not seen. I approached the nest and he swooped very close; eventually, at the nest, the splendid male swooped within a foot of my head, the closest he has ever come and quite fantastic. In long heather beside the nest three young were found, plus one dead in the nest, another dead near by, neither much developed, if at all, since last visit. One young bird gave high-pitched whine as male swooped at me. Also hissed when approached; stood up surprisingly tall, with bill open and wings

Lapwing and redshank chicks.

spread wide. The other two, more concealed, crouched, with head turned towards me, bills open; reared up when approached. The very active bird lashed out like lightning with its feet, catching my finger and drawing blood as I tried to retrieve some prey remains. I soon managed to drag away the prey, by placing my boot in front of the bird so that it could claw at that. All three had very dark brown eyes (one fractionally paler but not grey) so all presumably female. Cere bright yellow, tongue bright pink with green tip like merlins'. Very well-feathered, richly coloured and patterned; white rumps had v-shaped brownish bars. Nest messy and smelly, plenty of prey – several young starlings. One dead passerine nestling seems to have been a ring ouzel; another dead bird was obviously a raptor, apparently merlin or kestrel. Adult male has brownish centres to scapulars and a few brownish bars on upperwing; outer tail feathers have grey and whitish bars near base. Eyes deep yellow.

Not far from here, I later found a pair of peregrines nesting on a tiny cliff, just an outcrop of rock, really, sticking up out of the heather. It was just big enough to be difficult to climb and get to the nest ledge under an overhang, but eventually

I tried as the female had been sitting for weeks into the late summer and nothing was happening – the eggs were clearly infertile. I collected them under licence. I was just able to reach them with the end of my extended telescope, as I hung on to a tuft of heather with one hand, and roll them back towards me. They were kept in a cardboard box at Newtown, ready for dispatch to Monks Wood laboratory for chemical analysis, but a cleaner knocked the box off the shelf and the eggs broke, so we never did discover the reason for their infertility. The day I found these peregrines in this wide, undulating, heathery area, I wrote:

> I saw a pale grey bird, assumed to be a male hen harrier, on the east slope. After only a momentary glimpse it 'disappeared'; but, thinking it must have settled, I looked at the spot with my telescope – perched on a rock was a grey bird, but in a very slanting pose and quite dark above, in contrast to its whitish flanks. I moved closer to investigate, under cover of a ridge; as I looked over the bird flew, but immediately turned and came towards me – a superb female peregrine! She came very close, sweeping by, with loud, repeated *kwaak kwaak kwaak* or *kwek kwek kwek kwek* calls. A male appeared, very low over the heather initially, swooping higher and then always keeping higher and farther off than the female, with less frequent, more croaking, lower calls. I thought they must surely have young. Looking quickly around I chose the nearest bit of rock, but found nothing. I moved to the northernmost of several tiny crags, as I had to return that way, intending to look at each 'crag' in turn as quickly as possible. In the event this isolated crag had a couple of feathers on the edge of a ledge, but I could see no young. It was 16–18 feet high (!), only a few yards wide and petered out at the side in a taper, with a gentle slope up to the top. I scrambled up this, looked over the edge and there, on a broad (18 inches?) ledge with dark soil and heather debris and couple of feathers, were three eggs. The eggs looked very pale but I did not try to describe them on the spot, having a few seconds' look before getting off out of the area as soon as I could. As I approached the 'cliff' the female swooped over it and back over me, calling with even higher, quicker calls than before, almost *kwee kwee kwee* in great agitation and excitement. As I left, both birds followed, high overhead, with less frequent calling, for a few hundred yards.

This was already the middle of June. I had expected to see large young, not eggs, partly because of the time of year and partly because of the adults' intense agitation and bold defence of the nest. Although I had my 'Schedule 1' licence, I was never very comfortable about visiting such nests, and left as quickly as I could. The birds continued to sit on these eggs until mid-July. I also took a clutch of merlin eggs, which was analysed and proved to have the highest level yet recorded of PCB residues, more than enough to render the chance of successful hatching nil. The fierce, feisty little birds tended their eggs for far longer than the norm and I felt sorry for them when their efforts came to nought.

From the spot where I camped the first night in April, I could hear black grouse cooing like pigeons across the valley, 1,000 yards away, above the general noise of sheep, cattle and traffic. They were on a slope covered with last year's bracken, fresh, green bracken growth and scattered larches, the sort of hillside that always looks so rich and colourful. Every so often as I walked across the hill I might flush one in a flurry of blue-black and white, the long wings with a broad white bar and long, flat-backed body and tail always striking as the bird usually made a rapid exit and flew right across a wide valley out of sight. Once I watched one feeding from the window of the Llangynog caravan, and yet I also trudged miles through young conifer plantations looking for black grouse and not finding them; this habitat, with its deep trenches, heathery ridges and spiteful, stiff, scratchy trees is particularly hard going. Red grouse were very few anywhere in the Berwyns, despite some excellent-looking habitat. One morning, after camping the night at the end of a high forest track, I awoke to the sound of a displaying blackcock right at the end of the tent. It was a while before it dawned on me what was happening outside:

A loud and peculiarly attractive sound outside the tent was that of a displaying blackcock. I listened for several minutes – an exceptional opportunity – before looking out and seeing a superb blackcock pursuing a greyhen, in full display posture, not 20 yards from me. The greyhen became alert and soon flew to a nearby bank, but the cock seemed unaware of me; he followed the hen and started displaying again, until she flew off. Originally in a small, flat, stony area with short grass immediately below a 15- to 20-foot face of rock. The cock gave a couple of very subdued 'sneezes' but, otherwise, a continuous series of loud, musical, bubbling/crooning phrases – not at random but in a distinct pattern. After a low, purring trill came a higher, louder 'bubble' impossible to write down, which was rapidly repeated – these phrases were repeated in identical form in the same '1,2,2; 1,2,2 ...' sequence.

I found scores of whinchats. Chasewater whinchats were well separated and rarely seemed to sing, but these Welsh ones, often close together at the head of a valley in deep heather and bracken fronds, sang to (or against) each other all the time – like robins, with churrs and rattles thrown in. Some gave remarkable performances, with grey partridge-like notes, whirrs and buzzy sequences between the soft, melodic phrases, always quite quiet, carrying about 100 yards. Wood warblers were in little patches of larch, as well as in the oak woods, and redstarts spilled out onto the hill on rocky slopes beside the trees. There were dippers and common sandpipers on the streams – common sandpipers singing and displaying with their complicated, rhythmic, passionate trills and whistles just beside my caravan.

The second caravan was close to a deep limestone quarry, with trees growing from the middle to the level of the rim. By standing on the outside, I could watch purple and white-letter hairstreaks at eye level and close up. White-letter hairstreaks often fed on the bramble blossom and, with care, I could get one on my fingertip and photograph it. Sometimes I counted more than 40 white-letter hairstreaks. I wonder if they are still there, or whether the ravages of Dutch elm disease put paid to their food plant. It was a great year for butterflies all round, with many large heaths and quite a few small pearl-bordered fritillaries. I managed to see three high brown fritillaries, beside silver-washed for comparison, near the Afon Vyrnwy.

A good find at Froncysyllte was a pair of hawfinches feeding recently fledged young, which I found on several days by following up their strange calls. Other surprising things included, for example, a saker falcon on the moors above Lake Vyrnwy, four bar-tailed godwits flying over the open hill and, of all things, a terrified fulmar, pursued by an acrobatic peregrine, heading even farther inland at Llangynog. One day above Llangollen I found a singing male lazuli bunting – a beautiful North American species, assumed to be an escape (although from where I know not).

There were many superb moments. I was seeing peregrines and harriers all the time, the harriers sometimes still performing their spectacular sky-dancing displays. One morning, a female harrier appeared, looking strangely pale against dark heather. It flushed a male merlin and pounced at it, but the merlin was too quick and sped away for 30 or 40 yards, before turning to come back and dive quite violently at the much bigger harrier. They agreed to differ and settled on posts on the moor. I walked over to the area and found a male merlin on a post, but he flew to settle on a low bank, where a female appeared and dived at him, before going off as if to hunt. The male flew after a meadow pipit but missed and, somewhat discomfited after all this, caught a big moth – probably an oak eggar – instead and settled down to eat it. A male hen harrier then appeared, flushing the merlin, which made no response. The light grey harrier hunted the area for several minutes, but then gained height, using what little breeze there was to help, hanging in the air with wings raised but quite steady for several minutes, with scarcely even a waver, before drifting closer to me, almost overhead, and performing two or three deep undulations, wings angled well back, rolling over sideways at the top of each swoop.

This bird was silent. It was only later that I heard a harrier call for the first time, when I came across a male hunting close to a road. It was probably not fully mature, being a little brownish-tinged on the back. It chased pipits, without success, using a faster, more purposeful flight than the usual light, airy drift. A much paler grey male appeared, flying just short distances and frequently settling in the heather. I lost track of it until a low, quick chattering call — wa-kek-kek — drew my attention to it overhead. It soared for five minutes or more in wide, slow circles. Then it sky-danced, in deep, smooth, semicircular undulations, beginning each with a headlong dive with wings flexed back, beating jerkily, before a smooth swoop and a near vertical climb. At the top of each climb it gave several wild, floppy wing-beats and rolled right over onto its back before righting itself again, like a raven; but sometimes it appeared to do a complete roll, its flapping wings making it hard to see exactly what it was doing. It repeated this exciting sequence more than 30 times, then broke off for a few seconds, before performing a further series of 17 more plunges, climbs and rolls, an exhilarating display of fitness and energy.

Over one valley I could see kestrels, buzzards, hen harriers, peregrines and merlins in the air at the same time. They had such remarkable freedom, crossing valleys and disappearing over open moors within minutes, journeys that would take me an hour to follow. I was struggling on narrow sheep-paths and once, high over a deep valley with a waterfall, I suddenly found myself on such a steep, open, smoothly grassy slope that I sat down for a moment to recover my senses and then could neither go back nor go on for a minute or two.

Peregrines were familiar before but now I was able to watch them much more intimately and so much more often than I had ever done, noting down differences in plumage, the considerable variations in size, bulk and power, as well as their quite extensive range of calls. I learned much more about dippers, the songs of pied flycatchers and redstarts, the behaviour of ring ouzels. My notes are full of short descriptions of all kinds of things.

Spring whinchats are brilliant: this male was as bright and smart as any I've seen — crown dark brown, streaked black, back black with a neat brown scaly pattern, wings nearly black and white, broad, pure white superciliary, pure white streak below blackish cheeks with small white 'whiskers' below each eye, contrasting with pale apricot chin, throat and breast. The purity of the white contrasted sharply with the blackish areas and the bright apricot colour below, especially when seen head-on. ...

In near-perfect silence, the singing whinchats were good, the curlews really loud and superb and the cuckoos really amazing! The latter were chasing about with the usual *cuc-coo* note sounding very loud but soft and wheezy, and higher-pitched, firmer *cuc-cuc-cooo*, quick *cuc-cuc-cuc-cuc-cuc*, the bubble of the female, harsh *aach aach, wach-achach* and softer, short *chuw* notes.

When I climbed to the top of the Berwyn range, I sat down in thick mist, unable to see more than a few yards, and found myself right next to a golden plover on eggs, just three yards away; she got up and gave a furious broken-wing distraction display to lure me from her nest. But it was the abundance of common birds that struck me so often – the valley-bottom fields with scattered trees and hedges were just great for pied and spotted flycatchers, treecreepers, nuthatches, mistle thrushes and various tits and finches.

In July, it came to an end: the money ran out, the birds moved away, the job was done. I was back home in Burntwood, unemployed and refused dole money. But by mid-August I was back in Wales, a four-week contract in Mold (based at Nercwys Hall) in my pocket, to do a desk study of the birds of the Dee Estuary. The end of the summer was hot and dusty and passed to the constant strains of 'Dancing Queen' by Abba, which would make it a desert-island disc for me for sure. And not far from the Dee, at the Point of Air, I had one wonderful afternoon with 50 Sandwich terns, 2,500 common terns, 100 little terns, a black tern and, best of all, two roseate terns at high tide. The only sad part about this month was the day my Reliant engine went bang and I ground to a halt in Mold. The local garage man said it had 'a dirty great hole in a piston' and offered me a pound to take it off my hands. So, that was that, the end of the job, the end of a beautiful friendship and the loss of my transport – all for a pound note.

Merlins and Mid-Wales

Was the line to the RSPB broken, after all? Thanks to Roger Lovegrove, no: he found some money from the Manpower Services Commission, and the RSPB employed me again. This time I was to spend the winter close to Newtown and do some work in the office, as well as assorted fieldwork, to keep me occupied and to give the RSPB some moderately useful data.

On 6 December 1976, three of us were installed in the little wooden-framed bungalow overlooking Llyn Mawr, both building and lake owned by the local naturalists' trust. We paid a pound a week rent, per head, plus electricity. It was quite a wild, windswept, snow-patched spot, although entirely farmed round about, set in green grass, not heather moor. Water was drawn from a well; a pump kept the supply going most of the time, except when the whole thing was frozen. I shared the cold cottage with Phil Dunning, another bird surveyor, and Roy Birch, a botanist from up north, who played Cat Stevens records a lot and wore clogs with metal toecaps. (These were to get him into a spot of bother once when he lost patience, for the umpteenth time, with the non-functioning lavatory, kicked it and smashed the pan.) Outside there were usually three Minis lined up, mine a smart aubergine van, a couple of years old, bought from Burntwood with a good finance deal – at something like 18 per cent interest over two years. (Interest rates then were horrific.) But it was part of the deal that I had transport for this job and, with my Reliant gone, this was a good solution.

The first real 'work' I was set to do was a precursor of the British Trust for Ornithology (BTO) waterways bird survey, and it involved surveying the birds of the River Severn between Caersws and Newtown. This meant that if I got a lift to Newtown I could do something in the office and then walk back along several miles of riverbank through a wide, attractive valley. The river was not alive with birds but there was usually something interesting. Best was the local flock of whooper swans in winter, which still appear every year. There were kingfishers in several places but, on the more eroded and intensively farmed stretches, lack of perches often forced them to fish by hovering over the river:

> The kingfishers move about a lot and are hard to count. Several close views. A pair together produced repeated calls, based on the usual *keee* and *chee-kee* but with fast, trilling variations ('song' from male?); later a single bird was equally noisy for a while and then I watched another pair, again giving a variety of calls including a thin *chik-weee* and more or less trilled sounds. They faced each other, very upright, but with heads drawn in or extended forward with bill horizontal and nape feathers ruffled. They reminded me very much of penguins at times! Often one would seem to fly at the other, which immediately flew in the opposite direction so that they seemed to exchange perches.

Goosanders were regular in small numbers; there were usually a few cormorants, herons, and a small variety of commoner ducks including goldeneyes; and in the fields there were always buzzards and good numbers of fieldfares and redwings. Now and then a green sandpiper or two would get up ahead and fly off while making their beautiful, yodelling calls. There were sometimes signs of otters, especially in the snow, when I found good tracks and slides close to Caersws.

One office job was to gather all the available information on waterfowl on all Welsh lakes and reservoirs. Sometimes I supplemented this by going to see a few myself: I ended up at all kinds of odd little pools and hidden lakes, often with interesting, if not spectacular, results. Whooper swans were scattered at some of these, and goldeneyes were often the only ducks on the higher, colder lakes. It was a good way to see a lot of mid-Wales, often in beautifully crisp, frosty conditions. After the long hot summer, the winter proved quite sharp, and at one point we were completely snowed in at the bungalow for three days.

Some weekends I could get back to Chasewater to study the Iceland gulls and once even dashed down to Blackpill to see a Mediterranean gull for the first time in a year or two. A trip south after the Christmas and New Year break took me to Llandeilo and Dryslwyn in the Tywi valley. There were still many birds there then, including 750 wigeon, 380 to 400 white-fronted geese, and 1,500 golden plovers. The goose flock was under half the number I used to see in my Swansea days and was soon gone altogether, a sad loss. Likewise, the white-fronted geese from Leighton, near Welshpool, quickly disappeared after decades of regular appearances there. My best count was 105, with four pink-feet.

The forestry plantations above Kerry proved to be good, especially as strong winds had felled a lot of trees and opened up some interesting clearings. Crossbills were often about, but I was after goshawks. When I had the day on the Berwyns with Derek Barber and Roger Lovegrove, I was fascinated to hear Roger mention that he thought there must be 50 goshawk pairs in Wales, which astonished me. 'My dear fellow,' said Derek, 'you really think there are as many as that?' So, I was always out to see goshawks, and Roger sent me to a number of places where there were suspected pairs, even likely nests. But I never saw the birds, even in the early spring display period. At one place on the border I found some huge goshawk nests in tall larches, some quite easily visible from a road, but couldn't see the birds themselves except occasional 'probable' males: never a whopping great female as big as a buzzard. It was a couple of years later, when I returned to see friends in Newtown, that I finally saw a superb female goshawk swoop by over the Kerry forests. Now, with much more experience behind me, I look back and wonder why I had so much trouble with goshawks (although the females I saw in the Wyre Forest, for example, were so huge and unmistakable that there was never any difficulty there).

Crossbills provided some interesting interludes:

The male was found by listening to a *very* faint song, or subsong, consisting of a tit-like phrase (*tidee tidee tidee tidee*) or almost goldcrest-like sound, which seemed to be distant but, as I moved, suddenly seemed to be coming from behind me – eventually I realized that the bird was in the tree above, singing extremely quietly.

At other times, the crossbills gave their usual loud, ringing, *jip jip jip* notes as well as much louder, varied, ringing calls with very loud *pip pip pip* sounds interspersed with song phrases that included prolonged, subdued twittering and tinkling, greenfinch-like trills and repeated whistling, musical notes. When two were together they often called with peculiar deep, guttural calls, and at times they used surprisingly great-tit-like *sitoo sitoo sitoo* notes; they have a remarkably varied repertoire.

Whooper swans were fun to watch and their behaviour was fascinating, hardly seeming to be 'bird-like' at all given their great size and dramatic presence. On 13 February 1977:

At 11 a.m., 11 whooper swans flew in to Llyn Mawr from the south. A few minutes later two more arrived to complete the usual 13. As they settled a fantastic display started. Two of the 13 are probably sub-adults, with very pale bills and faint greyish smudges. Within 2–3 minutes six more arrived, the pair with four young. All four young are now whiter, one particularly so, although still duskier than the adults. The 'greeting' displays included vigorous, rhythmic head-bobbing with, at the same time, rapid flicking of half-open wings. Often a bird would fully open its wings, rear up and flap, settling slowly down with neck gracefully curved. Or a bird might rush at another, settling with curved neck before swimming alongside and stretching up its neck behind that of the other swan. All the while the whole group called loudly with wide-open bills. Apparently they all left later, to return again in the afternoon, with an extra five. All 24 were present when I came back in the evening.

Then on 24 March:

Eleven adult whoopers flew over this morning in a single, regular, diagonal line. Later they flew in to the lake and I approached through a willow thicket and watched and photographed them from 30–40 yards. While I sat on the edge of the lake, half-hidden, there was clearly a conflict between wariness and curiosity and sometimes the whoopers all swam directly towards me, calling all the while. They have a habit of rising up out of the water, hind end uppermost, like a coot.

Early in April I went to a little, wooded hillside near Builth Wells. It was a traditional site for woodlarks, going back 70-odd years, and we wondered if they were still there, although it seemed unlikely, as this was a period of withdrawal for British woodlarks and they had become remarkably scarce. Almost the first bird I saw, though, was a woodlark, singing beautifully, and eventually I found three singing males plus another individual. I'm not sure they were seen again after this spring, although they may have persisted for another year or two. I visited a few times and found them again in April and late May. It was such an ordinary-looking bit of hill: why could there not be woodlarks all over Wales if they could succeed here?

At this point I started regular badger-watching at several setts:

On April 7th the sett entrance in the field, away from the hedge, was so small and insignificant that the emerging badger's head appeared to come up out of the grass. Now [11 May] there are two holes, six feet apart, with a broad triangle of earth and bedding between them and spreading about eight feet away. From one of these, at 9.20 p.m., a badger emerged very rapidly, almost like a giant rabbit. It moved to the other, looked in, withdrew, paused and then went down. Despite heavy cloud and intermittent rain, the light was better than on any previous watch – from 25 yards or so the animal appeared surprisingly brown, there being a good deal of yellow-brown mixed with the grey above and a tinge of buff in the tail – almost a brindled effect. It re-emerged and went back to the right-hand hole and this happened with or without a pause on top several times. Once it leapt out of one hole and was down the other in two bounds, remarkably quick. Once it went down the left hole and another emerged from the right, later both were in view together and eventually were side by side. One began to heave earth out of the smaller, right-hand hole, with a shuffling backwards movement and backward thrust with the forelegs. It went down for a minute or two then started digging again. I moved to within ten yards and the badger appeared and began to dig. One moved from the left-hand hole to the big entrance in the hedge; there was possibly a third badger. The upper white bands on the head were a purer white than the side bands (though sometimes smudged with soil). Watched until 9.40 when the light was still better than it was when the animal had first emerged last time. Silent throughout. When I first arrived the closer [badger] looked towards me for a few seconds then carried on digging: otherwise, took no notice at all. When a badger comes up head-on and stands high on the edge of the hole it looks particularly impressive, showing the head to perfection but also the broad black chest and thick black forelegs.

Later, in autumn, I was badger-watching at a different sett:

A short, extraordinary badger watch. A fine evening, the sun having gone down bright red through haze and broken, thin cloud (sunset after 8.30). Reached the sett between 8.25 and 8.30 – only the slightest breeze coming towards me, as I stood against a tree halfway down a wooded bank. Ahead of me the bank became larger, extending both farther up and farther down; the nearest large holes were 20 yards away near the top, with others just over the top in the flat field beyond. Calm and quiet generally but several calves running about, once or twice right over the sett, plus a really fearsome bellowing from a nearby cow (in the narrow valley this seemed amazingly loud, with a rasping intake of breath between each bellow and the general impression that the cow was either exceptionally angry or in mortal agony). As I was wondering whether this would deter the badgers, I saw one approaching the holes along a track from the other side – this was barely 8.45 when it was still very light. It soon reached the largest hole (often out of sight) then appeared lower down the bank. It appeared quite unconcerned at the loud report of a shotgun but I think it scampered up to a hole (out of sight) when a wood pigeon clattered off above it. It then ambled along towards me, looking from side to side or pausing to reach up and sniff tall grass seed-heads, coming along quite unaware of me. It followed a rough track down the slope, then back up to a point no more than five feet from where I stood, but it then turned back down and went below me a few yards away, so that I had to look over my shoulder. It came right behind me and up the other side as if to reach the level spot next to the tree where I was standing – it reached a point no more than three feet from my heels before it finally detected me, then went in a mad dash back round me and off up the bank, slipping on the loose earth. It paused by the large hole, then went away more slowly. I was back indoors before ten past nine having decided to leave the badgers alone after that.

There were stories of terribly inhumane treatment of badgers around here: one was found tied by its hind legs to a tree, with its front legs just about able to touch the ground, and left hanging to die. Badger-baiting was reputedly rife (and continues still). We tended to keep the location of the setts to ourselves.

The farmer who owned the caravan I was staying in ran a pack of hounds, followed on foot. He shot most of the foxes on his land but encouraged a couple of pairs with their cubs: 'I'll leave those so we can have some fun with them with the hounds in the autumn.' Hunting was, as everyone knows, purely about fun, nothing whatever to do with pest control. One day in February I was in a wood and saw the surprising sight of a fox running directly towards me on a path as I heard the noise of the hounds in the distance. The fox paused, just a few yards away, looking back towards its pursuers, then ran towards me and continued on its way. A few minutes later I was surrounded by the hounds, which were in pursuit. If I could have said in hound language 'He went thataway' and pointed in the wrong direction, I would have done it.

One day in early May I had a memorable view of a fox on the open hill. It was just before midday, in bright sunshine. The fox ambled down to a stream and drank, then wandered over several hundred yards of soggy moor, giving a wide berth to an aggressive-looking sheep (rarely can a sheep look aggressive) before going out of sight. I walked towards the area and, at about 40 yards, it reappeared and bounded away. It was a richly colourful creature:

> Blackish nose and ears. Bright tawny-orange around base of ears, rear of head, rear and sides of neck and shoulders. Blackish on legs; back pale brown with an admixture of reddish and yellow-ochre, especially on flanks; pure white throat and chest, pale belly. Pale orange-buff either side of base of tail, redder down rear of hind legs. Tail grey-brown, much greyer beneath, becoming buff and finally mid-grey on the tip. The patch of orange around the neck stood out brilliantly in the sun; black around mouth and white teeth also striking. A long, slim, elegant animal, broadest about the shoulders, with long tail and, despite 'long and low' effect, quite long, springy legs – a very handsome creature.

As with my birds, I needed to do justice to this beautiful fox and, as a frustrated artist, unable to paint it, I resorted to a description in the notebook.

A peculiar event I had not previously seen was a gathering of lampreys in the River Ithon at Penybont. There was a calm stretch in this mostly hurried, tumbling river, only a foot or 18 inches deep, and lampreys were evidently spawning over the clean gravelly bottom. There were groups of 20, 40 or 50 or more, the largest forming dense, writhing groups. Many were exhausted or even dead, but most were active and determined. They grasped pebbles with their sucker mouths and anchored themselves to the bottom, or were lifted up, pebble and all, and washed downstream. Those that got a fix on a heavier stone vibrated their tails, creating sizeable hollows and sending streams of sand away behind them.

The area around Penybont Common was really good that year, with pied flycatchers in the riverside trees, ravens nesting in tall pines rather than on cliff ledges, the odd barn owl and still good numbers of breeding lapwings, a few snipe and some redshanks – these waders have all but disappeared from inland Wales as breeding birds now. This was a period of great intensification of farming so, while I hugely enjoyed watching the displaying lapwings ripping through the air above the fields, the nests I later found on farmland were usually destroyed by rolling and reseeding or by trampling by sheep. It should have been easy to mark the nests and warn the farmers to avoid them – but we didn't, then. The advance of the smooth, green field, good for nothing but sheep, in place of the heath and scrub on the hillsides that had been noticeable in the Berwyns, was far more obvious here; but at least there were no windfarms then.

Up on the hills it was a dream. These are mostly quite low, rounded hills but ideal for a long day out walking, exploring the valleys, the little rushy hollows and heathery banks, the peaty pools where a pair or two of black-headed gulls might nest, the gullies with hawthorn trees containing old crows' nests that might be occupied by a merlin (and once, to my great surprise, by a sparrowhawk on eggs). I found a larch copse with long-eared owls in it, but short-eared owls were oddly absent in both of my hillwalking summers. Again, whinchats were everywhere – much more characteristic of many hills than wheatears – and there were moderate numbers of ring ouzels.

One particular day at the beginning of May gives a flavour of that spring of 1977. The day began with two long-eared owls in a copse. There were old nests in larches, but they all seemed unoccupied. The owls were present, but they were simply sitting in the trees, neither on nor near a nest. I saw the usual buzzards, a sparrowhawk, redstarts, two marsh tits. Then my main walk of the day produced eight buzzards, including one on a nest, four kestrels, two curlews, fantastic close-up views of a tawny owl in a yew tree, three wheatears, 26 singing male whinchats (making 41 plotted so far on this hill), three red grouse (always scarce), three male and two female ring ouzels, several cuckoos, seven singing reed buntings, and many chaffinches. The whinchats were virtually all associated with bracken on the peripheral slopes – the very areas that were being converted to grass for sheep – and never in pure heather or in the heather/bilberry or heather/rush mixtures. Most remarkable were 60 ravens, mostly in one roaming, nomadic flock:

> Like buzzards, ravens were constantly in evidence. Three or four birds as I set off, odd ones over the first hill and elsewhere. Then two, often battling with crows, giving all kinds of popping, cronking, rattling and machine-gunning calls and flying around for long periods 'duetting', flying almost totally together, turning, soaring, diving and rolling in unison, like a bird and its reflection, frequently with head and neck feathers raised to create a hugely top-heavy impression. Then they became extremely agitated, flying close overhead, calling constantly; one chased a swallow several times. I noticed the nest, with young just visible, in a slightly odd site – 40–45 feet up in the central fork of a large sycamore, an isolated tall tree in a hedgerow. It was a large, very deep nest. Later ravens were all over the hills, odd ones and twos, then the 'usual' noisy ones back near the road. I scanned the trees for their nest, flushing the brooding buzzard instead, then one or two more flew from the valley-bottom trees into a field – young

ones perhaps? As I watched, a great flock of birds issued from the trees and, incredibly, all were ravens. They gathered up into a very noisy flock above the slopes and all soared, rolled and dived about in a wheeling mass – at least 55 birds together! The flocks eventually split up, some birds going north and west, others flying low over the hill and 15–20 settling on a heathery slope. Surely this is unusual for early May when some young ravens are not yet fledged?

Two weeks later, 'I saw another huge congregation of ravens, virtually all adults, settled on the ground or periodically flying up to soar around and fill the air with their really beautiful calls, which carry for miles over the silent hills.' This time, there were around 65 of them, along with two merlins:

As I approached the area [of a merlins' nest I had found previously] I saw both merlins fly from the vicinity to chase crows (the female most actively). Then both returned. Later, the male circled with loud chittering calls. The female was only briefly seen flying near by, silent. Later on, after I had been well away out of sight, I saw the male chasing crows and ravens, using the same calls but with some longer, nasal notes. Later on I watched the female on the nest; the male was absent, but returned, calling, then settled on a fence post. The initial views of the male as he circled me, calling loudly, were superb – with his head raised, looking back over his shoulder at times, and wings flickering downwards, he looked more cuckoo-like than like any other raptor. Wing-beats often fluttering, but flight usually fast and dashing.

There were many good times with merlins, which in my notebook I tended to describe in considerable detail (although the plumage descriptions are largely left out of the following samples):

Male merlin briefly seen chasing a crow. Later, at the same spot, a female flew out from some trees, giving a very clear, close view in bright sun. The trees proved to contain an old crow's nest, so I moved away uphill 100–150 yards and lay down in the heather to look at the nest with my telescope. I was unable to see into it. However, loud calls announced the arrival of the male – he flew in over the trees, banked, with trailing legs, and settled near the nest. In bright sunshine he looked a little cracker, as bright as any I've seen – bright blue-grey above with darker tip to the tail, bright rusty-orange beneath and on the cheeks, contrasting with brilliant yellow legs. He called several times, a repeated, musical whistle unlike the *kee kee kee* display note – *wit wit it it it*. He moved onto the nest and settled as if incubating eggs. Soon afterwards the female flew in and settled on a fallen branch near by; there were quieter, longer calls all the time – a whining *weeeet weee weee weewee* or *keeee keeee keeekeekeekee* ...

The female merlin was brooding on the nest [one of several found that spring]. As she watched me 30 yards away it seemed pointless and perhaps risky to disturb her, especially in such unusually cold weather – still brooding when I left. However, the male was altogether different. He really is a spirited bird. At frequent intervals he flew around in a wide circle, low down, calling loudly all the time. On most circuits he flew over the nest tree and swooped down in a wild swerve right past the nest. Between these flights he perched on nearby trees or posts, at anything between 30 and 75 yards from me. I was able to watch with my telescope and fill the field of view with the bird – really supreme views. With head held well up and forward while calling, narrow, pointed wings, set well forward, with a rapid fluttering action and long tail, the male could at times look quite cuckoo-like. At other times, his flight was the typical low, fast, dashing variety. Wings sometimes held well back in towards the tail and flicked in and out [typical hunting flight before the final pursuit]. When perched (in dull light) the colours ... were rich, but not really bright, but in flight, especially swooping down off a perch with legs trailing, the combination of blue-grey, bright, almost orange-buff and rust, banded tail and bright yellow legs made him look very fine indeed ...

As I approached the nest, the female was perched in a bush on the opposite side of the gully. After a few calls, I saw the male on the bush – evidently they had changed over at the nest. I sat and watched as the male preened for several minutes, then approached openly as usual, so as not to surprise the birds at the last minute. He flew off at 200 yards' range, going away silently, circling and gaining height, drifting far away with the wind. Soared like a small peregrine but with wings slightly drooped, lacking the slight uptilt beyond the angle [of peregrine]; tail fanned and appearing broad, like peregrine but probably longer, and wings looked both narrower and shorter; occasional bursts of fast, flickering wing-beats unlike peregrine. Perhaps less buff and rufous below than [the other male described above] but very blue above with broad black band on tail. I found the female on the nest, obviously not warned by the silent male – she sat tight while I watched from 15 yards, staring back at me without a movement. Even when I looked down from the bank at 8–10 yards the bird sat still, but then twice made a move as if about to leave; finally left very reluctantly, flying to a nearby perch, silent. The views of her on the nest were really incredible – I could see the bristles on the lores [between the eye and the bill], broad lemon-yellow eye-ring, dull lemon cere with greyish ridge and large nostrils, the 'tooth' on the upper mandible, etc. As I climbed up to the nest the male called near by. Still three eggs, no sign of hatching [well beyond the due date].

It was from this last nest that I later took the eggs for analysis, which proved them to be heavily contaminated with chemical residues. The female flew off quietly when I was 300 yards away, the male left the nest when I was within 20 yards; but neither called much and, as I walked away with their clutch of eggs, they were silent. Perhaps they had given up on them, anyway, after several weeks' pointless incubation. When I gently shook the eggs it was clear that they had very liquid contents; no doubt the merlins could have detected this when they turned them at intervals.

It was unusual to compare a merlin with a peregrine: normally there is little real similarity. I sometimes find a hobby looks very much more peregrine-like and not at all easy to tell from the larger falcon. The place and the time of year are helpful indicators, although there was one day in July, which I spent on the moor on these mid-Wales hills, when I saw a hobby, a peregrine, two merlins and two kestrels, a fine set of falcons, a male hen harrier plus a pair with five young in the nest, and four buzzards. This particular moor was really good for everything: 10 to 12 curlews, a family of red grouse, whinchats, ravens and an abundance of butterflies, including 235 small heaths, 36 large heaths and 14 small pearl-bordered fritillaries.

Some hen harriers were especially aggressive and clearly had a nest; sometimes the female dived to within a foot of my head:

The nest was a raised, round pad of heather stems at the foot of a six-foot bank, ten yards from a stream, in long heather. Five chicks (one a poor runt) in shade of heather beside the nest – all in grey-buff down, primaries just beginning to show. They panted in the heat with wide open bills; sometimes hissed and pushed forward a long, pale custard-yellow leg with sharp black talons. The female dived at me time after time and I quickly left the vicinity. Only prey remains [were] half a meadow pipit fledgling. Adult female had very dark eyes, rich orange-yellow legs. In moult – on one wing one inner primary missing, on the other one middle primary … Needless to say this [the presence of a second male near by], in bright sunshine and still air, produced a whole series of superlative views of both male and especially the female harriers.

I watched peregrines, too:

Female watched soaring above a crag from the end of a road. Later, from across the valley, seen to fly down and perch on the crags – prolonged views, but in haze. Began to call loudly and almost continually; male flew in and female came up and circled – magnificent views for several minutes of very big falcon, very broad and thick-set – a marvellous bird. I moved to get a closer view of an old raven's nest, which contained a 'white blob' – a single, fairly small, downy chick, largely very inactive. Meanwhile the male flew around, calling, flying in circles overhead or coming along the cliff, 'stalling' and turning or banking steeply over to come in head on, then banking away again – a superlative exhibition of flying at very close range. Tremendous views of bright yellow cere, blackish 'hood', blue-grey back with thin, pale fringes to scapulars and coverts, whitish underparts with fine, regular dark barring, big yellow feet, etc. Later the male was perched by the nest, with the chick at times more active, and the female a few feet away. She turned to show off the big, powerful, brilliant yellow feet, then sailed off across the valley with a few calls. The male remained but called repeatedly for several minutes. The view of the male perched on a rock by a raven's nest holding its chick, on a superb crag, was a very fine sight.

Wales in summer can be an enchanting place. Even the roadsides are abundantly colourful, and journeys home via the West Midlands were stark indications of the difference as I headed east:

Grasshopper warblers in an unusual and attractive spot. Male sang first from a very small clearing on the edge of a deciduous wood, with short bracken, red campion, bluebells and broom. Then crossed the road to sing openly from the top of a short, layered hazel hedge. On this side of the road was a six-foot wide sloping bank, with the hedge below, then a meadow and a stream. The bank was grassy with scattered umbellifers, meadowsweet and a fine show of red campion and bluebells. Sharp, metallic calls drew attention to a second grasshopper warbler in the hedge, then both were watched at close range running about on the layered hazel poles.

My interest in the stars and planets continued a little hesitantly. I had seen Venus in daylight before, having searched for it deliberately when I knew it should be possible, but I hadn't happened to notice it by chance until now: 'Venus – at 2.10 p.m. in bright sunshine I noticed, high in the sky, a tiny white spot. It was visible to the naked eye quite easily despite the bright light and a telescope easily revealed a pure white crescent.' Later in June: 'At 10 a.m. with the sun high in the sky, sky bright clear blue with slight haze, Venus was extraordinarily bright – visible to the naked eye with ease, showing a broad crescent through the telescope.'

The Welsh hills – especially the Berwyns in the previous year, but often even here, in Montgomery and Radnorshire – could be lonely and remote. On the main Berwyns ridge I reckoned that, apart from the shapes of dark conifer plantations on some distant hills, I could neither see nor hear any sign of people, not so much as a fence post. The chance to experience such seclusion is rare, and I am grateful for having had it. The Radnorshire hills did not always equal the Berwyns scenically – they were generally a little less exciting – but at their best they were wonderfully rich and beautiful places to be. The border country towards Presteigne and Herefordshire was also, in its way, quite exceptional. Yet sometimes I needed a break, a day or so in the office, to see some people again. I was never alone for very many days at a stretch, but it was enough; and, although I had always thought that I was most happy in my own company, it was obvious that the company of other people was equally necessary – something that perhaps came as a surprise.

By late July the fieldwork was largely over and I returned to Newtown to live in a small room in a tall, red-brick, warehouse-like building overlooking the main Welshpool road. Facilities were few – a bed and a chair – and there was little money, but living in Newtown and getting out and about from there was good fun. Roger, tall, spare, almost gaunt, full of energy and urgency, and Graham, kind, generous, very hard-working but much more relaxed, complemented each other remarkably well in the RSPB's rickety offices above the National Farmers' Union in the high street. (Such was the state of these offices that the walls grew fungi; in fact there were so many fungi above one particular desk that we threatened to have it declared an SSSI.) Graham had been thrown into the deep end when he first joined the staff, as Roger had suffered an enormous car accident returning from an RSPB film show (he had hit a lorry head on). Graham would therefore spend the morning collecting RSPB sales goods from the adjacent field before taking on pretty much everything. However, the accident did not manage to slow Roger down for long (he was refused permission, on medical grounds, to do a sponsored parachute jump because of the large metal plate in his thigh). The two of them did a great job and it was a good time to be in Wales, working in the Newtown office.

Roger was always innovative in his RSPB work in Wales. Getting money to employ people was just one thing he was good at, much better than most other regional or country offices. Before me he had employed people such as Tim Inskipp, who later worked full time for the RSPB in investigations and then moved to TRAFFIC, studying the international trade in endangered species. After me, he gave a job to Keith Vinicombe. Keith, who had once braked hard on his bicycle to avoid a song thrush, and as a result fallen off and broken his collar bone, proved still to be accident-prone. He rode around on a motorbike. One day in the Newtown office he had put on all his motorbike gear, helmet and a heavy pack – ready to leave – and he overbalanced, falling backwards down the stairs with a great clatter, much to Roger's amusement.

One of Roger's interesting ideas was to count common scoters in Carmarthen Bay from the air. So it was at the beginning of June that I drove up to an airfield on the Shropshire border where I met Roger and his pilot friend and hopped into a little four-seater Cessna. We flew down the Swansea valley and out into the Bristol Channel, then across to Carmarthen Bay, where we did several transects at very low level. We also circled St Margaret's and Caldey islands before heading west. We looked closely at the islands of Skokholm and Ramsey, then flew out to circle Grassholm, site of a huge gannet colony (some 30,000 breeding pairs). We stayed out far enough to be sure that the birds didn't panic and leave their nests, but we nevertheless had a grandstand view of the huge colony and it was a sensational sight. On our return, we flew along the north Pembrokeshire coast as far as Newport Bay, then around the Taf/Tywi estuaries, along Llyn Brianne and around the Gwenffrwd/Dinas reserve.

We repeated the exercise (just the Carmarthen Bay count this time) at the end of August, counting 900 common scoters from the little plane. We went again early in September, with a further tour over Grassholm. This trip had been prompted by disturbing reports of severe oil pollution in the area. We saw an abundance of gannets and mercifully no sign of the oil. On the return, in a beautiful sky with puffy cumulus clouds, we sailed up and over the tops of the Brecon Beacons and Black Mountains – the pilot was a glider pilot and flew his Cessna in a way that came close to his gliding – and sometimes we rose to clip the top of a cloud, tipped over and dropped down the other side, in a marvellous half hour of pure enjoyment.

Following on from this, in mid-September, a small group of us travelled to Dale Fort and boarded a boat to head out to Grassholm by sea. Luckily, David Saunders, Operation Seafarer organizer in 1969 and great seabird enthusiast, was able to join us. Only the day before I had collected a storm-blown Manx shearwater from Llandrindod Wells, so this was an ideal opportunity to release it. Once we were well out to sea, I took it from its cardboard box and it sat on my hand for a minute or so, where it gathered its wits and whereabouts before flying off steadily towards Skokholm.

Grassholm was sensational. It was my first close-up visit to a large gannet colony. Despite their numbers, they had not yet spilled up over the top of the island and onto its other side, so we could still climb to the top and overlook the colony. I conservatively put down 20 to 30,000 gannets, as well as a surprising 800 great black-backed gulls (mostly adults heavily in moult), 100 kittiwakes, four purple sandpipers, and a few migrants such as redstarts, willow warblers, chiffchaffs, garden warblers and goldcrests, topped off nicely by a lovely juvenile red-backed shrike. How amazing it is that such a small, barren rock should attract birds of this sort, several miles out to sea.

The atmosphere, with constant noise, the smell, the air and surrounding sea full of gannets and the fantastic numbers of gannets on the ground, is absolutely tremendous. The colony is an amazing sight. There is a constant clamour, with an almost mechanical, clattering effect as a whole (*uck-erruck erruck erruck erruck* ...) with individual deep *urrah urrah* calls and whistling from the young birds. A too sudden close approach will set the edge birds [not nesting] thrashing away in noisy confusion, tumbling about in a heap. One group on the edge of the colony, non-breeders, swept away, half flying, half scrambling, throwing up a huge cloud of strong-smelling dust, 'guano' and feathers. However, a careful approach allowed me to get within eight feet of the nearest birds on the edge of a continuous densely packed crowd – I was too close to focus on them with my camera (which focuses down to 8ft 6in). Adults would even fly in to land within a few feet of me and all kinds of greeting displays, bill-scissoring, fighting, tossing of nesting material etc would go on a few yards away as if I wasn't there. There were some flying young and several on the sea, but many still in the colony. Several were still completely covered in down, yellow bundles with a beak at one end, only showing minute feathers when spreading their wings. Many more had a good deal of down on the head and neck. [I was surprised at the number of downy chicks, as gannets are supposed to be so well synchronized in their breeding.] Birds on the sea stretched out maybe a mile north and west of the island – several thousands at a time – with maybe 5,000 more in flight. At times many more would be in flight in a vast cloud of gannets, while those on the island still seemed undiminished.

By late November either the money, or the work, or both had once more run out, and chances were I could end up back on the dole in Burntwood. I had had two glorious summers in Wales, but this could not really go on. Roger, bless him, gave me details of a job at The Lodge, the RSPB headquarters in Bedfordshire, and encouraged me to go for it. It was not the first I had applied for: I had once gone for a job as conservation planning assistant (thank God I didn't get that!) and had been to see people at The Lodge, including Peter Conder and James Ferguson-Lees, to talk about future possibilities. Nothing had come of that, but people remembered me and Roger put in a good word. So, I was asked to go for interview for the post of RSPB librarian, which would become available when Dorothy Rook retired.

I was interviewed by a daunting panel, including conservation director John Parslow and public affairs director, Frank Bailey. Also sitting in on the interview was Trevor Gunton. It went well enough, but I was not at all used to interviews; I wasn't used to being in offices, or working indoors much, either. The decision, when it came, left me very much in two minds. I was not offered the job of librarian (that went to Ian Dawson, who is still there), but Trevor, who was trying to fill a post after a series of interviews had failed to find anyone suitable, offered me a different job, in the development department. Well, it was a job; it was with the RSPB; and, although it was in the dull depths of Bedfordshire, it would surely see me 'in the door' (I might soon get something better, perhaps something based somewhere else). With encouragement from Roger Lovegrove, a great confidence boost from Trevor and welcome agreement from my parents, I accepted.

Scilly in the Seventies

Finding a rare bird gives every birdwatcher a rush of adrenalin. Going to see one that has already been discovered by someone else (the true meaning of that grossly misused term, twitching) is not to everyone's taste, but I feel no need to apologise for it, criticise it or justify it, even though, in its more extreme forms, I have no sympathy with the competitiveness and nastiness that sometimes permeates it. I enjoyed twitching in moderation for many years; and seeing a rarity — albeit that you may not have 'discovered' it yourself — can be interesting or exciting on many levels.

To begin with, there is the simple enjoyment of seeing a species — rare or not — that you have not seen previously, perhaps never even heard of before. Enjoying birds is what this is all about. It is hard to understand people who are so very much opposed to it and are not really interested in seeing a new bird. If I had never seen a Pallas's warbler, or struggled in my attempts to do so, I would be much the poorer for it. Then there is the excitement of seeing something that you have been aware of for years — perhaps read about and dreamed about — but never seen; you know it is exceptional in Britain, or that few other people have seen it, and it may never come again. Put into such a context, rare birds are more exciting than those you have never heard of before and simply add to a list.

Many rare birds happen to be difficult to identify — some of the warblers, the pipits, the female and immature buntings, or passing seabirds that fly by but never come back. Identifying a bird is just one small stage in understanding it; but, nevertheless, it is sometimes extremely hard and a lifetime study in itself. Some of the much-maligned people who like rare birds have become remarkably expert in this small, chosen field. A few are exceptionally brilliant 'in the field'.

There are places in the UK that are much more likely to produce rare birds than most. Fair Isle, between the Shetlands and the Orkneys, is so far out on a limb that any passing, off-course, exhausted bird is likely to make landfall and be seen, identified and recorded. Extreme geographical points – long headlands, offshore islands – are more productive than long, even coastlines or anonymous landscapes inland. The Isles of Scilly, far to the west of Cornwall, make one such hotspot, where migrants of all kinds, common and rare, are often abundant, especially in autumn. My own brief dalliance with the Scillies rests almost solely with October visits in the 1970s. The early years of the observatory on St Agnes were well before my time and I missed the 1960s and the early 1970s' years of discoveries, excitement and controversy, but the late seventies had their share.

Like many others, I had been enthused by a strange but exciting paper in *British Birds* by Ian (D. I. M.) Wallace. It was unlike anything else *BB* had published, as it seemed to deal purely with the magic, mystery and pure enjoyment of seeing rare birds. 'An October to remember in the Isles of Scilly' was a great read and many of us wished we had been there. My idea of offshore islands was based largely on those of Wales and those seen mostly from the mainland of Scotland, so in my mind I had some vague image of rough, open, maybe heathery islands, with little dips and valleys where a few bushes might grow, each full of rare birds surrounded by perhaps ten or a dozen birdwatchers.

Pallas's warbler.

It must be relatively easy: how else could anyone find these American and Siberian vagrants that seemed to turn up, side by side, with amazing regularity?

It was Peter Lansdown who booked a cottage behind the post office on St Agnes in 1974 and suggested that I share it. The post office was ideally situated near the centre of the island, close to the main junctions of all the little unmade lanes and tarmac roads, which saw no more traffic than an occasional tractor or bicycle. The high-tech information system – a blackboard and piece of chalk – was also at the post office, so that anyone could write down what they had seen and where it was. This was a few years before CB radio, and it would be some years after that before birdlines (which you phoned for regularly updated, recorded information), mobile phones, pagers (which give you instant news straight to the pocket) and websites came along.

The islands must have shocked me. On the first day, we visited St Mary's and stood at the end of the long wood that runs down Holy Vale, looking at a real wood – a big one at that – and a vast thicket of tall willow, with rough fields behind, more thickets of willow, bramble brakes and large pools complete with reed-beds. This was not somewhere to find a bunch of rare birds in an isolated hawthorn bush; it was more like trying to find an individual warbler on the Gower peninsula or in a lump of the New Forest. It must be impossible.

We crossed Lower Moors, the rough, damp, low-lying ground behind Hugh Town, running east towards Porth Hellick. A yellow-browed warbler had been seen by other people; but I saw only a bright-green warbler showing 'at least one broad yellow wing bar and a long, pale, yellowish superciliary'. It was deep inside a thicket of grey-green sallows, silent and refusing to give a good view, but pragmatically I put it down as my first ever yellow-browed warbler. These islands must, after all, be all they were cracked up to be: I'd hardly started and here was a yellow-browed warbler, a bird I had so long wanted to see, a tiny waif from far off Siberia. The origin of such rare birds, and their vast migratory travels, are not the least part of their appeal. In a line of trees near by was a red-breasted flycatcher, and there was a second in a hedge near a pool. These were different from the elusive yellow-browed, and quite magical – another new bird added to my list with full descriptions, sketches and excellent views. They impressed me greatly: 'Neat, attractive, no striking colours but still beautiful.' Someone said a red-breasted flycatcher (or an 'r-b fly') would make a fine pet – he'd like to take one home. Later one was to sit on my friend Eric Phillips's bobble hat.

The main target for the day was in this great thicket at the end of Holy Vale. I got the idea that the bird would do a circuit around the wood, perhaps with a flock of tits and warblers, and eventually come to 'our' end before doing another circuit that might take a couple of hours. It was a case of standing, waiting, watching. And there it was! A Pallas's warbler. This was a real rarity then. Rumour had it that even Ian Wallace had never seen one, nor even strung one (that is, made it up, or put two and two together to make five or even more). Someone had seen one in Kent a few years before, but most of us were on for a tick. The bird was at 'our end of the wood' for 17 minutes, and I reckoned it was in view for about ten. There to watch was a mass gathering of 40 or 50 people – it seemed a lot then, it would be 500 now (a greater rarity on the mainland will attract 2,000). The bird appeared, tumbled through a sallow, flicked across a gap, shot up, dived down, went into the dark depths of the thicket and reappeared moments later, sometimes flicking out to catch a fly or dart out, turn back and hover with face to the bush, revealing its stunning lemon-yellow rump. What a magical bird. In my notes written up that night, I recalled:

> The superciliaries looked extremely long and the main wing bar very bright and prominent – when flying, the pale rump was conspicuous so the whole bird looked a mass of brilliant lines, bars, stripes and patches! All on so tiny and sleek a bird. It was really outstandingly beautiful, slightly reminiscent of a firecrest but otherwise quite in a class of its own.

Subsequent Pallas's warblers occasionally perched next to a goldcrest and I swear they were noticeably smaller – really minute birds. Firecrests have more colour, but Pallas's always have been special and always will be.

On St Agnes, as we sat in the Turk's Head that evening, Tony Smith, one of the 'incredible string band' (alluding to their reputation for stringing and derived from the name of the popular rock band), in his usual blue denims and shiny black cap, glanced across at the bar with a satisfied grin on his face. 'I keep looking at the bottles and thinking of the Pallas's – all those greens, all those stripes.' I liked Tony from the start. It was a special bird for everyone and it was rumoured that Ian Wallace was arriving the next day in an effort to see it, the most exciting vagrant Siberian warbler of the lot (it was not, quite, his first). Pallas's warbler has since become so regular that for many years it has been taken off the official rarities list (much against my wishes, when I was on the rarities committee, but in the end it had to be done), but it remains unique in its sheer charisma and ability to generate excitement.

The next day we returned to St Mary's and saw the Pallas's again; we also saw a yellow-browed, properly this time, for several minutes. More remarkable was a pale, elusive warbler in a reed-bed by Porth Hellick Pool, a small pool behind a beautiful sandy bay almost totally enclosed by rocky headlands. It was a peculiar bird, a touch like a sedge warbler crossed with a whitethroat – I did my usual bit-by-bit description without coming to any conclusion. The general feeling was that it might prove to be an aberrant sedge warbler, but other possibilities, including booted warbler, were mooted. On my visits to Scilly I was very much the beginner and there purely to watch the birds, learn what I could from others, listen intently and keep my mouth firmly shut. A poser like this, which stumped pretty well everyone, was not for me to get involved with, but plenty of others with even less experience added their two penn'orth. The mystery was solved (and some observers' firmly held views fully confirmed) when the warbler was trapped next day and proved to be a paddyfield warbler, another extraordinarily rare bird at the time. To put it into context, there had been just three UK records of Pallas's warbler before 1958, with six individuals in 1963 altogether exceptional, and 18 in 1968 just a hint of what was to come; in this year, 1974, 13 were recorded. Of paddyfields, there had been a mere three seen in Britain before this one (oddly enough, a few days later another turned up in Northumberland). It was an amazing start to my Scilly adventure.

And so it went on: days of rain and gales, sun and showers, in the most wonderful setting with such varied islands, all different, all thick with tall and dense cover – from the woods, farmland, reed-beds and pools of St Mary's to the small bulb fields, high hedges, pinewoods and gardens of Tresco and the beautiful island of St Agnes, which had a character all its own. Almost any bird might appear in front of you, any time. When the clouds parted and the sun shone, the air was fresh and clear, the light sparkling, the sun warm on our backs, and all was most certainly right with our world.

Lapland bunting: scarce in most parts of the UK but regular in Scilly.

We spent most of our time on St Agnes, with its pub by the quay (the Turk's Head), the Bar, a thin neck of sand exposed at low tide leading across to the adjoining islet of Gugh to the east, a narrow road winding up to the centre of the island with its cottages at Higher Town, then Middle Town with its post office, lighthouse and parsonage, where birdwatchers were welcome to walk in quietly and carefully to peer up into the trees for rarities. The lanes continued on in a circle, more or less, downhill past the 'fruit cage' to Lower Town and, beyond that, Troy Town, and various narrow concreted routes ran around the western end of the island, with a gap leading out to the pool between little rocky headlands and white sandy beaches. 'Big Pool', small and round as it is, is set in a patch of grass and rushes with bumpy, stone-walled fields by a small headland at Browarth. From the post office, Barnaby Lane, closed in on each side by tall, dense hedges, ran out through a gate to the open heath of Wingletang, across the narrow waist of the island to the tumbling granite rocks of Horse Point (the southernmost tip of the inhabited islands of Scilly), and Grandfather Hugh's Point. Far to the south-west were the Western Rocks, so dangerous to shipping, with isolated reefs beyond even those: Bishop Rock, Crebnicks, Peaked Rock, Round Rock of Crebawethan, Retarrier Ledges, the Gunners ...

Everywhere were thick hedges of evergreen *Pittosporum*, wispy bushes of tamarisk overhanging hidden beaches and coves, tiny bulb fields, a small rubbish tip, open pastures between stone walls, every corner likely to hide a small, skulking bird that would set the heart racing. A small beach south of the Turk's Head was a favourite of mine: Covean, with fields of root crops behind it, had given rise to stories of half the *Hippolais* warblers in the book being seen together in the tamarisk billowing around its upper edge, and to hopes that some, at least, would make a reappearance one day. Here I watched yellow-browed warblers and red-breasted flycatchers, both sometimes feeding on the ground, even amongst seaweed on the beach, on windy days.

My notebooks are full of descriptions of yellow-browed warblers – like Pallas's, no longer so rare but still extra special – my first serin, my first little bunting, on Tresco, before my first wryneck, four red-breasted flycatchers on St Agnes. One day, however, was almost birdless. We were on St Agnes in howling gales with driving rain, our post office cottage almost as wet inside as it was out, with condensation streaming down the windows, and the bedding damp and steamy when we risked switching on electric blankets at night. We cheered up at the thought that such weather might even now be bringing a new first for Britain to our windswept little island, but such days were wretched, especially in view of how little time we had each year to indulge ourselves in Scilly.

But then there was another Pallas's warbler — on St Agnes, our island this time — found by Pete Lansdown (who would later become chairman of the British Birds Rarities Committee). I arrived ten minutes later and found my own yellow-browed, and we watched the two together. The yellow-browed came out to preen in the sun and I watched it at 60× with my Nickel Supra. My notes read almost like a description of a museum specimen. A little bunting appeared a day or two later. My first, on Tresco, had been elusive but extremely well marked; now we had one on Agnes, close to Barnaby Lane, watched by luminaries such as Paul Dukes. It was in a small field, half bare earth, half cabbage and marrow plants, so it spent much time out of sight under cover, only occasionally popping out into full view. It could be only 15 or 20 yards away and yet out of sight for 10 to 15 minutes at a time; but it also sat happily on a gate, preening, in full view for a minute or more. Some people had real difficulty; one, later quite well known in rare bird circles, several times asked which was the little bunting, and Paul Dukes, exasperated when his precise directions again failed to lead him to it, muttered rather loudly, 'It's a pity it isn't five feet tall and orange.' Birdwatching has its terraces humour just like football.

My next visit to Scilly was in October 1975. We took the *Scillonian*, from Penzance to St Mary's. A red-breasted flycatcher before we made the crossing was a good start, surely? En route were 20 grey phalaropes, raising my life's total to 23. At St Mary's, there was no relaxed change to a little boat to St Agnes: we set off straight to Tresco, where we would land either at Crow Point, at the southern tip, or farther up the west shore at New Grimsby, depending on the tide. In the event we arrived at Crow Point quay and set off on a route march past the Abbey Pool to the pines at the eastern end of the Great Pool. David Hunt (the RSPB's representative on Scilly) had found a real cracker a few days before. Would it still be there? Excitement, anticipation, dreadful nerves; worry that it might have gone or that we would be unable to find it. But, no, a strange, mottled bird flew across the corner of a small field from a tall, thick hedge, to disappear almost immediately into dense cover. Later I saw a brief silhouette in a treetop. This added little to the initial impressions but it was clearly 'the bird' — Britain's first yellow-bellied sapsucker. Wow, what a start. Eventually we had excellent views from 30 to 40 yards away, allowing me time to describe and sketch it, although its complex pattern was difficult to get down. David Hunt had a pretty good black and white photograph of it, but it was a little soft; he kindly asked me to make a line-drawing based upon it, for publication in the Isles of Scilly bird report. The yellow-bellied sapsucker remains one of the rarest of UK birds, one that few younger twitchers have had the opportunity to get to grips with.

Long-billed dowitcher.

Tresco is a big island, second down in the zigzag that starts at St Martin's (north-east) and ends at St Agnes (south-west). It is a wide north to south rectangle with a long, broad headland topped by Castle Down and Tregarthen Hill. The southern part is cut in two by the Great Pool and the Abbey Pool, with a narrow neck of land between the freshwater lake and the sandy beach at either end – Pentle Bay and New Grimsby Harbour. From New Grimsby small clusters of houses and the occasional shop run across the waist of the island to Old Grimsby on the other side. New Grimsby, Towns Hill, Dolphin Town, Green, Old Grimsby – any of these can turn up birds in gardens and allotments. The little grocery shop usually had a blackboard by the door, with birds and locations noted on it: the best information system we had.

A walk back from Old Grimsby to the Great Pool on a high, sweeping trail, with magnificent views eastwards across the whole archipelago and over vivid turquoise and azure Crow Sound, was worth doing, but it was always a bit risky as most birds were discovered in lower, more sheltered spots – would we find something fantastic, or miss something tremendous? It was also a gamble time-wise as the walk took up a fair part of the restricted time available before the boat returned to St Mary's or St Agnes. St Agnes, when we did eventually get there later that first day, after the sapsucker, had plenty of promise: I saw my first buff-breasted sandpiper (with a limp) near the rubbish tip along Barnaby Lane, a red-breasted flycatcher, and a barred warbler, which was also near the rubbish tip and also my first!

Sunday was another day to fill in a few gaps. After three new birds on Saturday, I saw four on Sunday: one on St Mary's (four short-toed larks) and three on St Martin's (a rustic bunting, a Lapland bunting – yes, rare and regular buntings both new on the same day – and a young rose-coloured starling). The rose-coloured starling gave a brief view but, as luck would have it, flew down into a field to settle in long grass ten yards from me just as I had heard and located the rustic. I peered over a low stone wall to try to see the starling, and the bunting shot out, so my views of the bunting, whose sharp *tsick* had attracted my attention, were brief and unsatisfactory in the general mêlée. I waved across to a bunch of people on the other side of the field and pointed down at my feet, to where the starling was in full view. Dave Holman thought I meant the bunting was there. Perhaps he had seen the bunting fly off, which would explain why he dismissed my efforts to attract people's attention. 'No, look down here, it's the *starling*, here, just down by my feet!' I remember the look of disdain from the others – what rubbish is he talking about? Then the penny dropped and everyone scrambled round to my side and got a good look at it.

As often happened in subsequent years, I didn't get as good a session – looking and sketching – with the starling as I should have done; this was partly because I was trying to see the bunting, but mainly because I wasted the best moments by waving at everyone else. Two similar instances come to mind, both from Holkham in Norfolk. A Radde's warbler once led us a merry dance all weekend – I spent nine hours trying to see it. Each time it appeared there was a mad rush, which, of course, sent it scurrying off into deep cover. I located it once or twice, but on each occasion I looked sideways and gave a low whistle to alert the others, only to start a cavalry charge that once more sent the bird to ground. Ray Turley said to me, 'Next time you see it, just keep quiet and watch it – it's the only way you're going to get a good view.' Years later, Britain's first red-breasted nuthatch appeared not far from the same spot. I got a great view. A couple of weeks later I was there again, with just a handful of other people about; I spent ages searching, finally found the bird, and again turned round to wave over some other people who were near by. 'It's here: look, that big pine, then go left to the forked branch, up a bit, right a bit – no? Well. Start again at the big red pine, OK? Then – oh, it's gone.'

There were phone calls from island to island to exchange information, mostly St Mary's to St Agnes, but with Ian Wallace, who was on Tresco, throwing in the odd titbit. It was a classic Chinese whispers situation, which degenerated to the point where unseemly comments were being made about other people. For example, if Ian saw something and didn't tell anyone, he was roundly criticized for keeping everything to himself; if he saw something odd (such as, one evening, 'A thrush, with a rufous tail, might be worth keeping an eye out for') and told us about it, he was condemned for stringing yet another fake rarity – 'He's claiming a Naumann's thrush!' – so he was on a hiding to nothing whatever he did. He said he'd seen what he thought was a greenish warbler, and when we duly collected on Tresco we had that in mind as well as several other possibilities. We did see a warbler that looked the part but most people dismissed it, for no good reason so far as I could see. Two other birds of Ian's were in view on Tresco that day. His claim of a surf scoter at sea off Tresco was greeted with derision. But we all ended up in a boat, up towards the peculiarly shaped little island of Tean, watching the surf scoter. It was a dull brown one – not some adult male with obvious white patches and multicoloured bill – and many people got excellent photographs. On the day we went to Tresco, the scoter flew in and landed on Great Pool, and there it was, close up and easy to see.

Ian had also seen an odd warbler in the reeds beside the pool and wondered if it might be a Blyth's reed warbler. Things were different then. Ian had watched and sketched it for hours, but no one photographed it. Not many people around knew much about Blyth's reed: plenty must have seen and heard them in north Europe, but, as an autumn vagrant, it was little known and its identification was tough, to say the least (it still is). The main reference made it sound like a tiny bird, with whirring, wren-like wings, a long, thin tail and a remarkably long, spike-like beak. Ian's bird was, well, just an *Acrocephalus*, looking much like any other *Acrocephalus*. I got a good but brief view, and didn't get anything to add to the discussion. I'm sorry that I didn't describe the head pattern much more accurately because the 'pale mark from bill to eye' that I noted was a whitish, blob-shaped patch that later became one of the more oft-quoted features of Blyth's reed; also, it was remarkably plain, uniform across its wings, as Blyth's should be. Most people were not then fully aware of the importance of such things as primary projections and so on, which in any case are hard to judge. Now, any controversial and difficult bird would be digiscoped by scores of people, photographs would be in three or four magazines, and experts in analysing pictures would tear it to pieces bit by bit; it is a different kind of expertise from knowing and identifying the bird in the field.

Tresco that year had more than its fair share of problem birds. In 1975 Richard's and tawny pipits were discussed as a difficult pair, and papers were being published about them. On St Mary's, I studied a tawny on the golf course for two hours. The day after, with John Fortey and Eric Phillips, we found another tawny pipit on St Mary's (a good day: long-billed dowitcher, buff-breasted sandpiper, and Dave Holman's fantastic bobolink), and we also saw a

Richard's, another new bird for me. This latter tawny was a 'classic' pale adult, much paler and less marked than the golf-course bird.

So, on Wednesday I ticked tawny pipit; on Thursday I found another tawny pipit and ticked Richard's; on Saturday, on the same golf course, I saw my first red-throated pipit (an adult, complete with red throat). Then on Sunday there was another big pipit on Tresco. It was in a field beside the pool, the day of Ian's 'Blyth's reed' as well as short-toed lark and other goodies. It was pointed out to me as a Richard's, but then Ian Wallace, Peter Grant and Nick Dymond came along. Peter (who had, with Nick, not long before published a paper on these pipits in *British Birds*) said, 'That's a dark one, as they go, isn't it!' (implying it was a tawny, as it was clearly rather pale for Richard's). Someone else came along and said 'That's a pale one, isn't it?', equally clearly implying it was a Richard's. John Marchant was adamant it was a Richard's pipit and, later, the three 'tawny pipit' protagonists agreed with this. It was my first 'difficult pipit' experience, and I was left confused by it all.

Back on Tresco again, Alan Dean and John Ridley, from the West Midlands, found two large pipits – which they announced to be tawnies – at Old Grimsby, a long way from the quay. It was late, but we had to go; pushed for time, we had not long enough to study the birds, but we did have excellent views. Alan Dean was, and is, as good as anyone in the field. I heard the pipits call and found their calls pretty much like the Richard's I'd seen, but not like the descriptions of Richard's in the guides and identification papers. I remained confused. These two pipits were more difficult than I had imagined. Other people arrived, heard a call and instantly said 'Isn't that an explosive *schreep*!' (the typical bird-book Richard's description). It didn't sound like *schreep* to me; what other people heard (or said they heard) as a loud, explosive, rising *schreep* was, for me, a soft, rolled, down-slurred *shrrew*.

These Old Grimsby pipits – pale, long-tailed, slim, horizontal, tail-bobbing birds – called *chree*, *cheeup* and *shrrew*; they behaved like wagtails (a tawny feature) but also flitted low over long marram before diving in (like Richard's). 'What do you make of these pipits?' Ian Wallace asked me the inevitable question. I gulped. 'Difficult,' I said, usefully. 'Too right!' said Ian, leaving me feeling that I had not added much to the debate. It was later that Ian brought up the idea that one at least might have been a Blyth's. One bird *did* look different: it was more horizontal, not standing up and leaning over backwards like some of the previous big pipits; it wagged its tail and hunched its head into its shoulders, giving a rounded, yellow-wagtail-like look. Peter Grant leaned on a gate and watched them with me, having said the two were undoubtedly Richard's.

'How,' I asked, 'does this one differ in shape and actions from a tawny, then?'
'Very little,' he replied. Back to the drawing board.

This two-week spell in October 1975 was full of good birds, controversies and challenges. Several birds, such as the dowitcher and the buff-breasted sandpiper, the surf scoter and the barred warbler, stayed around and gave repeated good views; there were Lapland buntings to learn, with their rich, varied plumages and rattling calls; several short-toed larks (Peter Grant impressed me no end by picking up one in flight from a long way off by its 'linnet-like' *chirrup*); red-breasted flycatchers, yellow-broweds and another Pallas's. While we were waiting for a good bird 'to show' we were sometimes entertained by Bryan Bland – known to some people, in earlier years, as 'the man with the upside-down head' (most twitchers had silly nicknames of this sort) as he was pretty nearly bald but had (and still has) a long and luxuriant beard. Bryan achieved some fame when parrot crossbills nested in Norfolk. He trimmed his beard and put the trimmings on the ground, which the crossbills collected for the purpose of lining their nests. As a result, Bryan claimed 'parrot crossbills nesting in my beard'. In the Scillies he would wander along lines of birdwatchers and draw marvellously accurate caricatures of them in his notebook – maybe he still has some. Mine, I remember, was complete with moustache, flared trousers and pointed shoes.

I learned more about Scilly and its birds, and also about how to handle the people. In my notes I have such items as 'brambling at 12 yards through telescope – fantastic!' But it was tricky to watch birds of this sort. For example, I watched juvenile chiffchaffs because I like chiffchaffs and their plumages are interesting, but there was always the chance that someone might look over my shoulder, see the bird and say to his mate, 'Oh, nothing, he's just struggling to identify a chiffchaff.' On one occasion, after a melodious warbler had been seen in the area, I saw a bird with suitably yellow underparts dash into a hedge at the right spot. With Eric Phillips, I stopped to watch in case it reappeared and we could identify it for sure, but out came a rufous-looking reed warbler. At that moment, Peter Grant appeared. 'Got anything?' 'No, just might have been the melodious in this hedge.' Peter saw the reed warbler, and it called. 'That one that's going *churrr*?' He turned and walked away, and I was forever embarrassed that I may have made Peter think that Eric couldn't tell a reed warbler when he saw one. Three or four other people gathered; seeing the little knot of people, along came several more – a bit like the Crazy Gang, who started talking into a pillar box and left a crowd of people thinking that a small boy was trapped inside. 'Oh, just people having trouble with a reed warbler in a hedge. They can identify one in a reed-bed but as soon as it gets out of its usual surroundings they're stumped,' and they all trooped off.

One night someone – I guess Ray Turley – played a tape of a scops owl calling by the lighthouse. He had half the island running about in their pyjamas chasing the scops; the best part of the joke was that several people claimed to see it. Ray was not above other tricks. On one occasion he dropped a dead American passerine on a footpath, hoping it would cause a sensation when someone 'discovered it', but he was disappointed (albeit amused) when all the birdwatchers on the islands just walked over it and trod it into the mud.

It was easy to miss birds that others were seeing, so there was a tendency for people to go around in little groups rather than risk going it alone. News was passed around each evening in the pub, but otherwise the communication system consisted of waves and whistles, constant, anxious, 'anything about?' enquiries whenever one group met another, and general agreement (somehow) about the time of the boat next day and where it would be heading. No pagers or mobile phones; a handful of CB radios would come a little later. On St Agnes, a small island, it was quite possible to be alone and out of sight of other observers, but usually it was like an extended flock, with individuals widely spread out but each in view of another. If one should find a rarity, the nearest person would notice and move over to the spot, the next would follow, the next would chase after and so on, until the whole flock had gathered.

My visit in October 1976 started badly. We had tickets for the *Scillonian*. We were sitting in the car park, with an hour to go to sailing, when the ferry gave a loud blast and sailed off out of Penzance harbour without us – we'd got the time wrong. We dashed off to the heliport where, luckily, we were able to buy helicopter tickets, but it was a financial burden I could have done without. But then things began to look up. On St Mary's, just off the boat, there was a blackpoll warbler from North America! *We* were just off the boat, that is: I think the warbler might have flown under its own steam. Quite how many small American vagrants come in off transatlantic steamers has never been worked out. David Hunt used to tell of a cruise liner coming by Horse Point; when it was adjacent to the island it blew several loud blasts and, later that day, a couple of American warblers were found. He was pretty convinced they had been scared off the ship and made for the first land they had seen in days.

On the Monday afternoon, having seen a blackpoll again, Eric, John Forley, Jeff Hazell and I walked into the parsonage together after John and Eric had heard a chattering call. We saw a small, brownish *Phylloscopus* warbler with a striking superciliary, heard it call again and said, in unison, 'Dusky!' What a find – a dusky warbler in the parsonage undergrowth. It subsequently made odd excursions into the adjacent field, but gave everyone great views over a couple of days. This was the time when Radde's and dusky records in Britain were neck and neck, perhaps 20:21, then 21:22, 22:22, 22:23 as the years went by. Dusky warbler was a great bird, one of the best of the vagrants from Siberia.

The very next day we went to see a Bonelli's warbler and two spotted sandpipers. I took reams of notes. The sandpipers were on Porth Cressa beach and very tame. At first we saw only one, which then disappeared. Someone played a tape recording of common sandpipers. Nothing happened. Then, at a recording of spotted sandpipers, one immediately flew up the beach to settle within 15 to 20 yards, and the other, as yet invisible, began to call. There was another new bird – icterine warbler – the next day on Tresco, with little egret, dusky warbler, firecrest and bluethroat on Agnes. Dusky, red-breasted flycatcher, egret and black redstart topped the list next day, joined by a yellow-browed warbler, a barred warbler, which I found in Barnaby Lane, and two firecrests on the Friday. I especially loved the yellow-browed warblers. Sometimes I would get a yellow-browed entirely on my own – especially at the end of the day – coming across it in a tiny garden where it would flit about in an apple tree and I would try to watch it without being too embarrassed about looking into a six-foot garden next to someone's front door. Yellow-broweds are beautiful little birds, more subtle than Pallas's, more about harmony and delicacy than bright colours and garish patterns.

St Mary's pipped Agnes on the Saturday: tawny pipit, bluethroat and red-breasted flycatcher were reduced to a supporting cast as we waited for a glimpse of a grey-cheeked thrush, another remarkable transatlantic vagrant. It took three hours. At 10.10 a.m., while searching for the thrush, I saw a bird hop up in a bramble bush 25 to 30 yards away. Others saw it, too. It was extraordinary. With the naked eye it recalled a redwing, but binoculars showed that to be a pointless comparison. White-throated sparrow was mentioned, but surely it wasn't a sparrow? By this time I had it in the telescope. Grosbeak came to mind; I had no real idea what white-throated sparrow looked like at the time. It dawned on us, gradually. It was a rose-breasted grosbeak. 'What a grimler,' Peter Grant said later when he saw it. 'Whatever did you think it was?' He was not surprised by the initial confusion. It was the sixth for Britain and a wonderful bird. When we returned to St Mary's a couple of days later we saw it again, along with the grey-cheeked thrush plus a spotted sandpiper and a bluethroat. Grosbeak sketches took on an in-the-hand quality again, as views were so good.

Rose-breasted grosbeak, the sixth for Britain, appeared before us as we waited for a grey-cheeked thrush.

Once or twice on St Mary's, if the best bird was two or three miles away, we would save ourselves the walk, and a bit of time, by hopping on the local bus. It was a ramshackle old machine with an equally ramshackle old driver who would take it full speed down a hill at about 20 mph and shout out, 'Hold on, lads, we're getting into a speed wobble.' John Ward, sitting in the back, made loud and uncannily accurate impersonations of an old-fashioned motor horn. This was a few years before his exceptional skill as a mimic of all kinds of noises was put to more sensitive use when he made a record, *Big Jake Calls the Waders*. It was easier, then, to have a long-playing record of mimicked wader calls than to try to produce a complete set of genuine sound recordings of the real thing.

Sunday on St Agnes: American robin! What? An American robin on the track down by the pool – get there quick. The St Mary's crowd happened to be over for the day. With me was David Hunt, calling to people 'Don't run! Don't run – you'll scare it away.' They took little heed. But David need not have worried, for there it was: a fantastic adult American robin, in immaculate, rich plumage, feeding on blackberries down towards Troy Town. My first view was brief – of a large, broad-winged, almost dove-like thrush in flight, with grey upperparts and pale rufous underparts, and a prominent white vent – but then it was around, often in full view, all afternoon and again for the next three days. It was a sensation.

On a day trip to Tresco a group of people discovered a superb olive-backed pipit along the track beside the Great Pool. It was spectacularly well-marked. If flushed, it moved up into tall pine trees, but otherwise it fed in an area of rough ground between the track and a field, in a mixture of coarse grass, nettles and docks. It tended to be in the thick of this low vegetation and was easy to overlook, but now and then it wandered out into the open. It walked like a delicate wagtail, bobbing its tail, picking food from the ground, leaves and stems. This was another 'Siberian' to balance the American trend. A feature of Scilly is that birds from all quarters can appear at once. My sketches of this bird were published in the Isles of Scilly report. Some time later, Peter Conder, retired director of the RSPB, published a note in *British Birds* about olive-backed pipit identification; this information derived from the time when he was warden of the Skokholm Bird Observatory. After his years at the RSPB, Peter was not particularly noted as an identification man, but he was the first to point out the importance of the 'split supercilium' effect on olive-backed pipit: a white ear-covert spot separated from the superciliary by a black line. He kindly asked permission to use my Scilly sketch to illustrate his point. I was delighted that my notes and sketches included this hitherto unpublished field mark, although it was such a well-marked individual that I could hardly have missed it.

Tresco was always a good day out, though I tended to view it with some apprehension. It is a sizeable island so there was never any guarantee of seeing anything. But we were after ducks, and ducks, as a rule, sit about on the pool and demand to be ticked – in this case, a black duck and a blue-winged teal, both new for me. By this time, the islands seemed like old friends, as indeed did yellow-browed warblers, red-breasted flycatchers, large pipits and the like. On the first day of the 1977 trip, we were on St Agnes by the afternoon, and my notes have plenty of red ink underlines: long-billed dowitcher (I'd seen quite a handful of these by now), two excellent red-throated pipits by the pool, and a melodious warbler. The following day, St Mary's seemed to have the better selection: rose-coloured starling, three blue-headed wagtails, three black redstarts, a merlin, whinchats, topped off by a beautiful male rustic bunting and a Pallas's warbler. The Pallas's was up by the ponds at Watermill. I had only brief views of it but all the distinguishing features were clear, including that splash of pale lemon on the rump as it hovered: my fourth Pallas's, but the briefest yet.

Back on St Agnes, a firecrest in the parsonage impressed me: '... amongst bright, sunlit sycamore leaves against a dark background, a vision of brilliant translucent and luminous greens and yellows. The crest was reddish orange, the forehead, chin and patch around the bill yellow-buff – often striking in a front view.' Later, we sailed through hundreds of shags on the sea as we puttered across to St Mary's in the open boat. Sixty sanderlings trotted about on the beach. Late migrants included wheatears, whinchats, pied and spotted flycatchers. The best birds, or at least the rarer ones, were tawny pipit (an immature on the golf course) and olive-backed pipit by the Watermill; the presence of the Pallas's there had attracted more people, and another rarity find was the inevitable result – a yellow-browed and 12 Lapland buntings. The Laplands were on the golf course, often beside the tawny pipit. I greatly appreciated a good, long look at their variety of rich, colourful plumages and heard a greater variety of calls than I had known from Laplands before.

Then, at last, a full day on St Agnes. What a joy. Lunch in the Turk's Head was a pint and a pasty; in the evening we had the usual session of darts and logbook, calling out what we had seen, guessing (sometimes quite wildly if truth be told) at numbers of migrants on the island, ridiculing other people's claims, listening for news on the phone from Tresco and St Mary's. The dowitcher was still about ('remarkably good views'), a Richard's pipit had appeared, and there was still the melodious warbler, the blackcaps, garden warblers and chiffchaffs, yellow-browed warbler, firecrests, whinchats, wheatears and wagtails, seven black redstarts (a good count), and three Lapland buntings. In addition there had been another new bird for me, a quail, which I had flushed from bracken and later flushed again at close range; it got up and flew over my head with what I described as a rippling *crree crree* call.

While watching the dowitcher down by the pool, I heard 'an odd pipit call' and a little later I flushed 'an obvious large pipit', which was assumed to be Richard's. Everyone on the island had good views of 'my' big pipit and it turned out to be very obliging, remaining in a sandy, ploughed field for some time – but it also proved a touch controversial. Was it, in fact, a Blyth's? It was never discussed at the time – who ever heard of Blyth's pipit anyway? – but the old Richard's/tawny debate raised its head again. Looking back at my notes and drawings now, I suspect it was Richard's, but some features hint at the possibility of Blyth's; correspondence with Ian Wallace confirmed that, but we eventually left it as a 'possible' at best.

I have often said that I can recall the details of a bird I have seen well, looked at very closely, and sketched in the field, better than I can some other species that I have not grilled so intently. This debatable Richard's pipit on St Agnes was one bird I had in mind. I had, after all, watched it for hours, closely, often with a telescope, and drawn many sketches of it while it was in view. But I wonder. Do I really recall the bird, or am I remembering my notes and drawings? If I sat down to draw it now, would I reproduce some reasonable idea of what the bird looked like, or just duplicate my notebook drawings? In a way, it doesn't matter, so long as the original drawings were done well enough to represent the bird with a fair degree of accuracy. It is essential to make good notes at the time; at least then you can refer to them later and, if you want to check the tertial

Olive-backed pipit: a well-marked individual.

pattern or the colour of the greater covert tips, you can do so. You can never go back: there is no way that I can decide now whether the coverts were tipped with white, cream or buff. Indeed, there is no way to go back even an hour after the event, especially if, in the meantime, you have talked about a bird with other people, or looked it up in a book.

Someone had the bright idea that the strong winds we were experiencing would bring rare petrels – well, a Sabine's gull, at least – within range of a boat trip, so we all booked a boat and set off on Friday morning. We passed Annet and the Bishop Rock with its towering lighthouse and headed on out to sea for what seemed like several miles, crashing over the heaving swell. The vessel was really only an open boat, and the 40-odd soaking wet people on board were hardly able to cope with such conditions. I well remember the boatman turning to face the swell head on so that we would launch over it and crash down the other side with a bang, but it was better than rolling over sideways. Most of us felt pretty bad quite soon, and Eric Clare's vomiting over the side not long after we started didn't do much to help quell our stomachs. It didn't do a lot in any sense, really, this extravagant boat trip: 50 gannets, 300 shags, a shearwater (maybe a sooty), a couple of great skuas. I'd seen 100 gannets from dry land on St Agnes. I think we could put that one down to experience, and not an experience to be repeated. My notebook has 'A quite horrendous trip of which the less said the better!'

So, that was that: Scilly no more. I've not been to the Isles of Scilly in autumn since, and I still miss them.

Real Work at Last: the RSPB

H aving applied for the post of librarian at The Lodge — to replace the long-serving and much-loved Dorothy Rook, who was retiring — I was offered a different job entirely by Trevor Gunton, head of the development department. On my first day, 2 January, I went to Chasewater instead of turning up for work. I had misunderstood the New Year holiday time and thought that was what everyone would be doing. So, I turned up a day late.

Dave Fisher was working at the RSPB then, living in a house owned by the RSPB and used as a temporary base by new staff and visitors. He said it would be good to get another birdwatcher in, so accommodation in the house at 147 St Neots Road, Sandy, was sorted. I paid my rent and collected clean sheets and pillow cases each week from the housekeeper/cook at The Lodge. This suited me fine. I could live quite happily, cheaply and lazily. As a result we outstayed our welcome by a year or two until we got a flat near by. Various interesting people stayed at the house known as '147' while I was there. One, who did not last very long as a staff member, refused to pay his full share of the shopping bill — he wouldn't pay for toilet paper on the grounds that he only used it at work.

In the same office was Carl Nicholson, who later became Midlands regional officer and set up an office in Droitwich, and Roy Croucher. The development department has long since been defunct, its responsibilities hived off to others, but at that time it was responsible for the recruitment of new members to the RSPB (partly through media advertising) and the retention of existing members through running local members' groups and events, including film shows. This was before there was a fund-raising department (later renamed marketing), which took on the responsibility, among many others, of membership recruitment. As assistant development officer, I was expected to appoint leaders and approve new committee members in the local members' group system; to edit and help publish the groups' newsletters and programmes of events; to give talks, both to RSPB groups and to bird clubs; to introduce RSPB film shows, which at that time were given at around 150 or so venues nationwide; and to help at national events such as the members' weekend and the members' day and AGM in London. As someone who would not say boo to a goose, I would have thought this job one to be avoided, but Trevor Gunton saw something in me that made him confident I could succeed. His encouragement was invaluable and I can never thank him enough.

Carl Nicholson ran the art exhibitions that were traditionally part of the big members' events. He took me on as an assistant so that I could organize the exhibitions myself and deal with the artists when Carl had moved on to bigger things. As for talks, I had nothing to talk about, surely? And I had little to show anyone, although, after two years in Wales, and all my years in Swansea, I had a good stock of slides of Welsh habitats, butterflies and flowers, if not birds. The bird slides were topped up from various RSPB sources – we used Woodmansterne duplicated slides a lot, so many talks about RSPB work in general seemed to have much the same pictures in them – and I put together a talk on the wildlife of Wales, from the gulls of Blackpill and the wild flowers and butterflies of the Gower to the merlins and harriers of the Berwyns. Later I added a regular talk on gulls, with an assortment of my own slides, others that I begged and borrowed and added to over the years, and my own drawings and paintings.

Both of these talks seemed to go down quite well, Wales being a more popular one than the more specialist one on gulls. It surprised me that I could give talks at all. But soon enough I was enjoying it. Giving a talk is a boost for the ego, and, using the pictures as cues, never any written script, the whole thing went surprisingly smoothly and easily.

Film shows were more daunting at first. Within a week or two of my arrival at The Lodge I was out with Roy Croucher. He introduced a film to an audience of children. After the interval, he said OK, on you go, and I had to introduce the second half. I had never been on a stage before; I had never spoken to an audience (except for a brief talk a few weeks before to the photographic society where my father worked, when I showed some of my flower and butterfly slides, which I had used as a bit of a practice run). Soon I was going out with two big spools of film in blue plastic boxes under my arms, and a few boxes of sales goods and programmes, to show RSPB films at halls of all kinds. Once I was used to it I enjoyed the experience – we were all showing off, to a point, and

Avocet, the RSPB emblem.

enjoying the 'glory' of standing in the spotlight. Some of the shows were huge. In Sheffield I might show films to three full houses of children and two evening shows to the general public, making something like 9,000 people in all, over two and a half days. OK, so the kids in the balcony had spitting competitions, but most of them behaved well enough, and the evening shows – with films of really high quality – were well received. My first season with the RSPB coincided with the first showing of a superb film on ospreys, by Hugh Miles, later a distinguished film-maker for the BBC, especially praised for his remarkable film on polar bears. Many RSPB film unit employees went on to television work.

These films, and to some extent the talks, could be in any kind of venue from a big theatre to a small village school or church hall. One night I might be dealing with a box office and taking the films up to the fully kitted-out projection room, and retiring to the café or bar, the next I would be helping to put the chairs out with a couple of local volunteers who didn't even realize I was the guest speaker for the evening. One thing that was soon needed was a suit. I had one made to measure for an extravagant £80 and didn't even like it, but it was a start. Soon after I acquired my second suit, I was at a show with a small audience in a particularly small hall. When I filled in my report sheet the next day (after each film show we were required to complete and submit a report form), I wrote 'Waste of my new suit', which thereafter became a byword for the smaller shows.

Usually the film shows were extremely well run and the detail was buttoned up long before the event by Kate Berry, who was in charge of booking the halls and projectionists. But occasionally things went wrong. The projector might break or the sound go off; radio microphones were particularly prone to fail. Once or twice the lights wouldn't go out or they came on again halfway through a film. At one theatre, Trevor was with me and there was difficulty getting the film onto the screen at the right moment for some reason – I think there was no sound in the projection booth – so Trevor agreed with the projectionist that he would give a wave to indicate that the film should start. He was just getting into his welcome speech when he absent-mindedly brushed his hair back: the film began, with Trevor's surprised silhouette in the middle of the screen. And then there was the time when he welcomed the audience with a flourish and fell into the orchestra pit ...

Part of the job at these film shows was to recruit members during the interval. Membership recruitment for the RSPB is tough, and finding 20,000 or 30,000 a year from press advertising was hard, although Trevor and his team succeeded remarkably well. But at a film show, we could hold up a copy of a cheap book, offer it as a free gift, and watch the queues back up down the aisles. Sometimes I could return from shows with 50 new memberships, and all the cash and cheques, paid up on the night. At a few large shows, such as Birmingham, we were close to a hundred. It was soon apparent, much to my surprise, that I got on with the women in the office better than I did with the men: they said they felt sorry for me. So when I got back from shows with cloth bags containing new memberships, a few hundred pounds from selling programmes and perhaps £1,000 from gift and Christmas card sales, they always said it was because the audience must have felt sorry for me, too. An incident one November proved that I couldn't count on this. I took boxes of sales goods to the Gateway theatre in Chester (we would take as many boxes of goods as the Austin Maxis would carry – sometimes a couple more! – for the sales tables run by volunteers at the show). On arrival I found that the boxes contained no Christmas cards amongst the other merchandise. Chester members always bought their Christmas cards at the film show: what the hell was I doing turning up without any? Dozens of people complained. I just about escaped alive.

Sometimes the 'membership plug' before the interval was interrupted by the sound of snoring from the front row. It was distracting to see wide open mouths scattered around the audience, although this was less humiliating to me in a film show interval than it was if it happened during the first half of one of my talks. Trevor was especially good at adding humour to his talks, and was generally loved by RSPB audiences, but sometimes even he would die an absolute death. The optional Sunday evening slot after a members' weekend, when most people had gone home, was usually a happy-go-lucky performance, fuelled by relief that we had got through it. One year we realized that one member, a Mr Blackburn – who used regularly to write letters of complaint about pictures of birds mating in RSPB films – was sitting up on the side of the theatre. On discovering this, one of the speakers, Peter Merrin, included all he could about birds displaying, courting and mating. Then it was Trevor's turn, and he included a long description of black cocks at the lek, then ruffs also lekking to attract females. He described how the white ruffs were there only to attract the females in, while the black ruffs 'got all the girls'. Our member friend didn't bat an eyelid. Trevor laid it on thick; then he got back onto the proper subject and began talking about his favourite birds, herons. He said that, if he could come back as a bird, he would like to be a heron. 'What would you like to be?' he asked the audience. 'A black ruff,' I shouted out. Mr Blackburn bent down, took off his shoes and socks, took out a box from his bag, and proceeded to eat a packet of sandwiches through the rest of Trevor's talk. Perhaps he hadn't got his hearing aid switched on that night.

Other times were not so funny. Very early on in my time at the Lodge, I was asked to talk at a meeting of volunteers in the south-east England region. For a start, at that time, no one liked being called a volunteer; it was strongly resisted, even though I had to edit and put out the *Volunteers' Newsletter*, which I illustrated with little drawings and designed with Letraset. I had no experience, so Trevor gave me some notes to use as a prompt and to get me through my talk, which was about the best way to run events and deal professionally with visiting speakers. Trevor had written this with feeling, because he had long experience of being dealt with very badly by some clubs, and knew how poor

Franklin's gull: Britain's third, in
Suffolk, 1978.

some group events could be, especially in cold, draughty halls in winter, with hard seats and no facilities. So I trotted out all he had said and told everyone how they must make the speaker feel welcome, might perhaps give him a meal or offer accommodation, should delegate someone to make sure the seating was properly arranged, the hall opened on time, the audience made welcome, the heating turned on; I told them that a thank you afterwards might be appreciated. I realized part way through that I was speaking to people who had been doing this sort of thing very professionally for years, and guessed, quite rightly, that I might be in for a difficult time come the questions at the end. Yet, as Trevor well knew, all of the things he had scribbled down were genuine enough and some of the groups were not getting the basics right.

On one occasion I was offered expenses by a northern bird club. 'How much petrol did you use? And what did it cost? Ah, well, it's ten pence a gallon cheaper up here, so we'll work it out on local prices.' Trevor himself had innumerable interesting experiences. After giving a talk at one bird club, the club secretary wrote to him and said: 'I was unable to attend your talk myself, but I have spoken to a few of those who were there and can tell you that some people enjoyed it.' There were little stories like this every week, after some show or talk or other, somewhere. Having said this, it's fair to say that we were not exactly infallible either. I once misread my wall planner and turned up for a talk on the wrong day. Fortunately it was a day early, so I went again the next night and no one was any the wiser. Someone else sent a mailing to members in Chesterfield, asking them to a meeting to set up a new local group in Macclesfield: well, one 'field' is pretty much like another.

Black-throated diver at Little Paxton gravel pits.

Members' group committee meetings could be difficult. There was a surprising amount of infighting, and factions grew up within committees, each determined to get the other one out. The appointment of group leader was actually made from The Lodge, which was usually just a matter of routine approval, while the committee was elected locally. One group committee announced that it had ousted the leader, so I had to go along to the committee meeting to insist that he was retained and that no one but us (me, in fact) had the right to change the leader without approval from The Lodge. One group leader, however, resigned. He said he had announced it publicly at the previous group meeting. I wrote to the local members and said that we needed a new group leader. Unfortunately, and inexcusably, I forgot to add the words, 'because the existing one has expressed his intention to resign'. I stood on the stage in front of a packed hall and assumed that everyone knew of the resignation. They didn't. They thought I had sacked the man, and he did nothing to disabuse them of that idea, standing to one side with a fixed grin. It was a difficult time, with people shouting and swearing at me from the floor, hating me for getting rid of their loyal and much-loved local hero.

The Chelmsford members' group was inspired by the inimitable Roger Jordan to raise huge amounts of money. Most groups had little raffles and sold pot plants and so on, as well as RSPB goods, and had a good programme of talks, films and outings, and at the end of each year gave the RSPB a cheque for a couple of thousand pounds. Their activities were all bird-related. Roger saw things differently. His raffles had nothing whatever to do with birds, but offered a new car as a first prize! He even began to do house clearances and sell old furniture. Why should there be a bird interest? If you wanted money, this was the way to do it – and Chelmsford knocked spots off everyone else. Chris Durdin (who now works in the eastern England office and also runs his Honeyguide bird tour business) had joined our team and took on responsibility for the Essex groups. At the summer fair in Chelmsford, he was given the responsibility of judging one fundraising event – the sixth form girls' squat thrusts competition – which has affected him ever since.

Talks to women's institutes and similar groups were frequently requested, but I avoided them as often as I could. I have nothing against women's institutes, but they weren't quite for me, and I wasn't quite right for them. At one, I had to judge the best bird made from a piece of food in the evening meal. I chose something, but three ladies thought I had ignored a concoction made from a jacket potato, obviously much better than my winning selection. It was not a happy meal. Then they organized a bird quiz in which they all stuck little labels bearing the questions on each other's backs before running around reading everyone else's back and handing me the answers. Another one made me judge the best bird picture: there were a couple of paintings, some copies of pictures in magazines, a cut-out photograph and some robin Christmas cards … I wasn't quite sure of the rules.

One thing that film shows and talks required was a great deal of travelling. Sometimes we organized them into mini tours so that we could keep the distances to a minimum, but that meant staying away. Usually I preferred to drive home even if it meant getting back at one or two in the morning and getting to work at about ten. We rarely ran up any great expenses, eating cheaply (if at all), staying cheaply if we had to, or staying sometimes with volunteers. Sometimes a volunteer invited me to stay, but then presented me with a bill for bed and breakfast before I left next morning. All this was best avoided. At one film-show location, a member would always invite us back for tea between the afternoon and evening performances. She had a big, shaggy, horrible dog that insisted on poking its nose into other people's business then trying to stick its dripping, slobbery snout into my coffee. 'Don't do that,' she would say to the animal. 'Wait until the cup's empty, then you can lick it out.' Hmm. Maybe not next year. Usually I made up excuses and went to the nearest fish and chip shop.

Our film shows were premiered at the Royal Festival Hall (a prestige show with two houses of some 2,400 people). I once did the interval there but my own 'film show circuit' ranged from places in the south such as Bristol and Bracknell to Sheffield, Nottingham and Solihull in the north. For several years, I also took films to Guernsey, where the show was jointly presented by the RSPB and La Société Guernesiais, and once also to Jersey, which we combined with a Young Ornithologists' Club (YOC) event. Guernsey was great, with short-toed treecreepers and black-throated divers as bonuses. I was sent a newspaper cutting showing a photograph of the eminent guests at one of the Guernsey shows; I was at one end of the picture, captioned as 'the man that brought the films'.

Another slightly different part of the job was to introduce celebrity speakers. When Tony Soper was to speak at the Assembly Rooms in Derby, to a large audience, I went on stage a minute or two before the talk was due to start, not knowing quite what to say because he hadn't turned up. Spot on time, he walked in, handed his roll of film to the projectionist, came up to the stage, clapped me on the shoulder with a 'Hello Skip' and started into his talk. Smooth, perhaps, but not easy on the nerves. Other speakers I introduced included David Hunt, 'our man from the Isles of Scilly', Eric Simms, a well-known author and BBC sound recordist and producer, Bobby Tulloch from the Shetlands, and Bert Axell, ex-RSPB warden at Dungeness and, most famously, Minsmere. The only real difficulty, or anxiety, with this part of the job was getting the speakers to the venue on time, although there were sometimes other complications. When Roger Tory Peterson was on his little UK tour, I had

Whiskered tern, Richard Porter's excellent find at Grafham Water.

to leave him at a Midland hotel and, at his wife's request ('Don't tell Roger, he'll tell you not to bother, but it really is important') drive to Heathrow to pick up a pair of his spectacles sent over on a cargo plane from the USA.

Members' weekends were good events, usually at York or Warwick, once at Exeter, which proved the biggest of all. There could be as many as 1,200 members resident from Friday to Sunday afternoon, plus hundreds, sometimes thousands, of YOC members and parents on the Saturday afternoons. We had guest speakers of the calibre of David Bellamy, Sir David Attenborough, Sir Peter Scott and once the Duke of Edinburgh. Robert Gillmor always came along to help with the art exhibition (and still does). There were members' days, too, at all kinds of places, such as Bournemouth and even Swansea University.

All kinds of odd jobs cropped up. Once I had to deliver a short film script, needed urgently, to the home of Robert Dougall, ex-BBC newsreader and past president of the RSPB. I found the house on Hampstead Heath but there was no one in; and it appeared, so far as I could tell after repeated close scrutiny, to have no letterbox. But there was a strange little cubbyhole with a small door, so I left the script safely in there and hoped Mr Dougall would find it. It was, apparently, where the milk was delivered, and the script stayed there for a couple of days before being discovered.

The job was certainly proving to be challenging as well as interesting. But what of birds? Were there any birds locally? Well, yes, and sometimes there were some rare ones. Pectoral sandpipers at Bedford sewage farm and a collared pratincole just across the A1 in Sandy were among the best really close by. A lot of staff left half an hour early to see a superb black-winged pratincole up towards Fen Drayton, not many miles away in Cambridgeshire and were taken by surprise when Ian Prestt, director general, pulled up on his way home and wondered what we were all doing out at that time – but after a good view of the pratincole he wished us all well and drove on.

On the first Saturday after I started my job, we travelled to Suffolk to see a new bird – a sociable plover. I have seen a couple more since, but may never see another, as this is now one of the world's rarest birds. Somehow, almost unnoticed, it suffered a catastrophic decline in the manner of the slender-billed curlew (in 2004 there were only about 200 pairs left). The very next day, we went to see another rarity, although this time not quite 'new' for me, as I had seen the first one in Britain: this was a Franklin's gull (Britain's third) at Lowestoft. Curiously enough, we heard about it on next door's television. Our neighbour, apart from sporting a glass eye (which he would, apparently, tap with a pencil or even a screwdriver at times when he was pondering his next words) was very deaf and had his television on so loud that we could hear every word; and, on the local evening news, there was a story about the gull. Unlike the sociable plover, I have not seen another once since. Not long after that, I was back in mid-Wales, looking over Llyn Heilyn, an old favourite from the previous spring. The purpose of this visit was to see a black vulture. In the light of more recent occurrences elsewhere in Europe, many people think this should be accepted as

Killdeer at Pwll.

a wild bird, but at the time it was treated as an escape, despite there being no reports of losses from any of the known places that had captive ones.

Early in March, I had to go to South Wales for a couple of talks and a film show. En route, I dived in to Cheddar Gorge, and also stopped off near Llanelli. This meant two more new birds: the magnificent wintering wallcreeper in Cheddar and a killdeer at Pwll. I failed to find the wallcreeper in its usual quarry, but moved on to the gorge and, fortunately, this being several hundred per cent better than the pokey quarry for seeing a great bird, I saw it there. It even basked on a ledge in the sunshine and sunbathed, giving fantastic views. That spring was pretty good for birds, with rarities (generally seen with John Fortey and Eric Phillips) at Portland Bill, Lodmoor and Radipole Lake, at Breydon Water (a broad-billed sandpiper in its classic British location), Stodmarsh (the UK's first pallid swift), and Minsmere (another broad-billed, a purple heron and a Savi's warbler), as well as a return visit to the Berwyns and a day at Bempton Cliffs to get a fix of my beloved seabirds. Grafham Water occasionally scored well, most notably with an autumn whiskered tern found by Richard Porter and, remarkably, a spring surf scoter found by Tony Marr. Both Richard and Tony lived in houses near by. Richard reputedly went out at night and pruned branches off ornamental trees planted around Grafham, so that he could have an unobstructed view from his window.

Although I saw other good birds at Grafham, including Sabine's gulls in the great 1987 storm, and occasional large movements of black terns and little gulls, I never did like the place much and eventually stopped going. It had no soul and was getting perilously close to dragging the soul out of me. The Ouse Washes proved more to my taste. Little Paxton was also better, and for many years it was my regular spot, the nearest thing I have had to Chasewater, but not really a patch on it to be honest, for me. Gravel doesn't do it as well as mud. I found some nice birds – ring-necked duck and three Temminck's stints, for example – and saw other people's finds (such as red-footed falcons and ferruginous duck); it can be superb for watching ducks, cormorants and herons, and it has a great population of nightingales in the summer and hobbies in spring and autumn. But it is not a great wader place and on the whole it held few surprises; I felt I could write my notes before I went there and get them more or less right. And it, too, like Grafham, suffered from country-park-itis, getting more and more organized, less and less free, with far less access off the approved routes, and busier and busier. It still has good birds and good numbers of common ones, and I should go back.

Paste-ups and Personalities

After five and a half years in the development department I was offered a new job at The Lodge – editor of *Bird Life*, the magazine of the Young Ornithologists' Club (YOC). It was an A5 colour magazine published six times a year for members up to the age of 18 – far too wide an age span. In recent years, the magazine has been split into three – for under-eights, eight-to-thirteens (this is still called *Bird Life*) and teenagers – but in my time we didn't have such luxury and had to focus more or less on the middle group.

One early development was to make the magazine bigger and more or less square. (It has since grown to A4.) Working on the magazine was an excellent grounding for an editorial job. I had no real experience, but now found myself in a department of editing and printing professionals under the direction of Nick Hammond. For a time, too, I was proof-reading *British Birds*, which was useful experience, at least in using proper proofreaders' terms and symbols. In the development department we had made do; everyone did, then, making the best of what we had for the least possible expenditure. We produced typed leaflets, adding headings in Letraset, rubbing them down from a transparent sheet and building up the words character by character. These were printed down the corridor in the print room on basic printing machines; only later did we get a paper-folding machine to create three-folded leaflets ready-folded, and a collating machine to staple the pages of newsletters. I made menus for Saturday evening dinners at the members' weekend, staff name badges and all kinds of other jobs like this, while Trevor Gunton, with his past signwriting experience, created dozens of larger posters and signs by hand.

This was not long after the RSPB had rented space on the Heinz computer for handling its membership registry and label-printing requirements, making redundant the 'bonking room' at The Lodge, in which address labels had previously been stamped out by hand using the 'bonking machine' (a continuous 'bonk-bonk-bonk' would echo around the ground floor and up the main stairs). Now things were a little different, but we still produced magazines by typing texts (with much use of correction fluid) onto marked-up sheets, with a rule to help count the number of characters per line and a set of numbers down the side to count how many lines had been typed. We would 'cast off' the text by drawing a line down the right-hand side and working out the average number of characters per line and, by using various tables and a special plastic ruler, we worked out roughly how much would fit in a certain space on the page, given the particular font and print size (in 'points') and 'leading' (the space between the lines).

The designer would then work this into designs for each page, drawing a box on a tracing paper sheet with margins pre-printed in blue. We would type out and mark up (with instructions to the printer) all the headings, subheadings and introductory paragraphs, then send the whole lot off to a typesetter in Bedford. The papers would be collected and then delivered back a few days later by a white witch on a motorbike. At the same time, designer and editor would choose pictures from a whole set of transparencies collected from picture agencies across the country. Sometimes we would have thousands to look at. They were all valued at £400 each should any be lost, which occasionally happened. Once we found one when cleaning the dust out of the inside of a typewriter.

The transparencies would have a piece of tracing paper taped over them and, on this, the precise area that we wanted to use would be outlined and the final required dimensions marked up. We used a huge piece of equipment, a Grant enlarger, which projected the slide up onto a glass screen on which we could put the tracing paper sheets and trace around the image, winding the projector up and down to make the picture larger or smaller until we had precisely the right degree of enlargement to fit the design we wanted. All this was taken to Norwich for colour reproduction. A first proof would come back a few days later and we would check the colour balance against the original pictures, bit by bit, and mark up '+cyan' or '−magenta a touch' or 'a fraction less yellow' until we got the balance about right. This might need doing a second time if things didn't work out, with more return trips to Norwich.

The typesetting would come back with the white witch a few days before the amended colour came in from Norwich, so we would be cutting and trimming sheets of text on shiny paper – bromides – ready to paste down onto the colour 'boards' when they came in. If the text didn't fit, we would mark up the words to cut or alter and send the thing back off to Bedford. Sometimes it still didn't work, so it had to go to Bedford a third time, with more amendments, or there would be a bit of final fitting by phone. Eventually, we would get the text to fit the spaces between the pictures and do a final 'paste-up'.

Magazine production was a long and slow process – a full-time job by the time you added the actual commissioning, writing and editing. As technology improved, it became quicker and other things were piled in to fill in the gaps in the job. I remember thinking that I didn't want a word processor when it was first suggested – I had a typewriter, two fingers and a thumb, what more was needed? We were all dubious, too, about fax machines. Now everything is computerized. We work with page-layout software on Apple Mac computers and create pages – including text, pictures and all the colour – on screen. Pictures are sent by email, taken from websites, or posted to us on a disk. Editors write, cut, add and alter words on screen, move text about the page, and change italics to bold with a keystroke; we get pictures digitally and can, at a push, create a new feature for *Birds* magazine in an afternoon if something is 'pulled' at the last minute. And *Birds*, a 116-page magazine is, despite all the politics and approval rounds that attend it, now only a part-time job. The rest of my time is filled in with leaflets, posters, reports, booklets, newsletters, displays, the RSPB annual review, appeal leaflets and letters – anything and everything. Even toilet signs. I once edited a brown paper bag.

I edited *Bird Life* for five years. We won a national award with it (giving rise to the first time I hired a dinner jacket for a 'black tie' do), then I moved up to *Birds*, the RSPB members' magazine. In spring, 1989, my first issue as editor of *Birds* appeared. At the end of 2004 I was working on my 65th, which, surprisingly, puts me way ahead of any other editor in terms of time served. (If only I had been better behaved, I might have had some time off.) When I first came to the RSPB headquarters in January 1978, *Birds* was quietly celebrating 75 years of the RSPB magazine. It began as *Bird Notes and News* in 1903, a simple, black and white, four-page leaflet, published quarterly, sent free to associates who subscribed five shillings or more each year, to keep them up to date with the RSPB's work and its thinking on issues of the day. This is still the aim of the magazine. For many members, unless they visit reserves or belong to a local group, *Birds is* the RSPB. It proved successful from the start and doubled in size to eight pages within six months. At that time the RSPB had 5,000 'members', and it took a very long time to develop into a more substantial organization. In autumn 1947, with a membership of just 6,000, it changed the name of the magazine to *Bird Notes*. The next big change came in 1953, with the first colour cover by Charles Tunnicliffe. He painted covers for 12 years until 1965 (by which time I was a member and enjoying his pictures).

In 1966 came a bigger change. The name was shortened again (to *Birds*), the magazine appeared six times each year and it was much bigger – a quarto publication with a colour cover photograph and some colour inside (there were several apologies for the poor quality). In 1974, the magazine was produced in A4 format (which lasted until a small enlargement in 1997). In 1976 financial problems caused the six issues to be cut to four. In the year before, only five issues were published because of rampant inflation but no one really noticed, so the decision to cut back was made more easily. Both photographs and paintings appeared on covers until 1972, when paintings took over for many years until one – by me – of a black guillemot, which was the last, in autumn 1988. It was not very good and highlighted my lack of technique, but I was proud to see it nevertheless. Photographs were reintroduced for the centenary celebrations (an avocet, then a great white egret) and have stuck, almost universally, until now, despite occasional efforts to resurrect paintings. So, oddly enough, I had the last painting in the regular series on the cover and presided as editor over the arrival and domination of the photographic cover.

So, in my first year at the Lodge, 1978, *Birds* had a regular 64 pages, four times a year, practically all in colour, and cost less than a pound per member per year. Now, it costs members nothing at all, as advertising revenue covers all the costs, which are huge (well in excess of £1 million a year) and include paper, printing and postage. The fact that not a penny comes from members' subscriptions to pay for the magazine is something we are, justifiably, proud of. Advertisements in the magazine included, as might be expected, binoculars and bird-food ads that had been going since the year dot – the first ever in the RSPB's magazine were Haith's bird food and Barr & Stroud binoculars – but there was also an infamous series of Damart thermal underwear ads, with one or even two pages full of pictures of people in their underwear. They went on for years; fortunately, their appeal diminished.

Advertising has an enormous effect on the appearance of a magazine and the way it is perceived by the readers (I will not say 'audience', still less 'customers'). From studying the advertisements in *Birds* it would be reasonable to surmise that the membership must all be elderly and in need of walk-in baths and stair lifts. There is nothing at all against such things (I'll need one soon), but we did, at last, make the decision to excise them from our pages as best we could. We have long had a ban on tropical hardwoods and, for reasons that presumably have little to do with birds, tobacco. Now and then a big company will do something we cannot agree with and it is consequently added to the blacklist, but otherwise we have few restrictions. This can get us into trouble now and then. There is a constant dilemma about advertising foreign wildlife holidays when we are campaigning for better management of demand for air transport in the face of global warming. It is hard to resolve this issue: in many countries, wildlife simply would not survive if it did not have a commercial value and that, in the main, comes from wildlife-related tourism. The future of most of Africa's mammals without such tourism would be bleak indeed. And we are realistic, I suppose, in accepting that people will still go on holidays abroad, whether we advertise them or not – I do so, myself.

The autumn 1978 issue had a superb Lars Jonsson whinchat on its cover. The original hung in our office for some time. A colleague complained that Lars 'couldn't do leaves' and made the nettle background blurred. There was another Jonsson original that was stored in our cupboard after it had been put on show at members' weekends but not sold. I could have bought it for £90 but foolishly didn't – a good Jonsson now would set you back several thousand pounds. That same issue has advertising for the members' weekend at Warwick in 1979 with a 'logo' designed by me. Now that there is such intense concentration on the RSPB brand, there is no chance of an event such as this having its own logo, and no possibility that I would design it. There were also several members' days that year, advertised with my line-drawings of flamingos, a hen harrier, a common gull (a second winter, notice!) and a black redstart. In 1979 I drew a guillemot, a ring ouzel, a crested tit, a Bewick's swan and a first-year Iceland gull (!) to advertise these events. And a puffin with a sandwich board, saying 'Please join us!' in best Letraset, then portraits of David Bellamy, Richard Porter, Roy Dennis and Eric Simms, speakers at the spring weekend.

Browsing through old magazines always brings back memories. In one issue there is an advertisement for a cruise with Tony Soper to the North Cape. Tony later sent a thank you postcard from the ship to my wife, Marcella, who had set the thing up, saying 'Birds, sea and dancing girls, this is the life!' A few years later, in autumn 1989, I commissioned Tony to do a regular page for *Birds*, which he did for 50 issues (all except one, which was actually written for him by someone else). Several pages were faxed or emailed to me from on board a ship somewhere as Tony had now become a frequent cruise leader – a 'nanny' he sometimes said – which took him all around the world.

Birds reported the retirement of Cecil Winnington-Ingram, after 14 years as one of the RSPB directors, at about the time I arrived. This was noted in the magazine. He had enjoyed a long career in the Colonial Service before that and retained a 'colonial manner' and way of speaking. He was also accident-prone. One day his car broke down and he had to be towed by a colleague. He forgot to turn the key in his ignition to release the steering lock so, at the first corner, the towing car turned right and CWI headed straight on into someone's garden. Another time he fell backwards while mowing the lawn and sliced the tops off a couple of toes. People enjoyed poking gentle fun at him, telling of the time, for example, when he stood on the edge of the pier at Aldeburgh, waiting to board the boat for Havergate, on a staff outing (they had them, then), with everyone already in the boat beneath trying not to let their eyes stray upwards beyond his knobbly knees to his wide-legged khaki shorts. On another occasion, fellow director, Anthony Clay, sent a memo to Cecil who signed, dated and returned it. By all accounts, Anthony was furious, banged on CWI's door and said 'I don't mind your commenting on what I write, but I do object to being given marks like a schoolboy – 3/10.' 'My dear chap,' said Cecil, 'it is the 3rd of October.'

Most RSPB presidents are well-known figures with more or less interest and involvement in the environment but often little knowledge of birds. During my years at The Lodge, one president was both ornithologically and environmentally a megastar, but hardly known to most staff, let alone members. Max Nicholson retired as president in October 1985, and his retirement speech at the AGM was reported in *Birds*. Max said:

> I must sadly confess that, with limited exceptions, I cannot admire
> the quality or performance of public or private management in this
> country … There was a time when voluntary societies, not excluding this
> one, were something of a byword for amateurish and inefficient conduct of
> their affairs … Having been privileged to see the working of this society's
> management at close quarters over a longish period, I am full of admiration
> for it. In fact as a former senior officer in the public service I can confidently
> state that if the management of Great Britain Limited in Westminster and
> Whitehall were anything near a match for that of your council and staff,
> and if its perception of problems and proportion of correct decisions
> were half as right, this nation would be much more prosperous and less
> depressed than it is now.
>
> It is the combination of wise and effective conduct of our affairs with a
> sense of proportion, of humour and of give and take with regard to others,
> and yet a certain tenacity, firmness and, when need arises even toughness,
> which wins the public respect now so evident for the RSPB. People see us as
> a body with a heart, a head and a backbone, working together in harmony,
> and they like that.

He also admitted his disappointment that he had not been able to find a woman as his successor, and wished to see more women in senior positions in the RSPB before long. That has certainly happened, at every level. It is rare for a retiring (or serving) president to make a speech of the kind that Max Nicholson did.

The variety of material in *Birds* was interesting. Now we are so heavily pressured to include RSPB projects and policy matters that non-RSPB subjects are rare and non-bird subjects almost non-existent. While we still agree that enthusing people and helping them to enjoy birds is an essential part of the job description, it is harder to do it with so many other 'priorities' taking up all the available space. But, with Nick Hammond especially keen on bird art, there were then frequent features on artists and a series by John Busby, 'How to Draw Birds' – the start of a process that led to the book *Drawing Birds* being published. (A completely rewritten edition was published in 2004, but sadly without the *Birds* features to back up its sales.) In one issue there is a picture of Robert Gillmor giving a painting demonstration at one of the many members' weekends held in York. Robert has now attended more members' weekends than anyone else, more than any of the staff, from the very first.

The winter 1988 issue celebrated the RSPB's first 100 years. The RSPB's 'Royal' tag has occasionally come in for criticism (not often, nor usually very strongly) but it seemed right that we should seek a message of congratulations from HM The Queen. This was published, together with a full-page photograph. But somehow the transparency was 'flipped' so the picture appeared reversed, giving the Queen a slightly odd expression; more importantly, for those who take an interest in such things, it showed her wedding ring on the 'wrong' hand. Fortunately editor and designer survived this indiscretion, without having to study ravens at the Tower. There were messages, too, from people such as Margaret Thatcher, Neil Kinnock, Malcolm Rifkind, Sir Derek Barber, Max Nicholson, Lord Home and an assortment of other MPs – the whole issue very 'political', as the RSPB always has been from its very beginnings, although, as a charity, it has to take great care not to take party lines. People don't like the RSPB getting 'mixed up in politics'. I sometimes wonder how they think anything ever gets done. Conservation is – and always has been – an intensely political business. There has sometimes been a suspicion, too, that many members would like the RSPB to 'get things done' so long as it doesn't cause any trouble: none of that nasty Friends of the Earth or Greenpeace stuff, please.

In the issue for summer 1990 there was a feature on the 'shame of Spain', about proposed tourism and golfing developments around the world-renowned Coto Doñana. When I heard about these, I felt able to make a difference by alerting a few people, who in turn were able to alert the likes of Max Nicholson, David Bellamy, Guy Mountfort and Eric Hosking, all of whom made statements in *Birds*; and Max Nicholson wrote to Prince Philip who got on to King Juan Carlos – direct access to the top! For all the good work of so many researchers, scientists and policy people, the ability to find someone who knows someone who knows the right person is still invaluable.

In winter 1991 there were features on estuaries. This was a chance for some editorial indulgence. I included one on the Burry Inlet and Bob Howells, written appropriately by Jon Gower from South Wales. It was a chance to give Bob something of a tribute – he was still doing the endless round of wildfowl and wader counts on the Burry and at Blackpill that he had already been doing for several years when I knew him in the early 1970s. Only occasionally does an opportunity arise for the editor to do someone a favour or pay back a debt while still producing a good feature.

The spring 1992 issue has a picture of the *Birds* team at an awards ceremony in the previous November, with the film critic Barry Norman. We won Best Corporate Magazine of the Year in *The Publisher* awards (the 'periodical Oscars') at The Brewery, London, and we won it again the following November. These awards are good to get, but otherwise of dubious value, especially as they cost money even for a charity to enter. At least we had our table paid for by printers and suppliers.

The cover of the winter 1995 issue represents a hiccup in the otherwise standard use of photographs. I put a painting on it! It is a picture of a golden eagle, by Keith Brockie, and it related to a feature inside about problems in the Cairngorms. It didn't lead to any revival of art on the cover, but there was also a little egret painting by Keith Shackleton inside the back cover (the paper was a little thicker and whiter, giving better reproduction, than the bulk of the magazine). I selected this as the RSPB award winner at the Society of Wildlife Artists (SWLA) exhibition that summer. Subsequent awards have been given to people such as Mike Warren, Andrew Haslen, David Bennett, David Binns, Dafila Scott, Paul Henery, Matthew Underwood and Kim Atkinson. Usually I would go down to London the day after the selection for the annual SWLA exhibition, more recently on the selection day itself, to see the pictures and choose a winner. For some years *BBC Wildlife* gave an award too, with editor Ros Kidman-Cox always inviting me along to their expensive lunch at Carlucci's in Covent Garden.

On one occasion the *BBC Wildlife*'s guest judge was art critic Brian Sewell, who made the day more interesting. I asked to see a painting again after it had been rather fleetingly shown. 'If you really want to look at that again, please take it away into another room where you can look at it by yourself,' said Mr Sewell. He had recently judged pictures at the Society of Portrait Painters and said the two groups were similar – both were trying so hard to make a likeness of their subject that they forgot the art. It was a good point.

In spring 1993 came something that I had been trying to achieve for years. I had done a feature on one artist, Colin See-Paynton, but the old-style features on bird art that were so frequent when Nick Hammond was in charge had long since dried up. However, to get Lars Jonsson to write for *Birds* was too good for anyone to turn down and I quietly pursued the possibility, until Lars finally found time and produced 'The Image of a Bird'. It was followed, too, by a short series, 'Looking at Birds', by John Busby, which was not about art so much as appreciating birds, illustrated by John's inimitable drawings. Some years later I put in a feature on Lars Jonsson's new book, *Birds and Light*. Lars came over to England for an exhibition to launch the book, held at the Wildlife Art Gallery, run by Graham Barker and Andrew Haslen in Lavenham, Suffolk. It was on the weekend of a violent storm and many visitors failed to make it; worse, all power was cut off in the town. Visitors looked around the exhibition by candlelight, and we took Lars to a house in Lavenham for lunch, soup cooked on a camping gas stove, all of which he took remarkably well.

In Spring 1994 there was another noteworthy event: Simon Barnes appeared, after two earlier one-off features, with the first of his regular columns, which are still running to increasing acclaim. Simon was an environmental writer in *The Times*, but that worthy publication cut its environmental output (perhaps Simon was too provocative) but retained Simon as a sports writer. He is now chief sports writer and several times Sports Writer of the Year, but he maintains a strong interest in environmental matters and his bird books are bestsellers. In the same way that Tony Soper would email me from on board ship, Simon will call from some outlandish place where he happens to be covering the Olympics or the World Cup, and send in his copy.

Birds is produced to a high quality with few if any typographical errors creeping in, but sometimes something gets through that none of us spot. David Saunders, long ago organizer of Operation Seafarer in 1969, wrote well about Ramsey and finished: 'Travel west and see for yourself: Ramsey never fails to disappoint.' Well, it was of course the opposite of what it should have said, but we all knew what he meant … Satisfyingly, members consistently rate *Birds* as one of the top benefits of RSPB membership (although, apart from visiting reserves, for many members there may be few others). Some, however, continue their membership without taking *Birds*. Market research is a bit frightening sometimes when it reveals that many do not read it, and most who do read it can't remember much about the last issue.

Trevor Gunton, who had given me my first proper RSPB job, featured quite often in *Birds*. He 'lived' the RSPB and still does. He was brought back after retirement to help with the successful push to bring the RSPB's membership to one million and, even after that, he remained an active consultant. He still turns up as a helper on some stand or other at the annual birdwatching fairs, still leads his groups. Another prominent RSPB figure, now retired to Norfolk, is Richard Porter. I was pleased to feature him in the magazine before he left The Lodge. Richard made a name for himself at an early age with his studies of birds of prey in the Middle East. Later, he recalled:

> When I first set foot in Turkey on an April day in 1966 and saw the mosques and minarets of Istanbul, with black kites soaring around them and the first white storks of the spring overhead, I was totally hooked. Lying in bed I listened to the sound of the muezzins echoing from the mosques, which was completely alien to my experience. This entry into the world of Islam was total and utter fascination.

Richard produced the first bird identification books in Arabic, of which he is justifiably very proud. He is one of those dynamic people who actually get things done and make a positive difference for conservation. He is now organizing surveys of birds in Iraq. I once asked Richard why he hadn't written a book about his travels and birds (he has written several excellent guides and innumerable papers), as he has so much to say. He said that anyone writing such a book must be very arrogant – a comment that has haunted me through the preparation of this one. Sorry, Richard.

From the very beginning of my time at The Lodge, I have thought that most RSPB members have little idea of the scope and scale of the RSPB's work. In particular, many of the active birdwatchers I knew had a poorer view of the RSPB than should have been the case. To help this a little, I negotiated the publishing of a 'special issue' of *British Birds* that would focus on the RSPB and its work, and John Parslow, then conservation director, agreed to help put it together; but he never did and it didn't appear. The feeling is still there. It is one reason why we produced a small section called 'Conservation Action', then 'The Action Pages', in *Birds*, so that we could supplement the news pages with far more information, in short items, about the work we do. Occasional features, such as one about the economics of coffee and cocoa (the chocolate trade) on migrant birds, reveal more about the sort of thing RSPB staff are involved in, especially internationally – I learned a lot myself about RSPB-supported projects in Brazil to help small coffee farmers, which in turn helps to maintain forest habitats that are hugely more useful for wildlife than intensive plantations. This kind of thing is interesting and important but rarely makes it to the forefront of RSPB publicity or membership awareness. At least, though, we have promoted RSPB science much more in recent years, the legacy of James Cadbury, Colin Bibby and others, and the work of a large department of scientists and specialists that does more intense study of birds (all with a practical conservation aim) than anywhere else.

The RSPB hit 1,500 members of staff in 2004 for the first time and has more than a million members. Its reserves holdings continue to grow, with the consequent (rather scary) permanent commitment to staff and expenditure that this entails. International work is already massive, especially as a leading force in the BirdLife International partnership, and also grows. Although rising costs and especially threats of vastly increased postage charges threaten changes soon, the magazine goes to more than 620,000 homes and is read by more than 1,700,000 people, which is a frightening thought.

Lammergeiers and Griffons in the Pyrenees

Birdwatchers have always travelled. Early scientists and explorers collected birds the world over. I often wonder how such people as Blyth, a birdwatching explorer, managed to identify Blyth's reed warbler and Blyth's pipit, when neither had ever been heard of before and when we still can't do it with all the benefit of the best books and identification papers. OK, he had a gun, but still …

There were of course great books on the birds of Europe, but it was not until the Collins field guide in the early 1950s, taking up where Roger Tory Peterson had left off in America, that there was a decent, simple, portable guide to the birds of Europe. By then, there were some hardy souls who trekked off around the world, and some of my contemporaries were birdwatching outside Europe. When I first met Tim Cleeves from Bristol, he had just come back from India (I remember his stories of being de-loused by the authorities when he got back). Richard Porter and his mates had long been investigating the bird of prey migration watchpoints in Turkey, and plenty of people had studied birds during the war or while abroad on national service. But ordinary birdwatchers didn't travel much: for the most part that was for more adventurous souls.

When I first began to become aware of birdwatching abroad, it was as if 'abroad' had just been discovered (each successive generation discovers everything); and it seemed that the popular destination was Spain. After that, people began to go to Greece and Majorca (which, despite its package-holiday reputation, is a great place for birds). Then Morocco became fashionable, then Turkey, then the Gambia and the Canary Islands. Then it was South America, Thailand, and eventually the whole world opened up – Siberia, China, Borneo, wherever you like. Yet there is still a lot to be said for Spain.

My first experience of Spain was with Dave Fisher and Steve Gantlett in 1978, during my first year as an RSPB employee. The trip took in the renowned Coto Doñana, which resulted in loads of new birds, from Spanish imperial eagles to marbled ducks, and page after page of notes. The visit to Doñana itself was not a howling success, although time spent on nearby roads and tracks was marvellous. In the reserve we were herded onto a large vehicle, with poor visibility, and driven around with a few non-birdwatchers, stopping occasionally to look at a rabbit or

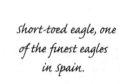

Short-toed eagle, one of the finest eagles in Spain.

a magpie! But we did get to see the famous Palacio, the centre of the Doñana research station, which was later out of bounds for visitors, and the lagoons near by with purple gallinules, although the edge was slightly taken off it by the ranks of captive birds of prey sitting on stumps around the car park.

I returned to southern Spain just a couple of years ago. It was a shock: vast areas had been despoiled, mainly to cater for British people living in giant, appalling resorts that plaster whole hillsides with ugly development. More often I have been to the north of Spain. It changes, for sure, but it is still stunning. The first trip with a hired car and a tent started from Barcelona, went down to the Ebro delta, then cut up through Zaragoza to the central Pyrenees. Since then I have been many times to the same area, leading groups for the RSPB and latterly Chris Durdin's Honeyguide company, and then going back without a group, just to enjoy it in a more relaxed fashion. We have always been based at Berdún, a little village on a sharp hill between the main east–west road from Jaca to Pamplona, looking north to the Pyrenees beyond the opening of the spectacular Foz de Biniés (a *foz*, or *hoz*, being a gorge or canyon).

Berdún has changed, but not a great deal in its essentials. A few new barns have gone up, a few old ones have been demolished. Gone is the rubbish tip that used to spew out into a long, stinking cone on the north side (I used to think Spain was a dirty, untidy place; now I think England is generally worse). Gone are nearly all the traditional Pyrenean chimneys from the massive stone houses that crowd in on the narrow concrete streets. There are now street lights, dozens of them, where there is really no need; there are benches and litter bins, a fountain, roofs of corrugated iron and plastic instead of ancient orange tiles. Gone are many of the grassy meadows and little cornfields down in the valley and so, too, their calling quails and crickets. Over the years we have seen the fields of the Berdún valley – the Rio Aragon valley – change to sainfoin, lucerne, oilseed rape and now wall-to-wall, intensively cultivated wheat. It all depends on what the subsidy is for. So the wild flowers are reduced, and the birds have changed. Even, in the village, the always dependable scops owls have recently disappeared. The Montagu's harriers that used to hunt the fields are no longer there. Yet, in 2004, in midsummer, there was an abundance of butterflies such as I had rarely seen before. And the griffon vultures are thriving.

When, on that first trip, we approached the southern foothills from the hot plains of Zaragoza and Huesca, it was a relief to climb to cooler, aromatic slopes, to see the dramatic *mallos* of Riglos, giant cliffs of red conglomerate, rising ahead. We drove over the Sierra de la Peña and dropped down the north side on a rough, unmade track. From a point on the way down to Santa Cruz de la Seros we looked back and saw our first awe-inspiring lammergeier. The lammergeier was still there in 2004, but the track has long since become a tarmac road with fenced viewpoints, and Santa Cruz is being turned from an ancient and photogenic village around its large church into some sort of tourist development. Now, at the top, where once there was nothing but the large, disused monastery and a puddle where crossbills and citril finches drank, there are road signs galore. Every few yards is a no parking sign, reinforced by a picture of a car being hauled away by a tow truck. No smoking, no fires, no dogs, no picking the flowers. There's a stall that sells drinks and snacks and plays loud music all day. Coach parties disgorge onto the meadow that is so good in spring for wild flowers, so the kids can play football and the parents can light their camping stoves, cook up a lunch and, in the Spanish way, shout at each other.

The monastery is surrounded by new building work, scaffolding, giant cranes. Vast hoardings explain what is being done: this is a special, sensitive site, a site of conservation and, above all of interpretation. People are to be brought here and shown things, to let them enjoy nature but be told not to damage it and, while they are here, stay at a new hotel, have courses and lectures in a new conference centre, to see the great new exhibition telling them all about this quiet, sensitive, delicate place that must not be disturbed; above all, I suspect, they are to be brought here to spend their money. In the woods the trails have new signs: this is an oak, this is a beech, this is a pine tree. Don't drop your litter. Keep your dog on a lead. Here are some birds you might see. Here are some animals. And the people wander about with their radios and kids with their footballs, all being interpreted to. Interpretation. Sometimes I dread it. Here, it risks killing the place.

What, I wonder, would John Boucher make of it all? John, now no longer with us, and his wife, Vivien, came to Berdún 25 years ago and set up a painting school. They had a house in the village and rented another and brought in groups of would-be artists each summer. It all went well until something went wrong with the printer who did the brochures and John decided that, no matter, it would run itself for a year with all their regular, returning clients, brochures or no brochures. The business collapsed. It proved hard to get it back again, so the painting school diversified. John and Vivien ran architectural tours and also opened up to groups bringing naturalists to Berdún. It was Martin Davies, of Birdwatching Fair fame, who went there with Cox & Kings travel, and told my wife, Marcella, and Trevor Gunton at the RSPB about it. They ran RSPB holidays then and could see the potential. One of the early leaders they sent out with a group was me.

John always said that his Spanish neighbours didn't know, or properly appreciate, what they had. Seeing the old chimneys, the old roofs, the old houses going from the village upset him. He gave talks to visiting groups, illustrating them with pictures of apparently insignificant things: window frames, doorways, lintels in barns, doors repaired with tin cans hammered flat and nailed into place, door knockers, roof tiles. They were trivial things that mattered. He took Marcella and me to remote villages that looked like something from Tibet, and whole villages that had been emptied, having lost their fields to a reservoir, and now stood dangerous and derelict, but that might, or might not, be converted into some sort of holiday retreat by a trades union. Now and then he wrote a letter and said that, in the middle of winter, the sky was clear, the air frosty, and griffon vultures hung above the village streets. It was, he said, still a remarkable environment. Of just two of the local, characteristic Pyrenean chimneys left in Berdún in 2004, John's was one. Inside, it still has the big conical vent and rattles and bangs furiously in a wind. Nobody else has room for such a thing now, but a few little concrete replicas with none of the works are stuck on new roofs in villages here and there.

When I first went to Berdún, there were lines of old men in black berets leaning on the village walls. I don't think there's a beret left, but the elders of the village still gather to watch television, play cards, drink a little and smoke a lot in the bars. They go on until four in the morning and start again at seven. We used to meet and eat in the bar and restaurant run by Prudencia. The bar's balcony overlooked the Rio Veral valley to the north. The television usually had 'dispatch of the day' in the evening, the televised bullfight, which always struck me as a pathetic and degrading spectacle. Prudencia had cancer; she fought it magnificently, but died a year or two later. Since then, groups that stay in the painting school eat their meals in the Rincon de Emilio – Emilio's corner – in the corner of the upper square next to the village church.

Emilio's follows much the same pattern, although it is more formal than Prudencia's was, with a more regular starter, main course and pudding. At Prudencia's you used to eat what was given, then find that something else had appeared on the table, then another dish, then another, in no particular order, as or when they were prepared. Then the regular call by the leader, how many for coffee (show of hands) – tea (smaller show of hands) – cognac (none, until perhaps the last night, when we all celebrated). There was and still is red wine for breakfast, lunch and dinner; you pay for the coffee, the wine comes free. This always was the happiest birdwatching tour group I led and I still think the wine had something to do with it. But it has become expensive and, in 2005, after a poor take-up in recent years, Chris Durdin for the first time deleted it from his programme. It is a great shame: it can be a cracking good holiday.

One of the drawbacks, though, has always been the unpredictability of the weather. Some years in April it was warm and sunny. In others we had deep snow in May, briefly even in Berdún itself; we had constant rain and cold in June, while on that first camping trip years ago it was roasting hot; an October trip was fine. The proximity of the mountains has a lot to do with it, but the regular, expected pattern seems to have been broken in recent years and no one knows what to bet on any more. However, birds of the area are rich and varied, so much so that any kind of list would be tedious. Let's just say there is always something good to see. I enjoy revising the identification characters of thekla larks, short-toed treecreepers, Bonelli's warblers and various birds of prey, as well as lapping up the unmistakable hoopoes, bee-eaters and red kites. Here, though, I will concentrate on just a few species that can be highlights of a visit.

Griffon vultures breed in nearby gorges, including the Foz de Biniés. If it is going to be a hot day, in summer, they stay put until late morning when the air warms up, then simply sail off their ledges and float away. Scores may be seen high over Berdún; sometimes they go so high that they are barely visible even with binoculars over open, flat ground. A glider pilot told me that they are frequently encountered up to the cloud base, whatever it is, often at 9,000 or even 12,000 feet. If, though, it is cold, and especially if there is a wind, they may be up and about almost before it is light. Then, Berdún is great for them and a pre-breakfast walk becomes the best part of the day. The wind sweeps unhindered along the broad, flat Aragon valley until it hits the slope of Berdún, where it must sweep round either side or rise over the top (or rush through the narrow streets past shivering birdwatchers). The vultures fly low, slowly, heavily, from Biniés to reach Berdún, where they exploit these complicated air currents. Then you can stand in the town square or on the 'ring road' that encircles the village and see vultures so low above your head that their wing-tips practically measure the field of view of your binoculars: you see every speck of detail. There may be 30 or 50 of them doing this, sometimes with an Egyptian vulture or two, and nearly always with a couple of red kites for company.

I could watch griffons for ever. I gorge myself on them as they gorge themselves on a dead sheep. Other birds of prey are usually around. Here's a day in early May 1991, dull, cold, windy from the north-west:

> Thirty or more griffons, many times several very low over the village; 2–4 Egyptian vultures, a buzzard, a kestrel, two honey buzzards (migrants here although they breed not far away), six red kites, six black kites, a peregrine hanging in the wind over the village, a pale-phase booted eagle, two Montagu's harriers. On a walk to the Rio Veral, nightingales, subalpine warblers, melodious warblers, Dartford warbler, spotless starlings, bee-eater, woodchat shrike, wheatears, whinchats, stonechats, redstart, black redstart (they breed in the village), eight pied flycatchers, a chough, four ravens, 15 serins, cirl buntings, crested larks and, strangely, a brambling. Normally we would expect tawny pipits and woodlarks, too, and at least to hear singing ortolan buntings.

I fancy the kites have declined; and now I remember, too, that most of the spotless starlings (and the village tree sparrows come to that) have gone. That year was cold and windy and difficult at times, but usually there are hoopoes, wrynecks and golden orioles. And short-toed eagles: it is good for short-toed eagles. They are among my favourite birds of prey, big and impressive, boldly patterned, often close enough to see golden eyes gleaming from deep sockets in the large, round head; their white undersides reflect the colours from beneath.

Griffons, like choughs, fly for the fun of it. Stand at one of the various viewpoints on the way up to San Juan de la Peña and look down on them, or marvel at their changing forms as they sweep by at head height, the wind

Wallcreeper, one of the great birds of the Pyrenees.

whistling loudly through their spread wing-tips, and you can have no doubt that they do it for sheer enjoyment. Frequently they perform the kind of expert formation-flying that the Red Arrows would be proud of. Two or three, sometimes five or six, will form up in a 'stack' like a parachute display team, each one a little to one side, a little behind and a little higher than the bird in front. In this arrangement they glide around a cliff or cross a gorge, sweeping round in wide curves while keeping their precise distance, then peel off, one by one, in the perfect 'griffon break'.

A bird we always hoped to see but as often as not didn't – bad for the nerves – is the wallcreeper. There was a place where they nested close to a road (amazingly close, and low down, just 12 or 15 feet above the tarmac). The first time I tried for them, nothing happened for half an hour and my tour group wandered off, cold, bored and wanting to see what was in the woods just up the road. I'm not sure if I was a good leader or a bad leader by persisting and not going with them (bad, surely). Eventually the wallcreeper appeared. Suddenly, spectacularly, it was there, bouncing, dancing, flicking its crimson wings, right by the nest. It dived inside and I was clenching my fists and hopping about in excitement, with no one to turn to, to say 'Wasn't that brilliant!'

Just then, some of the group reappeared. I got them all together and made them watch the hole (good leader, now). It took a while. But then, as quickly as before, there it was, outside the nest hole, bouncing, flouncing and dipping, spring-heeled as any dipper, before it spread those glorious wings, caught the wind and spiralled upward like a dead leaf to disappear over the cliff top. It brought the house down. Everyone said it was the best bird they had ever seen; how could anyone imagine something so beautiful?

Knowing how much a wallcreeper would do for them, I took every group to the spot after that, and tried hard to make them stick with it. Half the times we succeeded, sometimes we saw nothing. But when we did manage it, we had outstandingly good views and wallcreepers, delicate and dainty, with wide butterfly wings of sooty black, crimson and translucent white spots, are among Europe's finest birds:

With little optimism I decided to try the 'wallcreeper gorge', where I had seen no sign of the bird last year. Previously on this road I had seen very distant chough flocks high over the peaks. Today I noticed a small flock of crows beside the coach, over a meadow, and they were clearly choughs. Then a larger group swirled up above the woodland ahead. When we stopped I was amazed to step out into a chorus of whistles and trills: Alpine choughs! We were surrounded by wheeling flocks, spinning and turning on all sides, all calling loudly in bright sunshine. A few choughs joined in, then came a larger flock of choughs, keeping more or less separate from the Alpines. They all rose up very high but gave prolonged views at close range. Later we saw them in a couple of small, roadside fields and, on our return, stopped and had a repeat performance.

As we stopped on the return trip someone saw a raptor which turned out to be a lammergeier, not very high up against the cliffs. It had its wings angled back, head pulled back and tail tilted upwards, swinging into the cliffs and losing height and speed. It carried a stick in its bill and settled inside a large cave where there was a second lammergeier. We then had wonderful views as both flew out several times, swinging out against the sky or flying several hundred yards against the cliff. Both were strongly orange beneath.

The old wallcreeper nest site was easily found. It was then cold, mostly dull and very windy, as we were getting up near the cloud and there were odd spots of rain. After only a few minutes I saw a shape on the rock face and, sure enough, it was a wallcreeper. It was quite high and very small but everyone saw it and, amazingly, it soon became clear that there were two. After several minutes both flew together. They scuttled up smooth rocks, disappeared into crevices, bounced like dippers on flat ledges, flicked their wings and spun out in short, bouncy flights. Now and then the sun came out and caught the velvety flash of crimson. Then one, and finally both, began to work gradually lower and closer, making looping, swooping flights out from the rock, tossed like leaves in the wind, and down to a new rock face. This was brilliant, and getting better. Both had obvious black chins, one a small black bib surrounded by white, the other, in closer views, showing a much broader, glossy black throat and upper breast [a male]. Finally, one at a time, they came right down to the nest crevice just yards from the whole group. One, the female, entered with a twig. Both settled a few feet from the crevice, danced in and out, flitted their wings and jerked around as if on springs. The male flew out and made undulating, floppy flights, perhaps a display. Then gradually they moved away again.

Wallcreepers and lammergeiers make an unbeatable pairing, all in a spectacular mountain setting. On another occasion I found a wallcreeper in Foz de Biniés, this time on the October trip (they are not normally in the Foz in summer). We all watched it for half an hour, then the group began to drift away, to have lunch in a meadow near by. I stayed put: this was too good to miss. Eventually, the wallcreeper, which had been performing stunningly on the opposite side of the gorge across the river, flew down to my side, above the road, and came much lower down – a five-star performance.

Lammergeiers have made a great recovery in the Pyrenees after years of decline. They are well protected and supplied with supplementary food in places, but there is no sign of this when you go to the valleys around Berdún and Jaca. They are certainly as wild and wonderful as ever, just a little easier to see now that there are more of them. They are often said to be the largest of the vultures and, purely in terms of wingspan, that may sometimes be so, but when they are in the air with griffons, they almost always look a little smaller. They have such a long tail that their bill-to-tail length is longer, but they don't have the weight and breadth of wing of a griffon, although this is not to say that a lammergeier looks lightweight or any less impressive; indeed, it is usually the most impressive bird in the sky.

Any large bird of prey, or stork, or pelican, will soar beautifully and show great mastery of its environment. What is it about lammergeiers that seems to take them a step above the rest? Even against a cliff face, or within the confines of a gorge, they sail along for ever without the merest trace of a wing-beat. And if there is a wing-beat (as sometimes there will be) it is a slow, deep, majestic one, the wing-tips almost meeting beneath its body. And then on it goes, wings straight and flat, just slowly, slowly floating on and round and up, or following the contour of the cliff face, swinging in and out with each gully and bulge of rock. Sometimes it will be close enough to show the bunch of twisted feathers dangling beside the chin, the 'beard' from which it derives its alternative name of bearded vulture. At a distance, in sunshine, sometimes a flat-winged shape will appear amongst the V-winged griffons high over a cliff and, as it turns, so the light catches a large, white head – lammergeier! A shout goes up so everyone can see it; the excitement is palpable. Lammergeier! I anticipate the moment, willing a lammergeier to appear – and feel dejected if it doesn't. Some days have produced as many as seven individuals; we used to feel lucky if we saw as many in a week. And these might be with, say, 100 or 150 griffons (if you go farther west, there might be several hundreds).

This area of the Spanish Pyrenees is exceptional for wild flowers and butterflies, despite the pressures of intensifying agriculture. A walk from Berdún to Biniés and on up the Foz is so full of interest to the all-round naturalist that it takes forever. There is so much to stop and look at. Apart from the griffon vultures – lammergeiers, too, very often – there are short-toed, booted and golden eagles, peregrines, buzzards, choughs, alpine swifts and so on overhead, not forgetting the lovely fat trout and barbel in the river below (I am usually alone in my fish-watching). We used to stop for lunch in a

A lammergeier and a red kite head over Agüero in the Pyrenean foothills.

small meadow at the top of the gorge. It can be full of flowers, including several species of orchid (lady, burnt-tip, early spider, bee), and butterflies, and the river chuckles by beneath a slope covered in intensely green trees. A visit in June, later than usual, was especially good, but the butterfly identification was, as usual, a bit hit and miss:

Superb lammergeiers – for a while both perched on a grassy knoll in the gorge, looking very orange. One flew, carrying something, like a bone, in its feet for several minutes. Excellent comparisons side-by-side with griffons (which themselves gave many wonderful views, whether on ledges, low in the gorges, high overhead in a blue sky, or sailing low over the Aragon plain in the cold morning breeze). Some good close views of alpine swifts and excellent red-backed shrikes were among other highlights.

The 'usual' lunch-time stop in the meadow above the gorge produced a truly spectacular show of butterflies. Many remained unidentified, even blues settled on fingertips. Roughly, though, there were: scarce swallowtails, cleopatras, painted ladies (frequent), Spanish gatekeepers, Spanish heaths, commas, dappled/Bath whites, marbled, small and wood whites, many black-veined whites, ilex (?) hairstreaks, small coppers, southern white admirals, small skippers and many other skippers of 'grizzled' patterns, perhaps two or three species, Adonis (?) blues, common, small and holly blues, Escher's (?) blue, Spanish chalkhill blues and several other blues of various patterns, both large and small, pale and vivid; meadow browns, clouded and Berger's clouded yellows, several niobe fritillaries, pearl-bordered type fritillaries, heath fritillaries, Shepherd's (?) fritillaries and perhaps two or three other fritillary species.

A highlight for most people would be the bee-eaters, which are often around the Veral and nest by the Aragon, not far away. Another might be the golden orioles of the poplars and willows around both rivers. One year we had some miserable wet and cold days and, on the last day before coming home, walked down to the Veral again for one last try for the orioles. Normally they can be heard easily and at least glimpsed as they fly between clumps of tall trees, but on dull days, if they are not calling, they can be exceedingly hard to find at all.

An unbelievable June morning: thick grey mist, no wind, pouring rain. At times the main road at the foot of the hill is invisible and nothing much beyond it has been seen at all so far. What to do?

Drove [in the coach] via Biniés, Anso, Zuriza, Isaba, Roncal and Anso [a lengthy excursion through some brilliant scenery] – constant rain, sometimes heavy, even very heavy! Nothing seen.

A good walk in the late afternoon at least finished the trip on a high note after a nearly disastrously bad day. Wrynecks calling almost all the time, but only distant views of them. Golden orioles: several brief flight views, then a male followed by two females flew into a dense stand of poplars. A little later at about this point a male and female appeared after several seconds of unfamiliar calls. These continued and were clearly from the orioles – a sharp, high-pitched, loud, double note (which I've already forgotten, but roughly *pit-chip* or *pit-chou* I think). [This is a good example of why it is a good idea to write these things down on the spot – an hour later is not good enough.] Then there seemed to be two males, and one began flying around a male and female perched together; the inactive male soon dropped down out of sight, now leaving two dull female types perched a few feet apart. Meanwhile, the 'main male' continued flying around a female. This was perhaps 20 feet up, on the edge of a broad, dense poplar. His oval, or elliptical, flights were of 5–6 feet in diameter, going in through the edge of the poplar and out into the open on our side. The circuits were undulating, like the rim of a big, broad, wavy-rimmed hat, and at each 'end' of the loop the bird banked on wings at full stretch, its tail broadly fanned. The sharp calling – totally unfamiliar to me – continued all the while. This went on for more than two minutes, perhaps more than three, giving everyone the most spectacular views. Then the male settled a few feet from a female, bowed his head and gave a couple of normal fluty calls. All finally disappeared. As usual the male looked nothing like 'lemon yellow' but was a full, vivid, buttercup yellow and glossy black.

This was one of those rare occasions when, as a group leader, things finally come right. I had felt so sorry for my group: they had paid so much money and looked forward so long to their holiday only to have weather such as we had endured. Follow me, I'd said, and at least we can see some orioles. But I hadn't expected anything quite like this, and members of the group were so excited that the wasted, washed-out days were momentarily forgotten. The orioles had done us proud.

Stetsons and Whooping Cranes in Texas

One December, some years back, I accepted one of the promotional press trips that are occasionally offered to the editor of the RSPB magazine (now we turn them all down). It resulted in a feature in *Birds* on birds and boat trips – ' "Green" tourism in Texas'. It was a short trip with other environmental journalists and writers.

Flying, as most people will tell you, can be tedious – hours waiting in airports followed by hours spent high over flat, uniform, grey cloud. But some flights can be outstandingly exciting and memorable if, like me, you revel in the sight of stunning cloud formations, blue sky, even endless, sparkling oceans. A flight to North America can be such an experience and this one reached north-eastern Canada at something like 35,000 feet just as the cloud suddenly broke, like the ragged edge of a dishcloth long past its best, to reveal snowy terrain somewhere west of Labrador, northern Quebec. We passed the southern end of Hudson Bay above a realm of frozen, snow-covered lakes and snowy, ice-bound rivers. Roads, tracks and gullies full of snow created intricate linear patterns while higher hills stood out dark and grey, with striking wind-shadow effects. Soon the snow was reduced to smaller patches but there was a fantastic abundance of frozen lakes.

Somewhere north of the Great Lakes was a very wide, dead straight, snowy-white line that must have extended for tens or scores of miles; other people that have taken the same flight route have described the same feature to me, but I've never discovered exactly what this is. Soon we were over Lake Superior, near Sault Ste Marie, then travelling along Lake Michigan, over Beaver Island, with a huge view over Green Bay and way beyond into Wisconsin. This was my first view of what, to date, had been little more than exciting names in an atlas.

Beyond Chicago was a vast plain, with huge, rectangular fields, all very open, exposed and covered with snow. In places the older, extraordinarily complex, drainage pattern could be seen for hundreds of miles, superimposed by square field boundaries that bore no relation at all to any of the natural features on the ground. After ten and a half hours, we reached the glitter and efficiency of Dallas-Fort Worth airport, with an afternoon of daylight still to come. It was my first experience of America.

My first birds in the USA were starlings – I suppose I should have expected it – and two grackles, which went sadly unidentified. We were quickly in the air again, in a twin-engined BeechCraft, on our way to Burnet (not, we were told, pronounced Bur-net, to rhyme with wet, but Burnet, durnit). At Burnet there were two new birds – American kestrel, mourning dove – then it was on to Lake Buchanan, more precisely to Lakeside Lodge beside County Creek. It was cold. We were welcomed, shown our rooms, made comfortable, given a little speech or two. I was itching to get out. There was not much light, but I went for a short walk through the lightly wooded lodge grounds to a little pier. I encountered three new birds (great blue heron, American coot, canyon wren), plus two I had already seen as vagrants back home (double-crested cormorant, spotted sandpiper), and two not properly identified (terns, which were later confirmed as Forster's, and a warbler, probably yellow-rumped). I could hardly wait to get among the birds of the Texas hill country (which, here, was not so very hilly).

Before breakfast, while everyone else stayed indoors, I was wandering along the road to a patch of scrub and back through a small cluster of raised wooden houses set in leafy gardens. It was cold, true, but superbly clear, the start of what would prove to be a cloudless day of sunshine and vivid blue sky. On this pre-dawn excursion, there was little other than still-bright stars, Saturn and Jupiter, but the 15-minute spell between daybreak and breakfast at 7.30 sharp was great. Not many birds but they were mostly new to me, so I could get a nice little list while seeing them all well. Five northern cardinals were splendid creatures and, could I believe it, right away I was seeing birds such as belted kingfisher, mockingbirds, Bewick's wrens, tufted titmice. I had a brief view of a rufous-sided towhee (a species that had strayed to Britain so it had a sort of relevance), a yellow-rumped warbler (that's another), and my old friends ring-billed gulls. Thirteen new birds before breakfast. This was going to be good!

We drove to the east end of Buchanan Dam, which holds back Lake Buchanan on the Colorado river. Here was another mixture of birds entirely new to me (such as American black vultures) and some I had seen before at home (killdeer, lark sparrow). It was like being a beginner again, with all the old excitement and uncertainty. Inks Lake State Park was next up. This small, separate lake south of Buchanan was much more birdy – now there were 40 or 50 black vultures, 50 lesser scaup, a bufflehead, a superb red-tailed hawk, gulls and waders, 50 or so eastern meadowlarks, an eastern bluebird, chickadees, kinglets, two species of warblers and two or three of sparrows.

I had trouble with the sparrows, not for the last time. Some were song sparrows, but others were difficult and I had too little time to work them out. We had a couple of local birdwatchers with us, so I asked about them, but there was a curious reluctance to discuss sparrow identification as if they really didn't know, didn't care and preferred (sensibly) to be looking at the mockingbirds. Why would anyone want to spend time identifying little brown sparrows? American sparrows, aside from the ones introduced from Europe, are not the same as house and tree sparrows, but a larger family of bunting-like birds with complicated patterns that are attractive but not always instantly obvious.

The afternoon was occupied by a cruise (the Vanishing Texas River Cruise) on Lake Buchanan and the Colorado river flowing in to its northern end. This is bang in the middle of Texas, on the northern edge of the central hill country in an otherwise low-lying, flat state. The cruise, complete with commentary, was sensational for me as my first experience of the USA and American birds. We stood out on an open, raised deck, which gave excellent all-round views, and saw a couple of hundred double-crested cormorants, an American white pelican, 100 ring-billed gulls, a few Bonaparte's gulls, and other odds and ends. My interest in terns – identifying common, Arctic and roseate at home – was satisfied by 20 or 30 Forster's terns (which turn up very occasionally in Europe in late autumn or winter), but the birds of prey were the birds of the day. These included a simply brilliant immature golden eagle, which put on a great show as the boat stopped under 'Buzzard's Roost', a range of red cliffs that rose from the narrowing river. The eagle sailed up and down the cliffs in the sunshine, settling now and then on rocks, branches and bush tops with half-open wings in classic 'heraldic' pose, floating up, down, backwards and forwards in the updraughts, tilting over and stooping – the whole works – in a splendid display at really close range.

Meanwhile, a young bald eagle had been sitting in a tree and a third eagle was close by. The bald eagle left, but then we came across another one perched on a treetop – this time a magnificent adult. It stayed put as we drew alongside, no doubt used to this sort of intrusion, then it heaved itself into the air and sailed away. The head had seemed smooth and white, but now, as the bird flew, the tail looked even more so – spectacularly bright and immaculate, a great wedge of the purest white. It soared high up, circled against the deep blue and came right overhead, as obliging as could be.

One bird that made a particularly lasting impression, being just so gorgeously coloured and patterned, was a golden-fronted woodpecker at close range on a roadside pole at Black Rock Park. Woodpeckers the world over are mostly spectacular, with a combination of bars and stripes and often red or yellow patches. This one is a stunner, with a golden-yellow forehead, a remarkably vivid, gleaming scarlet cap, a nape patch of soft, velvety, flame orange above a narrowly barred black and white back, and pale buff face and underside. Dark-eyed junco was another new bird. Later, I had the merest glimpse of a blue jay flying away, pointed

Golden-fronted woodpecker: an immaculate bird.

out by Stephen Mills just before it took a left around the back of a house. I've never seen another blue jay, so it is a disappointment that I didn't get a better view. At the west end of the dam, late in the day, there were 200 or more black vultures and the best view yet of an American kestrel, a bird that impressed me no end by its richness of colour and pattern. Great-tailed grackles were 'exciting' at the time, according to my notes, but I can't remember quite why. They are certainly different, like large, glossy purple-black blackbirds with sharp, pointed bills and long, broad, rounded and strangely keeled tails, V-shaped in cross-section.

Part of the cruise included a tour around the Fall Creek vineyard and winery. It was a good break from the boat and good for birds, too, with belted kingfisher, loggerhead shrikes, 70-odd meadowlarks (perhaps of two species, eastern and western, which look very alike and are best identified by voice), and half a dozen northern cardinals. At that time I was not aware of the campaign to maintain the use of corks as wine-bottle stoppers to help conserve the cork-oak woodlands of Spain and Portugal. (This campaign would later become a feature of RSPB work.) I had, though, heard a bit about the change from cork to plastic and even metal as the new and better way to seal wine bottles. Texas seemed a long way from Spain and I asked whether the winery used plastic. Our host told me in no uncertain terms that, if you wanted to produce a fine wine and market it in competition with the established names, there could be no question of using such artificial materials. It had to be cork. As usual, I felt a bit silly and hid in a corner, but perhaps I was ahead of the game: cork is increasingly being tossed aside as the more modern sealing materials are being taken up all over the world, and the cork-oak forests seem destined to be grubbed up unless another use can be found for their remarkably sustainable products.

It was a clear night with a penetrating frost, followed by another cold, flawless day without a hint of cloud or even distance haze. If December was an odd time to be here, it was nevertheless coming up trumps. I was up and about early around the lodge and nearby housing once more and found a further four new birds: to Bewick's and canyon wrens I added cactus (briefly) and Carolina wrens, seeing all four during a short wander around the place. To see such a variety of wrens, when we are used to only one, was quite something. The three seen well were all lovely little birds, impressive in their way. Bewick's is sharp-faced, long-tailed, with a long, thin, white stripe over the eye; Carolina is bulkier, much more rusty brown and orange-buff, with a shorter tail; canyon wren is a larger bird, more like a half-size dipper, rusty brown spotted with black and cream, with a big white bib and a long, needle bill. Cardinals were again brilliant, the males rich strawberry red with black bibs and upstanding, pointed crests, and a ladder-backed woodpecker was particularly obliging. Ruby-crowned kinglets struck me as being more like yellow-browed warblers than goldcrests, with neat, broad wing bars as well as striking eye-rings.

Under a sunny azure sky the birdwatchers among us were driven via Burnet, Marble Falls and Round Mountain to Dripping Springs. Seven more birds that I had never seen before showed themselves, and we stopped for a cracking view of a scrub jay before seeing sharp-shinned hawk, 200-odd American robins and 50 to 100 cedar waxwings. Most of these were flying over us as we walked through open woodland at Dripping Springs, with the soft, shrilling calls of waxwings everywhere, but for a time we walked along surrounded by robins and waxwings that had settled beside us.

From Austin, we took to the air in a small plane, flying south to Rockport. From the cockpit, I had great views of the Gulf of Mexico coast, stretching north to south with its long, narrow, barrier islands running parallel to the shore – Matagorda, San Jose, Mustang and San Padre island, which tapered on right down to the Mexican border at Brownsville and Port Isabel. The barrier islands offshore run for 350 miles from the Mexican border north to Port Arthur. At Rockport, we were ushered out of the plane and seated in a row of red and orange plastic chairs lined up beside the runway for official photographs. At each end of the row posed a cowgirl on horseback, each wearing a big, black Stetson hat and blue jeans, one in a starched white shirt and black waistcoat, holding a Texas flag, the other in a blue denim jacket, with the Stars and Stripes. Then we were greeted by the Daughters of the Empire, ladies with connections to families back in Britain, waving Union Jacks. The mayor of Fulton was there to make a welcoming speech, followed by the mayor of Rockport, who said 'Doggone it, you-all have a good time and you-all come back, d'ya hear?' (It's true – I wrote it down.) It was great, although a little surreal.

A couple of local birdwatching guides came aboard our bus and we were driven around the Rockport area, north of Corpus Christi. It reminded me of parts of the Netherlands, with its wide waterways, little marinas and harbours, fish quays and piers, groynes covered with gulls, lakes dotted with wildfowl, all intermingled with low, flat ground and the built-up areas of the town itself. Rockport sits on the seaward edge of a long block of marshlands, with San Jose Island offshore across the Aransas Bay channel and an almost wholly enclosed inlet, Copana Bay, inland. A bridge going north, across the mouth of this inlet, reaches the Aransas National Wildlife Refuge. Aransas is huge: 54,829 acres of the Blackjack peninsula, with 16 miles of roads and six miles of hiking trails within its boundaries. It is a mixture of grasslands, blackjack oaks, live oak and redbay thickets (America has all the best tree names) and tidal marshes.

The birdwatching was just fantastic, if a little rushed. I was over the moon. Two species of pelican, five of heron and five of egret (great blue, little blue, snowy, reddish, great), grebes and divers, hundreds of ducks including American wigeon, 500 redheads (like dark pochards), a fine male canvasback (larger and paler), which was a real bonus, buffleheads and whistling ducks, and many waders including semipalmated and piping plovers, willets, long-billed curlews and marbled godwits. Gulls, which were mostly ignored – except by me for whom they held a special appeal – included ring-billed gulls and American herring and 1,000 laughing gulls, and there were 36 royal and 100 Forster's, as well as Caspian, terns – glorious stuff. To round off the day, I saw many of these all over again from the hotel balcony. As usual, a simple list does nothing to distil and preserve the experience.

We could not have been made more welcome at Rockport, and the local guides did their best for us (even if they were not so hot on their sparrows). The local birdwatchers with us would leap out with tape players that they would drape on the nearest bush and play full blast at every opportunity, belting out bird songs, the calls of screech owls, the squeal of a dying rabbit. If that didn't work they would hiss, squeak, noisily kiss the backs of their hands and generally have a good time in their attempts to lure birds into view. They were desperate to give us the best of their birds. Yet we were left with slightly mixed feelings. Even these people, it seemed, were not so aware as they might have been of the need to protect all of this. The coastal marshes are extensive but their size leads to a dangerous complacency. There were plans for gigantic 'landscape gardening' schemes along the Texas coast, draining vast areas of marsh to create golf courses and resorts. The marshes were thought of as 'wasteland', or at least they were considered so large that no one gave a hoot – and that went for the birdwatchers, too. 'This place was going to be turned into a big health farm, golf course, sports pitches, the lot, but the money ran out and it's been shelved. A real shame.' This was a birder talking, one who had just pointed out roseate spoonbills, pelicans, a long list of herons and egrets, vast numbers of waders, thousands of American wigeons and redheads. The idea that such a place might be lost did not appear to register as significant.

The spread of houses with big backyards, each on a sizeable plot away from its neighbours, goes on and on and on, for miles around Rockport. The occupation of space is overwhelming. Often one of the guides would say, 'This used to be open marsh when I was at school' or 'We all used to bird here a few years ago but now you can't get into the parking lot.' But, they said, it was OK, because you could still hunt between the houses. But what about the birds that needed a proper refuge and extensive habitat? 'Well, you can still hunt the others.' It seemed hard to talk about birdwatching without somehow veering on to shooting instead. Yet the editor of the local visitor guide told me, 'We're proud of our peninsula and everything the Good Lord provided us with,' and there was no doubt that he was.

The local oil boom has passed and Rockport is necessarily now heavily into tourism and fishing. As one grinning Rockport businessman told me: 'Usually we have more business in the summer and less in winter, when the winter Texans come. They come from the north to miss the winter weather, in recreational vehicles and trailers. We say they arrive with one set of underwear and a $50 bill in their pocket, and don't change either until they leave three months later.' Birdwatchers were beginning to offer a better income.

As we drove along one evening just after dark, the lights of all the houses came on to reveal a veritable reef of corals, starfish, crayfish, sea urchins and shells of all shapes, colours and sizes, and giant marlins, sailfish and swordfish, stuffed and varnished, decorating the walls of scores of homes and staring blindly out into the night. There was a hugely acquisitive and exploitative edge to Rockport: sea life was there to be hunted and fished and stuffed and shown off, nature appreciated if it was obtained and possessed. It left us feeling a little uncomfortable, despite all the good things we had heard about the birdwatching conventions and hummingbird festivals that take place here every year.

The next day was to prove a really special one. For much of the time, and for the next couple of days, too, we were joined by Victor Emmanuel, one of America's leading bird tour operators. To say Victor is an enthusiast would be the understatement of the year. It was hard to keep up with his slender, cowboy-booted figure. He proved to be a great help during the next couple of days and was especially patient and understanding of a birdwatcher seeing new birds. While it would have been so much easier to say, 'Don't worry about that, we'll see plenty more later', he took endless trouble to make sure I got a good view of something dirt common without wasting too much time over it. And he oozed enthusiasm, even over a bird he must see practically every day – 'Over here, here, through there, just left a bit, yeah, there – look, look here, you'll get a really good look – wow.' I felt satisfied, he was pleased, and if we then turned a corner and saw 500 more, it didn't matter. My experience, both as a 'beginner' in new countries and as an occasional tour leader myself, tells me that this balance is exceedingly hard to achieve.

The day produced pages of lists and notes. We were, after all, seeing the best birds on offer around Rockport, Copana Bay and Goose Island, Cape Valero, and then by boat around the creeks and channels of the world-renowned Aransas National Wildlife Refuge. (Later on we looked over the refuge on land, too.) It was a great day and included one of the rarest species I have ever seen or am ever likely to see: the whooping crane. Apart from the birds, we saw bottle-nosed dolphins, several alligators, fox squirrels, white-tailed deer, raccoons (at really close range), a nine-banded armadillo (amazing) and, sensationally, three bobcats sitting out on a dirt track. These – an adult and two well-grown young – were in full view for five minutes as they dozed in the sun. Victor told me that, after 30 years in Texas, he had seen only about five bobcats and these were mostly just scooting off into the brush. As they stood up and walked away I was amazed how long-legged they looked, almost monkey- or baboon-like in the way they stretched up and strode off.

More new birds came thick and fast, and they were as varied as sandhill crane, white ibis, loggerhead shrike, eastern phoebe, solitary and white-eyed vireos, hermit thrush and American goldfinch. American avocet, roseate spoonbill and great horned owl were other highlights. But the ones I had seen before were stunning too; there was an abundance of wildfowl, waders, gulls and terns, for a start. The whole region was extraordinarily rich in birds and, as usual when faced with this kind of situation, it was difficult (and hardly necessary, to be honest) to differentiate between what was perfectly normal (or even disappointing) and what was unusual or unexpected. I was just happy with everything, be it eight species of egrets and herons, hundreds of red-winged blackbirds, flocks of snow geese, 50 stilt sandpipers, 100 Caspian terns or 2,000 American wigeon. My old notebook system of annotating the 'best birds' with asterisks was strained somewhat – nearly everything could have been starred, and most were.

It would be good to go back for a week (or a month) to study the waders. Greater and lesser yellowlegs were mostly straightforward, especially with both of them about (some solitary vagrants to Britain have proved less so), but I could never get the dowitchers sorted out (so often they wouldn't call and wouldn't fly and usually were quite distant – not ideal conditions for separating the notoriously difficult long-billed and short-billed dowitchers). And while I

Whooping crane at Aransas.

asterisked 50 stilt sandpipers, because they were practically new to me and gave such excellent views, I see that I did not mark out either 50 least sandpipers or 100-plus westerns, no doubt because I had to more or less pass them over in the general mêlée of good birds in a particularly rushed stop.

Victor's wows got longer, softer, more reverential as the birds got better and more impressive, even for Victor. Clearly, the whooping cranes (two extra large, fat asterisks) demanded to be bird of the day, bird of the year – bird of the decade … At the time the world population was reckoned to be 142 individuals. We saw 31 of them – almost a quarter. Three were juveniles. They were in groups of two (14 birds), three (six birds), four and six, plus a solitary bird. 'You're so lucky, so lucky – I've never seen them better than this. Wow,' said Victor. We did, as he said, get some pretty good looks. Some were seen well in flight, but the best were feeding on the marsh and seen really well; some, indeed, were close enough for 10×40 binoculars to reveal the black pupil and bright gleam in the eye – again, Victor (honestly I think) said these were some of the best views he could remember. To round things off, a pair even called, quietly, as we went by. According to my notes, 'And everything else was wonderful, too' – it certainly was.

So much caught my attention – tricoloured herons, for example, were frequent, and there were perhaps 150 American white and 50 brown pelicans. Even 'our' birds such as great northern divers, black-necked grebes, 100 goldeneyes, red-breasted mergansers, hen harriers (marsh hawks, here, and a bit different), were exciting, as well as more brilliant views of my gulls and terns – ring-billed, laughing, Bonaparte's, 100 Forster's terns, 100 Caspians, 30 royals, even a gull-billed. This was all seen from a boat on the channel. The local guidebook has a huge ad for Whooping Crane Tours, chartered boats from Lucky Day, Inc: '$20 per person from Rockport harbour in the largest capacity, most comfortable boat in the area, complete with glassed-in, heated observation lounge.' The First National Bank sponsored a full-page ad for a local birder's guide. The Sandollar Pavilion restaurant and bar advertised coastguard-approved whooping crane tours alongside its 'famous shrimp salad, broiled flounder and char-broiled steaks'. Capt. Ted offered 'The Most Extensive Whooping Crane and Bird Trip in the world, with complimentary coffee or wine and full narration.' There were whooping crane stickers, whooping crane badges, whooping crane T-shirts and caps. The birds came second only to the fishing, the hunting and the real-estate ads.

Victor wondered how anyone ever saw anything from the giant gin palaces, swathed with banners and pennants, sailing along the waterway beside chemical barges. 'I much prefer the little boats,' he said, 'they get in much closer but don't disturb the birds half so much.' As we eased up beside a small quay and disembarked, we were greeted, as at Rockport airport, by the delegation from the Daughters of the Empire, who had trestle tables set up on the grass by the trail, with chocolate cakes and cups of tea and coffee.

Seeing birds from a boat can be a great experience, as this so obviously was, but it is a bit like watching wildlife on a game drive in Africa when getting off the vehicle, getting your feet back onto the ground and being able to birdwatch properly again – walking round, getting closer, moving to get a better angle of view – is a bonus. So it was on the land-based exploration of Aransas, albeit a little short. A vast flock – 2,000 or more – of American wigeons ('You-all see those Amer'can weee-jans?'), 1,000 redheads, pintails and mottled ducks, as well as real Canada geese instead of our imported ornamental ones back home, held up the wildfowl end pretty well. Birds of prey included red-tailed hawks and a short view of a passing merlin, which I knew well from home but was a good, apparently unusual and more difficult bird for our guides. It was good to see small birds such as eastern phoebe and, especially, white-eyed vireo at close range, but now the light was fading fast and the short days of December became something of a disadvantage. You can't have everything.

After the riches of Rockport, things might have tailed off; but no, we drove south, via Corpus Christi, to explore some of the sites in the lower Rio Grande valley. The first port of call, though, was the King Ranch, Kingsville – the Santa Gertrudis section, home of the Santa Gertrudis pedigree cattle herd, with by far the most impressively equipped bulls you will ever see. The ranch also breeds quarter horses, which are used for cattle work, especially for singling out and separating an individual from a herd; these horses must have speed, strength and great agility in equal measure. When we were there, the ranch was suffering from a long-lasting drought, so many of its cattle had been moved far to the north, although not, perhaps, via the traditional cattle-drive routes that had been made famous by so many western films and that had fascinated me since I was a kid. It was from here and San Antonio, just to the north, that the great trails began, heading north to take cattle to Dodge City and Ogallala, Wichita and Abilene (the Chisholm Trail) and through Forth Worth to Abilene and Kansas City (the Shawnee Trail).

First we toured the farmhouse, itself a fascinating place, with wonderful bronzes of cowboys and cattlemen and a series of trophies from races such as the Kentucky Derby. Then we sat out on a bench at a long table and had lunch and 'coffee with the cowboys', the coffee said to be so powerful that it would melt a horseshoe. It was, sad to say, more like thin dishwater and a big disappointment but, as the cowboys looked like they could use a horseshoe to practise their knots, none of us said so. Afterwards we drove around a sample of the flat, dusty, huge ranch and stopped at likely spots, seeing a superb selection of southern USA specialities. There were some good new ones here for me, such as crested caracara, white-winged dove, curve-billed thrasher, pyrrhuloxia (a strange cardinal, halfway to a parrot, with a red crest, bib, wing- and tail-flash but otherwise pale buffy brown and white), great kiskadee, Sprague's pipit (courtesy of Victor, who got it on call as it flew over and chased over to see it with me, even though it was time to get aboard and go), green jay and lark bunting. The kiskadee was stunning, a massive flycatcher with bold black and white stripes on its head, a yellow breast and red-brown patches in the wings; in the USA it is a speciality of the southern tip of Texas. Stunning, too, were ladder-backed and golden-fronted woodpeckers and northern flickers.

A group of 20 sandhill cranes impressed, too, and we studied flocks of great-tailed grackles, red-winged blackbirds and brown-headed cowbirds to be sure of Brewer's and bronzed cowbirds. On some pools were various waders; once again, I could have done with an hour or two to study them, but had to be satisfied with shorter views (or, as Victor would say, looks) of western and least sandpipers, stilt sandpipers and still unidentifiable dowitchers. In the Muerta Pens area of the ranch, we found a concentration of Santa Gertrudis bulls surrounded by 300 or more sandhill cranes, crested caracas (large and striking birds of prey), turkey vultures, 2,000 brown-headed cowbirds, 1,000 red-winged blackbirds, 100 Brewer's blackbirds, three bronzed cowbirds and 1,000 great-tailed grackles – as I put it in my notebook, 'a strange and amazing sight'. The cowbirds are quite unlike any European bird: they are middling-small, blackish – so they seem pretty much as, say, starlings or maybe blackbirds do – and yet somehow contrive to be entirely different. They feed in tight flocks, heads down, tails pointing up, as if drawn by E. H. Shepherd. Just beyond their flocks were the cranes, some bold and allowing a close approach – 'altogether wonderful birds'.

To finish the day came a small selection of birds of prey, the best of which was a Harris' hawk, perched at close range on a roadside pole. It was an impressive creature, with massively powerful legs and feet, much more eagle-like than, say, a buzzard. Roadside poles, for all their faults, are unmatched for giving good views of birds of prey. We also encountered a couple more nine-banded armadillos, one of which was caught and shown to us 'in the hand' – a most peculiar and extraordinary creature, very big and heavy, with amazing piggy ears and a long, pink nose.

Down here in the south it was now getting warm and sunny, compared with the clear, frosty days in the hills. High, broken cloud had replaced the spotless blue void. It was a long, straight drive south from Kings Ranch on Route 281, heading for McAllen, through some of the emptiest parts of Texas. Just east of McAllen, Santa Ana Wildlife Refuge, near Hidalgo, in the Rio Grande valley, proved a brilliant place. Nearly everything got an asterisk. New birds were thinning out but still they came: least grebe, cinnamon teal, red-shouldered hawk, solitary sandpiper, black-necked stilt, white-tipped dove, green kingfisher, plain chachalaca, common yellowthroat, house wren, long-billed thrasher. But it was ducks and herons that gave some of the finest views, tricoloured herons especially, and green-winged and blue-winged teals, redhead, ring-necked ducks. Woodpeckers were again evident, with golden-fronted and ladder-backed and yellow-bellied sapsuckers brilliant. As in most places I visit far from home, I was very much aware of spectacular butterflies but made little or no mention of them in my notes beyond 'monarchs, red admiral types, and vivid yellow and copper ones'. But here, zebra longwings were especially spectacular, with their very long, slender black wings banded with lime green or yellow.

If the single great kiskadee at King Ranch had been great, now there were ten, drinking just a few feet away, then flying around and calling; and the chachalacas, strange birds of the far south, numbered at least 50. Think of a hen pheasant, longer-legged, with a rounded, white-tipped, dark-greenish tail and otherwise plain, beige-brown to dark-brown plumage, and you get the right idea. Chachalacas are a special species of the tall chaparral thickets of the Rio Grande – they are essentially Latin American birds – and I think we expected them to be scarce and skulking, hard to see, but they make such a racket – calling their name in a rapid, ebbing and flowing chorus – and are so abundant that they proved to be impossible to miss.

Another southern speciality came our way afterwards, in the shape of a Chihuahuan raven, like a smallish, desert raven with (usually invisible) white on the base of the neck feathers. This was on the road east along the north side of the river, on our way to another reserve, the Sabal Palm Grove, near Brownsville. Later on, we visited Brownsville tip and found 100 or more of the ravens, plus 50 Mexican crows (handsome birds, I thought, very glossy crows), as well as a black-shouldered kite. Mexican crows were unknown in the USA until the late 1960s when they began to appear in winter in the Rio Grande valley, particularly at Brownsville dump. Later still, 150 to 180 snow geese added an altogether different touch. At the Palm Grove, the day was made really special by my first ever hummingbird – a buff-bellied hummingbird, at the reserve entrance, coming to a feeder. I had seen a few hummingbirds in captivity, in the tropical house at Slimbridge, but this was my first wild one and so remains a milestone event. Its visits to the feeder were lightning-fast but several times it perched just above it, for 20 to 30 seconds at a time, so I could see it properly. It is not one of the most colourful species, but it is tiny, remarkably long-winged and also quite long-billed. Buff-bellied is essentially a Mexican species, another one that just creeps across the river here to edge onto the US list.

Sadly, the last day of this short and hectic trip came around all too soon. In the morning I wandered around for an hour or so on my own, watching birds at South Padre Island near Port Isabel and Boca Chica. It was warm, sunny, a little humid – a far cry from December at home. When would I next see pelicans, little blue herons, reddish egrets, a single canvasback with 700 redheads, lesser scaup, piping plovers, western sandpipers and willets, American oystercatchers and royal terns? Of my 158 species identified in a dash around a little bit of Texas, 108 were birds I had never seen before; quite a few I have not seen since.

We packed and got ready to fly north from Harlingen to Dallas/Fort Worth and on home. First, we had a late breakfast. This was the time I chose to shake the ketchup bottle when the top was loose – it flew off and half the contents landed on my shirt and in my lap. Still, it amused the rest of the party so I can't complain. It was a sticky flight home.

California in a Wet January

New Year is not the time a sensible birdwatcher would choose to go to California. No, California is warm and sunny in spring and summer, full of lovely New World warblers and hummingbirds. But in winter? Well, there is a chance it might be fine and dry and quite warm, and the thought that it might be a change from the dismal English winter makes it worth a try. So, we did. It was quite a trek. Marcella and I left home at 9 a.m., flew from Heathrow at 1.30 p.m. and reached Chicago at 10.10 p.m. (UK), 4.10 local. It was not until 9.45 local (3.45 a.m. UK) that we left Chicago after long delays. Our plane was overbooked and they were trying to pay passengers to give up on it and fly later. So we reached San Francisco at 2.10 a.m. Chicago time (8.10 a.m. UK). We got to Vagabond Inn by 1.40 a.m., 24 hours and 40 minutes after we left home.

San Francisco was in the middle of the wettest weather it had been served for years, with two and a half inches of rain in a day. Inland, where we had thought of heading first, the mountains were under many feet of snow. Roads were blocked everywhere. People were rescued from cars buried in snowdrifts; some had been missing for days, making headlines on the evening news. But we had nothing booked beyond the car and the flight home so, in between times, we could do as we liked.

Overnight, that first night, there was rain and thunder, much to our amusement. The first day, 29 December, was cool to cold, dull and drab with spells of rain but, luckily coinciding with our arrival at the best places, scraps of fine, sunny weather. I saw a new bird from the car park of the Vagabond Inn – California gull, appropriately. We drove a little way and stopped for a breath of fresh air in a suburban area, with plenty of wooded gardens; it might have been the edge of an English town, a little hilly suburb. This is what I like about entirely new places in the world: anywhere, the most ordinary sort of spot, can bring new birds, new experiences. With no interest in birds – with nothing to note – it would be ordinary, or at least unexceptional but, if you like birds, you are on your way immediately.

This was San Mateo, an open, sloping area surrounded by trees and bushes and with berried shrubs in the gardens. I recalled my walk at Dripping Springs in Texas, for, as happened there, we were suddenly surrounded by American robins and cedar waxwings. It was extraordinary: 100 or more robins (as big as blackbirds) and 150 waxwings (very like 'our' waxwings that come from northern Europe), many of them in a roadside bush feeding on fat red berries. There were northern flickers – 'red-shafted' here (northern flickers are colourful woodpeckers with yellow-shafted, gilded and red-shafted forms) – scrub jays, a mockingbird, yellow-rumped warblers, house and purple finches, pine siskins and golden-crowned sparrows. And there, look, just there, for a moment, was a hummingbird. It just 'appeared' in my binocular field of view while I was watching something else, a minute green apparition that hovered, settled for a few seconds and then was gone. It was the second hummingbird of my life and must have been an Anna's hummingbird; being sure would have to wait.

We drove south to Santa Cruz and stopped at the Seacliff State Beach. The birds were brilliant already! Just offshore the sea was surging, crashing, foaming up to the beach and, dotted all over it, were several hundred surf scoters, living up to their name in amazing fashion. Riding the waves with them were several black scoters and western grebes, a red-throated diver (loon, here), double-crested cormorants and brown pelicans. The gull-watching was fantastic; I could have indulged myself all day. Glaucous-winged gulls, perhaps including a few hybrids, western gulls as close as five feet, California gulls, ring-billed and Heerman's gulls. A small, flycatching bird swept about by the wind near the beach turned out to be a black phoebe.

We went on south, along a spectacular bit of coast, towards Monterey. Moss Landing was the next stop, where there were roaring waves, crashing surf and a cold, biting wind, under brilliant sunshine – a truly wonderful combination, the wild Pacific coast as I imagined it could and should be. There is a long list of birds in my book, with the comment 'great views of everything' – everything including great northern and Pacific divers (Pacific being very like a black-throated but rounder-headed, smaller-billed), 150 brown pelicans, black-necked (eared), Slavonian (horned) and western grebes, three species of cormorant, 100 surf scoters, 100 buffleheads, a fine list of waders including grey (red) phalarope, marbled godwits, willets and Hudsonian whimbrels, hundreds of gulls of seven species, even a pigeon guillemot. The scoters dived headlong into the base of huge, breaking rollers, as shags sometimes do at home in waves breaking onto rocks – suicidal surely, but bobbing up safely every time.

This was an exhilarating day, but not quite what we had expected. The weather reports had predicted more heavy rain and hail and heavier snow inland than there had been for 40 years; on this one day there had been six feet of fresh snow. The next day continued and expanded on the theme, with a wonderful stretch of coast under bright sun, a cool wind and immense breaking waves swathing the whole shoreline in a haze of white mist and spray. Black oystercatchers gave remarkable, exaggerated piping displays that seemed to out-oystercatcher European ones. Black turnstones and surfbirds were at home in the wild conditions. At least 50 phalaropes rode the seas. Auks, or auklets, and a single, all-dark, shearwater flew by far offshore, while brown pelicans – rapidly becoming favourites – took heart from the wind and came along the coast, riding the updraughts from the waves, skimming the wave crests and sinking into the troughs with scarcely a wing-beat between them. Pelicans are often portrayed as big, silly birds, but they – including, especially, the white pelicans of Europe and Africa – are truly among the world's finest.

Again the gulls caught my eye and notebook. They were high on my list of good, if easy, birds to see here and I was not disappointed: eight species this time, including Thayer's. Heerman's – so very smart, so different from the usual white and grey ones in their dark plumages – were practically hand tame, and westerns and glaucous-winged were within arm's length. Why so amazingly bold and tame here? Our gulls in the UK will dart down to pinch a sandwich or take a scrap, and some will walk up to be fed within a few yards, but you don't see flocks of them, just sitting there, letting you get close enough almost to stroke them.

And offshore, too, there were six or eight or maybe more sea otters. They were mostly heads bobbing in the water but they gave good views, even performing the classic sea-otter behaviour of hammering shellfish on their chests as they lay back in the bobbing black weed.

We took the '17-mile drive' along the Monterey Coast as everyone must:

Quite stunning. A magnificent place, for a start, with woods of Monterey pines and a remarkable coast with an even more remarkable and sensational sea. It is amazing how birds such as the Slavonian (horned) and black-necked (eared) grebes and surf scoters survive in the middle of the biggest, heaviest rolling waves and crashing surf.

For a gull-watcher this is paradise, albeit full of tricky situations. Heerman's and westerns watched within four or five feet, just waiting to be fed. I've always wanted to see a Say's phoebe! A black oystercatcher was a long-held ambition; Anna's hummingbirds simply unreal. The Townsend's warblers, however, rate among the more beautiful birds I have seen — absolutely sensational birds, far better than any illustration conveys.

Indeed, there were both Say's and black phoebes, Steller's jays, two male Townsend's and a female hermit warbler, and yellow-rumped warblers. Phoebes are small flycatchers, neat and upright. Black phoebe is black with a white belly, Say's is pale brown, brightening to tawny orange under the broad, black tail. Townsend's warblers are streaky black, yellow and greenish, boldly striped green-black and bright yellow on the head, with two white wing bars; hermits are greyer, whiter beneath, with black bibs and unmarked bright-yellow faces. While most North American warblers migrate south, both these species winter in small numbers in the California coastal strip. Yellow-rumped warblers are much more widespread in winter in the southern USA. There were scores of tame Brewer's blackbirds, wren tits and bush tits, pygmy nuthatches and chestnut-backed chickadees, and three Anna's hummingbirds, as well as all the sea- and shorebirds you could wish for.

And that's not all:

**Grey whales – 4 – a couple showed quite well, one being very mottled, but usually just large spouts of spray – excellent all the same [my first great whales].

**Californian sea lions – 500 – all over a large, rocky island, both a magnificent sight and creating an unbelievable sound. I've never seen anything like it – they rate with African big game, certainly.

From here we turned back north and visited San Francisco proper, crossing its great bridges, scanning the harbour across to Alcatraz, driving the steep hills of Steve McQueen's *Bullit* car chase, admiring the bulk of the Golden Gate bridge in the rain and seeing a brilliant Anna's hummingbird there, along with white-crowned and golden-crowned sparrows. Hummingbirds dart by like big bumblebees at full speed, stop dead to perch upright on a twig, or turn on their tails to hover, almost vertically, and move back and forth across a bush full of flowers, before dashing off again whence they came.

Going north over the great bridge, we drove to Muir Beach Overlook and
Stinson Beach (highlights included 75 American avocets) and Point Reyes. We
saw California quails, red-shouldered hawk, turkey vultures, maybe a varied
thrush – it surely was, but was merely a glimpse – thousands of red-winged
(mostly 'bicolored') blackbirds, tricolored blackbirds, towhees and sparrows.
San Francisco was good, but after that the weather was dreary in the extreme,
the views spoiled by the conditions. Point Reyes was open and bleak and birdless,
and the Point Reyes forests, though wonderful, were by then in gathering
gloom and rain.

We decided to head south again, plans for going east curtailed by the
weather. We drove steadily through the murk before getting stuck, in the
middle of nowhere in particular, for hours in a traffic jam on New Year's Eve.
Finally we saw a neon sign, a place to stop, took it in desperation and tried
to get some sleep. On the television there had been appeals to people not
to go out on New Year's Eve and fire guns into the air, as every year people
were injured, even killed, by falling bullets, but such appeals went unheeded.
Despite pouring rain there were fireworks and gunshots everywhere. We were
on the ground floor overlooking the parking lot and, in the next room, there
was evidently someone with a young, crying child. Outside in the car park,
the father came to take the child away. It turned into a huge argument and

American bittern.

shouting match. Then – a sudden shock in the middle of the night, just a few feet away – a window smashed. The police arrived. We gave up on sleep and turned out again to escape all of this.

The drive south next day, on 1 January, was a long one, unfortunately impaired by constant dull light and drizzly rain. Still, there were birds: yellow-billed magpie for a start (another new one), then good numbers of waders including 100 long-billed dowitchers. Tree swallows seemed a bit incongruous in such weather. Then a surprise. I didn't know how unusual or ordinary it was, but there, crossing a field by the road, was a coyote, an impressive looking animal, too. We saw another three later on: not so unusual, then.

We found San Luis Wildlife Refuge and did our best to make a go of it, but all our birdwatching was done from the car in pouring rain. This had not been part of the plan. That had included vast flocks of geese and cranes, but of these we saw nothing. Nevertheless, it was good, very good: American bitterns; pied-billed grebes; red-tailed and red-shouldered hawks (smaller than the common red-tailed hawks); white-tailed kite (very like the African black-shouldered kite); Californian and rufous-sided towhees; chipping, fox, song, golden-crowned and white-crowned sparrows (200 of these); and another black phoebe. By now, only fox sparrow was actually 'new'. I had seen American bittern before – in South Wales! Another new bird came later, in the entertaining and curious shape of a burrowing owl. In Delano, after dark, hundreds of American crows flocked to roadside trees to roost. But at 9 p.m. it was still raining.

Next day was a complete mixture, a lucky dip for weather and scenery, from thick fog to occasional sun and a clear, very cold night, and from the flat, central valley with its extensive vineyards and splendid orange-orchards to quite drab, hilly grassland. Then we reached much finer hills with open oak woodland and parkland landscapes, and climbed up into forests of dark pines, all under snow, in the most beautiful and spectacular winter wonderland you could imagine. After that, we were back on dull, flat ground before reaching semi-desert beneath a clear, blue sky with distant mountains sharp and crisp in the thin, cold air. After dark, we rolled up into Lone Pine, under the stars, a large moon and the brilliance of Venus, all reflected from snow on the high peaks of the Sierra Nevada. It was just fantastic.

There had been a new bird from the room window before we set off for the day – a flock of lesser goldfinches were feeding near by. East to Glenville produced a whole stream of fine birds, with close, beautiful views of most: acorn woodpecker (patterned in large blocks of black and white with a red cap) and Nuttall's woodpecker (more typically barred black and white), and hundreds and hundreds of American robins in the lowland vineyards, dozens in the higher forest. There were 30 or more mountain bluebirds (almost unreal in the brilliance of their colours), 40 Oregon (dark-eyed) juncos, 50 western meadowlarks, 200 house finches, towhees, ravens, flickers, scrub jays – and two more coyotes. We were driving on through increasingly beautiful countryside, to more than 4,000 feet above sea level, almost to Lake Isabella before turning back because of increasingly dangerous snow and ice on the roads. Every twig of every tree was thickly lined with snow in the still air.

Between Glenville and Bakersfield a group of large birds over a hill brought us to a stop. Two golden eagles were in view for the next 20 minutes, soaring and diving over a ridge with a group of ravens. At one time they sat side by side on the ridge, until they were spooked by a coyote.

The next day was a day of days, even though my bird notes are short:

Hard frost; bright, clear, cloudless morning. Bright clear day with warm sun, cloudless all day; very cold wind and cold night. All day in Owens Valley. Mount Whitney above Lone Pine up to Alabama Hills, scene of hundreds of westerns and a dream of a place – Roy Rogers Flats, Lone Ranger Canyon, Hopalong Cassidy Ranch! The valley was cold; hills to the west rising to more than 14,000 feet, covered in snow. To the east, a little lower, bleaker, snow-capped, all blue, purple and pink. The scale is awesome and misleading – from Big Pine, Mt Whitney looks like the next peak along the ridge, above the Alabama Hills, which are in fact 40 miles away. Even at Independence we seemed to be 'alongside' the peak, while still 15 miles from Lone Pine – yet we could see the other hills, far to the south, all day long. Despite huge amounts of traffic on the main road, anywhere else is deserted and unbelievably silent. I've never been to a more wonderful, magical place.

At one point we reached 7,000 feet up, on Westgard Pass, where the best birds were lovely little sage sparrows, their appearance, their name and their environment blending together perfectly. Sage sparrows are pale as bleached sage-stalks, grey on the head with a neat white eyestripe and broad white moustache, and a small, central black spot marking the white breast.

It became too dull for decent birdwatching after 4 p.m., with the sun behind the Sierra Nevada, but there followed an hour of pink and purple twilight, making the drive back south to Lone Pine really magical – it is an extraordinary place.

Sage sparrow: a subtly beautiful bird of the semi-desert.

The following day provided another example of the tameness of birds here, compared with similar or even the same species back home. A large bird of prey stood on top of a Joshua tree stump. I pulled up as close as I could and found that, as I suspected, it was a rough-legged buzzard, a scarce visitor to the UK, but a bird I knew well, particularly from the Netherlands. I got out of the car and walked closer, getting the most spectacular view I had ever seen of this species. Eventually, the hawk flew. But it came *towards* me and then went by to settle on the next tree. It had been sitting quietly, ignoring me – or perhaps taking a mild interest? – just 17 paces away.

This was something of a pattern for the day, as I stopped at several places and walked out into the semi-desert habitat, cut across to make a wide triangle of it and then wandered back to the car. The environment was outstanding, with enormously expansive views, still of exceptional clarity, although there was more cloud than before. The varieties of 'desert' were fascinating and I sampled several, but, this being January, I found them to be almost, or sometimes absolutely, birdless.

Feeding the wildlife is not a great idea anywhere. But near Panamint Springs, I broke the rules. Far ahead there was some kind of animal on the road. We stopped and it came towards us. It was a coyote, obviously an experienced scrounger, here to greet the tourists and take its reward. Other coyotes, which we had seen from a greater distance, looked surprisingly big and impressive, wolf-like in their general conformation. This one, so close, seemed small and

delicate, with a decidedly 'pretty' expression, and at first I thought it was some
sort of fox; but it was certainly a coyote, a beautiful animal. It circled the car
several times and I gave it some biscuits and an apple before deciding enough
was enough and we ought not to encourage it to wander around like this on a
road. Apart from us, though, the road was empty, for scores of miles. Later in
the trip we saw another coyote cross the road ahead. We pulled up to watch it.
A pick-up truck roared up from behind us, skidded to a halt and disgorged a
bunch of rough-looking men with an assortment of rifles and shotguns. They
took off across the fields in pursuit of the creature. We left.

Furnace Creek to Death Valley Junction proved to be endless miles of
birdless desert, not even a raven. Yet, here in one of the driest parts of the
world, there seemed to be copious amounts of vegetation, and there were
even puddles of water, appearing like spots of greasy perspiration on the face
of the vast grey salt-flats. Then suddenly there were three birds at one spot – a
white-crowned sparrow and two black-throated sparrows – which were new
and extremely smart. However, on this occasion birds were really a secondary
consideration: this was all about one of *the* great drives. The Lone Pine to Death
Valley route was just magnificent, awesome all the way, with remarkably varied
and colourful hills of cream, yellow, brown, green, red, grey and purple rocks.
Distance often lends a slight blueness to the scene. Perhaps it was simply the
scale of things here that made more distant hills look so much more intensely
blue than I'd ever seen before.

We were intrigued by the distances here, and the straightness of vast
stretches of road. Ten miles without the merest hint of a curve was quite
normal, and sometimes we would go up or down a steepish hill for five miles,
dead straight. On the stretch between Death Valley Junction and Indian Springs
we did 66 miles with two birds, a raven and an unidentified hawk, and that
included several stops and walks. Just beyond that, there were five more birds:
four sage sparrows and a rock wren, a fine little bird with a particularly long bill.
After a walk through such birdless terrain, the sudden movement, a scratch of
sound, a flick of a tail, generates a little tension and excitement. What will it be?
Can I get a good view? Will I identify it before it flies off and disappears?

Travelling from Owens Valley, over Toune Pass (4,956 feet), through Death
Valley into Nevada – with a quite different kind of scenery now, full of Joshua
trees and yuccas, along the edge of the snow-topped Spring Mountains in really
freezing air – made it a sensational and memorable day. And then we entered
an altogether different universe: Las Vegas. My walks into the desert had had
a particular objective, but clearly I had been going about things completely

the wrong way, or had conceived an entirely wrong notion about my quarry, because at Boulder Beach, Mead Lake, I finally saw the bird I was after. It was in a trailer park, where it walked between a car and a pile of bicycles, dodged under an occupied caravan, and then emerged to sunbathe, on an upturned boat. This, then, was the mythical roadrunner. It was not quite the wilderness experience I had been hoping for, but there you are.

The lake and its associated areas, such as Las Vegas Wash, pulled in many more birds. The notebook began to fill again. Prairie falcon and verdins were the first new ones of the day, followed by Gambel's quail, greater roadrunner and red-breasted sapsucker. In between were grackles, assorted gulls, western grebes, mockingbirds, loggerhead shrike, kinglets and hummingbirds, Say's phoebes, house finches, yellow-rumped warblers, and white-crowned sparrows – flocks of them. At Hoover Dam, I started an Arizona list, with rock wren amongst the five species on that side of the gigantic structure, where you can leap forward an hour and back again by hopping over the Central Time Line.

A Wednesday in Las Vegas, where it never rains. It was appalling. We drove south-west to Barstow, through thick fog, low cloud, snow and freezing rain on the higher stretches, dreary rain and leaden skies lower down. We later heard that an inch or two of rain had fallen along the coast, with several inches at Monterey. Over the middle of the desert I saw a ring-billed gull. Gone were the extensive views; most of the time we could scarcely see half a mile across flat desert flooded by shallow pools of rainwater. When we reached the Twenty-nine Palms visitor centre, we were told that black-necked grebes had flown down and landed on the roads, mistaking them for rivers – rivers that ran dead straight for 9.6 miles at a time. Even so, the variety of landscape and vegetation here was wonderful to see. At Twenty-nine Palms it was different again from anything we had yet encountered. But all day long we saw almost no birds. Phainopeplas were new, but so wet and bedraggled they were hardly at their best – a great name to go into the book nevertheless. And late in the evening, when it was a little drier, I had the best view yet of a cactus wren.

Next morning began cool and wet, although it dried out a little by late morning. At the visitor centre there was a much better roadrunner, excellent Gambel's quails, three superb cactus wrens, more warblers and sparrows (including black-throated at about five feet). We moved on to Joshua Tree National Monument – prairie falcon, coyote – and Barker's Dam. A canyon wren was the star turn here, active and noisy around a bunch of rocks by a small lake. The desert itself became more extraordinary yet. Joshua Tree is like something from an alien planet, eerily strange but wonderfully beautiful and haunting. It was enhanced, if anything, by the wreaths of grey cloud and damp fog that clung to the hilltops and sank into the valleys, penetrated at times by searchlight beams of sunshine.

But we reached Palm Springs – the capital of the desert – in pelting rain. Several of the roads around town were closed, and those that we could access were under several inches of running water. The windscreen wipers on our hire car gave up and I got out to fix them; I was drenched by the rain, almost washed away by bow waves from passing trucks. It was said to be the worst rain here since 1979, and yet twice as much had fallen in San Diego! We had half intended to visit San Diego, farther south on the coast, but it was declared a disaster area, suffering huge and damaging mudslides, so, like the great national parks inland in the mountains, it was crossed off the itinerary, relegated to 'next time'.

This series of wet, birdless days was becoming too long a chunk out of the middle of our visit to California. With Palm Springs mostly impassable, we drove on to Brawley in the Imperial Valley. The rain did nothing for it. But then joy, oh joy! A dry, sunny day. Lists and lists of birds. This was better. Brawley had cattle pens, reminding me of the King Ranch pens in Texas where I had first seen flocks of cowbirds and blackbirds. Here there were a couple of hundred cowbirds, 500 red-winged blackbirds and two yellow-headed blackbirds, my first – stunning birds but remarkably elusive amongst all that lot. There were 150 cattle egrets, too, and a white-faced ibis with 100 or so long-billed curlews. Twenty buff-bellied pipits, meadowlarks, mourning doves, grackles and sparrows all made the place very 'birdy' in comparison to the places we'd visited in the preceding couple of days.

The Salton Sea is a famous bird area and high on the list of attractions in California. It is, though, huge and difficult to 'manage' on a short visit. We hadn't a great deal of time. The area around Calipatria and the Salton Sea Wildlife Refuge headquarters proved a fine start. Wetland birds were obvious, including, for example, 40 great white egrets, 1,000 shovelers, some buffleheads, lesser scaup and green-winged teal. But it was the geese that we were after and that really caught the imagination. It was hard to get where we wanted to go, because the roads were often wet and impassable, but I saw a flock of snow geese and got pretty close. I was searching for a Ross's goose amongst them, but a light plane came over and put them all up. Then I found a larger flock in a field beside the road, and had better views. I was surprised and delighted to find a Ross's goose straight away. But then, with a scan through, it seemed that they were nearly all Ross's! This was unexpected: had they moved in because of the strange weather? I read a couple of neck collars and reported them to the headquarters, but heard nothing on them. Altogether there were 200 Canada geese, 500 to 1,000 snow geese (only three being 'blue') and around 4,000 Ross's geese (which look like snow geese but a little smaller, with different bill details). I couldn't complain.

And now I encountered another roadrunner – giving good views – along with northern harriers (hen harriers/marsh hawks, whatever), 15 American kestrels, killdeers, mountain plovers, yellow-footed gull (distant, but a new gull for me), Say's and black phoebes, 50-odd shore (horned) larks in a field, six Abert's towhees. The yellow-footed gull was a mile off but obviously a big gull, very dark on its back, with a large, vivid yellow bill and, even at that distance, I could see the large, pale-yellow feet – good enough! This sort of rich birdwatching continued, despite several false starts along flooded trails, as we explored the area of the vast lake. Birds were abundant almost everywhere: ibises, herons, egrets, birds of prey, shorebirds of many kinds, goodly numbers of ducks, thousands of distant snow geese, white-throated swifts, phainopeplas, phoebes, shrikes, black-tailed gnatcatchers, verdins, cactus wrens. Strange birds with strange names; colourful birds, instructive birds, impressive birds.

The weather reports held our attention that evening. It had been mercifully fine and dry where we were, in an area that can be oven-like in the intensity of its heat in summer, but there were floods in Palm Springs, severe damage in Los Angeles and San Diego, six or seven inches of rain in the hills. There was another inch or two forecast for the next day, and three to six the day after. What next?

Anna's hummingbird.

We travelled via Indio and Indian Wells on Route 74, then on to Hemet Lake. I had earlier seen a red-breasted sapsucker but it had puzzled me a bit, being dull with a complex pattern (a young one?), but now I found one right beside the road, giving a great view of its really bright colours – another example of a splendid woodpecker. A little patch of trees proved to be worth the few minutes' exploration, for it yielded scrub jays, plain titmice, towhees and a hundred or more sparrows – mostly white-crowned and very bright, breeding-plumage chipping sparrows. Hemet Lake had 15 or so white pelicans on the water, then 90 flew over heading west. They circled, grouped up in a shapeless mass, then re-formed and went overhead in a magnificent double V, a most impressive sight. Far off, big and impressive – but unfortunately offering only a very brief glimpse – a young bald eagle headed up the lake. Hairy woodpecker and pinyon jays kept my list ticking along, the jays in noisy, busy groups in treetops around the picnic area, some bright blue, others greyer, all looking very long-billed for jays. Western bluebirds again reminded me how shockingly bright blue they can be. On the next stretch we came across another new bird in the shape of mountain chickadees. We were up over 6,200 feet by now, in the Indian Hills, through thick fog and rain which sometimes cleared miraculously to reveal fine forests and wonderful snow scenes. Two coyotes dashed across the road in a snow-filled forest, between houses; again I was surprised by their tameness – or boldness – in such situations and impressed by how beautiful they were.

We were well and truly back among the birds now after days of scratching around for a species or two in the winter desert. Lake Matthews and Lake Perris, despite the weather, proved exciting. The former had at the very least 2,000 western grebes – I found four or five Clark's grebes amongst the two or three hundred birds closest to me – while the latter had 200 westerns, plus 100 black-necked, a calling Slavonian and a couple of pied-billed grebes. Wildfowl were good, especially lesser scaups and ruddy ducks; there were many gulls and terns about and quite a varied list of birds of prey; and there were all kinds of small birds from rock and Bewick's wrens, western bluebirds and yellow-rumped warblers, to California thrasher, Anna's hummingbirds and hundreds of house finches.

After my earlier efforts to see a roadrunner, it seemed to me that they were now having a bit of a joke: here was one, ringing wet, on a strip of rough grass beside a roundabout slip road. Then, on a muddy field, there was another, if anything looking wetter and more sorry for itself than the first. On another muddy field there was a flock of shore larks (horned larks), which I am used to seeing in fours and fives; astonishingly there were 500 here, perhaps as many as a thousand. At least, there were more than a thousand small birds flying over the field and, when less than half the flock settled, all of them, 500 or so, proved to be shore larks.

We returned that evening to Hemet. The next day, for whatever reason, the two of us took turns to be ill. It was a pity, as this could have been a big day for birds. In the event, it was cut down to half a morning. Prominent in the notes are bush tits, wren tit, acorn woodpeckers, rufous-crowned sparrows. Despite a good series of birds I was moved to write: 'Most species continue to behave like difficult Dartford warblers or rarities in Wells Wood: everything here seems so difficult to see!' But we were soon back on the coast and birds became easier. Heerman's, western and glaucous-winged gulls were often too close to photograph; why, anyway, do they always move *just* as you press the button? Next morning we were soon out at Newport Pier. A black-vented shearwater showed off beyond the brown pelicans and the flocks of gulls, but most of the time we were watching from the car, in rain. It rained, too, at Bolsa Chica and even more so at Long Beach.

Another aspect of birdwatching around here was the difficulty of getting to where we wanted to go. Flocks of birds on lakes and beaches – glimpsed as we drove by on the highways – were often difficult, or even impossible, to reach. When we did get to a beach or a pool, it was often blocked off by barriers or we were directed to places we didn't really want to stop at. Everything seemed so organized, so inflexible: walk your dog here, jog there, birdwatch over this way, trailers that way, cars there. It is the kind of thing I so dislike at home, and I rebel against it. It was taking the cycle-track syndrome several stages too far.

The next day was much the same, coming on to rain heavily early on and severely impeding the birding aspect of the day. Bolsa Chica clearly had potential though. Wildfowl (including blue-winged teals) and waders (American avocets, 50 willets, 50 long-billed dowitchers, 40 marbled godwits, 500 western sandpipers, 30 leasts), gulls and terns (40 Forster's) were excellent. All of these and several others were seen well enough to fill the field of view and count the barbules on their feathers. Obviously, this sort of place would do for a lifetime, let alone a fortnight or a week; half a day was just plain silly.

We went to Hollywood. Low, grey cloud hid the famous name on the hills. There were few birds about, although I did find yellowthroat (only the second I had ever seen). At Beverley Hills we saw only mourning doves, but I wrote them down anyway – you have to get something to put the place in your notes. I stopped to buy a 'star map' (not an astronomical chart, but a map of

Pied-billed grebe.

the Beverley Hills houses, showing who lived where). We were tourists, after all. The Getty Museum was good once we braved the downpour and waded through the running water on the roads. It was wet, wet, wet …

Now things took a turn for the better, although it was not to last, weather-wise. Los Angeles proper was really not for us; San Francisco was a hundred times more appealing, but the Palos Verdes peninsula in Los Angeles was great. Bird of the day – I know it's always there, taken for granted – was brown pelican. You can't not enjoy brown pelicans. They are, for a start, big bruisers, impressive in every respect. They swim like battleships and they fly like heavy bombers, or Sunderland flying boats, but with a delicacy all their own. And you can walk in amongst them:

The coast has little of the drama of Monterey but the Pacific, nevertheless, produced a wonderful succession of giant breakers and crashing surf and the pelicans often sailed inches above the foam, along the length of the curling wave crests. In sunshine, with both reflection and shadow beneath them, they looked magnificent. Others sailed along the cliff edge, coming by at head height, like gigantic fulmars. Others scrounged fish at the marina quays which we overlooked while having lunch.

Black-vented shearwaters [we saw 500] were passing a few at a time all the while, in an interesting session at the whale-watching point in the morning and again, even more, in the afternoon.

A female Anna's hummingbird gave excellent perched views and then a sequence of miraculous hovers in and out of the dense foliage of an evergreen shrub.

Frequent views of a female grey whale with a calf, over perhaps 15–20 minutes. Like the first [of three], a little before, they often merely made a disturbance in the water, like a long-lasting dark ripple or ring around a calmer patch. The first just occasionally gave a glimpse of a dark back, but nothing else. The later couple were much better, the small one often rolling over to show the full length of its back, followed by a bumpy snout, a misty spout, then a long, curved back, a small, fin-like bulge, then a series of bumps or knobs towards the tail. Several views, however, were of long, flat backs lying within the ring of disturbed water, but some seen well through the telescope were much higher, arched rolls.

Another dreadful morning after a night of rain. Wind, heavy grey cloud, steady rain. This actually became worse as there was a steady downpour and low cloud or mist until mid afternoon; later very dull, damp, with showers. Los Angeles has had 14.6 inches of rain this month – an inch a day – and it is still raining again tonight, with 2 inches forecast for tomorrow.

This had been a day of pelicans, gulls, terns and waders on the beach. The following day was wet, too, and we simply watched a few birds from Redondo Beach. I had a few biscuits and scattered them for the gulls. A Heerman's gull pecked my hand in its rush to grab a piece. It was the last event before we left for the airport and home.

Wild Africa

A single trip to East Africa yields enough wildlife and sensual experiences to fill a book. For this reason I had intended not to include Africa in this book, being wholly incapable of doing it justice and claiming nothing that has not been seen and experienced by any other occasional visitor on a wildlife safari. I open my notebooks and find pages and pages of tightly written lists and descriptions, efforts to get something down on paper that will evoke a little of the experience. It is impossible to do so, and yet it is impossible to leave it out. So here, chosen almost at random, are a handful of days spent in places that have thrilled me.

I have not been to Africa now for several years, and yet only now am I beginning to get through the withdrawal symptoms. I have even avoided African wildlife programmes on the television for years. It is dangerous to open my notebooks, to relive the visits. It risks bringing on the yearning to go back. Africa, you see, gets its hooks into you – it is totally addictive – and yet news of that complex continent, its troubled peoples and cruelly abused wildlife is likely to be utterly depressing and horrific. As I turned on the computer this morning, to write these pages, there was an item on the radio about illegal bushmeat being sold in London markets. An investigator was interviewing pygmy hunters who would give him gorilla hands and feet free – so long as he gave them the bullets – and would sell whole gorillas and chimpanzees for the right price. They had killed so many gorillas, they said, that they could not say exactly how many it might be. As editor of *Birds* I receive a daily summary of media reports of environmental interest from the RSPB media office, and items such as these and many other disasters and deeply disturbing reports – just think of Zimbabwe, for example – provide an almost daily diet of despair.

All my visits can be put down to good fortune. On one occasion, when Marcella was organizing RSPB holidays, a phone caller out of the blue offered a trip to Kenya. Really, he said, we would like to take you to Kenya. No, you don't need me; you need a birdwatcher, someone who can write about it when he gets back. I know just the man, Marcella said. So came about my first trip to East Africa, a different world from the Gambia where, like many people, I had my first taste of African birds. Gambia was a press trip, a promotional visit, and a hideously rushed affair but a whirl of excitement. While others had lunch, it was just possible to pick up a chicken leg and a piece of bread and walk around the hotel or lodge gardens to see what was there; the frantic pace never let up – even in such fantastic places as Lake Naivasha, where we stopped for just an hour. But we visited some of the great parks, including the Mara and Amboseli, roaring along in a cloud of dust to reach them, and also flew to the coast, at Mombasa, which I have not visited since and where the birds were terrific.

On another occasion I was invited to join a group of birdwatchers on a visit to Zimbabwe. This led to a feature in *Birds* and then to the setting up of an RSPB holiday, which I co-led with the local top bird guide, Rhett Butler from Harare. Nine years later, out of the blue, Rhett asked me to return to Zimbabwe to do a set of drawings for his tour company there, which was about to produce a series of guides and brochures for safari lodges scattered around Zimbabwe's wonderful national parks. It was perfect timing: with a sabbatical due and a project with quite a strong link with conservation, I was able to spend three magnificent weeks in Zimbabwe. Sadly, as things developed, the brochures may never have appeared; certainly I never saw any results, despite sending sheaves of drawings of birds, mammals, flowers, lizards, lodge buildings and details of the rooms, inside and out, from soft furnishings to sculptures and piles of African pots, and wonderful places such as the ancient city ruins of Great Zimbabwe.

Other visits have been as a wildlife tour leader or co-leader. There's a lot to say about tour leading but I will resist most of it. A good tour is largely down to the leader; for the leader, a good trip is largely down to the people on the tour, and sometimes the co-leader too, especially in Africa where it is hardly possible to have 'a bad time' with the wildlife. The local drivers and guides were invariably brilliant. All the trips were sensational for the wildlife; one or two were not so good for the people. It is sometimes, oddly, a problem that I am as enthusiastic as anyone on the trip, often more enthusiastic than most of the people I'm leading. You can get a lot from an excited leader, but less enthusiastic travellers who are apt to be bored will not be enamoured of a leader that appears to be having a good time. Frankly, I found it difficult when, for example, I was genuinely enthusing about 400 zebras standing in the dawn light beneath a belt of acacias beside a river, just as the morning sun burned away the mist and brought their stripes into sharp focus, with fish eagles calling overhead and impalas coming in to drink, but my passengers looked at the floor of the minibus and said they had seen zebras before. And, after seeing surprisingly few wildebeest in the Masai Mara for two or three days, it puzzled me to find that when at last we came across 50,000 and I stopped the bus so that we could see what wildebeest in huge numbers were like, everyone looked blank – even looked the other way – and asked if we could perhaps find a lion. But there were also tours, in Kenya and Tanzania, that went swimmingly with people who were a joy to be with and who still ask when I am leading another trip so they can join me again.

Much of Africa, for a wildlife-watcher, is overwhelming on a first visit. Well, let's say it is overwhelming for a birdwatcher. Birds survive better than mammals. In Zimbabwe, there were always a few birds about even in the suburbs, usually a new species or two, probably multi-coloured or huge and impressive, even though we travelled (by super-efficient, air-conditioned, very cheap Blue Arrow bus) for mile after mile after mile through barbed-wired ranchland without a mammal in sight. Even in my few years of visiting Kenya I would find that on one trip I would see open grasslands with giraffes, zebras and kori bustards, and then, by the time of the next trip, discover that the same area had been turned into cultivated fields with nothing. The pressures on Africa to produce food, to occupy even those parks that are still full of animals, are so intense that I can see no way out of it that doesn't send the remaining wildlife into a spiral of decline. So, let's say that Africa in parts, in its game parks that are still safe, is for the moment overwhelming for the wildlife-watcher.

In recounting some of my experiences of Africa, a famous name seems a good place to start: Lake Nakuru. (It horrifies me that this – one of the world's great wildlife spectacles, an area made known worldwide through endless films, television programmes and books – can be allowed to deteriorate through over-exploitation and pollution and excessive silting from adjacent deforestation, but this is the case. As a species, mankind seems unable to protect even the very best places in the world. From now on, though, I promise to be positive ...) It was September; we drove from Naro Moru, west of Mount Kenya, via Thomson Falls at Nyahururu, across the Equator (where we stopped to take our photographs and see the obligatory display of water spinning clockwise down the plug hole on one side and anticlockwise on the other) and down to Nakuru town. The drive goes through extraordinarily rich, cultivated and wooded land, so wonderfully green, green in all its multitudinous forms, so densely, toweringly vegetated, with swathes of emerald tea, miles of pineapples, coffee and banana plantations, groves of pyrethrum. Close by the scruffy town, we entered the national park and drove in, tired and dusty, to our lodge.

My bird notes are extensive; asterisks dot the page to pick out the top birds, from marabou storks and thousands of pelicans to red-breasted wryneck and arrow-marked babblers. Several were new for me.

> A great view over the lake, the waterbirds distant but an exciting taster of what was to follow. Far from being the shy, well-hidden birds of the textbooks, the francolins [Hildebrandt's, a local speciality] were trotting about the camp between the apartments, as were the babblers and anteater chats, which were numerous and very tame – and fine songsters, too.
>
> I was able to sit beside my room door, on my first visit to Lake Nakuru, shaded from the hot sun, and see thousands of pelicans in swirling corkscrews against distant hills along the far shore of the lake, with more scattered through the marsh on the near shore.
>
> Baboons 40–50; waterbucks *c.* 1,000; hippos 3; impalas 40-plus (several very close old rams); warthogs 5.

In the afternoon we drove around the lake:

> This was an overwhelming place. The sheer numbers of birds and the ability to see so many of them at very close range made it a wonderful experience, sensational. Practically all the waders, the ducks, herons and egrets, pelicans and flamingos were within a few yards at times – as well as the waterbucks.

My lists include: '** White pelicans, thousands, perhaps 10,000-plus; **lesser flamingos 300-plus; **greater flamingos 3–4,000.' The supporting cast was extensive: little egrets, 150 cattle egrets, 20 great white egrets, black heron, night herons, sacred, glossy and hadada ibises, 600 white-breasted cormorants, Cape and hottentot teals, red-billed ducks, Egyptian geese, fish eagles, blacksmith plovers, avocets and a host of other waders including marsh sandpipers, 150 black-winged stilts and 1,000 ruffs. Over the water were 500 white-winged black terns, whiskered and gull-billed terns, 500 grey-headed gulls. Other star birds were Nyanza swifts, southern ground hornbills and a Verraux's (milky) eagle owl.

At the camp there was the fabulous, mesmeric chorus of frogs and crickets at night. Minute tree frogs, with their high-pitched, metallic clicking, plinking and plonking sounds, were everywhere. The next morning dawned cool and sharp: 'A beautiful clear morning, with an upside-down full moon, screaming and barking baboons about the camp, pelicans all over the lake.' Baboons are not to be taken lightly. In some camps they wander around too closely for real comfort. On one trip there were two ladies, one in her late eighties with a companion in her late seventies who looked after her. They were indefatigable, as elderly ladies on wildlife tours very often are. One lunchtime, I went into my room and looked out of the open window at birds in the trees opposite. A massive male baboon materialized on the window ledge. The suddenness of his appearance made me back off involuntarily, then I waved and shouted, but in he came, swinging right past me. I was suddenly on the wrong side of the room, with a male baboon, between me and the door, baring huge canines that would have put any Doberman or Rottweiler to shame. I jumped over the bed and across to the door, while the baboon began to rifle my suitcase and shoulder bag. While he was focused on that, I squeezed out, shouting at the baboon from outside the cracked-open door, until he made off out of the window with a tube of insect repellent. The room stank of baboon as I went over to close the

Two-banded courser: beautiful inhabitant of very short grassland.

Long-tailed widow bird in breeding plumage.

window, shaking with the shock. 'Excuse me, Mr Hume,' came a little voice from below. 'Is this yours? You may have dropped it.' The two ladies were on the ground below, outside the security fence, holding up my insect repellent.

That day at Lake Nakuru was quite accidentally improved for the birdwatchers of the party, but spoiled for those who 'never want to see another red, green or blue bird again', as we were 'stuck beside the lake with a broken suspension – what a place to be stuck! Hot, sunny, flat calm, with unbelievable birdwatching.' Everything was, in fact, too wonderful to be true, giving one of the best day's birdwatching I've ever experienced. Flamingos and pelicans have long been among my favourite birds, anyway:

White pelicans were simply sensational. They were everywhere. They gradually moved around the lake during the morning, flying very low over the water in long, ponderous lines. Then there were great flotillas fishing, often forming great flocks, scores of birds synchronizing their movements and ambushing the fish shoals. Others came by just a few feet overhead, with a great noise of beating wings, or flew low over the surface, dappled by reflections from the water below. At 10.15 the first thermalling flocks began to rise [using rising currents of warm air to take them aloft]. Other groups were loafing about on land, preening or stretching and it was fantastic just to be with them for several hours. By walking to the shore I could practically be surrounded, on three sides anyway, by pelicans and flamingos, plus all the waders. During the day, as flocks on the shore immediately adjacent to our stopping place got bigger and closer, so the views got better and better. Finally, a small creek close to us, where a tiny stream ran into the lake, was chosen as a bathing place by a few pelicans and others rushed to join them. They bathed, then scrambled out and preened on the dry land alongside (all just yards from us). Eventually, perhaps four or five hundred giant birds were crammed into the creek, squashed in like sardines in a tin, a boiling, thrashing mass of wet, shiny, beating wings and waving beaks, pouches wobbling in all directions.

Both greater and lesser flamingos, meanwhile, were also at close range (too close to focus binoculars on) and all around the lake. Most of the closer lessers were dull immatures, but every so often an outstandingly pink adult would appear. Even the greaters seemed pinker and brighter than ever.

My estimations for this period include 'thousands' of white pelicans, 15 pink-backed pelicans, thousands of greater and 300 to 500 lesser flamingos, many egrets, herons, African spoonbills and ibises of three species, various eagles and vultures, 50 blacksmith and two or three three-banded plovers, 100 stilts, 17 avocets, many marsh and curlew sandpipers, little stints and ruffs, thousands of gulls, hundreds of white-winged black terns, and then a lengthy list of more or less land and woodland birds, from grey-backed fiscals (big, striking shrikes) to hundreds of wattled starlings.

With suspension repaired, off we went around the lake, seeing all of this again and much more besides. I revised my pelican estimate to 8,000 to 10,000, greater flamingos to 5,000-plus (maybe as many as 10,000) and lesser flamingos to 3,500. This was a good greater flamingo count; but, while I have also been to Nakuru and found hardly a flamingo and no pelicans at all on days of low water and swirling dust devils, I have also seen lessers there in hundreds of thousands, so this was a poor day for them.

There were perhaps 1,000 waterbucks all told, a few reedbucks, 50 Thomson's gazelles, 65-plus impalas, 30 warthogs, 50 baboons, rock hyraxes, 50 buffaloes (some old bulls very close, mightily impressive), two bushbucks, three zebras, and 13 giraffes of the strikingly marked, rare Rothschild's race. Evidently we failed to find either white rhinos (which have been introduced to Nakuru and look wonderfully prehistoric and magnificent), or leopards, although the next morning, as we left the park, we did see leopard tracks on the dusty road.

Not only is Nakuru good for wildlife but it is a wonderfully beautiful place, in a scenically outstanding country, especially at its southern end:

To the south of the lake is some of the most beautiful parkland savanna and acacia forest, with abundant big fever trees, that I have ever seen. To the east is a strange, out-of-this-world euphorbia forest – where we missed leopards by a matter of seconds.

Many kinds of forest have a particular beauty all their own. These soaring yellow-barked acacias, beneath which even the tallest giraffes are dwarfed, hold their own with any.

Here's another visit to Nakuru – just a morning drive – this time in August:

Nothing to add to the list really: it says it all. Just sensational flamingos – continual action and noise and great splashes of colour. Altogether an amazing experience. [Greater flamingos – 200–300, a few in superb breeding colours; lesser flamingos 150,000–250,000.] Pelicans far less rewarding than before but still good [200–300]. I've never seen so many yellow-billed storks before [380–400] – many at just a few feet range, as were many marabous [230–250]. Woolly-necked stork was good for me and also Horus swifts, which I have rarely seen, and the knob-billed duck, which was certainly my best ever view [this was a species I came to know much better in Tanzania].

The list includes three saddlebilled storks, 48 African spoonbills, 2,000 to 3,000 white-breasted cormorants, 100 Egyptian geese, lanner, fish eagle, many waders including Kittlitz's and chestnut-banded plovers, rather few gulls and terns, 100 Horus swifts, Nyanza swifts, green wood-hoopoes, and several kinds of shrike, flycatcher and oriole.

The leopard was wonderful. It walked into some bushy undergrowth but fortunately came into full view in a clearing and gave a series of clear views, side-on and tail-on, for several minutes, at about 40 yards. It looked a really big, heavily built animal, much the most impressive I've seen for size, and also very heavily spotted with large, round, black spots, especially on its legs, and big rosettes on the flanks.

Farther south, right on the border of Kenya, is the great Masai Mara game reserve. It has its problems, but it is still phenomenal:

In the middle of the day, under a flawless blue sky, I sat by the Aga Khan's viewpoint [at the Mara Serena Lodge in the Masai Mara] and felt that I had never been happier. Early in the morning, at the same spot, alone in perfect peace and quiet, I sat and looked out towards the sunrise, but downhill towards the Mara river, below the level of the sun, so all the colour and detail was clear but everything was edged with a reddish light. A hundred or two zebras approached a pool, outlined in rust, their swishing tails red-brown, drinking with wildebeest and elegant impalas. In the afternoon there was a steady stream of animals in the same area, in some ways giving views – from a distance, but from a high viewpoint – which were better than the closer ones from a vehicle. These were lively, active, unhurried, undisturbed animals, totally unaware of their admiring watcher. I looked out to the Olpunyata Swamp, Governor's Camp, Paradise Plain, Rhino Ridge, the Loita Plains and the Loita Hills.

A little while after this, a friend of mine who had been here with a birdwatching group told me that one of the guards, standing alone in the lodge, had been killed by a leopard. You never quite know what is around the corner, or behind that bush. On one trip, we were at a tented camp in Tarangire park in Tanzania. I had two excellent characters in my group, both of whom had a stammer. One evening, we left our tents to make our way to the dining room, which was in the middle of two long, straight rows of tents. Ours were out near one end. It was remarkably dark and we had torches. 'Oh look, we've got j-j-jackals in the camp tonight.' As usual, I was interested in seeing which species of jackal they might be and we all crept up to the shapes held motionless in the torchlight.

'That's not a jackal,' I said. 'That's a lion cub.' And then another lion cub appeared, followed by a wonderfully fit and handsome lioness and then, at some distance, another cub. We turned tail and dived towards our tents, all thumbs, fumbling with the zips.

'C-c-can you run faster than a l-l-lion?'

'I d-d-don't know, but I really don't c-c-care so long as I can run f-f-faster than you!'

Another night at this tented camp was memorable. Marcella was with me on that trip and we were in the same tent as before, the one farthest from the lodge. It was our last night there, after some superb drives. Long after dark, I heard some baboons and an impala begin to bark. Then the baboons, seemingly coming closer, began to make an infernal noise. Their alarm calls are loud, staccato, reverberating barks and screeching yaps in a rhythmic, hysterical chorus – *waa, waa, wak-up, WAA-uh, WAA-UH, waakup, waak, waak-uh*. The sound was coming towards our tent ...

Soon I heard the unmistakable sound of a leopard. It was a heavy breather all right, and gave the strange, sawing, rasping sound that I had heard before, a deep, rough *aah-woo aah-woo aah-woo* that strikes me as a really awesome, powerful sound when heard close up. I confess I was getting quite worked up about it when it seemed to be a matter of inches outside the tent (I wonder how far it really was – probably some way off).

'What is it?' Marcella asked.

'A leopard.'

Aah-woo, *AAH-WOO*, *AAH-WOO*. Quiet snuffles and lip-smacking seemed even worse than the rasping. My hair stood on end and, what was not already, instantly turned grey. The deep, boomy sound seemed enough to scare any potential prey to death; it might be me. All the while the baboons kept up their chorus of emphatic, shouted barks, surely making the whole camp ring with their fear and excitement.

The sound of the leopard seemed to recede. At last, the baboons had moved on and their noises were quietening down.

'I think it's gone.'

'*OOOOu-UMPH!*' My God, a lion! It sounded as if it were under the canopy by the door of the tent. I didn't get a lot of sleep that night.

I notice from my notes at the Mara Serena that I listed some place names, just as I did when I was in Scotland in my teens. I was still fascinated by names on a map. I'm not sure that 'Paradise Plain' and 'Rhino Ridge' are quite up to it, but some of the European names are somehow as evocative as the African ones. I soon found 'Archer's Post' on maps of Kenya, a tiny spot in the middle of nowhere not too far from Samburu, north of Isiolo. It has a ring to it; it makes me wonder about Archer, who he was, what he did, why he was setting up a station there, how very remote it must have seemed from any European. On some trips I was pleased to find that we drove through Archer's Post, but it is a small place, a row or two of typical poor houses along a wide central street, filthy 'hotels', butcheries and hardware shops, a post office and a police house. It seemed so much better on the map.

The Masai Mara is the Kenyan extension of Tanzania's Serengeti, and both are outstanding places. They are extraordinarily rich in bird and other animal life, although both would be utterly beautiful to be in even if there wasn't a bird to be seen. Coming down from the highlands around Ngorongoro, towards the Serengeti, rates as one of the truly great drives. When we stopped to look out scores of miles – perhaps a hundred miles – across the Serengeti, a woman in my bus said, 'It makes you want to weep.' She was not the first.

Indeed, I have found other people with a tear or two on their cheeks, and I, too, have felt the awesome, emotional power of such places very strongly, many times. Not least, at the Mara Serena. From the Aga Khan's viewpoint I could see hundreds of zebras, scores of topi, perhaps 80,000 to 100,000 wildebeest (I tried several times to make more than an educated guess at their numbers), a waterbuck, 50 buffaloes, two spotted hyenas, two giraffes, 100 impalas, several baboons, 13 elephants, 30 to 40 hippopotamuses, some warthogs, and several very tame rock hyraxes.

> After some brilliant game watching already, now [on entering the Masai Mara] we are getting into the indescribable stuff. This drive was stunning. Every species is beautiful individually – topi, impala, Thomson's gazelle – and in large groups they were just fantastic. The occasional groups of 1,000 or 2,000 wildebeest looked magnificent – then we saw two vistas with maybe 20,000 each and then more slopes with 5,000, 2,000, another 2,000. All figures very rough but I tried hard not to overestimate like everyone else – their 'thousands and thousands and thousands' wildly over the top but giving a good idea of the effect! [I put down 60,000 to 70,000 wildebeest on this drive, plus scores of corpses in the Mara river.]
>
> The hyenas [ten] were very close, in a gutter, which ran into a pipe beneath the track (exactly the same situation – I wonder if it was the same gutter? – in which I saw some closely before). The big mother stood staring at us, her mouth open, revealing large teeth and vivid pink gums, a smile 'from ear to ear', saliva dripping and drooling from her chops. I would not argue.

I have always liked hyenas, which are, in their own sweet way, lovely creatures, with the most beautiful and evocative night-time noises. Other highlights included 800 Thomson's gazelles, hartebeest, 750 zebras, 225 topis, three lions and a superb serval, a beautiful, small and exceptionally elegant striped and spotted cat, the first of several on that trip. On another drive we saw 1,000 topis: gorgeous, big antelopes with amazing red-brown eyes, glossy rusty-pink backs and a large, oval, oily-grey patch on each thigh. My asterisks and double asterisks and repetitive superlatives try to pick out the most astonishing of a long list of astonishing things: wonderful elephants, which I am totally in love with; impressive lions; giraffes, which have the most amazing long, black, upswept eyelashes you will ever see; but also '**Zebras – hundreds – immaculate as ever – the best!'

There were other days like this in the Mara – I could pick any one at random:

Splendid stuff: brilliant zebras [hundreds], often all around us in some of the most scenic wooded valleys of the Mara between Sarova and Keekorok. The lions [nine, two males] were sleeping off a good meal in thin bushes about 20 yards by 10 – from one end all were quite invisible, showing just how dangerously inconspicuous they often are.

The caracal was a first for everybody – and we had quite prolonged and clear views despite the long grass. It was darker than I had imagined – the neck is short and head rather angular and tilted downwards, without the supreme grace of a serval, but the finely attenuated ear tufts give a beautiful touch to the quite stripy face.

Six more lions in the evening at a newly killed wildebeest, one male very big but with little mane. All fed for a long time, then a female walked away, limping. Another walked over and the two licked the blood from each other's faces. The fit one went to a nearby gully and returned with a long, black stalk or stem, dropping it in front of the injured one, which then chewed on it. The male then left the kill and licked one of the females, cleaning its face, then moved a few yards away, by which time all three were within about 15 yards of us – the male eventually came closer still. This was magnificent (the male, especially, looked wonderful, but all, panting open-mouthed, looked magnificent, especially compared with the indolent lot earlier) – but more was to follow.

**Black rhinoceros. Very soon after leaving the lions we came across a vast female rhino. Extremely close views, easily my best ever of any rhino. It had a long, curved, shiny frontal horn but the upper [rear] horn was much longer, straight and upstanding. Distance according to focus on camera was 35 yards.

** Leopard – to cap it all, a leopard in a sausage tree. Extremely close. It was far more obviously aware of us than the lions, on the verge of a menacing snarl several times. Like all the earlier lions, it was breathing heavily; unlike the sleepy ones, open-mouthed. It stared at us with splendid orange eyes, but soon settled down, lying along a branch with dangling legs and tail [a classic pose]. It was completely unblemished, in brilliant condition – with enormously long whiskers but the whole of its fur like the softest, closest pile of a deep carpet – no trace of coarse or wiry hair as on a lion, just like velvet.

Another day:

> ** Cheetahs — an adult with three cubs. These were seen soon after we were
> turned away from Mara Serena [it was overbooked and half our group had
> to go on to Kichwa Tembo], so we had a real stroke of luck. Also in an area
> singularly devoid of anything else for miles. We first saw the adult lying
> down, then noticed the cubs about 100 yards off. They looked at the adult
> but 'she' gave every impression of ignoring them, even when she walked off
> and lay down again, facing away. The cubs were brilliant, under half grown
> but not kittens. They still had traces of a fluffy mane, They were very alert
> but moved only a few yards all the time we watched, but two frequently
> played together, pawing each other, rolling and tumbling down a bank.

Cheetahs look fabulous, and distance creates a misleading impression of size,
especially as they look so long and tall, despite their small, round heads. Lions
are often doing nothing all day, unless you come across a mating pair, in which
case they mate every few minutes but do little else. At dawn or dusk, though,
you may see them on the move and sometimes one will roar not far away
with the impressive, booming sound that is nothing much like the popular
notion of a lion's roar (courtesy of MGM); it is more a deep, expressive moan,
strangulated at first, as if requiring a lot of effort to squeeze it out, then repeated
several times and fading away in a long series of short grunts. Each lion has its
own vocal pattern, something along the lines of *AAowh; eeAAAOWH! EEOWH,
yow, oh oh oh uh uh uhuh uhuh uh* ...

Not the least remarkable thing about lions can be their inconspicuousness.
Some I have seen have been blindingly obvious: great, heavy-maned males
standing or sitting proud on a high ridge. But most are lying about in little low
thickets, overgrown with tall, brown, wispy grasses, where they are practically
invisible from 20 yards and sometimes hard to point out to people next to you
in the vehicle at even closer range. Never get out to go behind a bush in such a
place: you might be in for one last surprise.

In fact, it is worth saying here, for those who have never been on one, that
an African safari, for all the high chances of success, is not necessarily easy. You
might see five leopards in a fortnight, or, more likely, none at all; it might take
several return trips to see a leopard or a cheetah. They are not just there for the
taking, as seems to be the case on television. The Mara, for example, still more
so the Serengeti, is simply vast and these large predators are not very common.
Go to the Ngorongoro crater and lions are pretty much guaranteed, but you

can't find them just like that in the Masai Mara; and, in places such as Samburu, you may not see one at all. This is one of the problems with tours as so many people, understandably, expect everything on a plate; however, those who realize the challenge get so very much more out of it when they succeed.

The Mara is a famous big game reserve, as severely pressured as any, but also a great bird area. The Serengeti is perhaps better still. It is easy to forget that these great gatherings of large mammals attract huge numbers of birds, some of them perhaps unexpected. Here are hundreds and thousands of white storks, migrants from Europe, feeding around the antelopes, but also sometimes scores of lesser kestrels, too, Montagu's and pallid harriers, bee-eaters and swallows. It is surprising, at first, to see flocks of gull-billed terns also exploiting the vast insect harvest that comes off these plains, disturbed by the millions of migrating hooves. And where might that common sandpiper nest – in mid-Wales perhaps, by a little brook in a green, wet valley? – the one that is now trotting about on the back of that hippo?

A game park I am particularly fond of is Samburu, well north of Nairobi. Here you are getting into some very dry country north of Isiolo, after dropping down from the high central plains with their endless fields of wheat and giant combine harvesters. It is not so far from the parks farther east where George and Joy Adamson lived with their lions. (You can visit one of Joy Adamson's houses, Elsamere, on the shore of Lake Naivasha, where you can get excellent tea and lovely home-made cakes, see an abundance of birds and black-and-white colobus monkeys, and see diaries and many original paintings of birds, animals and Africans made by Joy.)

The country in and around Samburu and Buffalo Springs, which together form a very large protected region, is remarkable, with strange and dramatic hills rearing up all around as a backdrop for everyone's photographs. It is little wonder these mountains have special significance for the local people (who, incidentally, are a branch of the Masai farther south, tall, imperious, with sumptuous jewellery and robes of crimson and penetrating blue).

There is also another of the 'great drives' I have been fortunate enough to enjoy. Instead of taking the usual route via Thomson's Falls to the Rift Valley lakes, through Nanyuki then Nyeri and zigzagging over the southern end of the Aberdares, it is possible to go north, via Archer's Post, on the unmade A2 under the sacred hill of Ololokwe, through miles of flat thornbush stiff with 'wait-a-bit' acacia (which hooks your clothes if you walk through it, hence the name); you then go on through bandit country with isolated cliffs and weirdly shaped hills, and on across the C79 and C78 over the northern end of the Laikipia

Plateau, through Tangulbei (just a dot on the map), and finally swing down to Lake Baringo on a track from the north-east. The views south towards Don Dol are awesome; then as the Rift Valley opens out before you the whole panorama, in an atmosphere of great clarity, ia overwhelming.

As soon as you enter Samburu park from the east, into Buffalo Springs really, it is time to look at everything that moves. It is so different: the birds, the mammals, all kinds of things are new here. There are many elephants, often red from a thick coat of caked mud. The giraffes are not the common, rather randomly marked, Masai giraffes, but the angular crazy-paving reticulated form. Suddenly, what seemed like an impala with impossibly big ears rears upon its hind legs and reaches an unexpectedly long neck to feed from the top of a bush; it is clearly a gerenuk. A large, pale animal strides from behind a bush to reveal gigantic, almost dead straight horns: an oryx! And then the zebras seem different: they have huge ears, an abundance of narrow stripes and clear white bellies – these are Grevy's zebras, rare and localized but, here, the usual ones to see. Look at the ostriches: not the pink-legged ones with lipstick-red shins you've seen elsewhere, but blue-legged, blue-necked Somali ostriches.

Samburu is usually very dry, often in the grip of a long drought that challenges people and animals alike. Once, when staying in the Serena Lodge, two women in my group came along to the evening dinner. One said that she couldn't seem to get much hot water from her shower. The other replied that she had the answer: she just turned the shower on full before she came to dinner and, by the time she got back, it would be running warm. What can you do? At other times, we have been to Samburu in dramatically different weather, with howling winds and heavy rain, the Ewaso Ng'iro river changed from a simple stream in a wide, flat, sandy bed to a rushing torrent with violent, foaming waves, threatening to wash away half of the camp and keeping everyone awake all night with the noise and the worry of it. It is a stark, hostile, dramatic environment, full of excitement. If I could go anywhere right now, it might just be Samburu.

On a walk along the river at Naro Moru (far south of the Samburu reserve) I came across a paradise flycatcher, not the usual rusty-brown one with a black cap, but a white-phase individual:

The star bird by far was the white male paradise flycatcher – the first white one I've seen. It was first seen in flight, by Marcella, quite unexpected, like a bird flying with a long white paper streamer [or a long, white, wriggling fish] – then good perched views. Its head and breast glistened bottlegreeny blue on black; the pure white back contrasted with jet-black lines on the tertials and secondaries, often exposed – as it spread its wings – as a series of thin, curved lines. The tail was sometimes fanned, revealing fine black feather shafts on the shorter feathers, while the central pair were exceptionally long, slender and supple, waving and rippling in the breeze, swaying with every movement. All in all, I really think this was the single most beautiful bird I have seen in my life. A glorious bird.

A day or two later in Samburu: 'New birds included golden-breasted starling. Perhaps *this* is the most beautiful bird I've ever seen, absolutely stunning.' There is no 'most beautiful bird' – there are far too many contenders for the title – but clearly this flycatcher and the starling are two that must be in the running, and Samburu provides several other possibilities.

In Samburu, as elsewhere, the typical touring pattern is a morning game drive followed by a rest period (or, if you are like me, a chance to find all you can in the lodge gardens – you can rest after dark), then an afternoon/ evening game drive until dusk. In Kenya and Zimbabwe, the norm is to make the morning drive very early, often while the air is still very cold, while in Tanzania the drivers usually start later, after breakfast. Typical of any Samburu game drive are the remarkably striking and really very handsome vulturine guineafowl, a tall, upstanding guinea fowl, with long, pointed plumes and large areas of vivid royal blue; you encounter it in the large, mixed, garrulous flocks – with the commoner helmeted guineafowl – that seem to overwhelm patches of dusty grassland scattered through the bush.

I have page after page of bird notes from Samburu, and there are many strange names, such as Donaldson-Smith's sparrow weavers, black-capped social weavers, cut-throat finch, Abyssinian scimitarbill, Von der Decken's hornbill, smaller golden-breasted bunting, pale chanting goshawk. Flocks of rufous chatterers move through the bush; there are several species of shrike, several kinds of nightjar, swift and starling, and new bee-eaters, barbets, sunbirds, flycatchers, pipits and mousebirds.

The mammal-watching can be unbeatable:

Grevy's zebras are simply stunning – the stripes literally dazzle and shimmer through binoculars, even at very close range. Great views, and very close.

Two magnificent cheetahs, watched for a long time, sitting upright, standing, walking about, searching for prey around bushes, often calling

White-phase African
paradise flycatcher (left),
with golden-breasted starling
(right), two of East Africa's
most beautiful birds.

to each other with a quiet, high cheep. They were everything I had hoped for, thoroughly beautiful. I was quite surprised, or at least felt a little less guilty, when several buses gathered and the cheetahs walked *towards* us and were not boxed in by the vehicles. They were apparently entirely oblivious of our presence. They gave very close views until we decided enough was enough and we left them, well satisfied – extremely exciting and moving. [A gathering of buses is often inevitable, but you can have good things entirely to yourself, especially if you have a driver who is patient and willing to wait a while until the others have seen enough and drive away.]

**Elephants – 15, 5, 77, 4 – and a couple of singles – 100-plus. Fantastic entertainment, especially from the 77 in and around the river (a long way from anywhere we have been before, so probably a new group) – all sand-dusting, mud-bathing, wallowing, pushing and shoving and generally having an amazing time – like we were!

Extraordinary views of everything – you can count the eyelashes on an impala – and all in a very scenic, evocative setting, the kind of Africa of your dreams.

Whenever we were close to anything, I always encouraged the group to look at the animals with their binoculars (and, especially, to look as well as take photographs — many people see little except through the eyepiece of a camera and then wish they had taken more notice). Animals at such close range provide a singularly impressive experience, especially if you can see every nuance of colour and texture.

Samburu in the late evening, back at the lodge, was always exciting, too. On the river's sandbanks, lit by floodlights, were roosting marabous and feeding nightjars, and sometimes dashing overhead would be the dramatic shape of a bathawk. Crocodiles pull themselves out on the shore and even come up to be fed; some are real monsters. On the other side of the river there is often half of an unfortunate goat hung out as bait for a leopard; thus the leopard's appearance is 'staged' in a way, but better than no leopard at all. Once, after the leopard had fed and left, and everyone else had moved away, I was amazed to see the unique shape and pattern of a striped hyena arrive to clear up the leftovers. That same evening, an African civet came foraging along the riverbank not 20 yards away.

Around the camp there are usually a few genets, which may be fed by hand and, with care, stroked as they come down to the bird tables. Not so cuddly, perhaps, are the elephants that sometimes feed on the lush green vegetation that grows inside the lodge grounds and hangs over the riverside wall; as you go to the bar or restaurant at night, a sudden presence makes itself felt and a noise like someone shaking a large rug means that somewhere, just there, in

Striped hyena waiting for leftovers at the Samburu leopard bait.

the darkness beyond the pool of light, just over the low wall, an elephant has just waved its ears. Then a trunk, two gleaming tusks, reach into the leaves alongside the footpath and pull away a great mouthful of nutritious food – all a bit too close for comfort. 'You haven't been to Africa until you have been close to an elephant,' said Ashley, our driver in Zimbabwe when I was on my sabbatical. My goodness, do you get close to elephants!

In East Africa you drive around in minibuses, with a roof that can be raised so everyone can stand and peer out. In Zimbabwe, around Hwange anyway, the usual thing is to drive around in open-topped Land Rovers: there is a roll-bar but otherwise you simply sit in the back on a raised seat. It makes conversation with the driver more difficult, but you do get an outstanding view. I'm pleased to say that in neither place, wherever I have been, is there a 'tracker' perched on a seat sticking out in front, which seems to me to be there just as part of the 'big white hunter' show and is something I would prefer to be without, but which is apparently usual in South Africa. Drivers we had in Tanzania said they could watch elephants all day, and in Zimbabwe the black Africans were the most gentle, most considerate and entertaining guides, not worrying about their guiding certificates and preferring to watch the elephants to learning how to shoot them. Perhaps I'm just being naïve.

Near the airport at Hwange, one elephant was particularly tricky. A researcher, studying Africa's few remaining wild hunting dogs, told us at lunch one day that she had encountered this huge elephant and had had to back off and race away in her small vehicle, unwilling or unable to stand her ground. But Ashley was adamant that the best way to deal with an aggressive elephant like that is to stand up to him, not to back away, otherwise you are admitting defeat and simply stimulating the animal to charge on, happy in the knowledge that he is the victor, the boss in that situation. No, he would rather rev the engine a bit, move forward, stop when the elephant stops, never go back.

That was OK in theory, perhaps. But when we drove along a narrow track, with no chance of deviating from it across particularly rough and overgrown ground either side, and found a giant bull elephant, in musth, standing just ahead, it seemed a little less obvious to us, sitting on the seat in the back of an open Land Rover, that standing your ground was the best plan. He was, indeed, a magnificent animal – animal seems far too weak a word, he was a towering presence, a god – black and shiny and steaming, a large wet stain from the gland behind his eye indicating his excited and unpredictable state.

'Oh yes, some elephants can be like this, sometimes they can be a little bit aggressive,' said Ashley. 'We'll just let him settle a bit, then we can drive by.'

'Can we not go back?'

'No, we'll just wait a moment and then we can go on by.'

'Please, I think we'd rather just go back.'

The elephant was advancing, shaking his head, waving his enormous ears, looking sensational, his massively thick trunk raised and rolled forward to present a solid mass of meat and muscle. I felt like sinking out of sight under the seat. I was a little bit ashamed, perhaps just a bit, when to my great relief we finally drove by and left him. The next day we saw him again, this time 300 yards away on Hwange airfield, far from the previous encounter but clearly the same formidable bull. He walked almost directly towards us, and began a series of threatening postures and strangled squeals, rolling his trunk over his tusks with loud bumping and slapping noises, before he backed into a clump of bushes and we left him.

This was close to the Dete vlei (pronounced something like Det flay), a glorious open valley with teak woodland each side on the Sikumi estate near Hwange national park, the only place where I have seen wild dogs. It grieves me to think of what it is like now. When I visited, on each of my three trips to Zimbabwe, it was paradise. It is also known as Sable Valley: one of the great glories of Zimbabwe is the sable, a brilliantly constructed, muscular, shiny black and white antelope, with big, powerful shoulders and great arched, pointed horns. The landscape here is quietly beautiful. The trees are deceptively tall, with a gigantic reach of great, arching beams. The vlei runs down from a wooded area into a widening, shallow, open valley, with very low, wooded hills either side and several pools and artificial waterholes at intervals in the middle. These are kept full, as far as possible, by small pumps, but the maintenance and operation of the pumps seems always to be a problem and it is now quite likely that they have been allowed to fall into disuse.

Breakfast at Sikumi Tree Lodge was taken around a large campfire, welcome in the cold early morning air, as the vlei and the woodland begins to wake up. On the first two trips it was heaven; on the third, we had rain and this brought out insects in their thousands and hundreds of thousands. It gives you quite a smack when driving along on the open seat of a Land Rover and you get a giant dung beetle full in the face, but perhaps that's better than having one crash down into your dinner or the butter dish. Huge, elongated, shiny-green beetles fell from the trees and the thatch and, as I walked to the bar, I crunched across them on the hard floor. These were blister beetles. Get one on your skin and you face a dilemma: to brush it off risks being left with a trail of liquid, exuded by the beetle in its alarm, which produces a series of painful blisters. If you then burst a blister, another trickle of liquid bubbles out to create more blisters. The poison from these beetles was used to poison arrowheads: six beetles produce enough for a fatal dose. Best to pick them off with care.

The camp was operated by Rhett Butler and his partners, principally Alan Elliott, who lived there when we first went but has since moved on. He has become enshrined in the language of our home. Once I was trying to tell the group of our plans for the next morning, but Marcella interrupted. I merely glanced sideways and she stopped. 'Rob,' said Alan from the end of the table, 'I'm going to practise that look.' That phrase has stuck with us for years. He was, on my last visit, one of just two white members of parliament in Zimbabwe, elected by an all-black constituency, and his wife was deeply worried. His predecessor had, like Alan, made noises in parliament about the corruption endemic in the running of the game parks in Zimbabwe. He had, she said, four road accidents in a week; the last one killed him.

Aubrey Pakenham was also involved with the lodges (Marcella and I met him at the stupendous Lodge of the Ancient City at Great Zimbabwe). He was another great character, older than Alan, with a feast of wildlife stories to tell. He frequently told them in his radio broadcasts, often he said, going out to

sable antelope: a big, muscular, powerful male.

shock the older ladies, gently, by broadcasting on subjects such as the specific differences in the size and structure of the genitalia of hyraxes, which prevented interspecies copulation and hybridization. Aubrey claimed to have been injured by all the 'big five' in Zimbabwe – charged by a buffalo, pinned against a wall by a black rhino, knocked to the ground by an elephant (which he had tried to stop eating the thatched roof of a tree lodge by throwing stones at it), mauled by a lion, and – perhaps this didn't really count – sent tumbling to the ground in shock when he climbed a tree and found he was sharing a branch with a leopard. Alan had only that week walked round to get into his Land Rover and found a pride of lions resting in the shade beneath it. By leaping in and shouting and banging the doors and beating his fists against the side panels, he'd shooed them off. 'Don't worry,' said Aubrey, 'so long as you don't get out you are just seen as part of the vehicle, not recognized as a human being.' There were tales, too, of a man who, when attacked by a lion, thrust one great red hand into its mouth and grabbed his gun with the other; he shot the lion through the head but blew a hole through his hand in the process. Aubrey, sadly, died in 2004.

Alan tells the story of the Hwange elephants in a splendid book, *The Presidential Elephants*, which details how he found a tiny herd of 11 terrified elephants – the remnants of what had once been a large population incessantly persecuted by poachers – and helped to build them up into the thriving herds in Hwange of a few years ago. In a clever move to get them protected, he called the herd the Presidential elephants and secured the personal backing of Robert Mugabe, who seemed to be one of the more enlightened African leaders at the time. (I often think Alan must have choked on that title many times since.) But by 2004, there were reports that the land had been appropriated by one of the president's deputies and elephants here were subject to appallingly indiscriminate snaring and shooting.

At one time it was possible to feed wild elephants in this herd from the back of the open vehicles, but it was clear that an accident was bound to happen eventually – if an elephant unintentionally swung its heavy trunk against the passengers – so the practice was stopped. Nevertheless, when Ashley drove the two of us into Hwange and found a big herd of elephants up ahead, including a lot of youngsters, the anticipation was intense. Indeed, the atmosphere was electric. We were driven closer than we had ever been to elephants, and then the engine was cut. All was silent, except for the gentle rumbling, grunting, sighing and rustling of elephants all around us. It takes a bit of time to get used to this; for a while I hardly dared move. Perhaps I couldn't move. Marcella was frankly petrified at first, especially as a young elephant came to say hello and mum came along behind to make sure all was well, reaching out with her trunk to within five feet or so of our faces.

> Stunning, stunning, stunning – the 'Presidential elephants' – one or two within ten yards, then a group of 15, some within 5–10 yards, then a group of 40, surrounding us, in our open-topped vehicle, often within 10–15 yards and some within 5 yards, one as close as five feet! All taking interest in us at times, rumbling, trumpeting a bit, waving their ears and trunks, but mostly just getting on with life, feeding, playing, rolling over – absolutely magnificent. One youngster was only a few weeks old at most. Another, a few months, was wrestling with a bush, getting bits into his mouth but not seeming to know what to do with them, then getting frustrated, swinging his trunk about with loud slaps against his side. Young bulls were sparring and pushing about – fortunately not so close! – while others were inquisitive and came over, with raised or waving trunks – the closest reached out and for a moment I thought he would touch me.

So we had been to Africa, then: we had been close to an elephant. This remains one of the most remarkable experiences with any kind of wildlife that I have ever had, or ever will have, and I treasure it. Eventually the herd moved slowly on, and drifted off into the trees either side of our clearing. I have always been impressed by the way that elephants can move so silently into what looks like an impenetrable thicket and, within a matter of feet, disappear so entirely from view as if they have somehow dissolved into the vegetation around them. They just leave behind their distinctive, pleasant, cold-tea odour and enormous round footprints in the sand.

There were other close encounters with elephants, some that were almost equally close and others that, in being a little less so, were in many ways a little more enjoyable, certainly more relaxed. One elephant, in particular, I remember was walking out from the forest on the open sandy strip beside the road. We drew up alongside, switched off the engine, and sat and watched. He was a large elephant, but took little notice of us. He lifted his left front foot and began to swing his leg gently to and fro, just a few inches each way, and lowered it back to the ground, still swinging it back and forth, the weight of his enormous foot giving it impetus, until he had begun to slice a narrow, shallow little groove in the sandy soil. Then, using his trunk in the most deft of movements, he reached down into the groove and pulled out a tiny, wispy root, transferred it to his mouth, and swallowed. He repeated this several times.

Elephants, for all their size, are marvellously adept at such intricate and precise operations and evidently particularly choosy about the little titbits they eat between meals.

One more place: Ndutu, on the edge of the Serengeti, is a small, simple, rather primitive camp, next door to the tented camp used by the late Hugo van Lawick (a great photographer and film-maker), not far from a large lake. To reach it means a long, hard, tiring drive from Ngorongoro, sweeping down from the mountain rainforest and vast open slopes, through a region that looks like Scotland but with ostriches and elands and Masai villages, on past the area of Olduvai Gorge where so many discoveries have helped elucidate the evolution of mankind, then finally across great open plains. Somewhere, nowhere, there is a fork in the road and a little wooden sign, a picture of a genet and an arrow to the left to Ndutu; but you are not there yet, it is still many miles away, into the edge of the open, dry, fascinating savanna woodland, which often seems to be full of various species of cuckoos.

The camp itself has a little central building with the reception, a bar and the dining area. Outside, in front, a rough path leads to the wide concrete bed of the campfire, from which, in the evening, you can sit with a beer and watch the incomparable night sky and see the flash and glow of lightning playing around the highlands to the east. To each side, in the usual pattern, runs a series of small rooms, each with bathroom facilities, beds, mosquito nets, a cupboard or two. They do not have the rich and fashionable decorations of the Zimbabwe lodges, nor the sumptuous quality of the big, newer lodges of Ngorongoro and Tarangire, but this is a much more intimate, exciting sort of camp, with lions on the doorstep – you may find their tracks next morning. For some people, it is an enduring favourite; for others, it is not what they expected for the amount of money they paid. For me, it was perfect.

Sit quietly at your door and there is a treasure trove of birds and animals out there, passing by at odd times during the day, visible from the comfort of the cane chair on your verandah. Take a stroll and you can see several kinds of birds that have not been encountered before, different weavers and finches, woodpeckers and cuckoos – Ndutu is always good for several species of colourful cuckoos. After you've gone to bed, you can hear lions roaring from two or three places near by, so you get up to make sure you did fasten the little wooden door.

On occasion I have been at Ndutu in drenching rain, and it seemed that the whole day would be washed out, that we surely couldn't move from the camp. We hadn't reckoned with the determination of our drivers, Tim and Golden.

It was in the schedule to go to the Serengeti, via Lion's Hill Gate, so, we would go to the Serengeti, come what may. The technique, quite the opposite of what I might have tried, seems to be to stick the thing in first gear, rev as high as possible, spin the wheels and make a charge at everything, even through deep wheel-ruts in soft mud, overflowing with running water. It is impossible to see anything as the rain lashes down outside and the wheels spray the bus, windows and all, with an inch-thick layer of mud. Anyway, you are concentrating too hard on trying to stay on a seat and not fall to the floor as the minibus slips, slides, bumps, turns broadside, tilts over and sinks to its wheels again, as a wet drive must be several times the average speed of a dry one. There may be a pause, as one minibus goes to the aid of another and tows it out of a particularly glutinous swamp; then the rope is swapped over as the rescued bus has to pull out its rescuer, now itself up to its axles in the ooze. But we get there. The rain stops. Windows are washed. And it is out of this world.

Here's a sample morning drive from Ndutu in March:

Extremely silent during the night. Hyena called at one point. Dawned still, cloudy, some streaks of brightness, cool. Became sunny, but a lot of cloud, several distant showers visible – beautiful. A glorious morning – absolutely beautiful, cool at first, becoming very warm but still, not fiercely sunny – in fact, the light was usually perfect. Stunning scenic effects with distant hills intensely green-blue. Large areas of the plains very open, with very short vegetation (after fires), all lush green and wet; in the wood areas mostly trees on short green grass. Only around the camp is it really coarse, tall, yellow grass under the trees. Herds of wildebeest and zebras crossing the river with a backdrop of acacia woodland and perfect reflections – a lot of action, many perfectly composed groups. Huge lines of wildebeest pouring out of the woods and onto the plains all around us. The plains covered end to end with animals, Thomson's gazelles by the hundred on the woodland edge; driving back through almost continuous herds of lovely mixtures of almost everything together – brilliant picture compositions time after time. Great views of bat-eared foxes and hyenas. Leopards – less action but, if possible, even better views than yesterday, one in a tree, another at its base. And all of this without another vehicle in sight.

My notes for that morning include scores of bird species, some familiar, others restricted to the local area, and a long list of mammals: 'giraffes 15; hartebeest 15; wildebeest 300,000 to 500,000; Grant's gazelles 100; impalas 20; Thomson's gazelles

1,000; zebras 1,000-plus; silver-backed jackals 4; bat-eared foxes 9; spotted hyenas 6 (very close); leopards 2.' And two tortoises for good measure.

These are notes made while I sat beside my room one morning, having seen giraffes, steinbock, 10,000 wildebeest, 500 zebras and two pairs of lions a little earlier:

When food is put out on the bar, typically 50–100 red-billed buffalo-weavers, 30–40 grey-headed sparrows, a couple of score rufous-tailed weavers, 20–30 helmeted guineafowl, 20–30 Cape turtle doves and 20 or so mourning doves join in the scrum – they occasionally burst up with a roar of wings. Also, today, speckle-fronted weavers (on the wet morning, but only then, a flock of wattled starlings arrived). A few fat, olive mice with pink ears and white eye-rings finish off the feeding group. Round about are African cuckoos (diederik cuckoos heard calling), an occasional sunbird and other odds and ends and, after a slow start, by midday the sky is well populated with four – no, five – species of vulture, marabou, bateleur and other big birds. Large butterflies float by; everywhere there are ants, but it is remarkably free of troublesome or irritating insects.

Hot and sunny, but breeze and cloud increasing, distant rain. Occasional murmurings of wildebeest herds, frequent loud drone of a passing dung beetle, trills of woodpeckers, cooing doves, chattering sparrows and weavers – but essentially, behind all this, a great, peaceful, silence.

Swans on the Nile

Trevor Gunton, with Marcella, Ken Swan and the redoubtable Miss Doreen Goodrick, of Swan Hellenic, arranged Swan's cruises in the Mediterranean and on the Nile, with an RSPB guest ornithologist, promoted to RSPB members. ('I only married him for his Nile Cruise,' Marcella often says of me.) On Mediterranean cruises, there were guest lecturers on any number of subjects, mostly geological, historical and religious, and their spouses could travel, too, free of charge, so long as they carried out occasional 'librarian' duties.

On the Nile, this was not possible, but the spouse might go at a discounted rate, so several of us took up the chance of 'leading' a Nile cruise and for several years they ran remarkably successfully, with many RSPB members aboard. There were Egyptologists and local Egyptian guides, so the birdwatcher simply pointed out things along the way and gave four or five lectures on deck or, using slides, in the main room inside. Several times, I was called on to identify birds on the walls of ancient tombs, as at Beni Hassan, and in paintings in Cairo Museum. This was not as difficult as you might imagine since the birds had been drawn so evocatively and accurately. It sometimes became difficult later, however, as the authorities insisted (rightly) that talks and guidance at the sites could be done only by Egyptians.

The *Nile Star* was a small blue and white cruise boat. It was not quite in the old-fashioned style of *Death on the Nile* – with cabins opening out onto the deck – but it was small enough and it had tiny, cramped cabins opening onto an internal corridor. It had the great benefit of being able to go through shallower water than could the great 'gin palaces' that plied between Luxor and Aswan. It was advertised as sailing 600 miles and 6,000 years into history, and that's exactly what it did. I did the full-length Cairo to Aswan cruise (or vice versa) a couple of times on this boat. I was fortunate to have been able to do this, as much of the best, most exciting and most satisfying parts of the cruise were on the Cairo to Luxor stretch, which is now so hard to do. And, being snobby about it, I was also fortunate that Swan's tended to attract the 'right sort' – people interested enough to want a few lecturers and guides and a full programme of visits, and who were not so likely (as some we saw) to scrape a rucksack across the face of a 4,000-year-old tomb painting, or give a mouthful of abuse to anyone getting in their way. Tourists, eh?

On later cruises we had the larger, plush *Nile Monarch*. To begin with, this managed the full cruise. But the water levels in the Nile began to fall; and increased silting – always a problem since the Aswan Dam prevented the famous annual floods – eventually prevented the full-distance cruise by any tour boat. Several times we were temporarily stuck on a sandbank ourselves. So Swan's cruises were, like everyone else's, confined to the stretch between Aswan and Luxor. And then came the terrorist attacks in Cairo, Assiut and at Luxor, and Swan's Egyptian operation failed altogether: a regrettable situation.

Naturally the cruises varied according to the time of year. On one trip, it rained in Cairo and the Fayum, and it was sometimes almost cold. On others, it was blisteringly hot (110 or 115°F in Aswan is, I have to say, too much for me). Going ashore in such conditions is like opening an oven in the middle of the Sunday roast and diving in. On one trip, sad to say, it proved fatal for one RSPB member. A long, hard, hot day around Saqqara was too much for him. The next morning everyone noticed that we had not left our berth on time, unheard of for Swan's. Then, as we watched the goings-on ashore, a white shroud was carried down the gangplank and loaded into a waiting van.

To start with, I knew little about the Nile or its history. I had seen most of the likely birds in Israel or elsewhere, and the Nile's birds are not, in general, especially taxing. It was, though, a matter of moments before I was thoroughly hooked on Egypt, both ancient and modern. I still say that if I were to select my top ten great places of the world, the Valley of the Kings would be the first name on the list. Although I have not been back to Egypt for a number of years, I'm still buying the books – there's a new one in the post as I write – and the Theban Atlas website is on my short list of 'favourites' on the computer at home. Egypt remains deeply embedded within me and endlessly absorbing. I love the place.

That said, each time I have been in Egypt I have been violently ill. Other passengers have eaten the same food and stayed fit and well, so I'm inclined to think that these afflictions have been caused by too much sun, too much standing at the edge of the deck scanning the banks for birds. After all, during the cruising, I scarcely let up, but it always seemed so perfect, sitting or standing on deck, binoculars in one hand, cold drink in the other, watching and scribbling feverishly in the notebook as we passed by scores of great birds. On the first occasion I was alone in my cabin. It had the usual two bunks side by side with a narrow gap between them. All one night I was on my knees, an elbow on each bunk, head hanging low, as it was the only way I could relieve the gut-wrenching pain. Next morning, I couldn't straighten up; I scrambled out to see a doctor, bent double on hands and knees. On another trip I found just how inconvenient it can be to be sick and have violently explosive diarrhoea on a trip in the desert. 'Drink Coca Cola,' the doctor said. 'It's cured more upset stomachs than most medicines.' Sachets of rehydration powders were doled out, too.

On the last cruise, being ill in Luxor brought its benefits. I couldn't believe it: it was the day of the early morning trip to the Valley of the Kings. (Swan's get you off the boat at 5 o'clock in the morning to avoid the worst of the heat and the crowds, which often means half a day free ashore, or three-quarters cruising on the river). It was the last place I would have wanted to miss, but I was too ill to move. Next day, the passengers were off to Karnak in the morning and then off again, for the fabulous son et lumiere, in the evening. Fortunately (for me at least) another passenger had also missed the Valley of the Kings. He wanted to go, so Swan's organized a taxi for the following morning. Marcella and I piled in with him. Quite remarkably, we reached an almost empty valley (apart from a few trumpeter finches), and we had the tomb of Tutankhamun entirely to ourselves. Not only did we stand and stare at the poor king's sarcophagus from the little balcony above, but the 'guard' – quite illegally I am sure – unlocked the gate and led us down to the floor of the burial chamber so that we could peer at the magnificent coffin a few inches from our quivering noses. Being ill has its rewards, now and then.

If you are the least bit interested in ancient history, Egypt is a magical place, and it is wonderful if you are at all inspired by brilliant scenery. Down towards Cairo the fertile valley is broad and always interesting; up towards Aswan it is narrow or non-existent and the river is crowded on either side by desert, cliffs or romantic hills. I've always found the people good fun, but then, I've only been as a tourist – I imagine that trying to organize anything is a nightmare. OK, we have been shown across the road in Cairo and ended up in a carpet shop instead of the hotel, but, so long as you're in no hurry, it doesn't matter. Most of the traders in the markets and at the ancient sites are good-natured and see tourists as a bit of a challenge: if you can resist them for long enough, they break into a broad grin, shake your hand, bid you farewell and wave you on your way, happy to have tried but acknowledging that they have failed. They are, after all, sure of another tourist coming along the street.

'Looky looky, no price for looking, best quality guaranteed.' The real, hard bargaining is done in private, as you are ushered into a shady corner away from the crowds, so that the best offer isn't overheard.

The children are great – bright, wide-eyed, always smiling, fed on local produce and seemingly fit. They usually got a good scolding from Eileen Walters, our excellent tour manager, if they asked for baksheesh, but they generally asked for pens. A couple of dozen always lined up ready to accost us as we got ashore at Beni Hassan, scarcely able to contain themselves before excitedly bursting ranks at some unseen signal and each choosing an individual who looked likely to buy a woven palm-leaf basket.

'Not now, thanks, maybe on our way back.'

'When you come back I will be at school, but my sister will be here and you can buy my basket then. What is your name?'

Two hours later, sure enough, there was the sister with the basket, making a beeline for me even though she'd never seen me before. 'Rob, you promised my sister that you would buy her basket.' I have quite a collection at home.

Other aspects are sometimes less appealing. Several times we have been stuck against a low bridge, waiting for it to be raised to let the boats through. The time for raising the bridge would be fixed for 10 a.m., arrangements made, payment given, forms completed, officials made aware. You can still be waiting at 4 p.m. Polite requests, entreaties, bribes, threats, violent arguments – none makes any difference. A day's birdwatching goes by the board (no great hardship); timings of visits to tombs and temples are thrown awry, scheduled transport is cancelled, Swan's officials and the boat's skipper are increasingly harassed. The bridge man will not budge. Patience: it is, in such hot and dusty and busy places, the only way forward. Best to calm down, take a few deep breaths, and watch the people instead, who are usually much more fascinating anyway, or haggle over the price of a wooden plaque inlaid with camel bone and mother of pearl, offered by a war invalid.

Egypt is full of life, noise, colour, smells; your senses seem hyperactive. Cairo is awash with traffic. Visitors say that, as in India, the driving is awful. In fact, it is often brilliant: cars and vans and trucks and buses speed in every direction, cutting each other up, shooting red lights, swerving in and out to avoid donkey carts, camels, goats and sheep, one hand on the horn, one foot firmly on the accelerator, and yet they never hit anything. Taxi drivers, with various obscene plastic icons hanging from their windscreens, play loud music from battered tapes. If, when taking a taxi, you show the least interest in the music – tap a foot or wave a hand in time to the rhythm – the driver turns round, raises his hands, starts clapping and singing – 'You like? You like?' – while continuing to plough on at full speed. But somehow you get there. Swan's used buses, taxis, horse-drawn carriages, donkeys, trailers pulled by tractors – anything to get passengers to the ancient sites. And feluccas. These are the sailing boats, like dhows, that ply the river, large and small, some passenger boats, others heavy freight transports, carrying great blocks of limestone or hundreds of sacks of lime or grain, as they have done for centuries. A trip on a felucca is immensely restful.

Cruising along late in the day is an especially satisfying and endlessly fascinating experience. It is like being transported back to biblical times; everyone says this, but it is true. People are going home after a day in the fields. Streams of people. And herds of sheep and goats and cattle and water buffaloes. Children everywhere. They pile into their little villages of square, mud-brick buildings, overhung by palms and flanked by huge, swaying reeds. Thousands of pigeons return, too, great flocks swarming to the domed dovecotes that are everywhere along the Nile. Muezzins, or at least taped recordings of them, call out from the minarets, a peculiarly satisfying, pleasing sound. And in the cool of the evening there is a magical hour for birds.

Things change fast, nevertheless. Even in the few years that I was going to Egypt, donkeys were replaced by tractors, water wheels driven by blindfolded oxen were exchanged for electric pumps, the number of shadoufs – the counterbalanced poles that raised water buckets from the river, which we all learned about at school – reduced markedly. But the essential qualities of Egypt remain. It was always a pleasure, tinged with excited anticipation of a new day, to wake in the little cabin, pull aside a curtain and watch the river rushing by inches below your nose, and see the sun rising, huge and orange through the peculiar pearly haze and thin low cloud, behind rows of palm trees and scattered minarets. Even the rapid, two-tone repetition of the boat's horns, as we approached a bridge or quay or passed a sailing boat, came to be evocative of Egypt and the Nile cruise experience. Only the prospect of yet another day of ferocious heat was at all daunting.

It was better, in many ways, to start a cruise at Cairo. There would be a night in the huge Rameses Hilton hotel, overlooking the river, with a stunning view of the city from perhaps the 36th floor. I wondered if there might be a roof tax, for half of Cairo looked to be unfinished: the tops of all the buildings bear spikes of scaffolding (as well as lines of washing, groups of children playing, foraging chickens, the occasional goat). The cruise ship was moored somewhere along the river not far away; scores of egrets would fly to roost in the grounds of Giza

Juvenile masked shrike at Philae.

Zoo or find a spot in the tall roadside palms, plastering the parked cars below with thick, white guano. Ring-necked parakeets added their squeals to the general din.

Before the cruise you would visit the pyramids. If you have no back problem, claustrophobia, heart disease – or anything else on the list by the entrance – you could go inside one of them to the strange, eerie, empty room at its core. They still have the power to raise the hairs on your neck and, should you let yourself drift off into thoughts of who built them, who lay in the burial chamber for thousands of years, you can dismiss the presence of other tourists and enter a different world. And on to the Sphinx – wiping away the odd tear, getting a bit emotional, because the Sphinx grabs people like that. Then perhaps the birdwatchers in the party would get on a bus to Lake Quran in the Faiyoum, stopping at a few archaeological sites on the way, seeing a few birds (sometimes a lot, such as hundreds of white-winged black terns and slender-billed gulls, waders, little green bee-eaters, even hoopoe larks).

Next day would be Memphis and Saqqara, with its magnificent pyramid of Djoser, the oldest stone construction in the world, which rises in a series of giant steps. Then there would be another pyramid to enter, that of Unas, little more on the outside than a rounded mound but still inspiring inside, and the first colossal statue of Ramses II, lying on its back inside its little exhibition building, tucked away under the blissful shade of a few eucalyptus trees. And then to the boat and the first evening meal served by blue-and-white uniformed staff with golden cummerbunds (one, you swear, identical to Ramses II – not his statue but his mummy), a cocktail party on deck, which you helped facilitate by bringing several bottles of drink from the duty-free, and a get-together for the lecturers and guides.

It could, though, be a cruise in the opposite direction: you would fly from Cairo to Aswan and then cruise back. This meant getting stuck into the hottest part of the trip right away – no time to acclimatize to the heat. It could also mean the best birds at the beginning, which was a bit of a shame, as it all happens so quickly. Here you are, in Aswan, with Elephantine Island and the Aswan Dam; the breathtaking temples of Philae (that were moved wholesale from their original sites to save them from rising waters as a rehearsal for the even bigger project at Abu Simbel); the gleam of the Nile in the evening light and the street lights along the corniche – and the realization next morning that the gleam comes from hundreds of thousands of discarded plastic water bottles jostling their way to the Mediterranean.

Already you are seeing scores of egrets, squacco herons, perhaps a little bittern or two. The corniche is alive with typically dark and richly coloured laughing doves feeding on the grain spilled from the nose bags of skeletal horses, which pull the tourist carriages around Luxor and down the road to Karnak. From the coach (Ken Swan always called it a 'motor coach') you might glimpse a little green bee-eater or a hoopoe as you head for the Aswan High Dam through a series of what a roadside sign announces as 'Dangrious carves'. You wonder at the swallows – why are they so short-tailed and so very dark? Later you remember they are of the local Egyptian race, with the dark red of the throat extended all the way down to the tail.

At the High Dam you find pale crag martins. Philae has gull-billed, whiskered and white-winged black terns and, depending on the time of year, migrants might be skulking in the tamarisks there – various warblers, perhaps a masked shrike. It is in any case worth stopping a moment in the bushy patch beside the temple because the heat of the sun, the travel, perhaps it's just the change of water, make you feel you need to sit down for a minute until the ground settles beneath your feet. White-crowned black wheatears are good birds on the island and there are sunbirds – worth another look, because you may not see many more of these farther north. On the way back to Aswan you stop to see a vast obelisk, still unfinished, still only three-quarters cut from the ancient granite quarries.

A fleet of feluccas takes the group to Elephantine, with its noisy egret colony. (Once I was photographing a young little egret on the ground – getting closer all the time, shooting the best pictures I'd ever taken – but each time I was in just the right position, a local man insisted on shooing the bird away from me; he then held out his hand for baksheesh.) The island is leafy and cool; there are olivaceous warblers, graceful prinias (tiny warblers with long, cocked tails), Nile Valley sunbirds, bulbuls, clamorous reed warblers. From the boat you see designer kingfishers in black and white – pied kingfishers – and must get a photograph, not knowing that there will be hundreds more to come. If you are sharp-eyed, and lucky, you might see a green-backed heron from the boat. Something of a newcomer here, it is almost true to say that this bird was first discovered in Egypt, at least on the Nile, by the guest birdwatchers on these Swan's cruises. Also from the boat, looking across to a reedy shore in the evening, you see a remarkable, dark, cock-tailed, cockerel-sized bird wander into the reeds – a patch of white, a hint of red somewhere. A purple gallinule. No worries, there will be many more of these, too, downriver, and you will soon get a great view. The local race is green-backed, deep violet elsewhere, with a splash of bright turquoise on the throat; these birds have enormous red bills and deep-pink-red legs with grotesquely long toes, with which they grasp long rush stems while they extract the soft white pith with their beaks. They are curious birds, a set of pieces that hardly fit together, yet they could be called handsome, in a way – I would argue that they are beautiful.

The temples, the tombs, the nilometer, the colourful markets of Aswan – all this is too much, so it is good to be back on board, cooling down in the cabin, finding a gin and tonic or a beer at the bar. Egypt assails you from all sides and you need time to clear your head. On one of my trips I was obviously so tired after such a start – which had followed hard on the heels of the long flight from home – that I wrote 'Cruising south' in my diary when we were, of course, heading north, downriver. I always kept good details of the birds on these cruises, timing the sections and making reference to towns and villages that we passed. These various lists and counts were sent off to people who record the birds of Egypt, and many notes from early cruises made it into the authoritative *Birds of Egypt*, a fine book by Meininger and Goodman. Birdwatchers in Egypt have always been relatively few, and my counts, for example, of pied kingfishers and squacco herons, even egrets, as well as records of rarer species such as the green-backed herons, proved useful to supplement the existing data. But keeping such notes could become something of a chore or, at least, a little disconcerting for the people you were with. Halfway through a conversation with a fellow traveller, for example, you must say 'Excuse me a moment', check something with your binoculars, note it down in your book, and then carry on as if nothing had happened.

Most of the species were expected and repeated each time. There were always huge numbers of little and cattle egrets, surprisingly many grey herons (often standing on sand dunes at the edge of the desert where it came down almost to the water's edge), hundreds of squacco herons, scores of purple gallinules, literally hundreds of pied kingfishers. Spur-winged plovers are common. On the stretch from Esna to Edfu there were 250 garganeys, dozens of moorhens, Kentish plover, and 50 collared pratincoles. But there are always excitements that get the adrenalin going. Sometimes we saw white-tailed plovers, rare and exciting waders with long, elegant, yellow legs, and I once saw a flock of yellow-billed storks over the valley far to the north of Abu Simbel, where a few had begun to turn up. A falcon on a desert dune looked like an Eleonora's, while sooty falcons and Barbary falcons were always a pretty safe bet. At one disembarkation point, the passengers climbed onto their donkeys, but I decided to walk; I was rewarded with a couple of Egyptian nightjars that I flushed from the riverside grass. Glossy ibises, flocks of Egyptian geese, migrating red-throated pipits, birds of prey, cranes, spoonbills, pelicans – all these and many more could raise the level of excitement on deck. One group of pelicans flew upriver, very low in a line abreast; they circled up and away to the west, where they were joined by a black stork.

'We've got pelicans back home,' said one of the Americans on the boat. 'They're bigger than these, too.'

'Sure they are and no doubt they all have university educations as well,' replied a Canadian lady, a little wearily.

The people on the cruises helped to make them, too. There were usually 15 to 20 RSPB members, sometimes more; but by the end of the cruise, most of the other people on board were taking some sort of interest in birds – it was hard to avoid them. Once, I found a blackboard, drew cattle, little and great white egrets on it in chalk, and parked it on the deck near the bar as an aid to identification for those who were new to birdwatching: little egret, black bill, yellow feet; cattle egret, yellow bill, black feet. It seemed too much for some of the passengers to comprehend and they were forever getting them wrong.

After so many false alarms from people who will insist that little egrets are 'huge' it was nice to find a really good, and obvious, great white, in a session with an excellent heron and egret list [great white, 60 little egrets, 100 cattle egrets, scores of grey herons, three purple herons, 30 squacco herons, 11 night herons].

The strong light and distances made things confusing for many people. Any grey heron in the shade was 'much too dark', any heron in the sun was 'much too white'. I was always being told, 'No, you're wrong, it's a crane' or 'Surely not, it's a white stork!' But this sort of thing can catch anyone out. I remember being on the north beach at Eilat in Israel on one occasion, with a bunch of birdwatchers from England; a few yards away stood Lars Jonsson, world-renowned artist and all-round expert from Sweden. A group of egrets flew overhead, not too high up. Some of us looked at each other; someone dared ask, 'Are they little egrets?' Another suggested they might be great white egrets. I didn't offer an opinion. Another leader said he didn't quite know for sure. Lars looked over and said they can be difficult sometimes, and didn't offer an answer, either. It was comforting.

On one trip we found eagle owls on a pyramid (not the great pyramids of Giza) and these I declared 'bird of the trip'. I had only ever seen one before, and that not very well. Here were two adults and two well-grown juveniles. On another trip, at Saqqara, six hoopoe larks were unexpected and wonderful, very tame, running about the entrance to the Stepped Pyramid complex. Perhaps most exciting of all were African skimmers, which we encountered on several cruises. These were so unexpected at first, but later always looked for again, somewhere between Aswan and Luxor, usually near Kom Ombo. The first time I saw some – 16 flying south in October 1983 – we were in the middle of lunch on deck, and the boat almost rolled over when everyone dashed to the side to see what the excitement was about.

> One bay, quite distant, had many of the egrets, including a great white
> egret, most of the waders and the pratincole flock (50) on the ground.
> Soon after passing that, still writing notes and remembering numbers,
> the great excitement of the whole trip came when eight Africa skimmers
> came downstream as we sailed up. It was all quickly over as the birds went
> on, over the birds in the bay. They flew very low over the water, almost
> line astern, in a fast, steady flight with regular, powerful wing-beats with
> high upstrokes but little movement below body level. Progress was direct
> until they crossed the weedy bay, when they swung one way, then the
> other, rising above the water in a synchronized, banking curve. No sooner
> had they gone than a smaller group appeared, then another and another,
> making another eight in all. They were totally unexpected and really

marvellous – all a bit quick, not much detail seen, but got the adrenalin flowing more than anything.

Skimmers are peculiar birds, like large terns with very long bills. The upper mandible is much shorter than the lower one, which projects like a deep, flattened blade; it isn't evident that this is so when the bill is closed, it just looks long and dagger-shaped, but then a skimmer will fly low over the water, open its bill and trail the tip of that remarkable lower mandible to slice the surface tension and detect the presence of an unsuspecting fish. But skimmers in flight are also wonderfully elegant and graceful, with very long, tapered wings, all black above and white below. To see a line of 15 or 20 of them, rising and falling in turn like a passing wave, is quite something; but, as they may simply pass by the boat going in the opposite direction, or fly over a distant backwater, you have to have your wits about you.

At Luxor, we used to moor beside the bank; later it was turned into a stone-faced embankment alongside the corniche. Then there were so many cruise boats that we were forced to moor up against another boat – sometimes third from the shore, so we had to disembark by walking through the reception areas of two other cruise boats ('Not as good as ours, is it?'). It was a shame, because we had previously been able to look out across the road to the floodlit Luxor temple at night, unimpeded by pesky tourist boats – who did they think they were? Swan's were a cut above the rest, after all. The tourism boom continues. I know I shouldn't take the cheap package, I know I shouldn't fly, I'm not sure it is a good idea to go back, but I will. I'll add to the ever-growing crowds.

Luxor is a good place to spend an evening or two ashore. We used to go ashore at Assiut, too, but it became a bit dodgy (tourists are not so welcome there). Marcella and I walked together down a street, she in jeans, and someone shouted 'Forbidden! Forbidden!' Maybe it was the sight of two people in trousers, arm in arm, I don't know. The next time we sailed through Assiut without stopping, with a police launch and armed officers keeping us company, after serious unrest in the town and attacks on tourists.

Just away from the river, running parallel to it, is the main Luxor market, the souk, where you can buy made-to-measure galabeas, the long Egyptian robes, which you think will look great as dressing gowns when you get back home but which will stay in the wardrobe, never to be seen again. There are jewellery shops full of Egyptian gold that gleams in the streetlights. Spices of every colour are laid out on stalls: saffron, powders of brown and green and orange and unexpectedly bright blue. Here is a shop full of farm tools, another full of nothing but aluminium pots and pans, another selling vegetables. The piles of vegetables and neat pyramids of colourful fruit change with the season, a bewildering variety of lentils, beans, grains and root crops. There are piled-up crates full of chickens and pigeons, baskets of ducks, little clusters of sheep and the odd donkey waiting to be sold. Egyptian boys are sometimes horribly cruel to their donkeys. There are stalls selling eggs, homemade butter and cheeses. Men come for a shave or a haircut or just sit on street corners smoking their hubble-bubble pipes. One shop has nothing in it but flip-flop sandals, the next seems to specialize solely in brooms and brushes of every description. There are pastries and bread rolls and stalls selling sandwiches, bags of popcorn, oranges and peanuts. Sugar cane is squeezed by machine into sticky cups, oranges crushed into glasses of bubbling juice. The heat has diminished, the air is comfortably warm, the streets have a not unpleasant aroma of spices, donkey, horse and humanity. It all passes too quickly.

The Nile is in turn wide and open or narrowed and compressed between pale cliffs; in many places there are broad sandbanks and shallow side channels, long grassy flats where boys tend water buffaloes, red-brown men bathe naked under white soap suds, spur-winged plovers and Senegal thick-knees line the water's edge and hoopoes feed under little vertical cliffs. Innumerable sheltered bays are thickly lined with rushes and reeds and dotted with ducks and coots. A common bird is the black-shouldered kite, which hovers over fields and marshes, especially in the cool of the evening. Black kites are frequent, too, and marsh harriers often hunt over belts of tall reeds. The sky is often hazy, not quite a full, clear blue, despite the intense heat. The days could be wearyingly hot and very sticky, punctuated by cold rain that seems to have no effect on the intense heat of the sun. Odd weather conditions can appear quickly and unexpectedly, as various extracts from my diary illustrate:

In the evening the hot sun soon turned back to a leaden, strange sky, with a 'metallic' look around the sun, a reflection of the desert under the clouds giving a pink-orange look, while in some directions it was just dark grey with all sorts of strange, swirling effects. Eventually a cloud of sandy buff colour rolled over, with occasional lightning, a sudden fierce wind, then blown sand and quite steady rain for a short time. After that it cleared and quickly became calm again …

In the Fayoum [October] it suddenly became very windy and dark, then there was heavy rain. On the return through the Western Desert it was very strange to see pools of water on the sands. Cairo was awash, with more rain, even flashes of lightning and a very dark sky. It was the first rain of the year in Cairo and quite exceptional ...

After the rain the atmosphere was quite clear and I wondered what this magical region [Saqqara] must have looked like. From a rise beside the Stepped Pyramid I could see at least 16 pyramids (one of the three at Giza being hidden from this angle) stretching south to Dahshur and beyond, and north to the Great Pyramids. They almost look their best from here, removed from the busy car parks and roads of Giza and the pylons of the desert to the west, so that they simply float magically up from clean desert sands. Also, Cairo was clearer than I have ever seen it, including the big suburbs on the hills east of the Nile valley.

Normally, though, it is just more sun, more heat. Sometimes, birds came fast and furiously and I was trying to look in all directions at once and keep the lists going. One bay had '30 purple gallinules, 80 glossy ibises and 40 Egyptian geese; later there were 200 Egyptian geese asleep on the desert sands, on undulating slopes'. This was in a spell during which there were also 50 ferruginous ducks, four ospreys, four black-shouldered kites, six marsh harriers, two white-tailed plovers, Senegal thick-knees, pallid swift, hoopoes, pied kingfishers, bee-eaters, and others. And this was quite ordinary, really. In one 90-minute spell I noted 350-plus squacco herons 'nearly all in superb golden breeding plumage' as well as a honey buzzard, 100 pied kingfishers, 40 white-winged black terns, thousands of swallows, a blue-cheeked bee-eater. That made more than 500 squaccos in just that one day, all scattered along the riverside or on floating weed – extraordinary really. If I didn't have my notebook to hand all the time, I had no chance of remembering what I had seen, certainly not any details of numbers.

My first Nile black-necked grebes. Night herons [18 to 20] in the depths of a big mimosa tree as usual. Quite good flight views of white-tailed plovers [five] including whiffling twists and turns from a bird about to land. African skimmers [18 to 20] again well away in a large backwater, often disturbed – by a marsh harrier? – and wheeling around in a tight, co-ordinated flock or in a long line astern.

In this spell there were also scores of egrets, 55 squacco herons, purple and grey herons, spoonbills, Egyptian geese, shovelers, pintails and wigeon, 14 black kites, two booted eagles, two ospreys, three sparrowhawks, 16 black-shouldered kites, two marsh harriers, many waders including marsh, green and wood sandpipers, 15 black-winged stilts, gull-billed terns, 130 white-winged black terns, eight purple gallinules, 45 pied kingfishers, hoopoes, sand martins, hundreds of pied wagtails and a red-throated pipit. I remember counting more than 100 pied kingfishers from one spot, and sections of river with 40, 60 or 80 of them were quite commonly noted. (On the stretch from Esna to Edfu there were 208 pied kingfishers – 80 in just one area, an amazing density near a shallow bay with fishing boats – as well as 50 garganeys, dozens of moorhens, Kentish plover, and 50 collared pratincoles.) We would usually moor at Kom Ombo for a while, where pied kingfishers would perch on the boat or on its mooring ropes, or hover alongside the deck.

> Nag Hamadi: cattle egrets. The colony beside the boat [where we moored] actually stretched for several hundred yards and had maybe 1,000 birds in it, both adults and large young. There were also small young and even nests with eggs (often visible, as the adults would stand up, shading them from the heat). We watched birds nest-building, mating, fighting, incubating, feeding young: in anything from a nearly-white plumage with dull yellow legs and yellow bill to full breeding regalia with rich golden-buff plumes and red bill and legs. Many (and this full range of colours) within just 30 yards at eye-level from the deck – really wonderful.

But there was more:

> The best 'egret evening', with streams of cattle egrets [2,500 or so] crossing the river and passing the boat, until it was practically dark. They looked especially good, almost blue, against dazzling ripples of orange, silver and black reflecting the black palms against a lilac and pale orange sky. The sunset was wonderful and up high in the clearest blue, apart from a few wisps of light orange, Venus was dazzlingly bright.

Sooty falcons are special birds of the Nile, not easy to find elsewhere. They often appeared towards dusk, when other birds were coming to roost near the river. A selection of notes recalls various sightings:

> As we were cruising late in the day, I was hoping for a sooty falcon going after a wagtail roost. Suddenly, over a reed-bed, with wagtails and marsh

harriers, a dashing yet graceful and relaxed grey falcon appeared on cue. Like a longer-tailed, relaxed hobby with long, angled wings (but 'soft' shaped, or slightly rounded at the carpals). All pale, milky slate or pale grey with a soft, dark terminal tail band and dark tips and trailing edges to the wings ...

Sooty falcon briefly in view over the cliffs above Hatshepsut's temple at Deir al Bahari. It must be one of the easiest falcons to identify with long wings and the instantly obvious pale blue-grey back and inner wings contrasting with blacker wing-tips as it banks over ...

Sooty falcons [two] a few minutes apart in the middle of the cruise [the three-hour stretch from Balliana to Sohag in the afternoon]. The first was very close, allowing details such as the large pale-yellow cere [patch on the base of the bill] to be seen and the dark tips to the primaries (primaries otherwise pale grey, like the rest of the wing). The second was more distant, going after a swallow in a very long, fast, level pursuit with rapid, deep wing-beats like a hobby, then chasing with sudden upward swoops and dashing power-dives and sudden twists. After several of these I think it caught the bird and broke off into a flat, slow, relaxed glide ...

Yet another sooty falcon. It flew over the river, then circled low over a clump of tall trees, dipping in and out, evidently trying to flush out prey – quite unlike the usual perception of a desert- or coastal-cliff bird. It was beautifully lit by the low sun; cere a lemon yellow, legs more orange-yellow.

The landscapes of the Nile are exciting, inseparable from the birds and inseparable from the people. Even the wildest riverside cliff is likely to have a little white-painted dome on some shrine or other, or a series of mysterious, black, rectangular entrances to long-emptied tombs. 'Stunning desert slope and cliff landscapes and broad, flat riverside plains edged by palms, backed by bare hills, like some east African pan lined with acacias.'

The future of the Nile in Egypt is uncertain. Some people predict the next major war will be over water. Countries upstream are extracting so much that too little is left by the time the great river reaches Egypt on its last stretch before the famous delta and the Mediterranean. Let's hope that the people and the birds continue to thrive, somehow, whatever happens.

The Double Rasp

What is your favourite bird? is a question that is often asked of any birdwatcher. What is the most beautiful bird? What is beautiful? What, let us say, is the most beautiful bird song?

Such questions have no answer. As I sit writing this I can look out across a small lawn to a tall, somewhat unkempt yew hedge. The lawn has, I guess (after estimating the number of blades per square inch, the number per square foot, the number of square feet in the lawn) perhaps a million or two sharp, gleaming green spikes, each of which catches the morning sun; after a frost, each has a sparkling diamond at its tip. Like the complex repetition of shapes and intricate patterns across the yew hedge, it produces an astonishingly beautiful effect, if I care to think about it. Sometimes I do; most times, although I am aware of it, and often appreciate it, I just look across the lawn — nothing more or less.

At the risk of being offensive or sounding conceited, I think that many people — perhaps most people — have little time to bother about the beautiful effects of the breaking day on the surface of a lawn. I have stood on Sandy railway station before dawn, in icy frost, staring at the Prussian blue sky slowly brightening in the east, with the quite extraordinary brilliance of Venus at its finest slowly being overtaken by the lightening sky, while everyone else on the platform stared at their feet. I watch sunrises and sunsets from buses and trains while no one else so much as glances out of the window. But they will perhaps be listening to a piece of music on their headphones — music that they think is the most perfect in the world and that I might pass off as a catchy tune. I look out at my yew hedge and, sitting somewhere near, is a song thrush, singing its heart out. If I care to, I can listen to the thrush and consider its repeated phrases the best, purest, notes of the bird world; if I think about it, it might contain strident, shouted, even screeched notes that reduce its quality in comparison with the blackbird. Yet I confess that, this morning, it was simply a background sound as I had breakfast, made my tea and switched on the radio. So far as I know, few people near by take much notice of it.

What is really beautiful depends so much on context, as well as concentration, however much we might think a sound to be wondrous and exciting. Play a nightingale song to the gathering on Sandy station on the way to work in London one morning, and I doubt that it would have any effect, whatever 'the books' might say about its supreme qualities.

I have several times toyed with the idea of conducting a poll in *Birds* to find the readers' favourite bird songs and then producing a CD of the RSPB members' top 20. But I wonder how imaginative the responses might be: similar polls always show the favourite bird to be the robin. In my top 20 bird sound favourites – not necessarily songs – I think I would have to have a seabird colony and, if a chorus of guillemots, fulmars and so on proved unacceptable according to the rules, I suppose I would settle on a kittiwake. I would probably include curlew calls, evolving into a song, and perhaps, also, the remarkable cackling of a red grouse flying low over some heather. As to songs, I don't know. Skylark would be high up, for sure, probably above the ranking it would achieve in a general poll.

Pondering this calls to mind a trip I made in 1969 with a small group from Swansea University, marshalled by Robin Woods. We hired the Union minibus and set off on the Swansea–Cork ferry, to take part in the great Operation Seafarer census of all the breeding seabirds in Britain and Ireland, helped by advice from its organizer, David Saunders. The crossing itself was made at night, the boat, the *Insifallen*, yawing and pitching and shuddering against big waves. Passing the lights of little clusters of silent fishing vessels otherwise invisible in the darkness, beneath swathes of brilliant stars and a fine Milky Way between showers, was itself a marvellous beginning.

From Cork we drove north and west to the little pier at Westport, at the end of Clew Bay in County Mayo, with our objective – Clare Island – all too obviously apparent: it made a brave show with its low southern shores rising steadily, then rearing up, to a high (around 1,500 feet) peak, which dropped sheer into the sea on the north side, in a fearsome but ultimately relatively birdless line of cliffs. The boat arrived to collect us, having made its way across from the island with its little mast rolling from side to side in what seemed like a neat 90-degree V. Surely, we thought, it can't be ours. But it was.

'Would you like some hin's iggs?' asked a man at the quay, whose apparent mixture of English and Gaelic was otherwise almost unintelligible to us foreigners. We added a dozen eggs to our provisions, which included a huge

Cheddar cheese bought in Cork, and an assortment of donated items assembled by Mike Goddard, such as a vast box of cereal, £3. 12s. worth of glucose tablets, a very large jar of barley sugars, several boxes of tins of soup, several more boxes of large tins of beans, a box of tins and jars of pickles, another box of stock cubes, another of cartons of Instant Whip, tins of fruit juice and so on. We had even negotiated, in lieu of our meals at the halls of residence, some food from the catering department. We set to, loading the boat with sacks of coal and other bulky items to be taken across to the island, as well as our own gear.

It was dark when we arrived and we dived into the pub – which was also the post office and shop, and seemed to be open for 23 hours of each 24. We were dropped at a suitable campsite in the middle of the island and put up the tents rather chaotically in pouring rain. We could see little of our surroundings until dawn, when there came an unexpected tap on the outside of the tent. A small girl in big black boots stood outside. 'Here's your bread.' We had seen no one and asked no one for anything, but already the islanders were giving us fresh food. The girl's father later trotted down to milk his cow and pour warm milk from his bucket into our bottles, which he did each morning while we stayed. One morning a complete stranger arrived to hand us a bucket of crabs' claws; others gave us bundles of rhubarb and bottles of home-brewed beer.

Clare Island at that time was a wonderful little island, where the people were friendly and talkative, and the main means of transport, other than Mr O'Grady's Land Rover, was the donkey. The tracks were unsurfaced, the whitewashed houses roofed with turf. The fearsome cliffs on the north side of the island were awesome from any angle. A footpath is supposed to cross the steeply sloping top just where it becomes a sheer face of 1,000 feet. A shepherd, leaning on his crook, pointed to a faint mark and said 'Ah yes, dere's the pat arl roit.' He said he had once taken a visitor along it, but he shouldn't have done it: he had to almost carry him most of the way.

During the Clare Island stay – in which, between us, we covered all the coasts and counted everything we could find, including good numbers of choughs (a pair of which nested within yards of our tent) – we sailed across to the adjacent island of Inishturk, a still wilder and rougher island than Clare Island, with just 17 families. Although the people were as friendly as those we met on Clare, they seemed generally quieter, more withdrawn. We dropped Robin Woods and Jerry Tallowin on a tiny islet, Caher, where they hoped to find storm petrels but spent more time fending off the local ram.

At Inishturk, we transferred from the Clare Island boat to one of the local curraghs, a little tarred boat, to reach the small quay. On the quay, arriving entirely unannounced, we were met by a young lad, who invited us to follow him. We had left our tents on Clare, so he would see we were put up somewhere warm and dry for the night. His mother ushered us into the cowshed at the end of her house, and shooed the cows outside. We arranged our sleeping bags fanwise on the straw, which did nothing to soften the concrete floor, so that our heads would be halfway out of the door, the only way that we could bear the stench. Then hoping for shearwaters and petrels, we set off late in the evening to walk across the island through its little central valley.

We had no luck with nocturnal seabirds, but the walk back under the stars was sublime. On each side a steep slope, with little, invisible hayfields at its foot, rose against the sky, the land distinguishable from the sky only as an extra darkness with no stars. From the fields around us, corncrakes called. At a distance, the song of a corncrake is a lightweight thing, a little, insubstantial, double rasp, little more than a grasshopper sound, the kind of thing that a tiny dry twig against a comb or a bit of rough sandpaper can more or less reproduce. It has a dry, thinness about it. Closer to, the sound takes on a weightier, fuller quality, the rasp roughens a little and seems altogether deeper and more solid. Up really close, in the stillness and blackness of the night, the corncrakes rasped and rasped like demons. The double note separated into minute, individual notes, in the same way that at very close range the reeling of a

Corncrake at dusk – a magical experience.

grasshopper warbler becomes a discrete series of rattles. The rasp was no longer a dry twig against a comb, but a sound with vibrance and depth, like a heavy object dragged hard against a grille, a metal bar across a cattle grid – and every note echoed and re-echoed as it bounced about between the hillside slopes. The effect was magnificent.

That night we had little sleep on the hard floor of the cowshed with the smell and the sound of the cows and the pre-dawn chorus of chickens and corncrakes. Now, according to reports (I have not been back) the corncrakes of these western isles of Ireland are all gone.

So, here, we have the least musical, most mechanical, most repetitive and least varying 'song' of all the birds in Europe, raised to a level at which it became truly beautiful. It is one that must find its way into my top 20 – if I can find a recording of it that goes even halfway to evoking that memorable effect on Inishturk as we walked wearily back to a cowshed one night in June 1969.

Further Reading

Attenborough, David, *Life of Birds*, Collins (1998).

Bannerman, D. A., and Lodge, G. E., *The Birds of the British Isles*, Oliver & Boyd (1953).

Barnes, Simon, *How To Be A Bad Birdwatcher*, Short Books (2004).

Blixen, Karen (Isak Dinesen), *Out of Africa*, Penguin (1937).

Cady, Mic and Hume, Rob (Eds) *The Complete Birds of Britain*, RSPB/AA.

Chipperfield, Joseph, *Greeka, Eagle of the Hebrides*, illustrated by G. Gifford Ambler, Hutchinson (1962).

   Rooloo, Stag of the Dark Water, illustrated by G. Gifford Ambler, Hutchinson (1955).

Darling, F. Fraser and Boyd, J. Morton, *The Highlands and Islands*, Collins (1964).

Elliott, Alan, *The Presidential Elephants of Zimbabwe*, Delta Operations Pvt Ltd.

Ennion, Eric, *Birds and Seasons*, Arlequin Press (1994).

Evens, Bramwell G., *Out with Romany*, Romany of the BBC University of London Press (1937).

   Out with Romany Again, Romany of the BBC University of London Press (1938).

   Out with Romany by Moor and Dale, Romany of the BBC University of London Press (1944).

   Romany Muriel and Doris, by Raq (presented by G. Bramwell Evens). University of London Press (1939).

Fisher, James, *The Shell Bird Book*, Ebury Press & Michael Joseph (1966).

   Thorburn's Birds, Ebury Press & Michael Joseph (1976).

   The Fulmar, Collins (reprinted in paperback 1952 and 1984).

Fitter, R. S. R., *Collins Pocket Guide to British Birds*, illustrated by R. A. Richardson, Collins (1952).

Grant, P. J. and Poyser, T. & A. D., *Gulls: A Guide to Identification* (1982).

Hayman, Peter, *Birdlife of Britain*, Mitchell Beazley (2005).

Hayman, Peter, and Hume, Rob, *The Complete Guide to the Birdlife of Britain and Europe*, Mitchell Beazley (2001).

The Pocket Guide to the Coastal Birds of Britain and Europe, Mitchell Beazley.

Hudson, W. H., *Birds and Green Places*, RSPB.

Hume, Rob, *A Birdwatcher's Miscellany*, Blandford (1984).

Birds by Character: A Field Guide to Jizz, Macmillan (1990).

RSPB Birds of Britain and Europe, Dorling Kindersley (2002).

RSPB Birdwatching, Dorling Kindersley (2003).

Huxley, Elspeth, *Nine Faces of Kenya*, Harvill.

Johns, Capt W. E., *The Quest for the Perfect Planet*, The Children's Book Club (1961).

Jonsson, Lars, *Birds of Europe with North Africa and the Middle East*, Helm (1996).

Birds and Light: The Art of Lars Jonsson, Helm (2002).

Ladybird books: Vesey-Fitzgerald, Brian, *British Birds and their Nests* (1953); *A Second Book of British Birds and their Nests* (1954); *A Third Book of British Birds and their Nests* (1956), Wills and Hepworth.

McClintock, David and Fitter, R. S. R., *The Pocket Guide to Wild Flowers*, Collins.

Moss, Stephen, *A Bird in the Bush: A Social History of Birdwatching*, Aurum (2004).

Mullarney, Killian, Svensson, Lars, Zetterstrom, Dan, and Grant, Peter J., *Collins Bird Guide*, Collins (1999).

Murray, W. H., *The Companion Guide to the West Highlands of Scotland*, Collins.

Nelson, Bryan, *The Atlantic Gannet* (second edition), Fenix (2001).

Nelson, Bryan and Poyser, T. & A. D., *The Gannet* (1978).

Observers Series: Evans, G., *The Observer's Book of Birds' Eggs*; Vere Benson, S., *The Observer's Book of Birds* (1937); Wells, A. Laurence, *The Observer's Book of Freshwater Fishes* (1942), Frederick Warne.

Peterson, Mountfort and Hollom, *A Field Guide to the Birds of Britain and Europe*, Collins (1953).

Prebble, John, *Culloden*, Penguin (1961).

Glen Coe, Penguin (1968).

Richmond, Kenneth, *Birds in Britain: A Practical Guide to Identification, Habitats and Behaviour*, Odhams.

Shackleton, Keith, *An Autobiography in Paintings*, Swan Hill (1998).

Tunnicliffe, Charles. *Shorelands Summer Diary*, Collins (1952).

Venables, Bernard, *Mr Crabtree Goes Fishing*, Daily Mirror Features (1950).

The Illustrated Memoirs of a Fisherman, Merlin Unwin Books.

Wallace, Ian, *Beguiled by Birds*, Helm (2004).

Watson, Donald, *Birds of Moor and Mountain*, Scottish Academic Press (1972).

One Pair of Eyes, Arlequin Press (1994).